RANDOM PUBLISHERS

* **WASHINGTON, D.C.** *

Death of the Rising Sun

A Search for Truth in the JFK Assassination

Kevin James Shay

ALSO by KEVIN JAMES SHAY

Operation Chaos:
The Capitol Attack and the Campaign to Erode Democracy
It's a Mad, Mad, Mad, Mad Trip:
On the Road of the Longest Two-Week Family Road Trip in History
Walking through the Wall:
The Adventures of a 6-foot-7 Reluctant Activist on a Mission from God
A Parent's Guide to Dallas/Fort Worth
And Justice for All:
The Untold History of Dallas (with Roy H. Williams)
Sex, Lies & Newsprint:
Tales from a North Dallas Police Blotter

Front cover photo by Shay taken in 2015 of JFK's grave at Arlington National Cemetery, below the Arlington House memorial to Robert E. Lee.

Published by Random Publishers
Copyright © 2022 by Kevin James Shay
All rights reserved. Parts of this book may be quoted in reviews and articles, and cited in academic works. This book is for informational purposes only. Every effort has been made to ensure that the information is accurate. The author and publisher disclaims liability to any party for any loss or damage caused by errors or omissions, or any other cause.
ISBN 978-1-881365-56-3
EBOOK ISBN 978-1-881365-55-6
LIBRARY OF CONGRESS CONTROL NUMBER: 2017946860

Library of Congress Cataloging in Publications Data
Shay, Kevin James, 1959-
Death of the Rising Sun: A Search for Truth in the JFK Assassination by Kevin James Shay.
Pages cm.
ISBN 9781881365563 [paper]
1. Kennedy, John F. [John Fitzgerald], 1917-1963 – Presidency, assassination. 2. Political assassinations. 3. United States politics. 4. United States history. I. Title.
E 842.9. 2022
973.922092 – dc23
LCN 2017946860
10 9 8 7 6 5 4 3 2 1
Printed in the United States [USA]
First edition, 2017, Second printing, 2022

To the kids

Don't give up
on us just yet

Contents

Introduction 9

Chapter One *Winning at all Costs* 19

Chapter Two *Fearing the Beard* 27

Chapter Three *From 'Get Castro' to 'Get JFK'* 49

Chapter Four *Enemies Unite?* 60

Chapter Five *Mystery Wrapped in an Enigma* 72

Chapter Six *New Orleans Connections* 99

Chapter Seven *Multiple Threats* 121

Chapter Eight *The Sun Goes Out in Dallas* 149

Chapter Nine *The Fix Is In* 187

Chapter Ten *Ghosts of Dealey Plaza* 219

Conclusion 245

Appendix *Acknowledgments, Notes, Resources, Index* 260

This photo was taken in 2016 of the site where John F. Kennedy was assassinated. The former Texas School Book Depository building is in the middle, with the grassy knoll to the left. An "x" marks the spot in the middle of Elm Street where Kennedy was in the car when he was hit with the fatal shot.
The "x" was put there anonymously. City workerswill wash it off, and the mark will return. [Kevin Shay photo]

Introduction

He never reached his meridian: we saw him only as a rising sun.
 — **JAMES RESTON**, "What Was Killed Was Not Only the President," 1964

They killed him on the altar of the rising sun.
 — **BOB DYLAN**, "Murder Most Foul," 2020

One of my first boyhood visions features a casket draped with an American flag on a caisson pulled by horses.

Uniformed soldiers ride the horses and walk next to the casket. I'm four years old, wondering what has happened to cause this scene, where so many adults wear somber faces. The crowd of thousands upon thousands along the procession route overwhelms me. Hooves clack against the pavement. Drums beat in the distance. I'm bundled up, feeling more confused than cold. The sun is shining, but somewhere, it is raining.

I don't remember the scene in color; it's etched in my mind as a black-and-white scene, part of a horror movie that fades to gray as the caisson pulls away, heading to Arlington National Cemetery. Sometimes, I'm not sure I was even in Washington, D.C., that late November day, though my parents said we were. I don't know if it's a dream, a nightmare, reality, or a combination. Somehow, I sense something is not right; it seems I am witnessing not a parade, but a charade.

I sometimes think I have been haunted by this scene for my entire life. There are times when I'm sitting alone, reliving some memory, and a clip from John F. Kennedy's state funeral flashes in my mind for an instant, disturbing my recollections.

Like many, I began to lose my innocence the day JFK died. That day robbed many of us of a good part of our youth. The late Texas journalist Molly Ivins noted that after JFK was killed, "everything went to hell. It all turned into manure." [1]

Many of all political stripes agree. "The whole country changed," said Bobby Hargis, a Dallas Police motorcycle officer who was splattered with Kennedy's blood as he rode next to the president's limousine. Before that day, "we believed that everything was going to be fine, even if things didn't go right. But now, you can't believe that." [2]

Broadcast journalist Jeff Greenfield added, "To understand that this supremely confident, self-assured man could be slaughtered in broad daylight.... was to understand the fragility of life, the powerful forces lurking just under the surface of life. What our parents learned in a war, or in a struggle for survival, we learned that November. No one was safe; if not John Kennedy, then definitely not any of us." [3]

In 1964, some 77 percent of Americans trusted their government to do the right thing at least most of the time, according to a national survey. By 1974, that percentage fell to 36 percent and was at 24 percent in 2021. Trust in banks, churches, the media, and other institutions saw similar patterns. [4]

The intense political divide of the late 2010s and 2020s can be traced to 1963, said award-winning director Oliver Stone, who released a factual documentary in 2021 called *JFK Revisited: Through the Looking Glass* about three decades after his based-on-fact drama, *JFK*. "The reason we're in this kind of disbalanced situation in the United States, that we have less and less trust, is because of the past," Stone said on Joe Rogan's podcast in 2022. "If we go to this particular incident in '63... it's a turning point for the country." [5]

Since Kennedy was assassinated, no president has challenged the military or national security state as JFK did, said Stone, who directed another documentary on the roots of the Cold War called *The Untold History of the United States*. "Kennedy was the last one who was trying to curb [the military and intelligence agencies' power]. And he made a serious effort towards peace. He was the last president to talk about peace, very nobly. And people have said, 'Ah, he just talks.' But no, he was doing things.... He kept us out of war twice."

At the time he was killed, Kennedy was not only withdrawing from Vietnam but was trying to help Indonesian President Sukarno, wrote James DiEugenio, the screenwriter of *JFK Revisited* and co-founder of Citizens for Truth about the Kennedy Assassination. Lyndon Johnson reversed course with disastrous results, he noted. As many as 3.8 million people died during the Vietnam War, while many also perished in Indonesia under the dictatorial rule of Gen. Suharto, that country's leader for three decades starting in 1967. [6]

Beginning a quest

A little more than a year after JFK's assassination, I lost more of my youth as my older sister died. Believed to be one of thousands of victims of Reye's syndrome – a tragedy fueled by more institutional lies and cover-ups – Sharon was buried not far from JFK in Arlington Cemetery. Regular visits to that cemetery opened up double wounds.

Somehow, my family ended up in Dallas. I gravitated to journalism, and a chance encounter with an eyewitness to Kennedy's killing mobilized me. In early 1978, I happened to be the only person present in the cramped office of the Richland Mandala, home of Richland College's student newspaper, when JFK killing eyewitness Bill Newman entered. It was during the midst of the U.S. House Select Committee on Assassinations' investigations. Newman, an electrical contractor who attended college at night, was standing on Elm Street with his wife and two young sons no more than 15 feet from Kennedy when he was shot.

"I caught a glimpse of the president's eyes after he was shot the first time, and it was like a cold stare, like he was staring right through me," said Newman, who later became a city council member in the Dallas suburb of Mesquite. "It was then that the final shot seemed to hit his ear and take it right off." [7]

Newman thought the shots came from over his head in back of the grassy knoll, though he later said it was hard to tell. He told his wife and kids to get down on the ground, and a famous photo shows the couple covering their sons. He was interviewed by the national media, FBI, and Dallas sheriff's office, but the Warren Commission did not call.

Though at the time I was more concerned with basketball and baseball games than crime-of-the-century investigations, Newman's chance visit spurred me to start reading JFK assassination books, attending meetings and conferences, and interviewing witnesses. The CIA, Mafia, high-level defense officials, oilmen, right-wing businessmen, Castro, the Soviets, anti-integration racists, Jimmy Hoffa, LBJ, and J. Edgar Hoover all became suspects.

Perhaps some of my interest was aided by sharing the same birthday as Kennedy. I wrote stories for my college papers and others. I didn't learn who really killed Kennedy, but as I delved into the question, it almost became lost in a maze of even larger mysteries about what governments and semi-secret institutions did in our names. As much as I was convinced that the Warren Commission and several subsequent panels did not get to the bottom of who killed JFK, I began to understand why they didn't. And that intrigued me all the more.

As a mostly sports reporter for the Park Cities News, a conservative weekly that covered the high-society Dallas suburbs of University Park and Highland Park – which have housed the likes of former President George W. Bush, ex-VP Dick Cheney, and former Texas Gov. Bill Clements – I attended a ceremony in 1983 organized by the local Democratic Party to commemorate the 20th anniversary of JFK's assassination.

The event didn't give insight into who killed JFK, but officials such as former U.S. Sen. Ralph Yarborough spoke about what Kennedy was like and how his assassination changed the country. People did not blame Washington, D.C., for the death of Abraham Lincoln so it was unfair to blame Dallas for Kennedy's death, said Yarborough, who rode in the 1963 motorcade with Kennedy. [8]

I later read a harrowing account by Yarborough of what it was like to be in that procession. He recalled the contrast between the reactions to Kennedy from people lining the street and the mostly businessmen who stood above them inside office buildings. The people outside were smiling and cheering, but most business types in the offices – who included right-wing extremist and oil billionaire H.L. Hunt – were staring in silence "with positive hate," Yarborough noted. [9]

My weekly column, which was usually buried in the sports pages among high school football and basketball results, mostly detailed that event. My editor later met with me to say, "Stick to sports." I argued that sports were inseparable from life, that sometimes even sports fans could not ignore the larger events that affected us all. He said it wasn't up to him, but the paper's owners and investors didn't like my meanderings. "Some of them could have been in on the conspiracy, for all I know," he noted.

I steered clear of mentioning Kennedy in future columns but continued to cover issues beyond sports. I increased my activism with the Dallas advocacy paper Hard Times News and embarked on a long walk project across the U.S. and Europe to Russia as a statement to end the Cold War. Through that, I met more people convinced that the full truth about JFK's death had not been revealed, especially those in Europe.

In 1988, I attended a few meetings of the Dealey Plaza Irregulars, a group that evolved from a conspiracy theory course taught by journalist Jim Marrs at the University of Texas at Arlington. I met witnesses such as Esther Ann Mash, a waitress at Jack Ruby's Downtown Dallas Carousel Club who claimed she witnessed Lee Harvey Oswald meeting with Ruby and others in that club before the assassination.

Mary Ferrell, an executive legal secretary who had amassed some 25,000 pages of FBI documents by 1988 in her Oak Lawn home, was another who I profiled. The likes of national journalists Jack Anderson and Geraldo Rivera had used her files. Jim Garrison called her. Her husband, H.A. Ferrell, had provided the Lincoln Continentals that rode in the presidential procession, while her station wagon carried some reporters.

"I have a firm belief that Oswald did not act alone, though I don't have absolute proof," said Ferrell. "I see my job as compiling all this information for others to use." Much of the information is catalogued online. [10]

'Not here to solve this crime'

In 1989, I covered the opening of The Sixth Floor Museum in the former Texas School Book Depository building, from where Oswald supposedly shot at the motorcade. I asked then-project director Conover Hunt why there was so little emphasis on conspiracy theories. "We are not here to solve this crime," said Hunt, who was not related to H.L. Hunt. [11]

That statement struck me as odd. Shouldn't a museum that promotes this crime of the century be at least mildly interested in all aspects of the case?

It had been a struggle just to preserve that building, which was renamed the Dallas County Administration Building in 1981. Many civic leaders, including influential billionaire Ross Perot and former Dallas Cowboys coach Tom Landry, called for its destruction. The structure survived arson attempts in 1972 and 1984. Preservation efforts received a boost when archaeologists unearthed Native American artifacts just outside the building. Admission prices at the $3.5 million museum, which included a reconstructed sniper's perch and the original stairway sign, rose from $4 in 1989 to $18 in 2022.

Gary Shaw and co-director Larry Howard opened the JFK Assassination Information Center in downtown Dallas soon after The Sixth Floor Museum to focus more on conspiracy theories. The center, among other duties, printed an informative brochure outlining problems with the official story, such as there were more bullet fragments in former Texas Gov. John Connally Jr.'s body than were missing from the bullet that the Warren Commission claimed caused his wounds. In addition, the CIA turned over a file on Oswald to congressional investigators that was empty as the military destroyed its Oswald file, according to the center.

In 1991, I viewed a premier of Stone's *JFK* film, attended by the director, who spoke about how many journalists in the corporate media considered him little more than a "conspiracy nut." In my 1991 review for The Addison/North Dallas Register, I was among the minority in the mainstream media to recommend the movie:

> The Warren Commission's conclusion that Lee Harvey Oswald was the lone assassin is about as believable as the theory that the world is flat. Stone's film is dedicated to the young people in this country who inherit whatever it is we've made of it. I just hope more of us wake up and demand that our government tell us the truth about this matter. [12]

The movie sparked Congress to create the JFK Records Act, which directed the U.S. National Archives and Records Administration to develop a collection of documents, photos, and other materials related to the assassination and fully release them publicly by 2017. Most were housed near the University of Maryland, College Park, campus. The Assassination Records Review Board worked to unveil the collection to the public until running out of funds in 1998. The National Archives kept releasing more records in ensuing years, though some were withheld primarily due to "national security" concerns.

The released documents lent more details on potential suspects or patsies in Chicago and Tampa who could have been involved in plots to shoot Kennedy in those two cities shortly before the one in Dallas succeeded. To me, those plots occurring at about the same time as the Dallas one is probably the most difficult aspect for lone-assassin theorists to explain away.

But Donald Trump and Joe Biden still declined to fully issue some documents, citing national security concerns. Why was the government still covering up information almost 60 years later? That's partly what makes this case so interesting.

In later years, I continued to write about aspects of the assassination. I joined and consulted with other researchers, such as SMU linguistic anthropology professor Bill Pulte. When Beverly Oliver wrote *Nightmare in Dallas* in 1994, I detailed her story in a lengthy feature for the Arlington News. I did more stories for The Dallas Morning News and other newspapers. A 1999 book on Dallas political history I co-authored with civil rights advocate Roy Williams called *And Justice for All* included considerable information on the assassination. A comprehensive story on Kennedy's autopsy for The Washington Post Co.'s Gazette in 2013 won a Best in Show feature writing award from the Maryland-D.C.-Delaware Press Association, beating out larger papers.

While I haven't been as dogged in pursuing the truth behind the JFK assassination as Penn Jones Jr., Jim Marrs, DiEugenio, Stone, Earl Golz, Jim Garrison, David Talbot, Jefferson Morley, and some others, it remains the most important and defining story I have chased in my more than four-decade journalism career. It haunts me today as much as it did in 1978.

Once you go down the rabbit hole, you learn that this is more than a detective story with high-level political and economic stakes. To truly pursue the truth, you have to suspend belief about most everything you have been taught about this country, big business, and international politics. You might have to risk your career, reputation, and sometimes even life. You definitely have to shuck off the "tin foil" comments. You have to walk down a slippery slope. It can be similar to a missionary's cause without thought of monetary reward, fame, or even redemption. You have to reach deep within yourself to find reasons to hold onto the hope that the sun will, indeed, rise in the morning.

No matter what you thought of JFK, his death profoundly changed America and the world. A 1999 Newseum survey of American historians and journalists ranked the JFK assassination as the sixth biggest story of the 20th century. The other events in the top ten were the 1945 atomic bomb droppings, 1969 moon landing, 1941 bombing of Pearl Harbor, 1903 Wright brothers flight, 1920 women's vote victory, 1945 Nazi concentration camps exposed, 1954 Supreme Court school decision, 1914 beginning of World War I, and 1929 stock market crash. The only top ten event with major controversy about what really happened remains the Kennedy killing. [13]

Though the U.S. government continues to blame one man, some 61 percent of Americans in a 2013 Gallup poll still believed Kennedy was killed as the result of a conspiracy. That belief has ranged from 50 percent in 1966 to 81 percent in 2001. A 2017 survey by FiveThirtyEight also showed 61 percent leaning towards the conspiracy side. To many, JFK's murder remains largely unsolved, and most conspirators have yet to be held officially responsible for their roles in this earth-shaking crime. [14]

After *JFK Revisited* was released in 2021, the usual critics castigated the film. The critics, including Noam Chomsky and Gerald Posner, regurgitated discredited sources and information that has been corrected. For instance, some said Kennedy's parade route was not changed, when it was. Some said attorneys for suspected New Orleans conspirator Clay Shaw did not receive help from the CIA or FBI. Not only did they, but they were also aided by Hugh Aynesworth, a journalist who also fed information to both government agencies.

JFK Revisited "leaves no doubt that the [Warren Commission] was wrong in its rogue prosecution of Oswald," wrote DiEugenio, author of numerous books on the JFK case and other political assassinations. "What the film deals with are the forensic facts of the JFK case, for example, Kennedy's autopsy and the ballistics evidence, which is how one determines guilt in a homicide." Robert Tanenbaum, a former prosecutor and major of Beverly Hills, was quoted in the film that Oswald would not have been convicted had he lived because of the circumstantial nature of the evidence. Even Posner said in 2010 that a good attorney like Mark Lane "would have won an acquittal." [15]

Norman Mailer wrote in *Oswald's Tale* that he was 75 percent sure Oswald committed the crime of the 20th century alone. So, he left the door one-quarter open to a conspiracy. And that was in 1995, before many more eye-opening documents have been released, detailed in compelling arguments by DiEugenio, Stone, Talbot, Lamar Waldron, and James Douglass, among others. Though a mostly lone-assassin supporter, Mailer pointed out that Oswald was not a crazed lone nut as the Warren Commission claimed, but an intelligent, articulate young man who believed in action, made many acquaintances, and had at least cursory ties to the CIA, military intelligence, FBI, KGB, and Mafia. [16]

The following account details much of the results of my research, gleaned from classified and unclassified government documents, reports, studies, interviews, meetings, books, and articles. As a longtime researcher, I heavily document sources, using footnotes that are at the end of the book in the appendix.

In this work, I give light to some associations unearthed by fellow researchers such as Pulte that have not received the attention they deserve. For instance, Pulte found a convoluted alliance between anti-Castro Cubans, right-wing businessmen, mobsters, and the CIA who operated out of "safe" houses and apartments in Dallas. Relatives and associates of anti-Castro leaders Rolando Masferrer and Antonio Varona lived in the same apartment complex in East Dallas as Silvia Odio, who was visited by a man named Oswald and two Cubans shortly before Kennedy was killed.

I highlight some information from government documents that I haven't seen reported elsewhere. Those include an FBI report that noted that an active Marine intelligence officer at the Naval Air Station in a Dallas suburb talked a few weeks before the assassination about how an attempt on Kennedy's life would be easy if the assassin "ordered a mail-order rifle." The latter was a specific detail that authorities attributed to Oswald. There is new information about suspects in the Chicago and Florida plots, including the FBI confirming an arrest in Chicago. There are new details about what CIA officials were doing and said shortly before and after the JFK murder. [17]

I also show how Dallas, despite having a Texan on the ticket, displayed the strongest anti-Kennedy sentiment in the 1960 election of any large city in the country – even stronger than smaller anti-integration bastions like Birmingham, Ala. Dallas probably deserved the title of the "U.S. Capital of Hate" in 1963, though the city has changed immensely since then. But as I show, the assassination could have just as easily happened in Chicago, Tampa, Miami, and other cities.

I try not to ignore the contributions of the lone-assassin crowd. For us to truly force the full truth of this crime to emerge, it will take cooperation from all sides, even if we are rivals at times. Of course, I can understand the wariness of someone like Garrison, who faced death threats, prosecution, infiltration, dirty tricks, media hype, and more in the late 1960s as he courageously pursued the only criminal case in this controversy that has tried someone for conspiracy in court. You don't just easily let go of the level of harassment Garrison experienced.

I recognize that there is so much information on this assassination that I have certainly left out many important facts. It is hoped that this book can contribute to weeding out kernels of truth among the massive amount of material on the subject and making the topic clearer.

A rising sun died in America and the world on November 22, 1963. Some say that we have never again seen such a rising sun in the sky as we did that morning. Even if it was cloudy or raining that day, the country and world were more innocent and optimistic at that moment than they have been since then. Some say that a piece of all of us – the hope that helps us get through another day – died that day. Others say the act just opened the eyes of many about what the U.S. government and other governments have done in our names for a long time.

How do we regain the hope and optimism many felt before the bullets struck JFK? Can we? Tough questions. All I know is we can't begin to glimpse that kind of rising sun again without being honest about what happened that day. If we can someday fully acknowledge the horrors behind the events of that day, then we can begin on that long road back to redemption.

Some of the newspaper articles on JFK that the author wrote are displayed.

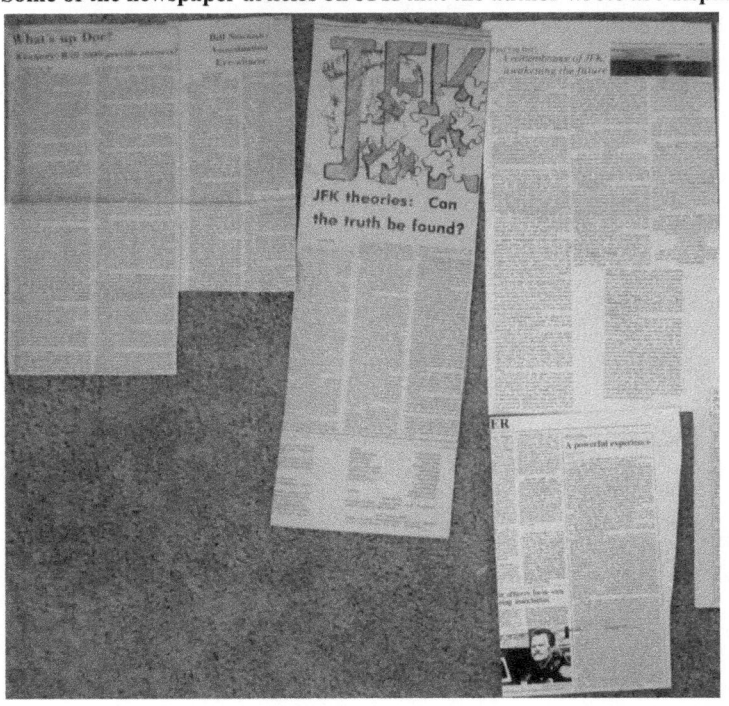

Chapter One

Winning at All Costs

But I've a rendezvous with Death
At midnight in some flaming town,
When Spring trips north again this year,
And I to my pledged word am true,
I shall not fail that rendezvous.
    – **ALAN SEEGER**, "I Have a Rendezvous with Death," 1916

As he stood in the Hyannis Armory on the sunny early November afternoon, John F. Kennedy seemed surprisingly buoyant.

After a brutal campaign and election, the New England senator had just received a telegram from Vice President Richard Nixon conceding the 1960 election, the closest in the popular vote in U.S. history. Kennedy's blood-shot, yet friendly, eyes darted across the crowded room at the Cape Cod armory, which hosted politicians, reporters, campaign workers, and a Massachusetts Army National Guard battery.

"To all Americans, I say that the next four years are going to be difficult and challenging years for us all," the new president-elect spoke. "The election may have been a close one. But I think that there is general agreement by all of our citizens that a supreme national effort will be needed in the years ahead to move this country safely through the 1960s. I ask your help in this effort." [1]

Not all citizens would join the effort to move the country safely ahead. More than a few thought the Kennedys had stolen the election. The popular vote came down to about 113,000 votes out of more than 68 million cast, a microscopic 0.003 percent advantage for Kennedy, who had used television more effectively than any other presidential candidate to that point. By the quirk of the Electoral College system, JFK had a much greater 303-219 edge. Even the contested 2000 election, where Al Gore polled 0.01 percent more votes than George W. Bush but lost the electoral vote, was more decisive in the popular tally.

Nixon had done well in late returns from the West Coast and Rocky Mountain states, but The New York Times still had gone to press at midnight with the headline, "Kennedy Elected President." Nixon made a speech at the Ambassador Hotel in Los Angeles around 3 a.m. but didn't concede since four states that could hand him victory – California, Illinois, Michigan, and Minnesota – were still undecided. "Why should he concede? I wouldn't," noted Kennedy, who maintained a friendly demeanor with his fellow wartime naval officer despite the nasty campaign. [2]

But by that afternoon, it was clear to most that JFK won enough states to gain the White House. Nixon's congratulatory telegram was gracious, alluding to how Kennedy "will have united support of all Americans" in the years ahead. But inside, the man some called "Tricky Dick" burned. At a 1960 post-election party, he was heard saying, "We won, but they stole it from us." Robert Kennedy – JFK's right-hand man who ran his brother's 1960 campaign – "illegally bugged more people than anyone," Nixon charged. "He was a bastard." [3]

Some – even members of his own political party – called Lyndon Baines Johnson worse names. But his presence on the ticket proved to be a key electoral difference, when the Democrats won not just Texas but important Southern states such as Louisiana, South Carolina, and Georgia. Previously, the Democrats had not won Texas since 1948. Republicans like Barry Goldwater thought Johnson ushered through less-than-honest electoral practices.

"I think Texas might have been stolen, frankly," Goldwater said. "I was through that state too much and too often to believe that they could have switched in the last ten days to the extent that the vote count showed they did." [4]

Democrats denied that, even though LBJ had won close elections in Texas under questionable conditions that included the hotly-contested 1948 U.S. Senate race in which opponents charged that Johnson's machine manufactured last-minute votes from dead people. LBJ competed with Kennedy for the presidency in 1960 and was angered, to say the least, that the party chose the less experienced, but more charismatic, JFK.

As a conciliatory move, Kennedy offered the vice president position to Johnson, expecting him to stay in the more powerful role as Senate leader. House Speaker Sam Rayburn, a close ally of LBJ, reportedly threatened to kill major legislation proposed by Kennedy if the tall Texan did not get an offer. LBJ saw the VP move as one step closer to his ultimate goal, saying in a Forrest Gump-like manner, "Power is where power goes." He told some friends that he had a good chance to ascend to the top position since roughly one in four of the previous 33 presidents had died in office. LBJ liked those odds. [5]

Shenanigans in Texas, Chicago

Sifting through the 1960 voting wreckage, Republicans claimed to find irregularities deep in the heart of Texas. In a precinct in Angelina County in East Texas, only 86 people voted, but the final tally was 147-24 in favor of Kennedy. Republican leaders demanded a recount, but the all-Democrat Texas Election Board denied the request. [6]

Even with such shenanigans, Republicans would have had to have found more than 46,000 new votes – or gotten more than 23,000 switched to their side – to win Texas. While some noted that LBJ's machine was capable of stealing thousands of votes, most experts agreed that overturning a 46,000-vote margin was a long shot.

Despite having the former Texas senator on the ticket, Dallas, in fact, provided Nixon with his largest margin of victory among any of the 20 most populous U.S. cities. Nixon won Dallas County by a whopping 25 percentage points, even larger than his victory margin in San Diego near Nixon's hometown. He won Fort Worth by ten percentage points and Houston by six. San Antonio and Austin balanced out those cities somewhat with more Kennedy support.

Many other conservative cities, such as Knoxville, Birmingham, Richmond, Wichita, and Salt Lake City, gave Nixon smaller victory spans than Dallas. One of the few that provided Nixon a larger margin was Southern anti-integration stronghold Charleston, S.C., at 28 points. However, Charleston only fielded some 33,000 voters in 1960, compared to about 240,000 in Dallas.

How anti-Kennedy was Dallas in 1960?
(Hint: Every other large U.S. city, even anti-integration stronghold Birmingham, Ala., showed JFK more support.)

City	Kennedy	Nixon
Dallas	37%	62%
Knoxville	38%	61%
Oklahoma City	39%	61%
Richmond	39%	60%
Phoenix	41%	59%
Birmingham	42%	57%
San Diego	43%	56%
Wichita	44%	55%

Fort Worth	45%	55%
Charlotte	45%	55%
Salt Lake City	45.5%	54.5%
Anchorage	46%	54%
Houston	46%	52%
Albuquerque	47.5%	52%
Seattle	47%	51%
Portland	49%	51%
Minneapolis	49%	51%
Memphis	49%	49%
Los Angeles	50%	49%
New Orleans	50%	27%
Denver	50%	50%
Atlanta	51%	49%
Nashville	53%	46%
San Antonio	54%	46%
Austin	55%	45%
Tampa	56%	44%
Chicago	56%	43%
Las Vegas	57%	43%
Pittsburgh	57%	43%
Miami	58%	42%
San Francisco	58%	42%
Milwaukee	58%	42%
Cleveland	60%	40%
Baltimore	64%	36%
New York	65%	34%
Detroit	66%	34%
St. Louis	67%	33%
Philadelphia	68%	32%
Boston	74%	25%

Note: Washington, D.C., did not gain voting rights in presidential elections until 1961. LBJ won the city with 85.5% in 1964.

Source: uselectionatlas.org

While Republican Party chairman and Kentucky Sen. Thruston Morton led recounts or investigations in 11 states, Chicago was ground zero for most "stolen election" charges. Kennedy won Illinois by a mere 8,858 votes, a significantly smaller margin than Texas. Cook County, the home of Mayor Richard Daley's notorious political machine, provided more than its share of votes for JFK, who won that county by more than 300,000.

Daley was known for giving ward bosses and precinct captains specific vote quotas. A report by special prosecutor Morris Wexler found "substantial" miscounts due to voting machine errors and unqualified voters in more than 1,000 precincts. Some precincts offered voters free meals, liquor, and raffle tickets for hams. [7]

Joseph Kennedy Sr. himself was alleged to have brokered a deal with Chicago mob boss Sam Giancana and other mafiosos to deliver thousands of votes. Kennedy had been a shrewd – some said corrupt – businessman who made a fortune through the stock market and reportedly received insider tips to sell most of his stocks before the October 1929 crash. He then invested in lower-priced real estate and Hollywood studios that later increased significantly in value. He wanted to become the country's first Catholic president, but that dream was derailed by questionable positions as U.S. ambassador to Great Britain from 1938 to 1940. The elder Kennedy supported British Prime Minister Neville Chamberlain's policy of appeasing Hitler and sought a meeting with the German dictator as late as 1940. He also made derogatory comments about Jewish people, including referring to the "Jew media" in the U.S. JFK once described his father as being "to the right of Herbert Hoover," the Republican president who led the U.S. into the Great Depression.

For the 1960 campaign, Joe Kennedy persuaded entertainer Frank Sinatra to meet Giancana on a golf course and relay messages, according to journalist Seymour Hersh. Mafia leaders aided Kennedy's campaign mainly because they believed he would "reduce FBI pressure on their activities," Hersh wrote. [8]

Media reports detailed serious election corruption charges. Earl Mazo, a reporter for the New York Herald Tribune, found a Chicago cemetery where the names on the tombstones were registered and votes marked. "I remember a house. It was completely gutted. There was nobody there," Mazo noted. "But there were 56 votes for Kennedy in that house." [9]

Mazo also investigated Republican areas in southern Illinois and found fraud. "The Republicans were having a good time, too," he said. "But they didn't have the votes to counterbalance Chicago. There was no purity on either side, except that the Republicans didn't have Daley in their corner." Democrats charged that the Mafia-affiliated International Brotherhood of Teamsters union leader Jimmy Hoffa reportedly performed illegal acts in Ohio to help deliver that state to Nixon. [10]

Mazo wrote numerous stories on Chicago irregularities but said his bosses called him off after Nixon lobbied for a halt. Nixon's main reason was reportedly because he didn't want to cause an electoral stink. However, some suspected he didn't want reporters closely examining his own campaign's misdeeds. [11]

Legal challenges failed to significantly alter results, but Wexler's investigation resulted in three precinct workers being convicted for vote tampering and serving short jail terms. However, about 650 indicted election officials were acquitted by a Daley-friendly judge. [12]

Charges of wholesale election fraud in Chicago were "baseless and unsubstantiated," concluded a 1961 study by University of Chicago professors Herman Finer, Jerome Kerwin, and C. Herman Pritchett. Most reports of fraud came down to human errors or were only allegations, they wrote. Eight other large U.S. cities, including Detroit, Cleveland, Philadelphia, Baltimore, and Buffalo, gave Kennedy a higher percentage of support than Chicago, the authors noted. Republicans pointed out that the professors were Democrats, with Finer even appointed by Daley to the Chicago Regional Port Authority. [13]

Subsequent studies of the 1960 race in Chicago lent a more mixed picture. "Excessive partisanship on both sides has complicated that analysis" of whether Kennedy really won in Illinois, wrote Ohio State history and law professor David Stebenne in 2010. "The most recent and fair-minded study [Edmund F. Kallina Jr.'s *Kennedy v. Nixon*] concludes that sufficient evidence does not exist to determine whether Chicago's Democratic machine stole more votes there than Republicans did downstate." [14]

In Texas, Jim Crow laws prevalent in the South, which included discriminatory poll taxes and literacy tests, made conducting fair elections practically impossible, Stebenne noted. "Voter fraud was fairly common, safeguards to prevent it were few," he said. "Thus, the most dispassionate analysis of this issue from the perspective of 50 years later is that we will never know whether Kennedy really 'won,' in the sense of what result an entirely honest and effective administration of the electoral process in Illinois and Texas would have produced on Election Day in 1960." [15]

Going postal

In such an environment, many more people than just opponents and their operatives thought the Kennedys pilfered the 1960 election. Among those was Richard Pavlick, a 73-year-old retired postal worker from a small New Hampshire town with no immediate family.

Pavlick turned his house over to a local youth group soon after the election. The right-wing conservative loaded his 1950 Buick with a few possessions and dynamite attached to a detonation device, then took off to stalk JFK across the country.

Kennedy had "bought the presidency," Pavlick wrote in a note he carried. In the former mail carrier's twisted mind, JFK deserved to die. Numerous supposedly more sane people would agree by 1963. [16]

Pavlick had been a fixture at town meetings in Belmont, N.H., complaining about the flag not being properly displayed, Catholics, and the Kennedy family's wealth. He had displayed a gun to a water company representative who visited his house during a billing dispute. [17]

Stopping at cities where Kennedy spoke, Pavlick followed the president-elect to his Cape Cod home, which he photographed. By December 11, his pursuits resulted in him parking the dynamite-loaded car in front of the Kennedy mansion in Palm Beach, Fla.

Pavlick's plan was to ram the Buick into Kennedy's car. From his vehicle, Pavlick observed Kennedy emerge with Jacqueline and their young kids, Caroline and John Jr., from the mansion. As JFK climbed in the car with his family, Pavlick delayed an attempt to kill him there because he later said he didn't want to harm Jackie or the children. He wasn't a complete lunatic. He looked for other opportunities to kill Kennedy, as he was even in his church at least one time. [18]

By that time, Belmont postmaster Thomas Murphy contacted authorities after noticing postcards from Pavlick with postmarks of cities where Kennedy had spoken. One claimed residents would hear from him "in a big way." The Secret Service contacted Palm Beach police to be on the lookout for Pavlick and his 1950 Buick. [19]

A patrol officer spotted Pavlick's car on a Palm Beach bridge on December 15. Police surrounded the vehicle and found the dynamite inside. After admitting to authorities that he wanted to kill JFK but that he would have targeted Hoffa if Kennedy had not won, Pavlick was institutionalized. He would be released in 1966. For a time, he would stalk Murphy, sitting in his car outside the postmaster's home. He would die in 1972.

Secret Service agent charges lax security

Such threats did not slow as Kennedy moved into the White House a month after Pavlick's arrest. In 1961, the Secret Service investigated 870 threatening letters, some 50 percent more than the annual average during President Dwight D. Eisenhower's term.

Despite that increase, training for the 36-member Secret Service team that guarded Kennedy did not seem to be a top priority, some charged. Agent Larry Newman was given a sub-machine gun on his second day, even though he had never used one. [20]

Abraham Bolden, whom Kennedy once referred to as "the Jackie Robinson of the Secret Service" for being the first African-American in that agency to guard the president, said he was told to wing it after he was handed an AR-15 semi-automatic rifle in 1961 that he was not trained to use. Bolden joined the Secret Service's Chicago division in 1960 and was transferred to Washington, D.C., the following year.

Bolden was shocked by how lax Kennedy's security was in D.C. and at the Kennedy compound in Hyannis. Agents were drunk on duty, chased women, and spoke openly of their contempt for JFK, he said. Many white agents used the "n-word," he said. When Bolden complained to superiors, they ignored him. Some would make him a target.

"I told the chief of the United States Secret Service that if an assassination attempt was ever made on Kennedy, it would be successful because either the agents wouldn't respond or would be slow to respond," Bolden said. [21]

Historical marker noting the 1961 invasion of Cuba outside the Bay of Pigs Museum, also known as the Brigade 2506 Museum and Library, in Miami's Little Havana neighborhood. The marker commemorates the men of Brigade 2506 and the Bay of Pigs conflict, which some believe sparked Kennedy's assassination. [Shay photo]

Chapter Two

Fearing the beard

Truth is stranger than fiction. Fiction is obliged to stick to possibilities; truth isn't.
  – MARK TWAIN, 1897

Before Fidel Castro took over Cuba, the Caribbean island nation 90 miles south of Florida had been "essentially, a colony of the United States," according to former MIT linguistics professor Chomsky. In fact, U.S. leaders in the early 19th century, including Thomas Jefferson and John Quincy Adams, first tried to annex Cuba as part of the country, but the British Navy temporarily halted that plan, he wrote. Finally, U.S. political and business leaders essentially controlled Cuba through puppet regimes until Castro's coup in 1959. [1]

With its mostly Mafia-run casinos, brothels, horse-race tracks, and high-priced resorts, Havana was "a mistress of pleasure, the lush and opulent goddess of delights," gushed tourism magazine Cabaret Quarterly in 1956. The likes of Ava Gardner, Sinatra, and Ernest Hemingway frequented Cuba's night clubs. [2]

JFK made several trips, noting that on a 1957 visit he was told that U.S. Ambassador Earl Smith was the second most powerful man there behind President Fulgencio Batista. As airline ticket prices fell, more Average Joes visited. Cuba became Vegas Southeast. [3]

By 1959, U.S. companies controlled almost all of Cuba's oil and cattle industries, 90 percent of Cuban mines, 80 percent of public utilities, and about half of the sugar production, Kennedy noted in a 1960 speech. U.S. leaders had "refused" to help lift poor Cubans from poverty, with "nearly all" aid in the form of weapons, which "merely strengthened the Batista dictatorship," he charged. Kennedy blasted Batista's reign as "one of the most bloody and repressive dictatorships in the long history of Latin American repression," charging that Batista "murdered 20,000 Cubans in seven years." [4]

"We used the influence of our government to advance the interests of, and increase the profits of, the private American companies, which dominated the island's economy," Kennedy said. "Our action too often gave the impression that this country was more interested in taking money from the Cuban people than in helping them build a strong and diversified economy of their own." [5]

Castro takes over

Under such conditions, with very little done for Cuba's poorest citizens, revolts naturally broke out. As a college student, Castro, a University of Havana-educated lawyer who came from a wealthy land-owning family, spoke out against corruption, U.S. influence, and gambling. He launched a failed attack on a Cuban military garrison in 1953 and was imprisoned for a year. Soon after getting out, he waged a guerrilla war from the mountains that lasted several years. [6]

The bearded one's army in January 1959 finally drove the Batista regime from power. He became prime minister and established a socialist government that eventually fielded close ties with the Soviet Union.

Castro implemented reforms in education, housing, health care, and other areas that resulted in higher literacy rates, fewer homeless people, and lower infant mortality rates, among other improvements. Poorer citizens generally supported the reforms, but some criticized crackdowns against press freedom, gay rights, and civil liberties. Middle-class Cubans, including doctors and engineers, began to leave the country in waves. [7]

While Kennedy was among Batista's harshest critics, he also noted in 1960 that Castro had broken promises of free elections and an end to "harsh police-state tactics." However, Castro was "an attractive and popular figure," and the U.S. "had no real alternative" but to support him initially, said a CIA officer who worked in the Havana station at the time. Most CIA agents in Cuba opposed Castro from the first day, seeing through his "democratic facade," the officer reported. [8]

Eisenhower was horrified at Castro's successful revolution. However, some administration officials who weren't fond of Batista convinced Eisenhower to formally recognize Castro's revolutionary government in early January 1959. Secretary of State John Foster Dulles wrote in a memo, "The Provisional Government appears free from communist taint, and there are indications that it intends to pursue friendly relations with the United States." [9]

Behind the scenes, Eisenhower – who had approved CIA covert operations that successfully overthrew Iran's prime minister in 1953 and Guatemala's president in 1954 – wasted little time rubber stamping a similar campaign against Castro. By March 1959, the National Security Council authorized the CIA to arm guerrillas inside Cuba. [10]

Since Castro did not really align with the Soviets until at least a year later, the main reason that U.S. leaders decided to overthrow him was that Cuba was "taking an independent path, which has always been unacceptable to powerful interests in the United States," Chomsky said. To Eisenhower and other U.S. leaders, the real crime carried out by Castro was making improvements in education, health care, and similar areas quicker than previous Cuban dictators, which could cause other Latin American nations to try to emulate him, he charged. [11]

In April 1959, Castro visited the U.S. under an invitation from the American Society of Newspaper Editors. Eisenhower was so opposed to the bearded one that he remained in Georgia playing golf while Castro was in Washington and New York. [12]

Nixon met with Castro and emerged with doubts that the Cuban leader could be steered away from communism. But he was impressed with his leadership qualities. "Whatever we may think of him, he is going to be a great factor in the development of Cuba and very possibly in the development of Latin American affairs generally," Nixon wrote in a memo to Eisenhower. [13]

Castro dismissed questions about communism ties. He told a U.S. Senate committee that he had "no interest in expropriating U.S. property." [14]

But some two weeks after returning to Cuba, Castro signed a law to seize foreign-owned property and bar foreign businesses unless they turned over shares to the government. He pursued ties with the Soviet Union, particularly in the military.

In October 1959, Eisenhower approved a program proposed by the State Department and CIA to support Cuban officials who opposed Castro and exiles who raided Cuba. CIA Director Allen Dulles speculated to the British ambassador the following month that Castro would only last "in the range of eight months." Officials were working on contacting Castro supporters who "had only recently become alienated," and there was "always the chance that Castro would get shot," Dulles said. [15]

That December, J.C. King, head of the CIA's Western Hemisphere division, wrote in a memo to his supervisors that "violent action" was the only means of ousting Castro and that "thorough consideration be given to the elimination of Fidel Castro." [16]

In early 1960, Eisenhower imposed embargoes on Cuban sugar, oil, and guns. Castro responded by further nationalizing U.S. business operations, including by the Coca-Cola Co. and Sears Roebuck & Co. In a March meeting with high-ranking security officials, Eisenhower authorized a more formal "Get

Castro" program led by Nixon under the code name Operation 40, and urged participants to keep the mission secret and deny its existence.

"Our hand should not show in anything that is done," President Eisenhower said. [17]

At the same time, Castro told some of his aides, "If there is an invasion, the war, they can be sure, will be to the death." [18]

'Get Castro' operation shifts into high gear

While Dulles and CIA Deputy Director Charles Cabell took on higher-level oversight roles in the operation, CIA operations director Richard Bissell Jr. was the main field general. Former Guatemalan station chief Jacob Esterline led WH-4, a specific task force. David Atlee Phillips, a Texas-born operative who was the CIA's propaganda chief for the 1954 Guatemalan coup, took on the same function for Cuba. [19]

Fellow CIA operative E. Howard Hunt, also a veteran of the Guatemalan operation, headed political action, primarily organizing a government-in-exile to replace Castro following the invasion. Nixon and Allen Dulles oversaw the recruitment of right-wing Cubans who fled Castro's regime for Miami. Other participants in Operation 40 included future Watergate burglars Frank Sturgis and Bernard Barker; CIA operatives Felix Rodriguez, Porter Goss, and Luis Posada Carriles; and Orlando Bosch, founder of the anti-Castro network Coordination of United Revolutionary Organizations. [20]

The operation had an initial budget of some $13.1 million approved by Eisenhower in 1960. That grew to as much as $50 million annually, according to Chomsky. CIA operatives began training troops at bases in south Florida and Guatemala about the same time Eisenhower authorized the project. Among the objectives was to train operatives on guerilla war tactics and "secretly infiltrate" them back into Cuba to resist Castro and "mount terrorist military attacks" on economic infrastructure, according to an affidavit by attorney Daniel P. Sheehan, co-founder of the Christic Institute. Rodriguez – who sometimes went by the alias "Max Gomez" – and Carriles – whose alias was "Ramon Medina" – were among the members of a secret "shooter team" that trained at a base in Mexico that taught a "triangular-fire" method of assassinating leaders, Sheehan said. Hunt was among the supervisors of this team, he claimed. [21]

Bombing and incendiary raids on sugar cane fields and even urban areas piloted by Cubans and supervised by CIA agents increased throughout 1960. In March, the French freighter La Coubre exploded in Havana harbor as munitions were being unloaded, killing as many as 100 people. Castro charged that the U.S. and exiles sabotaged the ship, while American officials denied any involvement. [22]

A month later, Phillips met with Bissell to discuss propaganda plans. "How long will it take to create the proper psychological climate?" Bissell asked.

"About six months," Phillips replied.

"Get Radio Swan up and running in one month." [23]

CIA front business Gibraltar Steamship Co., which didn't own any steamships and whose president was former State Department official Thomas Dudley Cabot, quickly formed the 50-kilowatt radio station on Swan Island. The contested island near Honduras had operated a similar station for the 1954 Guatemalan coup and even had some left-over equipment from that operation. Radio Swan started operating in May, the first of several stations to broadcast anti-Castro reports throughout the Caribbean.

Meanwhile, Hunt visited Cuba clandestinely and reported that the CIA should destroy Cuban radio and television transmitters to curb mass support before an invasion. Also in May, Cuban soldiers shot and killed Matthew Edward Duke, an American pilot who flew Cubans out of the country reportedly for $1,000 per job. The ex-husband of tobacco heir Melody Thompson, Duke landed on a highway west of Havana and was killed in an ambush. The CIA denied Duke was employed by the agency, but some suspected otherwise. [24]

By July 1960, Cuba documented some 20 bombings with details that included plane registration numbers and called on the United Nations to intervene. But U.S. Ambassador to the UN Henry Cabot Lodge Jr. assured other representatives that his country "has no aggressive purpose against Cuba," and Castro's concerns were ignored by most. [25]

Enter the mob

A mere month after Lodge made such assurances, Bissell met with CIA security director Sheffield Edwards. They proposed that Mafia members be recruited to kill Castro, according to the Rockefeller Commission, which would investigate the CIA in 1975. The only other government officials who knew about the plan were Dulles and Cabell, reported the commission led by Vice President Nelson Rockefeller.

Edwards first consulted Robert Maheu, a former FBI agent who also worked for the CIA and billionaire Howard Hughes. Maheu knew "Handsome Johnny" Roselli, an influential mobster in Chicago and Hollywood. Edwards and Maheu hatched a plan to tell Roselli that Maheu represented Cuban businessmen who sought to eliminate Castro to help them recover investments. Maheu was authorized to tell Roselli that his "clients" were willing to pay $150,000 for Castro's removal, according to an internal CIA report. [26]

FBI agent James O'Connell and Maheu met Roselli in New York City in mid-September 1960. Roselli initially was reluctant to become involved, but eventually introduced Maheu to Chicago boss Giancana. The mafioso said he might be able to arrange to have an associate in Cuba "take care" of Castro. "No monies were ever paid to Roselli and Giancana," Edwards wrote. [27]

Edwards kept top CIA officials, including Dulles and Cabell, briefed on the Mafia involvement. While Dulles and Cabell did not formally approve the plans, Edwards "felt that he clearly had tacit approval to use his own judgment." Giancana turned to other Mafia leaders, including Florida boss Santo Trafficante Jr., who had operated casinos in Cuba that Castro closed.

In late 1960, CIA operations chief Edward Gunn laced a box of 50 Cuban cigars with botulinus toxin. The cigars were so heavily contaminated that just putting one in your mouth could kill you. Gunn delivered them to Cuban agents in February 1961. However, the lethal cigars were never used, CIA officer Jacob Esterline told the agency's inspector general, because agents could not figure out how to deliver them without evidence leading back to the CIA. Esterline said he destroyed them by mid-1961. [28]

Giancana then suggested poison pills. While CIA officials preferred Castro was shot, Giancana opposed using firearms. He said that no one could be recruited to do the job because the chance of survival and escape would be quite small. Trafficante knew a Cuban official with access to Castro named Juan Orta who needed money.

O'Connell received the pills in early 1961 and gave at least three to Roselli, who passed them on to Trafficante. Orta kept the pills for a few weeks before returning them due to losing his position and his nerve. He eventually left Cuba. "While the agency thought the gangsters had a man in Cuba with easy access to Castro, what they actually had was a man disgruntled at having lost access," reported the CIA internal memo. Orta suggested another candidate, who made several attempts without success. [29]

Trafficante then turned to Cuban exile Antonio Varona, head of the anti-Castro, CIA-backed Cuban Democratic Revolutionary Front. Edward Moss, Varona's public relations consultant, allegedly had a mistress, Julia Cellini, whose brothers represented two of the largest gambling casinos in Cuba. Varona was "very receptive" to the idea of helping with the Castro plots, as he sought funds to purchase ships, arms, and communications equipment. [30]

Roselli delivered the pills, $10,000, and some equipment to Varona to start the scheme. Varona gave them to an employee in a restaurant frequented by Castro, but the plan failed when Castro didn't show up.

Kennedy talks tough on communism

While Nixon obviously was well-versed on the "Get Castro" plan during the 1960 election campaign, Kennedy was kept updated by Dulles. Kennedy sounded like a liberal on issues such as civil rights, but in foreign policy, he was decidedly on the right-wing side, even as he made remarks about needing to do more to help Cuba's poor.

In an August campaign speech at a high school stadium in Alexandria, Va., JFK seemed to support the plan. "The communists are determined to destroy us, and regardless of what hand of friendship we may hold out or what arguments we may put up, the only thing that will make that decisive difference is the strength of the United States," he said. [31]

While criticizing Batista, JFK also regularly denounced Castro as a dictator. "We must attempt to strengthen the non-Batista democratic anti-Castro forces in exile, and in Cuba itself, who offer eventual hope of overthrowing Castro," Kennedy said in one speech. "Thus far, these fighters for freedom have had virtually no support from our government." Nixon, who knew more about what the Eisenhower administration was doing, called that position irresponsible and proposed a tougher military quarantine of Cuba. [32]

The Miami Herald heard about an August 1960 arrest of Cubans at a camp near Miami. That occurred after a teenager tossed firecrackers over the fence and was shot with a .30-caliber machine gun. Police arrested 15 Cubans, but they were released, reportedly at the urgings of federal officials. [33]

Reporter David Kraslow looked into the matter and learned how CIA operatives were training Cuban exiles to invade Castro. He also discovered that FBI Director J. Edgar Hoover, a staunch anti-communist who had targeted "radicals" since World War I, objected to the scheme, saying the training on U.S. land violated the Neutrality Act. Kraslow prepared a story, complete with denials from Eisenhower's press secretary, James Haggerty.

Finally, Kraslow's editors told him to talk with Dulles, who he met with Knight Newspapers Washington bureau chief Ed Lahey at the agency's headquarters. Kraslow detailed his story to Dulles, who told him, "If you publish that kind of information, you'll seriously damage national security." [34]

Kraslow told his editors, who discussed the situation with Herald publisher John Knight. An editor told Kraslow the story was dead a few days later. "I've always suspected that the minute I left his office, Dulles called Knight and said, 'Don't publish that story.' Knight was a big Republican and a very patriotic guy, and I think Dulles probably believed a direct appeal to him would work," Kraslow said in 2015. Though the story wasn't published, Kraslow believed it helped convince officials to soon move training of the Cubans to Guatemala. [35]

At a September public demonstration, Castro stated, "If they continue the economic aggression against our country, we will continue nationalizing U.S. businesses." By the end of the year, most U.S. enterprises in Cuba, including oil refineries and banks, were under Castro's control. [36]

In perhaps a sign of upcoming events, a CIA-funded aircrew attempted to drop a pack full of weapons attached to a parachute to a waiting agent in Cuba that same month. The crew missed the target by seven miles, dropping the pack on top of a dam. The weapons were confiscated by Castro's forces, and the agent was caught and shot. The plane became lost on the way back to Guatemala and landed in Mexico. In addition, exile Carlos Rodriguez Santana died when he fell off a cliff on a training hike in Central America. [37]

Full speed ahead

When briefed on more details of the invasion by Bissell and Dulles shortly after winning the November election, JFK voiced few concerns about the plot. Some say he couldn't, that he was basically told if he pulled the plug on the Bay of Pigs, there would be grave political repercussions.

"[Kennedy] was kind of sandbagged by the CIA," Talbot wrote. "He did go through with it, but he had no intention of widening it into an all-out U.S. military assault on the island."

Stone added, "The Bay of Pigs was a setup. The CIA controlled that operation. They knew that operation would not work unless the U.S. came in militarily to back up that invasion. Kennedy made it very clear that he would not put U.S. combat troops into Cuba unless they established a beachhead, if [they] would succeed. But it didn't succeed because Castro knew it was coming." [38]

Meanwhile, Eisenhower would have likely supported using the military to back that invasion. In his final days, he lobbied for stronger action against Castro. "Are we being sufficiently imaginative and bold, subject to not letting our hand appear? Are we doing the things we are doing, effectively?" Eisenhower asked.

When an aide noted that the operation was apparently known across Latin America and even discussed in UN circles, Eisenhower discounted that development, stating, "We should be prepared to take more chances and be more aggressive." [39]

A few days later, leaders of Operation 40 ran with Eisenhower's suggestions, infusing new officers into leadership positions, such as CIA assistant operations director Tracy Barnes. U.S. Ambassador to Costa Rica Whiting Willauer, another of the fresh leaders, called for direct U.S. involvement in the invasion, saying that the previous plan "might not succeed" in overthrowing Castro. [40]

Leaders tried to contain even internal queries. Navy Admiral Robert Dennison sent the CIA more than 100 questions about planning for the operation, and only about a dozen were answered. Meanwhile, Castro arrested more Cubans who he termed traitors and even executed some. In a speech, Castro warned that an invasion "will not be a military cakewalk." [41]

About two weeks before JFK was slated to take over the White House in January, an adviser told Eisenhower that the Cuban exiles were "the best army in Latin America." Gen. Lyman Lemnitzer, chairman of the Joint Chiefs of Staff, who became more involved in planning the operation and called for the direct involvement of U.S. troops, agreed. Another aide said that citizen support for Castro within Cuba had drastically declined to about 30 percent.

"I would move against Castro before the 20th [when JFK took over] if the Cubans provide me with a really good excuse," Eisenhower announced. "Perhaps we could think of manufacturing something that would be generally acceptable." The group soon agreed to formally break diplomatic relations with Cuba. [42]

A day before his inauguration, Kennedy met with Eisenhower, who reported that Operation 40 was "going very well."

"Is it your recommendation that we support the guerrilla operation in Cuba, even if this support involves the United States publicly?" Kennedy asked.

"Yes," Eisenhower said. "We cannot let the present government there go on." [43]

Just a few days after settling in, Kennedy met with the Joint Chiefs of Staff. General Lemnitzer reported that Cuba was receiving "heavy" shipments of weapons from Czechoslovakia and other Soviet bloc nations. "Clandestine forces are not strong enough," he said. "We must increase the size of [the Cuban exile] force, and this creates very difficult problems. What is required is a basic expansion of plans." The Joint Chiefs sent a memo to new Secretary of Defense Robert McNamara stating that the main U.S. objective in Cuba should be "the speedy overthrow of the Castro government." [44]

In a wider meeting involving LBJ and numerous other Kennedy Administration officials, Lemnitzer and other Pentagon officials reiterated their call for expanding the operation. But new Secretary of State Dean Rusk warned that any overt military action that was not authorized by the Organization of American States would have "grave political dangers." Kennedy authorized defense officials to work more closely with the CIA and Rusk to gain support from other Latin American countries. [45]

In Guatemala, about half of the more than 500 Cuban exiles resigned in late January, citing various grievances such as lack of supplies. Many members had not served in a military combat situation before, while others were in Batista's former army. Jose "Pepe" San Roman, commander of the exiles, called Brigade 2506, was among those who resigned. The CIA operative in charge of the base, a man known only as Frank who could have been Gerard Droller, convinced San Roman to remain.

Pepe and his brother, Roberto San Ramon, had served in Batista's army with their father in the 1950s. But they weren't supporters of the regime and, in fact, were among a group of officers arrested for conspiracy to overthrow Batista. Within two months, Castro ousted Batista, and the San Ramons were released. While Pepe was commissioned to restructure the army, Roberto hid because he had fought Castro's guerrillas in the mountains and thought he might face war crimes. Pepe helped Batista officers like Ricardo Montero Duque escape to the U.S. until San Roman was arrested by Castro. Upon being released in 1959, Pepe and his brother left for Florida. Their wives, children, and parents soon followed. "We were thinking we'd be back in Cuba in a year or six months," Roberto said. [46]

But they would not return for about two years, and only in an invasion. They joined the group of Cuban exiles in Miami plotting against Castro and soon were flown via CIA aircraft to Guatemala. Pepe was chosen as commander in November 1960; CIA operatives recognized his people skills and leadership ability. Rather than order around troops, Pepe took time to explain what he wanted and solicited suggestions.

As plans changed from guerrilla warfare to an inclusive invasion with the support of American troops, they thought, "There is no chance Castro can win." Pepe trusted his CIA supervisors to a fault. "One of the things that always bothered my brother later was that he never questioned any of the American plans," Roberto remarked. [47]

Debate over the invasion intensifies

In Washington, Operation 40 leaders were not as optimistic. Lemnitzer assessed the invasion's chance of success as only "fair" in a February 1961 memo to McNamara. But, he wrote, "even if it does not achieve the full results desired, [it] could contribute to the eventual overthrow of the Castro regime." [48]

A Joint Chiefs committee headed by Brig. Gen. David Gray put the chance of success at about 30 percent. The Cuban exile force could last at most four days given "complete air supremacy," and success would depend on uprisings in Cuba, the panel reported. But Sherman Kent, a Yale University history professor and chief of the CIA's Office of National Estimates, argued that the Cuban population was "not eager" to stage such uprisings. [49]

Others gave conflicting reports, making it difficult for Kennedy to know who to believe. The CIA's Bissell said the Cuban force had a "good" chance of overthrowing Castro. National Security Adviser McGeorge Bundy said that defense and CIA officials "now feel quite enthusiastic about the invasion... At worst, they think the invaders would get into the mountains, and at best, they think they might get a full-fledged civil war in which we could then back the anti-Castro forces openly." [50]

But Bundy admitted that State Department officials were not sold and thought political consequences were still grave. Bundy himself supported a trade embargo to "let internal opposition build for several months," followed by an invasion.

In a meeting with top advisers, Kennedy asked for alternatives to a full-fledged invasion. "Could not such a force be landed gradually and quietly and make its first major military efforts from the mountains?" he asked. "Then taking shape as a Cuban force within Cuba, not as an invasion force sent by the Yankees?" [51]

Some officials argued to halt the operation. Arthur Schlesinger Jr., a special assistant to the president who focused on Latin America, said there was "no way to disguise U.S. complicity" in the plan. "At one stroke, it would dissipate all the extraordinary goodwill which has been rising toward the new administration through the world," he wrote. [52]

Sen. J. William Fulbright, chairman of the Senate Foreign Relations Committee, agreed it would be virtually impossible to conceal U.S. involvement. "The prospect must also be faced that an invasion of Cuba by exiles would encounter formidable resistance, which the exiles by themselves might not be able to overcome," he said. If U.S. forces entered the battle, that would undo "the work of 30 years in trying to live down earlier interventions," Fulbright said. [53]

But abandoning the plan could cause "explosions in three or four countries in Central America," CIA officials said. Most Latin American leaders would "at least privately" support a move against Castro as long as the U.S. was "assisting the Cubans themselves" and not "imposing a new regime," reported the CIA

Board of National Estimates. While it would remind many of the Soviets of sending troops into Hungary in 1956 to crush an uprising, the Soviets would "avoid a direct military confrontation with U.S. forces," the board believed. [54]

Some, particularly top Pentagon officials, pushed for an early March invasion date. But Kennedy argued for more time to consider alternatives in a mid-February meeting, delaying the March timeline. Meanwhile, more planes dropped pamphlets urging the violent overthrow of Castro on cities, and some targeted cane fields with incendiary bombs. Some bombs were set off in cities, reportedly by internal resistance members.

Castro took measures to crack down on rebels and guerrillas operating from the mountains. In early March, he announced that more than 400 guerrillas were arrested in the mountains and claimed they were killing teachers in a terrorism campaign. [55]

Bissell argued in a mid-March meeting for a splashy assault that would seize a beachhead "suitable for guerrilla operations." Fewer than 20 percent of Cubans supported Castro, Bissell claimed. He expected the large majority of soldiers to defect shortly after an invasion. Kennedy said he preferred a more low-key invasion at night that would be less likely tied to American forces. [56]

Jim Noble, a former chief of the CIA's Havana station, organized a mid-March meeting of scattered Cuban exile leaders in a Miami motel. "If you don't come out of this meeting with a committee, you just forget the whole fuckin' business because we're through," a Noble assistant told the Cubans. Three days later, the Cuban Revolutionary Council was formed with José Miró Cardona as coordinator. [57]

In late-March meetings, JFK questioned the plan more vigorously. "Do you really have to have these airstrikes?" he asked Bissell.

The CIA officer replied leaders would keep air invasions to a minimum.

"The tide is flowing against the project," noted Schlesinger.

At one point, the adviser asked the president, "What do you think about this damned invasion?"

"I think about it as little as possible," Kennedy responded. [58]

In early April, officials hammered out a compromise plan involving limited airstrikes two days prior to the main invasion and a diversionary landing of troops. The planes were to be painted with Cuban military markings so people might believe the attacks were from Cubans. The Joint Chiefs disagreed with prior air bombings since they would tip off the invasion and give Castro's forces more time to mobilize. Military troops shipped 15,000 weapons packs to Central America despite the force only having 1,500 troops.

At an April 4 meeting, only Fulbright and Rusk opposed moving ahead with the invasion. Schlesinger warned Kennedy that the operation could turn into a "protracted civil conflict.... Cuba will become our Hungary." JFK told the adviser he had "reserved the right to stop this thing up to 24 hours before the landing. In the meantime, I'm trying to make some sense out of it." [59]

Castro sniffs out invasion plans well beforehand

As D-Day approached, Castro and Soviet officials learned when the invasion would occur well beforehand through a communication interception or deep source, according to a June 1961 government report whose authors included Gen. Maxwell Taylor, Robert Kennedy, and Dulles.

More than a week beforehand, Castro began concentrating troops near Trinidad, where guerrillas were captured. When he later learned U.S. officials changed the location to the Bay of Pigs about 100 miles away, it wasn't too difficult to move operations. He also foresaw prior airstrikes, putting broken-down planes outside as targets and camouflaging working aircraft.

On April 7, The New York Times ran a story about the planned invasion that overestimated the size of the exile force. The report said training had wound down, and D-Day was believed to be imminent. Kennedy had successfully lobbied Times editors to tone down the story, but upon reading it, he stated, "Castro doesn't need spies in the United States. All he has to do is read the newspaper." At a press conference a few days later, JFK stated that U.S. troops would not, in any circumstances, intervene in Cuba. [60]

While top CIA officials were aware of the leak, they apparently did not tell JFK, said Peter Kornbluh, a senior analyst with the National Security Archive. The investigative journalism and research institute worked to get the government to release the full 1961 report, which was not done until 2000. [61]

CIA officials claimed that Castro did not know exactly where the invasion would occur and proceeded with the attack. Dulles and other organizers thought Kennedy would cave in during the heat of battle and authorize waiting U.S. Navy jets and Marines to invade Cuba – as Eisenhower had done in the successful Guatemalan invasion seven years before. There, similarly CIA-trained rebel forces had seen their initial bombers shot down by the Guatemalan army, and Eisenhower quickly agreed to provide additional planes. That support intimidated the Guatemalan army, which eventually stopped fighting.

Invasion planners expected to secure a small area of Cuba and then citizens would revolt against Castro's forces, driving him out. If the latter did not occur, they expected to set up a provisional government in the area and thought that U.S. troops would invade to oust Castro.

But a CIA memo about nine days before the invasion seriously overestimated internal support for the invaders.

"The great mass of people....place great reliance on [an invasion]," said the report. "Travelers through the interior of Cuba have reported that the disenchantment of the masses has spread.... It is generally believed that the Cuban Army has been successfully penetrated by opposition groups and that it will not fight in the event of a showdown. It is also certain that the police, who despise the militia, will not fight." [62]

That report could not have been more wrong, since Castro would organize as many as 20,000 Cuban troops to meet the roughly 1,300 exiles of Brigade 2506. [63]

Top military officers agreed to ground rules, including not allowing U.S. destroyers within 20 miles of Cuban territory. U.S. troops were also to be told not to fire on Cuban ships or aircraft unless the ships carrying the exiles were directly attacked. They also planned a series of diversionary actions, including landing fake exile planes in Florida to make it appear the airstrikes originated in Cuba.

The compromise plan was not well-received by CRC leader Cardona and led to revolts even within the CIA. About a week before D-Day, Esterline and Jack Hawkins, another CIA officer working closely on invasion planning, told Bissell they wanted out. "By pruning away at the operation, [politicians] were making it technically impossible to win," Esterline said. [64]

Bissell noted that the invasion was moving ahead with or without them and convinced them to stay. In a meeting with Robert Kennedy, he somehow put the chance of the mission's success at 67 percent.

On April 10, the exile forces began moving from the Guatemalan camp to Puerto Cabezas, Nicaragua, where they boarded ships bound for Cuba. "Bring me a couple of hairs from Castro's beard," Nicaraguan dictator Luis Somoza Debayle told the exiles as they departed. [65]

From Nicaragua, Hawkins reported to Esterline that "without exception, [the exiles] have utmost confidence in their ability to win. They say they know their own people and believe after they have inflicted one serious defeat upon opposing forces, the latter will melt away from Castro." [66]

Bissell sent Hawkins' message to the White House, which helped convince JFK to proceed. But Kennedy still wanted the operation curtailed. "How many planes will participate?" he asked Bissell.

"Sixteen."

"Well, I don't want it on that scale. I want it minimal." Kennedy replied.

Bissell agreed to reduce the number to eight. But he later wrote, "I believe the president did not realize that the airstrike was an integral part of the operational plan he had approved." [67]

On April 13, seven-story El Encanto, the largest department store in Cuba, was destroyed in a bombing and fire. Fe del Valle Ramos, a Cuban civil rights activist and Castro supporter, died in the fire as she tried to extinguish the flames and retrieve money. Castro had nationalized the Havana store in 1959.

Employee Carlos González Vidal, who had an uncle with ties to the CIA, confessed to setting off incendiary bombs. He was executed by a firing squad. Castro's forces also made more arrests of resistance members suspected of setting fire to cane fields and refineries.

The El Encanto bombing was a "CIA sabotage operation," said former CIA agent and author Philip Agee, who would live in exile and receive death threats after leaving the agency and writing a book. He believed the CIA was also behind the March 1960 bombing of the French freighter Le Coubre. At that time, Agee was training at a secret CIA base in Virginia, learning the arts of sabotage, bugging, and explosives. [68]

'Chico is in the house'

On April 15, eight CIA-supplied B-26's – piloted by exiled Cubans and painted with Cuban markings – flew from Nicaragua and bombed three Cuban military airfields.

Thus officially marked the start of the Bay of Pigs battle.

The strikes only destroyed five Castro planes, though others sustained some damage. One of the CIA planes landed in Miami, and the Cuban pilot said he and his comrades stole the plane and defected. They claimed to be hit by anti-aircraft fire and had to make an emergency landing.

Reporters noted that the craft's machine guns did not appear to have been fired, and the nose was solid metal while Castro's planes had plastic noses. Cardona issued a statement that the strikes were carried out by Cubans inside their country. "Even Hollywood would not try to film such a story," Castro later commented. [69]

Castro blamed the U.S. for the strikes and ordered pilots to sleep under their craft's wings so they would be ready to take off immediately. American officials, including United Nations Ambassador Adlai Stevenson, denied involvement. Stevenson even presented photographs of the planes before the

UN, claiming that they were from the Cuban Air Force. "The fundamental question is not between the U.S. and Cuba but among the Cubans themselves," Stevenson said. [70]

Concerned about the public glare and believing the first strikes did enough damage, Kennedy canceled more airstrikes planned at dawn April 16 and 17, despite protests from Cabell and others. JFK acted "partially on false reports" that the first airstrikes virtually destroyed Castro's air force, journalist Haynes Johnson reported. But Kennedy agreed to allow more U.S. destroyers as long as they remained at least 30 miles from Cuban territory. [71]

A group of almost 200 exiles tried to stage a diversionary landing on the far eastern edge of Cuba near Guantanamo about 500 miles from the Bay of Pigs that same day. But they lost some boats, and their contacts did not meet them. They attempted to land again April 16 but sunk another boat. They were ordered to join the main invasion but would not get there in time.

That same day, Juan Almeida, one of Castro's field commanders, inspected the Bay of Pigs after hearing reports of suspicious activities of internal resistance members in that area. He ordered troops to line the bay.

Exile forces traveled on the ships through the night of April 16, reaching the coast of Cuba to rendezvous with the USS San Marcos. The U.S. Navy ship transferred landing craft to the Cubans by midnight.

Radio Swan repeatedly broadcast a nonsensical message written by Phillips and Hunt designed to confuse Castro's troops: "Alert! Alert! Look well at the rainbow. The fish will rise very soon. Chico is in the house. Visit him. The sky is blue. Place notice in the tree. The tree is green and brown. The letters arrived well. The letters are white. The fish will not take much time to rise. The fish is red." [72]

Around midnight, a Castro officer near the Bay of Pigs observed a red light in the sea. Thinking it was a lost boat, he climbed into a jeep and turned the lights on and off. The invaders fired at the jeep, and the officer fired back. The main invasion was on.

CIA agent Grayston Lynch, a commander of the Cuban exiles aboard the landing craft Blagar, received an order from Washington to "unload all troops and supplies and take ships to sea as soon as possible." Exiles, led by San Roman, started landing at 1 a.m. Some Castro forces fired on them as they finished unloading one ship by 3 a.m. About that time, Castro was woken up in Havana and told that the main invasion had begun. He ordered all available troops to descend upon the Bay of Pigs and left for the area himself.

A battle commenced around 4 a.m. with a new message from Radio Swan to exiles: "Take up strategic positions that control roads and railroads! Make prisoners or shoot those who refuse to obey your orders! See that no Fidelist plane takes off! Destroy its radios! Destroy its tail! Break its instruments! Puncture its fuel tanks!" [73]

Castro ordered pilots to shoot at the retreating ships at dawn. Some pilots attacked exiles who landed on the beach after dealing with aluminum-boat motor failures. Many exiles failed to land. Few supplies reached the shore, although all vehicles and tanks landed.

Pilots in Castro's planes, which included T-33s made by U.S. defense giant Lockheed Martin and secured during the Batista regime, hit one of the exiles' freighters. The Houston became grounded like a "big mortally wounded fish" with about 200 men on board, as well as fuel, ammunition, and weapons. Troops evacuated to the shore using ropes as they ducked Castro's planes, but most could not participate in the battle since they lost their weapons.

Captain Enrique Carreras Rojas, known by his comrades as "Grandfather," then directed his British-made Sea Fury fighter towards the exiles' Rio Escondido freighter, also carrying ammunition and fuel. His rockets struck the Rio dead center, and the ship erupted in flames. [74]

CIA agent William "Rip" Robertson, who commanded another landing craft, Barbara J, and disobeyed orders by going ashore, heard the explosion from the beach. "God Almighty, what was that? Fidel got the A-bomb?" he exclaimed into his radio.

"Naw, that was the damned Rio Escondido that blew," replied Lynch. [75]

Exiles from the Rio successfully transferred to the Blagar, from where troops shot down a T-33. An exile battalion on the beach advanced about four miles before Castro forces blocked further encroachment and drove invaders out of the town of Palpite.

When told his forces had secured the village, Castro declared, "We've won! We've won the war! We've sunk two ships and three launches. And if they don't realize that they need to defend Palpite, then they've lost." [76]

Castro's forces continued pushing the exiles back closer to the beach, despite attacks from B-26s. Firing bazookas, the exiles damaged some Soviet-made tanks, and they retreated. Exile parachutists secured a main road about ten miles away and established outposts. Exile battalions in other areas gained ground as well, controlling two of the three main access roads.

The events caused Radio Swan announcers to suggest the exiles were winning: "The invaders are advancing steadily on every front! Castro's forces are surrendering in droves!" one exclaimed. [77]

Others knew the odds of success were bleak. The situation seemed even more dire at sea, as exile ships retreated under increasing attacks. The Caribe freighter continued out to sea more than 200 miles and was not available to resupply exiles fighting on the beach. The Atlantico freighter reached some 100 miles and would not return to resupply troops until the following afternoon.

Exile B-26s struck Castro ground troops and reportedly inflicted several hundred casualties. Several B-26s were shot down, while Castro's force lost craft as well. Castro definitely had the homefield advantage; his planes were within a half-hour of the front, while brigade pilots took four hours to fly from Nicaragua and usually had enough fuel to only stay at the front for 30 minutes.

An exile battalion led by second-in-command Erneido Oliva, numbering less than 400 men, reportedly defeated a Castro division of more than 2,000 men and 20 tanks. Some 500 Castro soldiers died in that battle, while less than 20 of Oliva's men perished. [78]

While Radio Swann and the Cuban Revolutionary Council continued to claim the exiles were winning that evening, aides informed JFK the force was in dire need of U.S. help. American ships might have to be used, the president told his brother. "I'd rather be an aggressor than a bum," JFK confided. But JFK continued to argue for not having blatant U.S. involvement. [79]

That night, CIA leaders ordered B-26 pilots to hit Cuban airfields with fragmentation bombs, but they failed to locate any in the darkness. At 3 a.m. on April 18, Castro's troops attacked exiles near Playa Larga with tanks, and the exiles retreated to Playa Giron some six hours later. Cuban troops also blasted exiles near the town of San Blas with artillery fire, causing a gradual retreat. At the same time, Castro's police arrested thousands of suspected resistance members in Havana, making sustained citizen uprisings extremely difficult.

Bombings by B-26s provided some relief for exile ground troops, but the vastly outnumbered invaders became more overwhelmed as thousands of reinforcements for Castro's soldiers arrived. By noon, the situation appeared more than grim for the exiles. Bundy told Kennedy that Castro's forces were stronger, and "our tactical position is feebler than we had hoped. Tanks have done in one beachhead, and the position is precarious at the others." He recommended U.S. air support "to eliminate the Castro air force, by neutrally-painted U.S. planes if necessary, and then let the battle go its way." [80]

Soviet Premier Nikita Khrushchev sent a message to JFK that his government would give Castro "all necessary assistance in beating back the armed attack on Cuba." Kennedy responded that the U.S. did not plan to intervene with its military but would "protect this hemisphere against external aggression." He added, "The people of the United States do not conceal their admiration for Cuban patriots who wish to see a democratic system in an independent Cuba." [81]

At a lunch with journalist James Reston, Kennedy confided that retaining Dulles as CIA head was probably "a mistake." The Cuban invasion "was a hell of a way to learn" how the CIA and high-ranking military brass really operated, the president said. At the same time, Kennedy brushed aside how the invasion was a violation of a U.S.-signed international treaty, the Charter of the Organization of American States that took effect in 1951, historian Howard Zinn noted. The treaty barred nations from intervening in the affairs of other countries, and the Cuban invasion was "all organized by the United States," Zinn wrote. [82]

That afternoon, Bissell defied JFK and authorized CIA contract pilots to fly combat missions. Two CIA pilots known as Peters and Seig took off from Nicaragua for Cuba with four other planes. They fired rockets and dropped napalm and bombs on Castro's forces, destroying tanks and causing hundreds of casualties. Top U.S. military leaders also ordered troops to prepare unmarked naval planes for possible combat use. [83]

Exiles fought off more Castro tanks at Playa Giron, the center of the invasion point, and were low on ammunition by the evening. In spite of heavy fighting, casualties appeared low among invaders.

A CIA official mentioned to San Roman that it would be a good idea to start evacuating that night. "I will not be evacuated," Pepe replied. "We will fight to the end here if we have to." [84]

At a midnight meeting in the White House, Navy Adm. Arleigh Burke made one last plea to JFK to unleash U.S. military pilots on Castro's forces. "Let me take two jets and shoot down the enemy aircraft," Burke requested.

"No," Kennedy replied. "I have warned you over and over again that I will not commit U.S. forces to combat."

Burke persisted. He suggested using unmarked military jets to fly over the beach to intimidate Castro's troops without firing. But Kennedy thought the U.S. jets might be hit and retaliate.

Burke inquired about using a destroyer to fire at Castro's tanks.

"Burke," JFK snapped, "I don't want the United States involved in this."

"Hell, Mr. President, we *are* involved," Burke exclaimed. [85]

Rusk continued to argue against any intervention from U.S. forces. Perhaps it was "time for this outfit to go guerrilla," stated Lemnitzer. But Bissell noted that the area swamps made that idea highly unlikely. Around 1 a.m., JFK relented slightly, authorizing one hour of air cover around dawn for B-26s by unmarked jets from the carrier USS Essex. Most B-26s that took off from Nicaragua early on April 19 were piloted by Alabama Air National Guardsmen secretly contracted by the CIA, said Albert "Buck" Persons, who provided training but did not fly in the mission. [86]

Getting more desperate

At the front, Pepe prepared to go down in flames.

"Do you people realize how desperate the situation is?" San Ramon radioed his CIA supervisors in the Blagar around 5 a.m. "Do you back us or quit? All we want is low jet air cover. Need it badly or cannot survive." [87]

An hour later, Pepe asked again, "Where is promised air cover?" And again at 8 a.m.: "Situation critical. Need urgently air support."

"Even his anger was quiet," journalist Haynes Johnson later wrote.

But as his pleas were largely ignored, San Ramon's voice became "edged more with anger and bitterness" yet still calm. "Where the hell is jet cover? Can you throw something into this vital point in battle? Anything." Then finally: "Out of ammo. Enemy closing in. Help must arrive in next hour. Send all available aircraft now." [88]

While some reports say the U.S. jets arrived too late to provide cover for the B-26s, others say they were there in time and escorted some pilots out. But the bottom line was that Castro's forces shot down two more B-26s. A bomber flown by Alabama Air National Guardsmen Riley W. Shamburger and Wade C. Gray sank in the water. Their bodies would not be found. [89]

The other downed plane was flown by two other Alabama airmen, aircraft inspector Thomas Willard "Pete" Ray and pizza restaurateur Leo Francis Baker. The craft fell in a cane field after making some bold strafing runs, a Cuban commander said.

A Cuban soldier shot Baker as he found him holding a grenade, while Ray was killed when he was also discovered armed, according to the commander. Cubans found fake CIA documents on Baker naming him as Leo Francis Bell – or Leo Francis Berliss, according to Cuban reports – of Boston, Mass. [90]

Baker's body was buried in a Havana common grave with others, and family members would not be informed by federal authorities that his remains could not be recovered until 1982. As for Ray, the Cubans would keep his body frozen in a freezer for almost two decades so they could prove that an American was involved in the invasion. U.S. officials would continue to claim Ray was missing until family members unearthed the truth and recovered his remains in 1979. The CIA would not admit that Ray was employed by the agency until 1998. [91]

The wives of the four Alabama airmen would be first told by government-hired lawyers that their husbands had died in Caribbean plane crashes as they transported cargo. Baker's death certificate listed the cause as "accidental drowning." They would be paid twice-a-month pensions through the Bankers

Trust Co. in New York. Widow Jane Shamburger, whose husband was an expert test pilot, would be told not to talk about the matter because doing so "might harm others." [92]

There were 18 men from Alabama involved in piloting planes and training Cuban exiles, said Persons, then a corporate pilot for a Birmingham construction company. "We felt we had been selected by our government for a job helping the national security," Persons would later write in a Birmingham newspaper, where he was managing editor. The pension payments were promised "in event of our deaths." [93]

Cuban exile Ernesto Castellanos was on one of several planes that left Miami for the Bay of Pigs invasion. But shortly before they reached Cuba, an American voice on the plane's radio said, "Turn back, the whole thing is off."

"It was all ordered by the CIA," Castellanos would say in 1963 at a John Birch Society meeting in the Dallas area. "I got another word for the CIA, but I wouldn't say it here." [94]

'I have nothing to fight with'

By 4 p.m. on April 19, San Roman felt completely disgusted and betrayed. Brigade 2506, numbering about 1,300, had held off as many as 20,000 Cuban troops. But they could do so no longer.

He dispatched his last message to the Blagar: "Am destroying all my equipment and communications. Tanks are in sight. I have nothing to fight with. I cannot wait for you." Then he retreated to the woods with what was left of his brigade. [95]

At the Playa Giron beach, Oliva stood and shook his fist at the sea in disgust at the American betrayal. While some of his troops climbed on small vessels to evacuate, Oliva shouted at his men that he would not abandon them. Castro's planes attacked the destroyers that were picking up the exiles, causing the larger ships to head out to sea. Some exiles on the beach shot in frustration at their fellow combatants who were leaving. Over the three days, Cuban planes shot down nine exile B-26s, and sunk two freighters and nine other boats.

On the beach, a soldier who had fought bravely at the San Blas front pointed his pistol at himself. "I didn't want my parents to suffer knowing I had been tortured and then executed," Amado Gayol later said.

"No!" Oliva yelled at Gayol. "You are a man! Not like those at sea." [96]

Oliva convinced him to join the batallion that was marching eastward to the Escambray mountains, from where they planned to mount guerrilla attacks.

But some Castro planes attacked them, and the men scattered into the woods. Castro took Playa Giron by 5:30 p.m.

In Washington, Allen Dulles told Nixon, "Everything is lost. The Cuban invasion is a total failure." Dulles blamed "soft-liners in the Kennedy administration who doomed the operation to failure by last-minute compromises." [97]

Almost 200 Castro troops died, compared to about 100 exiles. Many more of Castro's militia and civilians perished. Some 1,200 exiles, including San Ramon, Oliva, and Manuel Artime, a former member of Castro's rebel army against Batista and the Cuban Revolutionary Council's liaison to the exiles, were taken prisoner. Roberto was wounded in the final hours and escaped to the sea. He would be rescued 20 days later.

On April 21, JFK faced the media and accepted blame for the failed invasion. "I am the responsible officer of the government," he stated. [98]

But in private, Kennedy remarked to a high-ranking administration official that he wanted "to splinter the CIA in a thousand pieces and scatter it to the winds." It was "the beating of our lives," Kennedy said, as he wondered aloud why nobody had talked him out of it. Kennedy also told an editor of The New York Times, which toned down a story on the invasion a few days beforehand, "If you had printed more about the operation, you would have saved us from a colossal mistake."

As a hero of World War II who earned the Purple Heart and the Navy and Marine Corps Medal for his bravery in commanding the destroyed PT-109, Kennedy was not intimidated by military and intelligence leaders. He made plans to rein them in more. But he was shocked at their boldness in the Bay of Pigs invasion to the point that he wondered if he really controlled certain parts of the federal government. "He told other people, 'I'm not sure I'm in charge of this government.' Because they have a secret branch, the CIA, the military," Stone said. "All the [military] chiefs of staff were wildly against him." [99]

Chapter Three

From 'Get Castro' to 'Get JFK'

[The U.S. plot against Castro] was one of the most extensive, sustained, and ultimately futile covert action programs by one country against the government of another in the post-World War II era.
  – **DON BOHNING**, *The Castro Obsession*, 2005

In the aftermath of the failed Bay of Pigs invasion, hawks in the CIA and Defense Department became more fixated on toppling Castro than ever. A mere week after Castro prevailed, Secretary McNamara and Adm. Burke presented JFK with a plan calling for a U.S. military-led invasion of Cuba. Kennedy rejected the idea, but McNamara still told the Joint Chiefs to prepare to implement the plan in case JFK changed his mind. The following month, Kennedy presided over a meeting in which the National Security Council agreed to "not undertake military intervention in Cuba now," but "do nothing that would foreclose the possibility of military intervention in the future." [1]

Kennedy was more interested in providing Cuba and other countries close to the U.S. with aid for education, agriculture, healthcare, and social programs, rather than military adventures. He unveiled the Alliance for Progress, which Congress funded in May 1961 with a $500 million initial grant. Johnson would defund the program. It would fade out by the early 1970s, with few Latin American countries emerging as real democracies.

In Cuba, many people rallied around Castro. The emboldened leader more openly adopted socialism and closer ties with the Soviet Union, according to a State Department report. By late 1961, the value of economic trade between Cuba and the Soviets was estimated at $580 million by the CIA-influenced U.S. Information Agency. [2]

In May, Castro offered to release Bay of Pigs prisoners for about $28 million worth of farm tractors. A committee headed by Eleanor Roosevelt attempted to raise money but was unsuccessful in securing that amount. Some exiles were executed, but San Ramon, Oliva, Artime, and others would remain in prison until freed in late 1962. Negotiations would be led by Navy officer and attorney James B. Donovan and CIA lawyer Milan C. Miskovsky, who would also help secure the release of U-2 spy plane pilot Francis Gary Powers from the Soviet Union in 1962.

Castro would demand $1.5 million in ransom to release the three main leaders. Cuba received another $51.5 million worth of food and medicine to free other Bay of Pigs prisoners.

In mid-1961, the Gen. Maxwell-led report and another by CIA inspector general Lyman Kirkpatrick placed significant blame for the failed invasion on the CIA. The agency had been overwhelmed in organizing the invasion and should have transferred coordinating duties to the Pentagon by late 1960 or canceled the operation, the Maxwell panel said. Other factors for the failure cited included poor "ammunition discipline" by invading forces, the loss of the freighters, sending supply ships too far out to sea, not using closer bases to fly than Nicaragua, restrictions on the use of napalm, and the cancellation of airstrikes at dawn on April 17. [3]

"Such operations should be planned and executed by a governmental mechanism capable of bringing into play, in addition to military and covert techniques, all other forces, political, economic, ideological, and intelligence, which can contribute to its success," the report said. [4]

Kirkpatrick accused Bissell and Barnes of "playing it by ear" and having a "disorganized" command structure with "frenzied" planning. The report also suggested that Bissell misled JFK; Bissell responded in an addendum that the operation would have worked if Kennedy had allowed airstrikes as planned.

Meanwhile, Kennedy tried to follow up on his desire to break up the CIA, pressuring Dulles to resign in November 1961. He attempted to sweeten the situation by awarding Dulles the National Security Medal the day before he left. But Dulles returned to Georgetown and acted like he was "still America's intelligence chief, targeting the president who had ended his illustrious career," Talbot wrote. [5]

By February 1962, JFK forced out Cabell, Bissell, Gen. Lemnitzer, and Adm. Burke. They publicly accepted their fate, but most, like Dulles, burned inwardly.

Cabell, a decorated four-star Air Force general, was particularly incensed. Coming from Southern political nobility, he viewed being fired by Kennedy, who he didn't much like before the Bay of Pigs, as a public humiliation. His grandfather, William Cabell, was a brigadier general in the Confederate Army and mayor of Dallas. His father, Benjamin Cabell, was also a Dallas mayor. And his brother, Earle, became mayor of Dallas just two weeks after the Bay of Pigs invasion.

Cabell returned to the Pentagon, describing Kennedy to others there as a "traitor." He would reportedly work as a consultant for Howard Hughes' aircraft company and NASA, and reunite with Robert Maheu, who was involved in the CIA-Mafia plots. Cabell's "subsequent hatred of John Kennedy became an open secret in Washington," wrote New Orleans District Attorney Jim Garrison. [6]

Of the three top CIA officials ousted, Bissell seemed the least vengeful. He would even admit to some blame in his memoirs, although he wrote that the ultimate fault for the invasion's failure fell on JFK canceling air strikes. "So emotionally involved was I that I may have let my desire to proceed override my good judgment on several matters," Bissell wrote. He would become the head of the think tank Institute for Defense Analysis in 1962 and later work for defense firm United Technologies and the Ford Foundation. [7]

Operation Mongoose

The CIA-Mafia Castro assassination plots were halted immediately after the Bay of Pigs. But after a few months, the hawks resumed the "Get Castro" program through a wider initiative called Operation Mongoose. The project involved not just the CIA, but the Pentagon, State Department, and Justice Department, and was led by Department of Defense official Brig. General Edward Lansdale. At times, Robert Kennedy joined the meetings to report back to his brother.

CIA officer and former FBI agent William Harvey, who some called "America's James Bond," was one of the leaders of Operation Mongoose. CIA officers Theodore Shackley and Thomas Cline were reportedly involved. The task force eventually encompassed about 400 CIA employees and 2,000 Cubans. The annual budget of the operation grew to some $50 million, working out of buildings on the University of Miami campus.

In September 1961, a team of Cubans armed with bazookas and machine guns reportedly came close to killing Castro in Havana. They were arrested in two jeeps parked in a garage near a visible intersection.

In early 1962, Harvey and the FBI's O'Connell met with Roselli and Maheu in New York City. After dinner, they went to the Copacabana, where singer Rosemary Clooney performed. They reportedly observed Phyllis McGuire, part of the McGuire Sisters singing trio and alleged mistress of Giancana, sitting with entertainer Liberace and journalist Dorothy Kilgallen. The latter, who also starred on TV game show *What's My Line?*, would suffer a suspicious death in 1965 after writing columns that questioned the Warren Commission.

O'Connell and Roselli left New York and met with Harvey in Washington a few days later. Harvey picked up some poison pills before leaving for Miami. Roselli phased Giancana and Trafficante out of the program, dealing with Varona and an Italian-speaking Cuban named Maceo, who also went by Garcia-Gomez and Godoy. This phase of the CIA-Mafia plots lacked the "overwhelming, high-level gangster flavor that characterized the first phase," wrote CIA inspector general J.S. Earman in a 1967 report. [8]

Upon securing the poison pills, Varona requested more arms and equipment. Harvey, with the help of Shackley, secured explosives, rifles, hand guns, radios, and a boat radar system. They loaded the weapons in a rented U-Haul truck and parked the vehicle in a restaurant's lot, handing the keys to Roselli to pass on to the Cubans. A while later, they picked up the empty truck with the keys under the seat.

Not even the CIA had cell phones during this time. Harvey and Roselli had to set up prearranged times if they needed to talk. For instance, Harvey could call a pay phone at the Friars Club in Beverly Hills, Calif., at 4 p.m. most days to reach Roselli. [9]

LBJ, who was kept out of the loop on most matters and would complain about not having enough to do, was among the harshest critics of the operation. Shortly after taking over the White House, Johnson would accuse the government of "operating a damned Murder Inc. in the Caribbean." [10]

Chomsky and other historians thought JFK supported the anti-Castro plots, but that was not really the case, Stone said. "Kennedy was in a tough position. Yes, he had to move against Cuba. At the same time, he wanted to save his Alliance for Progress," Stone said. "He wanted to put money into education, into agriculture, not the military." Historian Arthur Schlesinger Jr. also disputed that JFK himself wanted to kill Castro. [11]

Others said the Kennedys exerted intense pressure on the CIA and other agencies to neutralize the Cuban leader. "We cannot overemphasize the extent to which responsible [CIA] officers felt themselves subject to the Kennedy administration's severe pressures to do something about Castro and his regime," Earman wrote. "The fruitless and, in retrospect, often unrealistic plotting should be viewed in that light." [12]

CIA agents "never did these things on their own," CIA officer Jacob Esterline added. "They were an instrument of U.S. policy from beginning to end." [13]

The actions of the Operation Mongoose team ranged from the sophomoric to the deadly. One assassination attempt reportedly included Donovan as he negotiated the release of Bay of Pigs prisoners. A CIA operative gave Donovan a wetsuit lined with spores and bacteria to present to Castro. But Donovan switched out the skin diving suit.

Harvey developed close ties with mobster Roselli. Besides the toxic wetsuit, their unit developed poisonous cigars, pens that could inject victims with poison, and thallium salts to make beard hair fall out. Harvey regularly briefed Richard Helms, who had replaced Bissell as operations director. Helms approved the assassination plan and told Harvey not to brief the new director, John McCone, who had taken over for Dulles in late 1961. [14]

Schemes include fake second coming of Christ

In February 1962, Gen. Lansdale detailed a six-part plan that hoped to culminate in an invasion of Cuba by October. One of his ideas was to convince Cubans that the "second coming" of Christ was about to occur and that Castro was the anti-Christ. Troops were to fire shells from a Navy submarine to create bursts of white light. Somehow, this idea was not executed.

Another idea involved dropping airline tickets to Mexico and fake photos of Castro gorging on food with women from airplanes. Then there was a scheme to blame Castro if astronaut John Glenn Jr. died aboard the Project Mercury spacecraft. Glenn averted that by successfully becoming the first American to orbit the Earth in February 1962.

In addition, officials discussed blowing up a U.S. warship in Guantanamo Bay and blaming Cuba, sinking a boat of Cubans traveling to Florida, and shooting down a civilian airplane and blaming Castro.

Actions that were actually carried out were mostly conducted by anti-Castro Cuban exile groups like Alpha 66. That outfit staged hit-and-run raids on ships transporting goods, a petroleum refinery, power plant, and other targets.

Robert Kennedy was briefed on most aspects, but it wasn't until mid-1962 that he was told about the Mafia involvement. RFK told Edwards and Lawrence Houston, a CIA founder and its first general counsel, to make sure they discussed Mafia involvement beforehand with him in the future since the ties would compromise his department's campaign against gangsters, according to the Rockefeller Commission. [15]

In July 1962, Lansdale reported that 11 CIA guerrilla teams had infiltrated inside Cuba, with one as large as 250 men. At the same time, Castro met with Soviet officials and agreed to allow the Russians to place nuclear missiles in Cuba as a deterrent to the U.S. harassment. The Soviets, who wanted to counter the U.S. putting nuclear warheads that could strike Russia in Turkey and Italy, started sending the missiles that August. [16]

Over the summer, the pill plan fizzled. In August, Harvey and McCone met with Lansdale, Gen. Taylor, McNamara, Rusk, and other high-ranking officials to discuss the operation. McNamara asked if assassination plans against Castro were being pursued, while McCone objected to such plans. Taylor said that military intervention was needed to overthrow Castro, but Kennedy remained steadfast not to use U.S. troops. Lansdale repeatedly asked Harvey about the assassination of Castro over the next several weeks, which Harvey avoided answering. [17]

In September, Roselli told Harvey that Varona was organizing another three-man team to attempt to penetrate Castro's bodyguards. But by October, JFK and other officials were engrossed in a larger situation that had even graver ramifications.

Cuban Missile Crisis

In mid-October, a U-2 spy plane took photographs of the Soviet construction of intermediate-range missile sites in Cuba. In response, some U.S. officials discussed options that included having Cuban exiles bomb the missile sites. A CIA sabotage team intent on destroying a copper mine in Cuba was arrested by Castro police in late October, and another team committed an act of sabotage in early November. [18]

The CIA and military were prepared to go to nuclear war to oust Castro. As officials like U.S. Air Force Gen. Curtis LeMay pushed for a nuclear confrontation, Kennedy tried a more moderate approach. He announced a naval blockade of Cuba on October 22, though he declared in a televised address that a Soviet nuclear attack launched from Cuba would result in a similar response.

"I call on Chairman Khrushchev to halt and eliminate this clandestine, reckless, and provocative threat to world peace and to stabilize relations between our two nations," Kennedy said. "I call upon him further to abandon this course of world domination and to join in an historic effort to end the perilous arms race and to transform the history of man..... Our goal is not the victory of might but the vindication of right – not peace at the expense of freedom but both peace and freedom, here in this hemisphere, and, we hope, around the world." [19]

As leaders of the superpowers negotiated, Castro sent Khrushchev a letter urging him to use the missiles and sacrifice Cuba if necessary. The U.S. was "extremely dangerous," and if the Americans invaded Cuba, "then that would be the moment to eliminate this danger forever, in an act of the most legitimate self-defense," Castro wrote. "However harsh and terrible the solution, there would be no other." [20]

Khrushchev essentially ignored Castro's offer and worked out a deal by October 28. The Soviets agreed to remove the missiles from Cuba, and Kennedy promised to take away U.S. missiles from Turkey and Italy. He also pledged not to invade Cuba with U.S. troops without direct provocation.

"President Kennedy basically...saved a lot of our lives because he did stand his ground," Talbot said. "He took a hard line against the national security people and said, 'No, we're going to peacefully resolve the Cuban Missile Crisis'." [21]

Meanwhile, many top military officers and lower ranking ones seethed with rage at Kennedy, considering him weak when they again had the chance to oust the communists from Cuba. "There was virtually a coup atmosphere in Pentagon circles" against Kennedy, said Daniel Ellsberg, then a defense analyst. In 1971, Ellsberg would leak the Pentagon Papers, a critical study on U.S. involvement in Vietnam.

Stone added, "This is what signed his death warrant. He didn't invade. Everybody in the Pentagon, including Eisenhower, his senior civilians, said, 'Go into Cuba, take them out.' But he didn't. The Soviets had 100,000 troops there. It would have built up into a nuclear explosion out of Cuba. We had far more nuclear weapons than Russia did. That's what the reason was that the Pentagon wanted the war there. They wanted to wipe out the Soviet Union.... The Kennedys and various people around them saved the situation at the last second." [22]

Continuing after Castro

Hawks in the JFK administration continued to try to kill Castro. By the end of 1962, thousands of Cuban exiles were on the CIA's payroll and the agency's station near Miami was its second largest behind the Langley headquarters. [23]

Helms, who became the CIA's director in 1966, would admit to the anti-Castro plots before the House Select Committee on Assassinations in 1978, though he blamed the entire government:

> We had task forces that were striking at Cuba constantly. We were attempting to blow up power plants. We were attempting to ruin sugar mills. We were attempting to do all kinds of things during this period. This was a matter of American government policy. This wasn't the CIA alone. [24]

In March 1963, a poison pill was supposed to be slipped into a chocolate milkshake by Castro's waiter but stuck to a freezer and was ripped open, former

Cuban intelligence chief Fabian Escalante said. By June 1963, Harvey would be reassigned to Italy. But the attempts on Castro would continue until at least 1965, according to the Church Committee, a panel headed by Idaho Sen. Frank Church that examined the CIA and other intelligence agencies about the same time as the Rockefeller Commission focused on the CIA.

While some in his administration had other ideas, JFK would make peaceful public overtures to the Cuban leader. Lisa Howard, a reporter for ABC News, would travel to Cuba in April 1963 to report on Castro. During the filmed interview, as well as in private conversation with Howard, Castro said he was interested in improving U.S. relations.

A meeting between U.S. and Cuban diplomats would be arranged at Howard's New York apartment, and UN diplomat William Attwood met Cuban UN Ambassador Carlos Lechuga there. Less than a week before his assassination, Kennedy would send a message to Castro that he was ready to negotiate normal relations and drop the embargo. JFK would have negotiated the agreement if he had lived, according to former Press Secretary Pierre Salinger. [25]

LBJ would close the government's ties to the Cuban overtures after he took office. But Howard would return several times to Cuba to broadcast ABC segments while lobbying for communication between Washington and Havana. At one point, Howard asked Castro about reports that JFK was having a change of heart towards Cuba before his assassination. "There was evidence," Castro said. Then he added that he shouldn't talk about it, according to a White House memo. [26]

Howard would openly engage in partisan political campaigns and be fired by ABC in late 1964. She would be found dead in 1965, reportedly of a drug overdose. [27]

LBJ would supposedly cancel the Operation Mongoose program by 1965, with the assassination program reportedly moving from Cuba to Southeast Asia and later Iran. But some said attempts on Castro's life would continue. Artime would participate in a failed assassination attempt on Castro in 1965. Cuban official Escalante would claim there were 38 attempts during the Eisenhower administration, 42 under Kennedy, 72 during LBJ's time, and 184 by Nixon's people. [28]

Some disputed those figures, saying the total number of attempts was more like one or two dozen. Whatever the exact number was, it was clear Castro came out ahead. By smarts or sheer luck, Castro would outlive most of his conspirators, remaining as leader of Cuba through the terms of nine U.S. presidents until 2008.

By then, the 82-year-old's deteriorating health would force him to hand over the reins to his brother, Raul. But he had proven that it was easier to kill the president of the United States than the president of Cuba.

"One day, the good Lord will take Fidel Castro away," President George W. Bush would say to reporters in 2007.

Castro, an atheist, would reply with not a small touch of irony, "Now I understand why I survived Bush's plans and the plans of other presidents who ordered my assassination: the good Lord protected me." He would live until age 90, dying of natural causes in 2016. [29]

Years after the Bay of Pigs, some CIA officers would admit their role in keeping Castro in power. "We may have prolonged his existence by encouraging and facilitating the mass exodus [from Cuba] of those who might have developed a viable resistance movement," said an officer who worked in the Havana station in the late 1950s and later in Miami. "This, of course, was a policy decision." [30]

Bay of Pigs leader can't shake demons

As Castro lived long, Bay of Pigs leader Pepe San Ramon tried to move on and work through the demons that whirled around the failed 1961 invasion.

"We all felt, and [Pepe] should have felt, that we were proud of having hit Castro the hardest with so little supplies," Roberto San Ramon said. "That was enough for me to survive the betrayal, but being in charge, Pepe just couldn't." [31]

Pepe wrote that he "hated the United States, and felt that I had been betrayed. ... Many times I had the feeling that we were thrown there to see what happened, because they were sure that Fidel was going to capture us and put all of us in the firing squad and we would be killed and there would be a great scandal in the whole world." [32]

His life and his men's lives were worth little more than cannon fodder to high-ranking American officials in their bid to create enough pressure for a U.S. military invasion of Cuba, without trying to appear that was what they were doing, Pepe believed. Put more succinctly, he thought his men were sacrificed for politics. [33]

Pepe, like Artime and Oliva, would develop a friendship with Robert Kennedy, who provided Pepe and his family with a furnished home for a few months. "There was nobody else in this hemisphere that wanted to help us," Roberto said. "The only open door for Pepe's men, whether financial help or education or another try at Cuba, was the American government – the same government that left us there. And so Pepe ate his words and his pride and went with them." [34]

Artime, a close friend of Hunt, would raise money for the Watergate burglars, a number of whom were American and Cuban veterans of the Bay of Pigs operation. He would die of cancer in 1977 at age 45. Some suspected he was planted with cancer cells, which the CIA reportedly experimented with starting in the 1950s.

Oliva would become a U.S. Army officer, rising to Major General of the Army National Guard in Washington. He would earn a master's degree in international affairs from American University.

Pepe would lay down on his bed in Miami one evening in 1989 and overdose on pills. His brother found him too late.

"I am sorry but I have to do it. There is no other way," Pepe wrote in a note. "This decision is taken after 20 years of struggle against myself. You all know that I have fought back with all my might, with all my will and tried every course available from the sublime to the ridiculous, to no avail. But I am not quitting. I am only dying so my death serves a purpose….. God does not punish guys like me to a life sentence of the soul." [35]

Did Castro send operatives to U.S. to hit JFK?

Roselli, the handsome mobster, would reportedly tell his lawyer, Edward Morgan, that he believed Castro turned some of the same Cuban operatives being used to try to kill him against Kennedy.

Morgan would tell FBI agents in 1967 that Castro became aware of plots against him by interrogating arrested plot suspects. The Cubans' lives were spared if they agreed to secretly work for Castro, while still publicly posing as anti-Castro operatives.

"Castro thereafter employed teams of individuals who were dispatched to the United States for the purpose of assassinating President Kennedy," Morgan said to the FBI. [36]

Journalist Jack Anderson would report that Roselli gave him a similar account in 1971, saying Castro had used underworld associates of Trafficante, who had tried to knock off Castro, to kill Kennedy. LBJ, Hoover, and Major Gen. Edwin Walker would be among those to accuse Castro of being involved in Kennedy's death in retaliation for the plots against him. [37]

There was little question in the mind of Andres Manso Rojas who was behind the JFK assassination. Rojas, a member of Brigade 2506, was among those captured a few days after landing in Cuba in 1961. He survived being beaten and eating food with rats in it. The humid prison had little ventilation and light. Most became quite ill.

"We were left for dead," Rojas would say in a 2016 interview. "It was a very tough ordeal. Many of my friends died."

After two years, he was released and moved to Miami, becoming a leader of the Brigade's Bay of Pigs Museum on a nondescript residential street in the Little Havana section of Miami.

The museum's walls were filled with portraits of those who died in the battle. Books, photos, medals, and other memorabilia were prominently displayed. The large yellow Brigade 2506 flag, presented to Kennedy in a Miami ceremony when prisoners were released, remained on the wall in a glass case. JFK vowed at that 1962 ceremony that the flag would fly in a "free Havana."

Rojas wasn't bitter anymore towards Kennedy. Too much time had passed. But he believed the full truth about his death had yet to be acknowledged by the U.S. government. "Castro got the best of John F. Kennedy," Rojas said. "I believe Castro was the mastermind of the plot against Kennedy." [38]

Bay of Pigs Brigade 2506 veteran Andres Manso Rojas survived some two years in a Castro prison camp before being released. He believes Castro was behind JFK's assassination. [Shay photo]

Chapter Four

Enemies Unite?

Any man is measured by his enemies. The list of those who hated Kennedy the day he died does honor to him.
— **THOMAS G. BUCHANAN**, 1964

Cubans, whether anti-Castro or secretly working for Castro to save their lives, could not have accomplished the kind of coup d'etat and cover-up that many believed occurred in November 1963 in the United States by themselves.

Their obvious allies were those who had assisted in the Bay of Pigs invasion and felt betrayed by the Kennedys, including CIA operatives and leaders, military officials, and mobsters. Less direct allies included right-wing Kennedy haters such as oil billionaire H.L. Hunt, Klansmen, and Birchers. Opportunistic political players like LBJ could have at least participated in the cover-up.

It is unlikely that all of those groups were directly involved or coordinated with each other. The CIA and Mafia had a natural process in place with the plots against Castro. It's possible that several plots existed at the same time, perhaps without each one knowing what the other was doing. Perhaps that is why attempts on Kennedy's life occurred in a variety of cities in 1963, including Chicago, Tampa, Miami, and Nashville.

The one thing the groups had in common with each other was they hated Kennedy. Whether that hatred really united them into a cohesive plot, or they operated in loose connection, was another matter.

The Georgetown 'government in exile'

Allen Dulles came from a prominent family. His grandfather, John W. Foster, was secretary of state under Benjamin Harrison, while uncle Robert Lansing held the same position under Woodrow Wilson.

With such connections, international diplomacy and spying came naturally. Dulles' first introduction to spydom arose during World War I, when he was an operative and diplomat in Europe. In World War II, he joined the Office of Strategic Services and oversaw spies in Switzerland, helping some German Jews escape Hitler. But Dulles later helped some Nazis escape who he thought might provide aid in the new Cold War against the Soviets – Mary Bancroft, one of Dulles' alleged mistresses who also spied on Nazi officers for him, once said his favorite word was "useful." A founder of an organization that later merged into the CIA, Dulles became deputy director for covert operations of the agency in 1950.

By the time Eisenhower appointed him to lead the CIA in early 1953, Dulles had developed a reputation for cunning, secrecy, and ruthlessness. He had "surface charm" that made him a "very popular party guest on the Washington circuit," Talbot noted. But underneath, Dulles was a "very cold man, a man who was capable of sending people to their death with the blink of an eye, a man who was capable of putting his own child, Allen Jr., in the hands of an experimental doctor who was working for the CIA in the notorious MKUltra [mind-control] program."[1]

Dulles was used to presidents who played along with his bloody international chess games. He immediately directed funds to overthrow Iranian Prime Minister Mohammad Mosaddegh in 1953 as part of British and U.S. plans to maintain control of oil fields. The CIA's involvement would not be widely discovered until the 1970s.

In 1954, Dulles, a board member of influential United Fruit Co., oversaw the Guatemalan coup that successfully deposed democratically-elected and social reformer Col. Jacobo Árbenz, whose policies angered United Fruit executives. Arbenz's successors banned political parties and halted reforms that aided the working poor. At the CIA's urging, Guatemala soon formed Latin America's first modern death squad to hunt alleged opponents of the new regime.

Eisenhower, Dulles, and others celebrated the coup at the White House in 1954. In 1999, Bill Clinton would issue a general apology for atrocities by the CIA and U.S. government in Guatemala without providing a financial settlement. In 2011, the government of Guatemala would officially apologize for its role in ousting Arbenz and make financial payments to his family.

In addition, Dulles and Eisenhower authorized a plot to kill Patrice Lumumba, prime minister of the Congo who worked for independence from Belgium, according to committee findings. In 1960, Dulles accused Lumumba of being "bought by the communists." But the CIA did not have a direct role in the eventual 1961 assassination, as Lumumba was captured by Congo opponents and shot to death by a squad believed to include Belgian mercenaries a few days before Kennedy's inauguration. In 2002, Belgian officials would formally apologize for their nation's role. [2]

Dulles never was known to apologize for anything that he did. He had the gall to brag about extramarital affairs in letters to his wife – something most men wouldn't do. He described the women in detail to Clover Dulles, who remained married to him until he died in 1969. Dulles wrote that one was "an attractive Irish-French female whom I took to Scheherazade, where we stayed until the early hours." In another letter, he admitted to being "rather too fond of the company of other ladies." Dulles even introduced Bancroft, the step-granddaughter of *Wall Street Journal* publisher C. W. Barron, to his wife. Clover reportedly approved of their affair, though she wrote in her journal that she wanted to "kill" her husband. She also allegedly took drugs and contemplated suicide at one point. [3]

Dulles never forgave JFK for forcing him to retire from the CIA following the Bay of Pigs invasion. Even though Dulles was likely most responsible for the Cuban fiasco and his ouster was justified, he still blamed Kennedy for not providing air support, said University of Texas professor James K. Galbraith.

"The exiles were [Dulles'] pawns, nothing more, in a bigger, bolder game," Galbraith wrote. "For a time, Kennedy took a political hit at the Bay of Pigs, but he won that particular round. He did not get trapped into an invasion of Cuba." [4]

Right after he was forced to resign, Dulles met regularly with allies in the CIA and military branches in his Georgetown home and at favorite watering holes. Cabell, Bissell, Helms, and longtime CIA counterintelligence chief James Angleton were among those who continued to meet with Dulles. Others, including William Harvey, Howard Hunt, and David Morales, communicated with Dulles through the phone and mail through at least 1963. He had a wide array of contacts throughout the world and even met with anti-Castro Cubans at times. "Dulles would turn his Georgetown home into the center of an anti-Kennedy government in exile," Talbot said.

As JFK approved other steps to erode the CIA's power, such as moving the oversight of overseas agents to U.S. ambassadors, Dulles' "government in exile" took note. It wasn't long before a "clear consensus" arose among the loose network of Dulles cronies that Kennedy "was a national security threat [who] must be removed," Talbot wrote.

Dulles was "the only man with the stature, connections, and decisive will to make something of this enormity [assassinating JFK] happen," claimed Talbot, who admitted that Dulles was skillful at covering his tracks and evidence against him was circumstantial.

Though forcing Dulles and a few other top officials to leave, Kennedy didn't go far enough to rid the CIA of Dulles loyalists and hire people more open to the changes in how he wanted the U.S. to operate in the world, some said. "His problem was he didn't clean house," Stone stated. "Most of those people were Dulles people. That's why we think Dulles was involved in the assassination because of the tremendous power [he] still [had in the CIA]." [5]

Dulles was also involved in the CIA's 1960s regime change scheme from Sukarno to Suharto in Indonesia, Australian researcher Greg Poulgrain wrote. A mineral-exploration business he helped form discovered a large gold deposit in Netherlands New Guinea. Kennedy's support of Indonesia taking over that territory in 1963 complicated Dulles' plan to control the gold mining and could have been another factor in JFK being targeted.

"Starting in the mid-1950s, Sukarno was on Dulles' list of leaders to be liquidated," Poulgrain wrote. "Both Sukarno and Kennedy had political predators and sharing the same one was to be their ultimate historical fate." [6]

The Kennedys crack down after using mob

As the CIA-Mafia plots against Castro show, Dulles and Cabell were no strangers to dealing with the mob. The Kennedys weren't either, though their relations were a little more confrontational.

The Kennedy family had reluctantly accepted aid from bosses such as Giancana to help JFK win the White House in 1960. They also welcomed help from Giancana, Trafficante, Roselli, and others with their "Get Castro" operation.

But despite such underworld support, Robert Kennedy, with the endorsement of JFK, legally prosecuted the very people who had helped his family get ahead. To Giancana, Trafficante, and others, that audacity was betrayal to the highest degree.

To be fair, RFK took on organized crime well before the 1960 race, having been chief counsel of the Senate Rackets Committee from 1957 to 1959. While he targeted corruption in unions representing truckers, bakers, hotel employees, postal workers, textile employees, and garbage collectors, RFK saved special zeal for the mob. He often described his pursuit as a religious quest in terms of good versus evil.

Giancana's dealings with RFK included several high-profile exchanges during Rackets Committee testimony. Born in Chicago to Sicilian immigrants, Giancana had started working for legendary mobster Al Capone as a teen and climbed the ladder to the top of that city's illegal gambling operations. By 1955, he controlled not only gambling and prostitution, but drug and other illegal industries in his hometown.

In one exchange with Kennedy, Giancana refused to answer questions and giggled as he cited the Fifth Amendment. "I thought only little girls giggled, Mr. Giancana," Kennedy retorted. [7]

Upon becoming U.S. attorney general in 1961, RFK tried to make Giancana "enemy number one" in his assault on the mob, wrote biographer Evan Thomas. The Chicago mobster was subject to "constant FBI surveillance and tax and criminal investigations."

The FBI under Hoover at the time officially denied the existence of organized crime, especially the Cosa Nostra Italian-American Mafia whose members had first entered the U.S. in the late 19th century. Among RFK's first moves as attorney general was to form a coordinated program involving all 26 federal law enforcement agencies to investigate the mob.

RFK beefed up the U.S. Justice Department's crime and rackets division, which in 1961 employed only 17 people. That small staff had to try to combat an industry that fielded an estimated 400,000 bookmakers, as well as thousands of drug dealers, pornographers, robbers, and murderers. Most mobsters operated front businesses like restaurants and dry cleaners that served to hide and launder their illegal main sources of income.

Besides more than tripling the crime and rackets division staff by 1963, RFK pursued anti-crime laws in Congress. One in 1961 sought to dismantle the nationwide betting system. In addition, Kennedy enlisted the aid of other government departments like the General Services Administration, which curbed the number of contracts awarded to Mafia-affiliated companies.

"The new laws, plus the close cooperative effort that is being made by all federal agencies, will result in significant action being taken against the leaders of organized crime," Kennedy wrote in a November 1961 letter to June Holloway, then GSA commissioner of the Kansas City region. "I believe that three or four years from now we will look back with pride on our mutual participation in an effort which has such great meaning for the internal security of our country." [8]

The increased enforcement resulted in organized crime-related convictions rising to 373 in 1963 from just 14 in 1960, Kennedy said before a Senate hearing.

But even RFK faced limits in his war on the mob. Some claimed that at times he didn't seem to pursue Giancana, who would not be convicted of a charge until after RFK resigned in 1965, with the same zeal as others. Perhaps the mobster sharing a mistress, Judith Campbell Exner, with JFK played a role in RFK easing up somewhat, they claimed.

"Prosecuting Giancana under federal laws was always going to be difficult, and not just because of the threat of blackmail," Thomas said. "Lacking the anti-racketeering laws of a later age, the feds had to stretch to find jurisdiction over crimes like murder and extortion." [9]

However, Ronald Goldfarb, a prosecutor on RFK's organized crime unit, said Kennedy did not let up on any Mafia figure. "Whatever private arrangements Kennedy may have had with mobsters such as Giancana did not, miraculously, get in the way of our section's aggressive pursuit of these men," he wrote. [10]

Giancana himself felt betrayed by RFK's pursuit. He thought his work in the 1960 election and against Castro would result in the government going easy on him. At one point, Giancana claimed he was not getting his "money's worth" from the Kennedys. [11]

Father's stroke lessens influence on sons

RFK's unit also pursued Florida-born, Sicilian-American Trafficante, who had a 1954 bribery conviction overturned by the Florida Supreme Court. He was arrested several other times in the 1950s on charges that included running illegal lotteries. As Trafficante fended off RFK's prosecution, the mobster became more agitated.

In addition, Kennedy tried to deport New York mobster Frank Costello and Italian-born Johnny Roselli. The latter man began working with Los Angeles crime boss Jack Dragna as a teen and was one of the few mobsters at that time to support civil rights.

RFK also pursued an income tax indictment against Paul D'Amato, a New Jersey nightclub owner and friend of his father's who had been influential during the 1960 West Virginia primary campaign. The elder Kennedy suffered a stroke in late 1961 at age 73, leaving him paralyzed on one side and largely unable to influence his sons' efforts against mobsters. [12]

Carlos Marcello, believed to be Cosa Nostra's top crime boss in New Orleans, was another huge RFK target. Born to Sicilian parents in Tunisia, Marcello settled with his family in New Orleans as a baby in 1911. As a young man, he was convicted of assault and robbery and served five years in prison. In 1938, he was convicted again of selling marijuana and served almost a year in prison.

Marcello then started an alliance with Costello, helping him place illegal slot machines in New Orleans. By 1947, Marcello controlled Louisiana's illegal gambling operation and joined forces with notorious mobster Meyer Lansky to skim money from casinos.

Marcello's annual income through gambling, drugs, and other means was estimated by the New Orleans Metropolitan Crime Commission to be at least $100 million in 1963. Still, he claimed he only made about $1,600 a month as a "tomato salesman." That admission in itself should have raised eyebrows since even as a lowly "tomato salesman," he would have been making more than three times the median family income. [13]

Marcello's passport claimed he was a citizen of Guatemala. So RFK worked to get him deported. In April 1961, Marcello was arrested while visiting immigration authorities in New Orleans and forcibly transported to Guatemala. While his lawyers secured Marcello's return to New Orleans within a month, Kennedy's people kept pursuing that legal avenue. That only made Marcello angrier.

War on Hoffa

Jimmy Hoffa, head of the powerful Teamsters union, was long linked to mob bosses,. He reportedly funneled a $500,000 contribution from Marcello to Nixon for the Republican's 1960 campaign.

Growing up poor in Detroit, Hoffa left school at age 14 to work to help support his family. He started union organizing as a teen at a grocery store, taking on issues such as low wages and abusive treatment. The Teamsters took note of Hoffa's skills, and he joined the union as a labor organizer in 1932.

Hoffa advanced through the ranks, becoming president of Local 299 in 1946, a national officer in 1952, and national president in 1958. The union was already aligned with mobsters before he joined, and Hoffa reportedly increased those alliances with the Mafia.

Robert Kennedy began going after Hoffa in the 1950s, pinning a charge of misusing union funds on him. But Hoffa was acquitted by a jury. Upon becoming attorney general, Kennedy formed a "Get Hoffa" team of prosecutors and investigators. The team would be successful in convincing Hoffa associate Edward Partin to testify against his boss, an effort that eventually resulted in a conviction for jury tampering in 1964. [14]

The mob strikes back

The mob crackdown, of course, had repercussions. In October 1962, Marcello told Edward Becker, a former casino public relations agent, that he was going to get a "nut" to kill JFK, which would effectively remove RFK as attorney general. The House Assassinations Committee would investigate Becker and find Marcello's threat to be credible, said G. Robert Blakey, chief counsel of that investigation. [15]

About the same time, Trafficante told anti-Castro activist Jose Aleman that JFK was "going to be hit." Mob lawyer Frank Ragano claimed he delivered a message from Hoffa to Trafficante and Marcello that requested that they murder the president. [16]

In addition, Hoffa and associate Partin discussed killing Robert Kennedy in 1962, Partin testified before the House Assassinations Committee. Partin passed a polygraph test, and the Justice Department later discovered Hoffa had spoken about killing RFK more than one time. Hoffa seemed to favor bombing RFK's Northern Virginia home at night, which he liked since it would kill "all his damn kids" as well, Partin said. [17]

RFK took few security precautions, despite the family receiving threatening phone calls. Longtime Washington Post executive Benjamin Bradlee said that JFK mentioned to him in early 1963 that Hoffa threatened to kill RFK with a "silenced weapon," according to the House Assassinations Committee. [18]

Other Mafia figures made similar statements against JFK in the eight months before his assassination. FBI electronic wiretaps of mafiosos in New York, Philadelphia, Buffalo, and other cities showed shocking and repeated death threats by them "that indicated the depth of their hatred for Kennedy," Blakey said. [19]

Most mafiosos seemed to dislike Robert Kennedy more than John. Some talked of planting a bomb in RFK's golf bag. "Bobby Kennedy won't stop until he puts us all in jail, all over the country," complained New York City mobster Michelino Clemente. [20]

Eddie McGrath, a gangster in Miami and New York, stated that he'd "gladly go to the penitentiary the rest of my life" for killing RFK. Buffalo mob boss Stefano Magaddino added that they should murder the "whole family, the mother and father, too." [21]

Drawing wealthy oilmen's wrath

JFK also drew the wrath of oil executives such as Dallas billionaire H.L. Hunt and Dallas half-billionaire Clint Murchison Sr. – who also had ties to the CIA, Mafia, and John Birch Society – by supporting a law in 1962 that significantly reduced earnings on investment in foreign oil operations. Then in early 1963, Kennedy proposed to end the industry's lucrative oil depletion allowance, which allowed oil operators to exempt up to 27.5 percent of their income from federal taxes. Doing so would have cost U.S. oil companies about $300 million annually back in the early 1960s. [22]

Hunt was a big supporter of anti-commie activists Joseph McCarthy and Gen. Walker. He was often heard saying that the U.S. would be "much better off without Kennedy," said John Curington, his special assistant for a dozen years. Furthermore, Hunt knew a conspiracy against JFK existed, Curington said. [23]

In 1960, as the Catholic JFK sought the presidency, Hunt had secretly financed printing 200,000 copies of an anti-Catholic sermon given by Rev. W.A. Criswell. He also published a novel through his H.L. Hunt Press about a supposedly utopian society in which the votes of wealthy citizens counted more and political discussion was prohibited on television and radio. Meanwhile, Hunt used the media to push his right-wing views through radio programs such as *Facts Forum* and *Life Line*. [24]

Moreover, H.L.'s son, Nelson Bunker Hunt, kept a list of political leaders to be "gotten rid of," Curington said. Those included Dominican Republic President Juan Bosch Gavino, that nation's first democratically elected leader who was overthrown in a 1963 right-wing coup after seven months in office. [25]

Murchison greased the wheels of high-powered officials like LBJ, Nixon, and Hoover, often having them stay free at his Del Charro resort in La Jolla, Calif., and gamble at the nearby Del Mar racetrack, which Murchison co-owned. They rubbed shoulders with mobsters such as Marcello and Trafficante. Murchison also counted the Cabell brothers among his close associates. The Kennedys were never invited to Del Charro.

'Kill any SOB who gets in my way'

LBJ's desire to be president was legendary. The tall Texan reportedly told some as early as the 1940s – when he was a representative before becoming a senator – that he would be president one day.

Richard Aubrey, a former Dallas County deputy sheriff who worked on LBJ's 1948 Senate campaign, said that LBJ made that boast before him and others in a staff meeting at a Dallas hotel. After Aubrey mentioned that Johnson wasn't even senator yet, LBJ reportedly replied that he'd "kill any SOB who gets in my way." Historians believed LBJ stole that Senate victory, which was marred by allegations of rigged votes, even by dead people. [26]

The enmity between Lyndon Johnson and the Kennedys grew throughout JFK's short term in office. Johnson continued to be excluded from key White House meetings. Staffers laughed at him behind his back, calling him, "Uncle Corn Pone," wrote his brother, Sam Houston Johnson. "He wasn't the number two man in the administration; he was the lowest man on the totem pole," Sam Johnson said. "He felt humiliated time and time again." [27]

By mid-1962, some speculated that JFK would dump LBJ from the 1964 ticket. Johnson faced legal problems related to alleged ties to businessman Billie Sol Estes, who was convicted for defrauding the federal government. Kennedy ordered the FBI to investigate Estes, and the probe extended to LBJ. While Estes was sentenced to prison in 1963, Hoover cleared his buddy, LBJ. [28]

Rumors swirled that Johnson was connected to suspicious murders, as LBJ political advisor Bobby Baker was investigated for bribery and kickbacks in mid-1963. Still, JFK publicly said in October 1963 he would keep Johnson, believing he could shore up support in Texas and other key Southern states.

Kennedy privately searched for a way to dump LBJ without drawing too much backlash. JFK told his secretary, Evelyn Lincoln, that he was seriously thinking about replacing Johnson as his 1964 running mate with North Carolina Gov. Terry Sanford. JFK also wanted to fire the petty, vincdictive Hoover.

Hoover's legendary blackmail files on politicians came in handy in 1963. He reportedly agreed with RFK to keep allegations that Bobby Baker had helped arrange a tryst between JFK and a woman who had been a Communist Party member out of the Senate investigations of Baker. Hoover allegedly was able to do that by threatening to release embarrassing details about senators. In exchange, RFK lent assurances that Hoover's position was safe and approved wiretaps on MLK so the FBI could investigate allegations that some advisors of the civil rights leader were communists, according to author Evan Thomas. [29]

Mac and LBJ

Out of all of LBJ's protégés, few were as controversial as Malcolm "Mac" Wallace. Some claimed Wallace would do anything for Johnson — even kill. But that reputation was overblown, author Joan Mellen wrote.

The Texas-born Wallace served in the Marines, then attended the University of Texas at Austin. He was popular enough to be voted student body president, a key position at the state's largest university. Wallace supported progressive causes, leading a protest march after UT President Homer Rainey was fired for allegedly having left-wing sympathies. He organized a visit by LBJ in 1944 to speak with students at the Austin campus.

Wallace earned a master's degree in economics in 1947 and entered a doctoral program at Columbia University. Two years later, LBJ reportedly helped him obtain a job as an economist with the U.S. Department of Agriculture in the D.C. area. He seemed to have a bright future.

But Wallace's family life wasn't right. Three years after marrying Mary Andre Barton in 1947, Wallace reportedly had an affair with LBJ's sister, Josefa. At the same time, Josefa was said to be sleeping with John Douglas Kinser, who operated a par-three golf course in Austin. Kinser was also suspected of cavorting with Mary Andre, who filed for divorce in 1950. It was a regular soap opera that became stranger and more complex over time. [30]

On a sunny October afternoon in 1951, Wallace walked into the clubhouse of the Butler Park Pitch & Putt course and confronted Kinser. Numerous golfers were just outside. They heard shots and observed Wallace, his shirt covered in blood, running towards his car. A golfer took down Wallace's vehicle license plate number, and police soon caught him. Police found the bloody shirt and a spent cartridge in Wallace's car. [31]

The case against Wallace seemed airtight. Most jurors pushed for a first-degree murder verdict. But one juror, reportedly a cousin and friend of one of Wallace's LBJ-connected lawyers, lobbied for acquittal. Several jurors said they had been threatened by "Johnson men," including one who pointed a shotgun at him and pulled the trigger. It had only clicked, being empty.

The jury compromised to recommend a suspended sentence in exchange for a first-degree murder verdict. Most jurors assumed Judge Charles Betts would overrule the suspended sentence, but he didn't. Wallace walked out of court a free man. [32]

The convicted murderer joined a company that eventually became part of Dallas defense contractor LTV in 1961. Right-wing oilman D. Harold Byrd, a major LBJ donor who happened to own the Texas School Book Depository building from the 1930s until the 1970s, was a principal of LTV.

Despite the murder conviction, Wallace was able to get a government security clearance and eventually managed the firm's purchasing department. A Naval intelligence officer handling the case said that LBJ had intervened to help Wallace obtain the clearance. [33]

In June 1961, U.S. Agriculture Department investigator Henry Marshall was found dead on his Texas family farm by the side of his Chevy pickup truck. Marshall had been shot five times with his own rifle. He suffered cuts on his head, evidence of a fight with someone. Carbon monoxide was found in his lungs.

The year before, Marshall had started investigating a cotton allotment scheme run by Estes. The scam allowed Estes to amass millions of dollars worth of federal cotton allotment payments on depressed land, some of which was owned by the federal government.

A local peace justice and grand jury ruled Marshall's death a suicide. Marshall's wife, Sybil, and other family members did not believe he had committed suicide. They offered a reward for information leading to a murder conviction.

Texas Rangers Capt. Clinton Peoples sided with them. He said that Marshall had "a terrific struggle" with someone, alluding to his head damage. Finally in 1984, a grand jury would rule that Marshall's death was a homicide. A state judge would affirm that ruling the following year. [34]

Estes would reportedly tell the grand jury that he and LBJ, who he claimed was involved in his schemes, had discussed Marshall's case back in 1961. Wallace, who had moved to California to work for Ling Electronics in early 1961, was recruited to kill Marshall, Estes claimed. Family members of LBJ and Wallace called Estes a liar. [35]

Others died suspiciously. The body of George Krutilek, an accountant for Estes, was found in his car in a West Texas desert soon after FBI agents questioned him about Estes in 1962. The windows were rolled up. A hose led to the vehicle's interior but was not connected to the exhaust pipe.

Krutilek had a severe bruise on his head and no trace of carbon monoxide in his lungs. A coroner ruled the cause was cardiac arrest. Several similar cases soon followed. [36]

By 1963, some thought LBJ – long associated with dirty politics   was going to face significant legal problems. That changed in a few fateful seconds.

Chapter Five

Mystery Wrapped in an Enigma

I did not find my ideal. Obviously, utopia does not exist. I could travel and change countries the rest of my life and never find it.
  – **LEE HARVEY OSWALD**, 1962

Raised by a mostly single mother who sometimes considered her sons to be burdensome, Lee Harvey Oswald bounced around from New Orleans to Dallas to Fort Worth to New York City, then back to New Orleans and Fort Worth. By the time he joined the Marines at age 17, Oswald had lived at 22 different addresses and attended 12 schools.

As a teen, he retreated from his chaotic upbringing by viewing an FBI-approved spy series starring Richard Carlson called *I Led Three Lives*. The 117-episode television show was based on the life of Herbert Philbrick, an advertising executive who infiltrated the Communist Party to inform the FBI in the 1940s. [1]

Philbrick spent much of the episodes lying about what he was actually doing, denying he was a spy or an FBI informant. "A communist will swear to anything," Carlson's character said at one point. "And why shouldn't he? What does the Bible mean to him?" [2]

Lee would "became really engrossed" in that anti-communist spy TV show, said his older brother, Robert Jr. "He liked the atmosphere that you could do anything that you wanted to do, that you could imagine you could do.... That was a training ground [for] his imagination." [3]

Oswald's insurance agent father, Robert, died of a heart attack in 1939 two months before he was born. Robert was "a very good man," said Marguerite Oswald, adding that the short marriage was "the only happy part" of her life. [4]

Marguerite struggled through numerous odd jobs to support her sons, including operating a storefront that sold groceries and sewing supplies called Oswald's Notion Shop. Robert and half-brother John Edward Pic were placed in various orphanages and boarding schools, including the Bethlehem Children's Home in New Orleans, when Lee was only two.

Oswald would refer to his poverty-stricken childhood and low-wage jobs held by his mother numerous times as reasons that he opposed U.S. capitalism and searched in vain for a fairer system in the Soviet Union. Some researchers said Oswald's background fit the pattern of CIA defector program recruits who came from low-income childhoods, meshing well into the Soviet propaganda machine. [5]

By putting her sons in orphanages and boarding schools or having others watch them, Marguerite conveyed early in their lives that she felt they were a burden on her, Robert said. Part of Oswald's problems stemmed from his mother, who attempted "to dominate" her sons, he said. Lee was "able to put up with her more" and was "more of a listener than a talker," but not an introvert, Robert said. [6]

Oswald's nomadic childhood and the three short marriages were not Marguerite's fault, she maintained. Marguerite blamed circumstances such as Oswald's dad dying, causing her to have to support her sons alone. "I often held two jobs trying to support my children," she said. [7]

At one point in New Orleans, Marguerite and Lee moved close to her sister, Lillian Murret, who watched Oswald for a time. Murret's husband, Charles, was a bookie "under the control" of Marcello, said Blakey. The House Assassinations Committee report called Murret a "minor underworld gambling figure" and "surrogate father of sorts throughout much of Oswald's life in New Orleans." [8]

Marguerite knew several Marcello associates, including a "personal aide or driver to Marcello," according to the House Committee. They lived at one time above a pool hall, though his mother said it wasn't that bad since wealthy people and "fine citizens" lived around her. [9]

Marguerite disputed that Oswald's upbringing caused him more problems than the normal child. "There have been so many psychiatrists saying Oswald was by himself, and he had a father image [problem]. There are many, many children with one parent who are perfectly normal children, and I happen to be one myself," said Marguerite. Her mother died when she was young, and her father raised her with the aid of housekeepers and relatives. [10]

Marguerite put Oswald into the Bethlehem orphanage for a year shortly after his third birthday. She became engaged to electrical engineer Edwin Ekdahl in early 1944, and the couple moved with Lee to Dallas. Robert and John joined them later after the school year was completed. Shortly after the couple married in 1945, Robert and John were shipped to a military academy in Mississippi.

Lee moved with Marguerite and Ekdahl to suburban Fort Worth, where he attended his first school, Benbrook Elementary. Marguerite and Ekdahl argued over money, and she suspected he cheated on her, according to the Warren Report. At one point, she recruited John and his friends to pose as telegram carriers at a Fort Worth apartment that Ekdahl reportedly also rented to see another woman. Marguerite said she found him there with a scantily-dressed woman when he told her he was out of town on business. [11]

They divorced in 1948, with Ekdahl claiming that Marguerite "constantly nagged" him, argued over money, and threw items at him. She denied those charges, but a jury found Marguerite guilty of "cruel treatment" while still awarding her $1,500. She and her sons eventually lived in the same home, where Marguerite would leave the boys alone when she worked. They moved to Fort Worth, and Marguerite enticed John to leave school to work in a shoe store to help support them.

After John joined the Coast Guard in 1950, Robert went to work in a grocery store to help support the family. He returned to school but did not graduate before entering the Marines in 1952.

Move to 'damned Yankee' town

Lee and Marguerite moved to New York to live with John and his wife shortly after Robert left. But Marguerite and John's wife argued, and during one confrontation, Lee intervened by pulling a pocket knife, according to the Warren Report. Marguerite said her son was whittling with the "small" knife and got between them during an intense argument to try to calm things down. [12]

They soon moved into a basement apartment in the Bronx. Lee reportedly missed many days of school, exacerbated by likely having dyslexia. A teacher reported that he spent most of his time in class "sailing paper planes around the room." An attendance officer found him one day at the Bronx Zoo, and Oswald reportedly called the official a "damned Yankee." Lee had to go to court for truancy and was put on probation. In early 1954, they moved back to New Orleans, staying with the Murrets briefly. [13]

Oswald supposedly started reading Marxist books and pamphlets as a teen, reportedly being handed such a pamphlet on a New York street at the age of 13. But Edward Voebel, a childhood friend in New Orleans, said reports that Oswald was already studying communism as a teen were "baloney." After he returned to New Orleans, Oswald had more interest in fishing and guns, Voebel said.

"We never discussed anything like [politics]," Voebel said. "The only things Lee would be reading when I would be at his home would be comic books and the normal things that kids read... He wasn't a great reader." [14]

However, Marguerite maintained that Oswald was "a reader" and eagerly devoured Robert's Marine manual after his brother enlisted. Oswald began to read communist material around age 16, getting books from the library, his mom said. "From early childhood, he liked histories and maps," Marguerite said. [15]

Oswald got in fights at Beauregard Junior High, but he didn't start them, Voebel said. "He was going to make sure that he ended it," Voebel said. "If you picked on Lee, you had a fight on your hands.... [Oswald] didn't like to be told what to do." [16]

Voebel helped encourage Oswald to join the Civil Air Patrol in New Orleans. The federally supported non-profit corporation served as the official civilian auxiliary of the U.S. Air Force, guiding young minds into the military. David Ferrie, who was two decades older than Oswald and later became a pilot and associate of Marcello, was a guest lecturer of the unit.

Oswald was gung-ho at first about the patrol but soon lost interest, Voebel said. "He even got a paper route to get enough money together to buy the uniform.... We were having classes then on the weather, and that can be a drab subject, although it is essential. But maybe that's why he quit coming." [17]

Upon being discharged from the military in 1955, Robert settled in Fort Worth, rather than in New Orleans. Lee tried to join the Marines with a false statement from Marguerite that he was 17, but that didn't work.

Oswald soon quit school to work for a few months as a messenger for a shipping company and dental lab. One of his bosses, Gerard F. Tujague, would become vice president of the anti-Castro group Friends of Democratic Cuba. In July 1956, Marguerite moved again to Fort Worth, where Oswald attended Arlington Heights High School. But schooling did not interest him; he had bigger plans. [18]

Oswald enlists to 'see the world'

As soon as he turned 17 in October 1956, Oswald left high school to enlist. He went into the Marines "not because I was a patriot, but I wanted to get away from the drudgery and to see the world," he told a friend. [19]

Oswald completed basic training in California and did well enough in rifle marksmanship to qualify as a sharpshooter. But in 1959 when he was discharged from the Marines, he scored 21 points lower and was only rated a marksman.

In 1957, Oswald received a "confidential" security clearance and finished seventh in his radar operation training class of 30 at Keesler Air Force Base in Biloxi, Miss. He soon left for a U.S. military base near Atsugi, Japan, that housed the CIA's secret U-2 spy planes. The high-altitude planes flew missions over China and the Soviet Union starting in 1956, taking high-resolution pictures of enemy military bases and other facilities.

For more than a year, Oswald served as a radar operator at Atsugi, with access to special equipment that could determine an aircraft's flight altitude. Few questioned his Russian studies, even as he snapped photographs around the areas where the U-2s were stationed and took a heightened interest in meetings on classified material by his unit's intelligence officer. [20]

In Japan, Oswald frequented a posh Tokyo nightclub called the Queen Bee, usually reserved for military officers and U-2 pilots. A night there could cost upwards of $100, but somehow the Marine private, making $85 a month, spent many an evening there. Oswald reportedly met an attractive hostess suspected of being a KGB informant and began a relationship with her after meeting with an intelligence officer who reportedly had him pass on false information to her. He supposedly lost his virginity to a Japanese woman. [21]

Oswald's intelligence contact could have been Richard Case Nagell, who did counterintelligence for the Army in the late 1950s and later for the CIA. Nagell learned that Oswald also visited the Soviet Embassy in Tokyo, meeting with Col. Nikolai Eroshkin of the GRU, part of the Soviet military intelligence apparatus. The CIA at the time tried to get Eroshkin to defect to its side. Oswald also met with Tokyo University political science professor Chikao Fujisawa, who was believed to have worked for both Japanese and Soviet intelligence agencies. Nagell claimed he tried to recruit Fujisawa to the CIA before the professor attempted to blackmail him into working for the Soviets. [22]

Fellow troops nicknamed him "Ozzie Rabbit" after a cartoon character and "Oswaldskovich" for his Russian studies, which some suspected he pursued as an intelligence mission. Several said he was not an outspoken advocate of communism. A few called him "Mrs. Oswald" and hazed him mercilessly, throwing him in the shower dressed. Unlike his younger days, Oswald did not fight back in most cases. [23]

One instance where Oswald did apparently retaliate was when he reportedly fired a gunshot into a wall with an unregistered pistol as some Marines taunted him. Oswald wounded himself another time when a .22 bullet grazed his arm. Some thought he did so to avoid leaving Japan; he eventually shipped out to Taiwan and the Philippines.

After Oswald dumped a drink on a superior officer who he thought put him on KP duty too much and threatened to fight him, he was sentenced to the military jail for several weeks. Fellow Marines said he was less communicative afterwards, associating more with Japanese friends. "Lee would rebel against the discipline of the Marine Corps when he had the opportunity to, when the leeway was there," Robert said. [24]

Back in the USA

In late 1958, Oswald transferred to the El Toro Marine base in California, where U-2s frequently flew. He showed interest in Cuba and expressed sympathy for Castro but was not a communist, said Lt. John Donovan, a commander of Oswald's radar crew. However, Oswald believed at that time that communism was a better system than capitalism, said fellow Marine Kerry Thornley. Oswald dreamed about joining the Cuban army and helping to "free" other Caribbean islands, Marine Nelson Delgado said. [25]

At the California base, Oswald was seen studying Russian while off duty. He also might have been recruited for an intelligence mission against Castro in Cuba. Gerry Hemming, who helped Castro's troops before becoming disillusioned and training anti-Castro exiles in Florida, said he met Oswald in southern California in early 1959. Oswald supposedly wanted to desert the U.S. military and join Castro's forces; Hemming suspected he was an intelligence plant. [26]

In August 1959, Oswald, who was not due to be released until December, asked for an early discharge from the Marines, claiming his mother needed him. He applied for a passport, saying he intended to travel to Russia and Cuba. He received the early discharge and passport.

"This did not square with the notion of going home to look after his mother, but there is no sign that the Marine Corps raised any query," noted authors Anthony Summers and Robbyn Swan. [27]

Part of fake defector program?

At times, Oswald was "all things to all people," observed Blakey. "Lee Harvey Oswald is a mystery wrapped up in an enigma, hidden behind a riddle....[He was] a Marine, working in a secure institution, having a security clearance. At the same time, you find him reading Marxist literature, defecting to the Soviet Union. Is he going as a defector or is he going as an agent for the American government?" [28]

Others speculated that Oswald was part of a covert intelligence program to send agents into the Soviet Union as fake defectors to learn valuable information about the superpower rival. In the 18 months before 1960, at least nine former military servicemen or National Security Agency employees made such defections, according to Summers. [29]

The raw 20-year-old Oswald was "an improbable candidate for a mission behind the Iron Curtain," Summers noted. However, intelligence agencies could have monitored him as an "unwitting tool" on how the Soviets handled military defectors, he said. The State Department in 1963 studied Oswald and other defectors, and officials had been unsure then whether Oswald was "one of ours or one of theirs," said Otto Otepka, a former chief security officer at that department. [30]

David Bucknell, a Marine who was stationed with Oswald in California, said Oswald confided to him that he was discharged early to go to the Soviet Union on an intelligence mission. But he told others that he was a Marxist or socialist who believed in acting on his principles, not sitting around talking, as he saw so many do. [31]

Jim Wilcott, who worked in the CIA's Tokyo branch as a finance officer from 1960 to 1964, said agents there told him Oswald was recruited by the CIA when he was stationed at Atsugi. Wilcott didn't believe them at first, but he eventually did after "six or seven" agents expressed that belief.

"I believe that Oswald was a double agent, was sent over to the Soviet Union to do intelligence work, that the defection was phony," Wilcott said to the House Assassinations Committee in 1978. [32]

An agent told him the cryptonym that Oswald used to obtain funds when he returned to the U.S. from the Soviet Union. Wilcott recognized the cryptonym as one he had authorized – his duties in Tokyo had included handling some $4 million a month in unmarked bills for dirty tricks and payments. [33]

"It was a cryptonym that I was familiar with, that it must have been at least two or three occasions that I had remembered it. And it did ring a bell," Wilcott said. [34]

'Do like Hemingway'

Before leaving for the Soviet Union, Oswald visited his family in Fort Worth. He told his mother and brother that he would be able to make more money working on a ship or in the exporting business, and he might go to Cuba.

"He wants to do like Hemingway," Robert said. "He wants to get some experience and write about it." [35]

Oswald's brother was shocked when he heard he was going to the Soviet Union. "That's almost unbelievable," Robert said. "The Cold War was going on. He was just out of the Marine Corps. It just didn't fit." [36]

In late 1959, Oswald obtained a tourist visa to Moscow in Finland. Once in the Soviet capital, Russian Intourist guide Rimma Shirakova showed him around the city. She suggested he use the name, "Alik," which was a common name in the USSR that was easier for Russians to pronounce than Lee. Oswald told her he wanted to defect, and she was "flabbergasted" but agreed to help. [37]

When told the Soviet government declined to extend his visa, Oswald cut his wrist in the hotel room, causing a relatively minor, yet bloody, wound. Shirakova reportedly found him unconscious and called for help. Oswald was taken to a Moscow hospital, where he told officials he wanted to become a citizen of their country.

"The most important thing for Alik was that he wanted to become famous," Shirakova said. "He was fanatic about it." [38]

On Halloween 1959, Oswald visited the American Embassy in Moscow and informed senior consular official Richard Snyder that he wanted to renounce his U.S. citizenship. Snyder said Oswald seemed "to know what his mission was. He took charge, in a sense, of the conversation right from the beginning." [39]

Oswald presented a signed note stating that he was taking "these steps for political reasons. My request for the revoking of my American citizenship is made only after the longest and most serious considerations." He "alluded to hardships endured by his mother as a worker, referring to them as experiences that he did not intend to have himself, even though he stated that he had never held a civilian job." He said he volunteered to give Soviet officials information about U-2 radar operations, adding mysteriously that "he might know something of special interest." [40]

Snyder, who worked for the CIA in 1949 and 1950 while waiting for a foreign service appointment, told Oswald to return in two days to make a formal renunciation when support staff was there. That would give them both time to think about it. Instead, Oswald wrote to Ambassador Llewellyn Thompson protesting Snyder's refusal to act that day. [41]

Snyder then sent Oswald a letter saying he could come back to the embassy to formally renounce his citizenship. "Privately, I took his letter [to Thompson] as a sign of waffling, a resort to rhetoric instead of action," Snyder said. [42]

Oswald's defection made news, and among the journalists who interviewed him at that time was Priscilla Johnson McMillan. She had applied to join the

CIA in 1952 and was not approved supposedly because she had been a member of the United World Federalists. McMillan worked as a translator for the U.S. Embassy in Moscow before obtaining employment as a reporter for the North American News Alliance. [43]

As her stories appeared in newspapers such as the Washington Evening Star, McMillan maintained contact with the CIA. "I think that Miss Johnson [McMillan] can be encouraged to write pretty much the articles we want," CIA officer Donald Jameson wrote in a memo in late 1962. "It would be important to avoid making her think that she was being used as a propaganda tool and expected to write what she is told." [44]

McMillan thought Oswald's knowledge about communist economic theories in 1959 was "very superficial." She noted that he had not returned to the American embassy to formally renounce his American citizenship and seemed to avoid doing so in case he changed his mind about staying in Russia. [45]

'Living big' in Minsk

The Soviets sent Oswald to Minsk, an industrial city about 450 miles southwest of Moscow, to be a lathe operator in a 25-acre electronics factory. The 5,300 employees, more than half of whom were women, made military and space equipment, as well as thousands of radios and televisions. Several radios, phonographs, and TV sets made at that plant were showcased – along with more famous items like the Sputnik satellite – at the 1959 Soviet National Exhibition in New York. The factory was a "vast enterprise created in the early '50s," Oswald wrote. [46]

Oswald lived in a furnished, low-rent apartment, which featured a balcony overlooking a river. He was kept under constant surveillance by tourist agency employees and others, including the KGB. He purchased a shotgun and joined a hunting club. He dated numerous women, who were thrilled to meet an American.

"I'm living big and am very satisfied," Oswald wrote. [47]

People were mostly friendly. The reconstruction of Minsk after World War II was an amazing story, "reflecting the courage of its builders," Oswald said. The 500-room Hotel Minsk was built in three months in 1957. Bread and meat were relatively cheap, but luxuries like chocolate could cost four times as much as in the U.S. Motorcycles and TV sets were snapped up immediately, but the process of buying a refrigerator or vacuum cleaner took about three months. A car could take a year to purchase, Oswald wrote. [48]

Higher education students could be paid to attend institutions, in contrast to the U.S., where students must pay tuition to learn, Oswald noted. As a result, the USSR had more doctors per capita than any country in the world, and turned out many more engineers and other specialists than the U.S. Medical care was covered by the government, and even vacations to resorts near the Black and Caspian seas were partly subsidized.

Oswald's defection concerned U.S. military officials enough that at the last base he had served in California, radar frequencies and other codes were changed. Officials in civilian clothes visited the base to question troops about Oswald. [49]

In May 1960, a U-2 plane piloted by Powers was shot down by a Russian missile. Powers questioned whether Oswald might have given information to the Soviets that helped them shoot down his plane. Oswald repeatedly denied doing so. [50]

At the Atsugi and El Toro bases, Oswald "had access to equipment which included height-finding radar" for U-2s and was a trained radar operator, Powers noted. While in the process of defecting to the Soviet Union less than a year before Powers was shot down, Oswald "intimated that he might know something of special interest," Powers wrote. [51]

The incident effectively ended peace talks between Khrushchev and Eisenhower. Powers noted that there had been no U-2 flights above the Soviet Union for two years before his. "Could Eisenhower have wanted Khrushchev to know of the flights?" he wondered. Others thought it could have been a direct attempt by military or CIA leaders to disrupt attempts at detente. [52]

Following almost two years in prison, officials swapped Powers and student Frederic Pryor, who had been arrested in 1961 by East German police, for Soviet KGB Col. Vilyam Fisher.

In mid-1960, Oswald began a relationship with co-worker Ella German and proposed to her in early 1961. She turned him down, saying she did not love him and was afraid to marry an American, who she thought might be arrested by the Soviets if relations with the U.S. didn't improve. When Ella would hear that Alik was the primary suspect in Kennedy's assassination, she would not believe it. "He was so gentle," Ella said. [53]

Around that time, the CIA's Special Investigations Group – known as "the office that spied on spies" – started investigating Oswald, CIA analyst Ann Egerter told the House Assassinations Committee. The SIG was part of a division headed by Angleton, who former Army intelligence and NSA officer John Newman believed worked to pin the JFK killing on Oswald. [54]

Souring on Soviet lifestyle

Oswald soon soured on Soviet life, writing in his journal about inequalities between average citizens and Communist Party members, the lack of food choices, and the inability to travel.

Party members were "opportunists" who were only interested in their own welfare, Oswald said. There were few places to have fun and too many mandatory meetings where the attention level of attendees was monitored by party members. Nobody likes these long lectures, especially after working hard for hours, but they are compulsory, he noted. 55

Information from the U.S. and other countries was controlled through towers that jammed foreign broadcasts. While some engaged in petty theft of piglets and lamps, large-scale embezzlement of government funds was problematic enough to cause the government to reinstate the death penalty in certain cases in 1961, Oswald reported. 56

Most work was "drab," with plants bogged down in bureaucracy and controlled by outside party members. Workers had little say about conditions, which could be health threatening, even dangerous. Noise at the stamp and pressing shop in the electronics plant where Oswald worked was "almost deafening," he wrote.

"Metal grinds against metal and steel saws cut through iron ingots at the rate of an inch a minute," he wrote. "The floor is covered with oil used to drain the heat of the metal being worked so one has to watch one's footing; here the workers' hands are as black as the floor and seem to be [so] eternally." 57

In the plastics department, 47 women and three disabled people "suffer the worst conditions" in the factory due to handling red-hot liquid plastic and breathing in poisonous fumes, Oswald noted. But they are given more vacation, 30 days annually, compared to three weeks for most workers.

Housing was tight with long waiting lists for apartments. Citizens sometimes faked having a baby to get their names higher on the lists. Voting was mandatory, and there were no choices other than the one party member per position. "The system ensures a 99% voter turnout and predetermined victory," Oswald wrote. Citizens could write in a candidate, but few dared to do so since party members monitored voters in the booths and knew which cards they used.

"If the entire population used the polling booth, they could beat the system," Oswald wrote. "However, years of mass discipline and fear have made the people afraid to attempt any such demonstration." 58

Visitors were mostly forced to take tours of prearranged sites that depicted a phony view of real conditions, Oswald noted. At times, police would order people out of their apartments and dormitories to welcome guests in the street with "yellowish waving hands." Visitors were often taken to a collective "show" farm about 12 miles outside Moscow, featuring automatic milking machines, feeders, and floor cleaners. The nice apartment houses contained cafes and stores built into the first floors.

Meanwhile, those who didn't "want to be duped" could visit a real collective farm some 24 miles outside Moscow, Oswald wrote. The huts of residents there did not have electricity, indoor plumbing, or natural gas. There were some 65.5 million people – about 31 percent of Russia's population – living on more than 50,000 such collective farms in the Soviet Union, he claimed. [59]

In February 1961, Oswald wrote to the U.S. Embassy in Moscow to request his American passport, saying he wanted to return to America if the government did not take legal action against him. He noted that he had not become a Soviet citizen. "I hope that in recalling the responsibility I have to America that you remember yours in doing everything you can to help me since I am an American citizen," he wrote. [60]

Marriage and 'maturing effect'

In March, Oswald met Marina Prusakova, a 19-year-old pharmacy worker, at a trade union dance, telling her his name was "Alik." She was not a party member, but an uncle with whom she lived was.

Oswald soon met Col. Ilya Prusakova, who worked in the Ministry of Internal Affairs and some believe could have been affiliated with the KGB, and Marina's aunt, Valya Prusakova. At one point, Oswald told Prusakova he had come to live in Russia "forever," despite recently writing the American Embassy that he sought to leave the USSR. The colonel said he would help him "organize" his life in Minsk. [61]

Marina and Oswald married in late April, about six weeks after meeting. Marina claimed she did not marry him in hopes of moving to the U.S. but was really in love with him and wanted to have her own apartment and a family. Oswald noted in his diary that he married Marina "to hurt Ella" but was also "in love with Marina," despite the short courtship that seemed suspicious on the surface. [62]

After a month or so of marriage, Oswald wrote that he told Marina he wanted to return to the U.S. She was "startled" and said she would miss relatives too much. She also was concerned that Oswald could leave her alone. "I don't have any guarantee that you won't abandon me there," Marina said, according to a transcript by the KGB, which had bugged the Oswald's apartment. "Then what do I do?"

"If you don't love me, then don't go," Oswald replied. "What do you have here? One room, and even that isn't yours. I want to live [in the U.S.] because the standard of living is high."

"And did you think you would come here and you wouldn't have to work and you'd just live?" Marina shot back. "Why didn't you study? You could study. You're just lazy."

"You don't understand anything," Oswald stated. "People leave this country by the millions. Here are crude people." Marina eventually encouraged her husband to pursue a move. But they argued over more than that. Oswald was not happy with Marina's cooking and cleaning skills. She didn't appreciate his criticism.

Marina wondered if she had made the right choice in marrying Oswald and reportedly reunited with an old boyfriend on a warm July evening, according to Mailer. She felt guilty about cheating but kept that secret. Lee maintained his own deceit. Sometimes she suspected he had only married her to make it more difficult for U.S. authorities to arrest him for possible treason if he had a wife and child. He regularly wrote in a journal, causing her to ask him if he was a spy.

"What if I were?" Oswald shot back. But when he saw her worried look, he said he was only joking. The KGB and secret police would later conclude that Oswald was not somehow affiliated with the CIA or other U.S. intelligence agencies; he had never tried to locate hidden industrial plants or do anything similar to raise suspicions. But others were not sure. The substantial notes he took contained minute details about factories, "phony" collective farms, and other aspects that could interest American officials. The Soviets continued to keep Oswald under reduced surveillance until the day he left the country.

"Oswald was to tell his wife many a lie over their years together, but no single deceit may have been as large as his decision not to inform Marina or Valya or Ilya before the marriage that in his heart he was already on his way back to America," wrote Mailer. [64]

Not wanting to tip off Soviet police in Minsk about his intentions, Oswald visited Moscow in July 1961 during a vacation. At the embassy, he reunited with Snyder, telling him he had not told Soviet authorities any confidential information and had not even been asked anything about it. Snyder believed him.

Oswald stated he had gained a new appreciation of the U.S. and the meaning of freedom. Snyder said he did not know any grounds for prosecution of him but could not give any formal assurances.

"Twenty months of the realities of life in the Soviet Union have clearly had a maturing effect on Oswald," an embassy official reported to the State Department. "Much of the arrogance and bravado which characterized him on his first visit to the [U.S.] Embassy appears to have left him." [65]

'Enemy of the people'

Marina soon joined Oswald in Moscow, where embassy officials interviewed her. When they returned to Minsk in mid-July, they were shocked to discover some Soviet officials had called Marina's work about their visit.

"There followed the usual 'enemy of the people' meeting, in which, in her absence, [Marina] was condemned and her friends at work warned against speaking with her," Oswald wrote in a letter to the American Embassy. "However, these tactics are quite useless, and my wife stood up well, without getting into trouble." [66]

Marina told her bosses and fellow members of Komsomol, the youth Communist Party association, that Oswald "longs for his homeland. I'm just going with my husband. It's possible it'll be worse there." The youth association kicked out Marina, but that was standard for anyone leaving the USSR. It also kept her from being promoted and getting a raise. [67]

Visits by relatives and friends declined. By the end of 1961, the Oswalds were told they would receive exit visas from the Soviets, but Marina still needed an entrance visa to the U.S. Oswald wrote to various places for aid, including funds to pay for the return trip.

In February 1962, the Oswalds had a daughter, June. They were both overjoyed with the family addition, and "Junie," as they called her, seemed to bring the couple closer. On her first night home from the hospital, Marina was left alone by Lee, who attended Aunt Valya's birthday party. She had to get a neighbor to help change Junie's diaper, and Lee arrived more drunk than Marina had ever seen him. He had been singing all the way home and swore his love to Marina.

Meanwhile, Col. Ilya told the KGB officer overseeing Oswald's case that Marina promised not to commit acts in the U.S. that would "compromise" her Soviet relatives. He also later spoke with "Likhoi," – one of two code names the KGB had for Oswald, meaning "reckless" – who promised not to conduct any actions "harmful to the Soviet Union." The other code name was "Nalim," which meant "sly." [68]

The following month, Marina obtained her U.S. visa, aided by a letter from State Department official Robert Owen to the visa office. Owen wrote that the department's Office of Soviet Union Affairs believed it was in the best interests of the U.S. to get Oswald and his family out of the USSR "as soon as possible." He called Oswald "an unstable character, whose actions are entirely unpredictable," adding that the Soviets could embarrass the U.S. by accusing the rival superpower of imposing a forced separation on the Oswalds by refusing to grant Marina a visa. [69]

In late May, the Oswalds boarded a train for Moscow from the Minsk station. No relatives appeared to see them off, only friends. They filled out the rest of the paperwork, and embassy officials interviewed Marina again. She received her visa, and the family set off on a long train ride via Poland, Germany and Holland, where they boarded a ship bound for New York.

The U.S. State Department loaned them $436 for the journey, which Oswald repaid by mid-January 1963, if under suspicious circumstances. He somehow paid off almost $400 in one month, even though he did not have savings and his weekly wages would not have provided excess funds to cover the debt.

Consuls commonly advance citizens funds in similar cases, Snyder said. "Worthiness is not a consideration," he said. [70]

The fact that Oswald didn't formally renounce his citizenship made it easier for him to return to the U.S., McMillan noted. "It was unusual to let him go back to the U.S. with a Russian wife, but I don't think it was a case of slipping through the cracks," said McMillan, who also worked for Kennedy at one time. [71]

Only greeted by anti-communist official

On the ship from Holland, Oswald wrote about his disillusionment towards both the U.S. and Soviet systems. He sought a third choice besides communism and capitalism.

"I have lived under both systems," he wrote. "I have sought the answers. And although it would be very easy to dupe myself into believing one system is better than the other, I know they are not." [72]

He also jotted down some answers to questions that reporters might ask, if any waited for him. His candid reason for going to the USSR was "as a mark of disgust and protest against American political policies in foreign countries, my personal sign of discontent and horror at the misguided line of reasoning of the

U.S. government and people." But if he felt a more evasive answer was needed, he would simply say it was to "see the land, the people and how their system works." He debated whether to admit he was a communist who didn't like the Soviet system but thought Marxism could be effective under different circumstances, or just say no. [73]

Upon reaching the New York area on June 13, 1962, the supposed Marxist Oswald was not greeted by any Communist Party members. However, Spas Raikin, the secretary-general of the anti-communist American Friends of the Anti-Bolshevik Nations, sought him out. Raikin, who also volunteered with an immigrant assistance group, wondered why there were not any government officials meeting Oswald, who had received fairly extensive media coverage when he defected.

"In my mind, there was the idea he could be a spy, and God knows what instructions he may have received from the Soviets if he's in their service," Raikin said. [74]

Oswald lied to Raikin that he had worked in the American Embassy in Moscow. "He did not want to meet me, but we had a way of finding people," said Raikin, who waited at baggage claim and introduced himself. "I thought I won his confidence, but I did not realize what kind of a man he was, that he was playing a game." [75]

Raikin contacted the FBI about Oswald, but he said he was not there as a government informant. "My obligation was to meet [Oswald], assist him through customs," Raikin said. "Once I delivered him to the office, my job was finished with him. He was passed to another worker, and I had no more contact with him." [76]

Despite telling Ilya that he would keep a low public profile, Oswald was disappointed when no reporters showed up at his re-entry into the U.S., McMillan said. He felt he had unique knowledge about both the Soviet and American systems, but at the same time, he was afraid of being prosecuted because he offered the Russians radar secrets, she noted. "He knew in his heart that he'd been disloyal," McMillan claimed. [77]

She later would call Oswald an "embittered psychological loner," a profile those trying to pin the assassination on him found helpful. McMillan continued to maintain contact with CIA officials and Marina for years. [78]

Some believe that Oswald was debriefed by a CIA contact, as were other defectors to the Soviet Union at the time. Robert Webster, a former Navy serviceman and Rand Development Corp. employee, also returned to the U.S. in 1962. Marvin Kantor, a defector and former Marine who was in Minsk at the same time as Oswald, was another named in CIA reports. [79]

There is a "huge amount of evidence that Oswald was a low-level asset for a U.S. intelligence agency, and not a communist," said author Lamar Waldron. "The Warren Commission claimed Oswald was a Marxist as a teenager, but how many communist teenagers join the Civil Air Patrol? And not only join the U.S. Marines, but try to join before he's even old enough? Oswald was under 'tight' surveillance by Naval Intelligence from the time he returned to the U.S. from Russia." [80]

Oswald declined to tell even his mother why he returned from Russia. Marguerite told her son that she planned to write a book on her life "because of your defection," and he replied, "You are not to write the book. They could kill [Marina] and her family." [81]

That, among other statements, led Marguerite to later tell the Warren Commission that she believed her son worked for a government agency:

> Many things bothered him in the United States. Race discrimination, harsh treatment of underdog, communists, and hate. Then on the other letter, he is going to Russia to write a book. And there is another story and another story. And all kind of stories. So what are we to believe, gentlemen? Is he throwing us off the track because he is an agent?
>
> Why does a man who wants to come back to the United States, five weeks later, marry a Russian girl? Because I say – and I may be wrong – the U.S. Embassy has ordered him to marry this Russian girl. And a few weeks later, he is coming home with the Russian girl. How does he get out of the Soviet Union with the Russian girl, with money loaned to him by the U.S. Embassy? [82]

FBI tails Oswald

Besides possibly Naval Intelligence, the FBI was outwardly interested in Oswald. Soon after settling in Robert's Fort Worth home, Oswald met with FBI agents. He reiterated that he hadn't given the Soviets information that could be used in a "detrimental way" against the U.S., according to an FBI report. He at first declined to answer why he had gone to the Soviet Union, then said it was to "see the country." [83]

"So what did they want?" Robert asked his brother when he returned to the house.

"Well, everything went all right. They even asked me if I'd ever been an agent of the federal government or the CIA," Oswald laughed.

Robert had his suspicions. He noted that Oswald's hair was thinner and of a slightly different texture. Perhaps he had undergone shock treatments in

Russia. Was he playing a high-stakes game like his boyhood hero, Herbert Philbrick? Was he in over his head? "What did you tell them?"

Oswald smirked. His only reply to the FBI agents had been, "Don't *you* know?" [84]

Not even his brother really knew. The brothers agreed to not discuss politics, though Lee would joke about how inept the Russians were in a non-political way. Later, Robert found it hard to believe that Lee defected for anything other than an experience.

"Maybe he just sowed some wild oats," Robert said. "He kind of went off to the far end of it, but I believe everyone of us at one time, especially around that age, might have done something or reached out far afield, so to speak, before we came to our senses and returned to a normal life." [85]

Bonding with an anti-communist

After settling in, one of the first tasks Oswald undertook was to hire a typist to convert his hand-written journal to a typed document. But he ran out of money to finish the job and searched for employment. He found work at a welding company, making $50 a week.

Marguerite offered to put up his family for a few weeks, but Oswald soon found her overbearing again. She claimed to have suffered financially due to her son's defection, that some people didn't want the mother of a defector working in their home as a nurse. She stressed how much she had helped Oswald return to the states, while her son thought he had done most of that work.

About the same time Oswald moved his family into a humble, lower-income bungalow near the Montgomery Ward warehouse, he called a Russian émigré named Peter Gregory. The engineer had left Russia in 1923 and supplemented his income by teaching Russian at the Fort Worth Public Library. Gregory was impressed enough with Oswald's command of the language that he recommended him as a translator or interpreter, even though others thought Oswald's Russian language skill was lacking.

Gregory introduced Oswald to other Eastern European émigrés. Most were staunch anti-communist White Russians. Some, such as Russian-born accountant George Bouhe, gave the Oswalds food and clothing, which Lee resented as emasculating. Marguerite agreed with her son.

"The Russian friends, who were established and had cars and fine homes, could not see this Russian girl [Marina] doing without," she said. "These Russian friends have interfered in their lives, and thought that the Russian girl should have more than necessary." [86]

While Oswald shunned most of Marina's Eastern European friends, he bonded with George de Mohrenschildt, a 51-year-old Russian immigrant and petroleum geologist with intelligence ties. In another age, de Mohrenschildt might have given Dos Equis pitchman Jonathan Goldsmith a run for his money as the most interesting man in the world. Mailer described him as possessing "an eclecticism that made him delight in presenting himself as right-wing, left-wing, a moralist, an immoralist, an aristocrat, a nihilist, a snob, an atheist, a Republican, a Kennedy lover, a desegregationist, an intimate of oil tycoons, a bohemian, and a socialite." [87]

With Russian, Swedish, Polish, German, and Hungarian ancestors, de Mohrenschildt's heritage went back to Swedish nobility. He was a real baron, driving convertibles, playing tennis, working on his tan by the pool. He was taller than average at 6-foot-2 and well-built. Many considered him likeable, though at least one acquaintance noted that he could get emotional. He had been a cavalry officer, lingerie salesman, and even filmmaker. He married four times. He knew anti-JFK oilmen Hunt and Murchison and spymaster Dulles. His links to Jacqueline Kennedy's family were so strong that young Jackie referred to him as "Uncle George." He earned a degree in petroleum engineering at the University of Texas and once worked for William F. Buckley Sr. [88]

In 1957, de Mohrenschildt provided the CIA with "foreign intelligence" on Yugoslavia, "which was promptly disseminated to other federal agencies in ten separate reports," according to former CIA Director Helms. The Russian applied to work for the CIA in 1942 but was rejected due to suspicions of being a "Nazi espionage agent." De Mohrenschildt also reported to the CIA about trips to Mexico and Panama in 1958. [89]

De Mohrenschildt had "on occasion done favors" for officials connected to the CIA since the early 1950s, he admitted to author Edward Jay Epstein. In addition, de Mohrenschildt worked for a company whose chief export officer, Pierre Fraiss, was connected with French intelligence shortly after he arrived in the U.S. from Russia in 1938. He collected "facts on people involved in pro-German activity" and contacted oil companies, including in Texas, to encourage them to sell oil to the French during World War II. [90]

De Mohrenschildt said he was given Oswald's Fort Worth address by an associate of J. Walton Moore, the CIA's head of domestic contacts in Dallas. Seeking aid from the CIA to obtain an oil exploration contract from Haitian dictator "Papa Doc" Duvalier, de Mohrenschildt met with Moore in late 1961. The CIA official brought up Minsk, where de Mohrenschildt had lived, and told him about the ex-Marine from the Dallas area seeking to return home.

Moore told him that Oswald was "just a harmless lunatic," and it was "safe to associate" with him. "I would never have contacted Oswald in a million years if Moore had not sanctioned it," said de Mohrenschildt. [91]

Oswald was complex, well-read, and a "seeker for justice" who strongly supported civil rights for African Americans and other minorities, de Mohrenschildt wrote. Oswald was interested, among other aspects, in de Mohrenschildt's 14-month "walking trip" through Mexico and Central America. De Mohrenschildt said he made the 1960-61 journey to help recover from the death of his son, who had cystic fibrosis. But he also submitted a written report on the trip to the U.S. State Department. De Mohrenschildt thought of Oswald almost like a son and was intrigued that he didn't seek money as much as ideas, he said. [92]

In turn, Oswald respected the older Russian, finding him smart and "very sympathetic," Marina said. Oswald opened up more to de Mohrenschildt, telling him he settled in Russia because he "was looking for an ideal." He liked that Minsk, where de Mohrenschildt also once lived, did not have "rich exploiters like [in the U.S.], no great contrasts between the rich and the poor." While Oswald criticized the Soviet government as "too regimented," he appreciated Russians who were not in the Communist Party who would talk philosophy and did not try to "make a communist out of me." [93]

Oswald told the older man he sought to reduce Cold War tensions on an individual level. He defended the U.S. in Russia and the Soviet Union in the states, according to de Mohrenschildt. Some wondered about the older man's interest in Oswald, suspecting he was feeling him out to see if he was a Soviet asset or agent and perhaps recruit him for American intelligence work.

Whatever de Mohrenschildt's interest in Oswald was, even Garrison did not believe he knew beforehand what Oswald's role would become. He referred to the older Russian as "an unwitting baby sitter." [94]

Working for spy plane mapping firm

About a week before the October 1962 Cuban Missile Crisis, de Mohrenschildt reportedly convinced Oswald to quit his job at the welding company and move to Dallas. The older man helped Oswald obtain a position at graphic arts firm Jaggars-Chiles-Stovall Co. The company did secret work such as creating maps of Cuba from photos where U-2 spy planes supposedly flew. [95]

While that was an odd place for a former Soviet defector who had reportedly promised to give the Russians U-2 secrets to gain employment, it fit if Oswald was also an intelligence asset. "Oswald's role as an intelligence asset explains why U.S. authorities weren't concerned when Oswald – a seeming former defector with a Russian wife – got a job in Dallas at a firm that prepared material for maps created from U-2 spy plane photos at the height of the Cuban Missile Crisis," Waldron said. [96]

The job required a high security clearance, but somehow Oswald obtained it within a week of moving to Dallas, Garrison noted. "If Oswald truly had no connection with our intelligence community, if he truly had leanings toward communism – as our government had assured us – then the nonchalance of the security clearance operation of Jagger-Chiles-Stovall represented great comic movie material gone to waste," Garrison wrote. [97]

Oswald had trouble keeping jobs for long, which could have been part of his deep-cover assignments. The graphic arts position was probably one of the few jobs Oswald really liked. He could enlarge his own photographs at work and make fake identification badges. He could offer his photography and graphic arts skills to make posters and more for the Communist and Socialist Workers parties in New York.

More and more, Oswald saw Marina as overbearing, similar to his mother. But then, Marina also "liked America" and "wanted to stay here," Marguerite noted. Still, Marina became discontented with Oswald because he "could not give her the things she wanted," and money was the source of many of their arguments, Marguerite surmised. She claimed not to have any contract with her son or Marina from late 1962 until the day after the assassination.

"When they get ready to let me know, I will see them," she said. "If not, I will go about my own business." [98]

Oswald found an apartment in Oak Cliff, a South Dallas area that was its own town in the late 19th century until Dallas annexed it in 1903. Marina and Lee continued to argue to the extent they soon decided to live separately. Marina and June moved in with friends for a few weeks but then returned to the Oak Cliff apartment on Neely Street.

Japanese connection

Oswald had a lighter side in front of friends, telling political jokes well and being sociable among people to whom he related, de Mohrenschildt said. Those included Yaeko Okui, a Japanese woman he met at a post-Christmas party hosted by Russian émigré Katya Ford:

They just....started talking and talking and talking. I thought that was understandable because Oswald had been in Japan, you see. But the interest was so overwhelming that Marina objected, and became very jealous. [99]

Okui, a 29-year-old store marketing representative and flower arrangement teacher who moved to Dallas in 1959, came from a wealthy family. An accomplished classical musician, she apparently played at some concerts by the Dallas Symphony Orchestra. Okui would say that she only discussed cultural topics, not politics, and that meeting Oswald "ruined her life." After being interrogated and investigated by the FBI, she would return to Japan in 1964. [100]

While Okui said that was the only time she spoke with Oswald, Marina found her contact information in one of his shirt pockets. "That Japanese bitch," Marina complained to de Mohrenschildt. She and Oswald fought over her, "and look at the result," Marina said, displaying a black eye. [101]

Sometimes their arguments were over heavier political matters and other times relatively trivial aspects like Marina not washing the floor to Lee's satisfaction. Marina told de Mohrenschildt that Oswald didn't satisfy her sexually, although she later said that claims he was impotent were false. They saw more bruises on Marina and fingernail scratches on Oswald, who later regretted the abuse while Marina rarely expressed remorse, de Mohrenschildt said.

"Sometimes it was my own fault," Marina said. "I wanted more attention." She said Oswald hit her once after finding out about a letter she wrote to a former boyfriend in which she said she was sorry she didn't marry him, rather than Oswald. "There was some grounds for [hitting her]," Marina claimed. [102]

Marina criticized Oswald as "puny," dull, and only interested in books, while Marina wanted more "things" but wasn't interested in working herself, de Mohrenschildt said. Oswald was always good to their daughter, June, de Mohrenschildt and Marina said. "He would walk with June, play with her, feed her, change diapers, take photographs – everything that fathers generally do," Marina said. "If I would punish June, he would punish me." [103]

Who shot at Walker?

By early 1963, Oswald became more of a "recluse" and regularly shot a rifle he had purchased through the mail, Marina said. He would be gone from home for hours at a time, and there were not many accounts of what he did and who he met. He supposedly made Marina take some photos of him holding the rifle and a communist newspaper, which became a controversial magazine cover after his death. He developed a "fantasy, which was quite unfounded, as to the fact that he was an outstanding man," his former wife said. [104]

When someone fired a shot at Major Gen. Walker in his Dallas home on April 10, many would pin that act on Oswald. The Warren Commission used it to show he had the capacity to pull off an assassination.

The far right-wing Walker was a suitable target for a self-described "hunter of fascists." JFK had relieved Walker of his command of an Army infantry division in Germany in 1961 after some accused Walker of brainwashing his troops with John Birch Society materials. Walker was identified as one of the leaders of the bloody 1962 riot at the University of Mississippi, which in the eyes of Walker and others committed the "cardinal sin" of admitting black student James Meredith. Robert Kennedy had Walker arrested for his role. Walker settled in Dallas and became a prominent Bircher and speaker at far-right conventions.

Oswald took photos of Walker's house before the shooting and "was planning this for two months," Marina claimed. On April 10, she said he left a note telling her where the mailbox key was and other instructions if he was arrested:

> That evening he went out, I thought that he had gone to his classes, or perhaps he just walked out or went out on his own business. It got to be around 10 or 10:30, he wasn't home yet, and I began to be worried.....
>
> When he came back, I asked him what had happened. He was very pale....He told me not to ask him any questions. He only told me that he had shot at General Walker....
>
> He said that this was a very bad man, that he was a fascist...I said that even though all of that might be true, just the same he had no right to take his life. He said if someone had killed Hitler in time, it would have saved many lives. [105]

De Mohrenschildt told the Warren Commission that he and his wife, Jeanne, visited the Oswalds in their Oak Cliff residence shortly after someone shot at Walker. Jeanne spotted a rifle with a telescopic sight in a closet, and Oswald said he did "target shooting," de Mohrenschildt said. As a "stupid joke" that later got him in hot water, the older man said he asked him without knowing that he might have fired at Walker, "Are you then the guy who took a pot shot at General Walker?" Oswald didn't answer, just "made a peculiar face," de Mohrenschildt said. [106]

Marina remembered that visit a little differently. She said that as soon as he saw Oswald, de Mohrenschildt asked him, "How could you have missed

[Walker]?" Marina later told McMillan that Jeanne had visited several days before the Walker incident, and she showed her the rifle then. [107]

Marina added that she kept the note and threatened to inform the police if Lee shot at anyone else. Oswald "said he would not repeat anything like that again." She said she didn't report the Walker shooting to police because "it was my husband," and if she knew Oswald would shoot at someone else, she would have reported it. [108]

One witness, Walter Kirk Coleman, reported men driving from the scene in two different vehicles. Two Walker aides saw men prowling or appearing to scout the house a few days before the shot. Authors Alan J. Weberman and Michael Canfield wrote that a "covert action team" did the deed as part of a campaign to "create the impression that a leftist assassin was running loose." [109]

There is the question of how Oswald, who could not drive, got to the scene carrying a bulky rifle without anyone suspecting anything. Authorities claimed he was adept at concealing the rifle under a raincoat while riding the bus.

There was another seeming contradiction here: How could Oswald – who de Mohrenschildt and others said admired Kennedy – do the dirty work for so many like H.L. Hunt and Walker who hated JFK, if he had tried to kill one of those Kennedy haters a few months previously?

If Oswald did shoot at Walker, some suspected it was part of his cover work as a supposed Marxist in the months before JFK's killing. The charge rested "on the unsupported testimony of Marina Oswald, after she had been threatened with deportation if she didn't cooperate," Garrison said. [110]

Mailer said it fit a pattern in Oswald's lifelong quest to be a famous, respected political figure, as he believed it proved he had the guts to take strong, risky actions. Blakey said the JFK assassination could be made part of a common effort with the Walker attempt if Oswald thought of JFK more as "the leader of right-wing America." [111]

Meeting the Paines

Another interesting association the Oswalds made was with Ruth and Michael Paine.

Ruth's sister, Sylvia Hyde Hoke, had worked for the CIA since the mid-1950s, including as a staff psychologist in 1961. The CIA had also considered employing Ruth's father, William Avery Hyde, for "a covert use" in Vietnam in 1957. In 1964, Hyde would receive a three-year contract to work as Latin American insurance adviser for the U.S. Agency for International Development, which employed numerous CIA assets. [112]

Michael Paine's family background was even more intriguing than his wife's. His ancestors not only came from the powerful financial-empire family Forbes, but included Declaration of Independence signee Robert Treat Paine and 19th century literary giant Ralph Waldo Emerson. His mother, Ruth Forbes Young, was a friend of Mary Bancroft and a member of the CIA-affiliated World Federalist Movement.

Lyman Paine, Michael's father, took up Marxist and socialist ideas after being influenced by the woes of the Great Depression. He divorced Ruth and remarried, cutting off close ties with his son. Paine was also related to Henry Cabot Lodge Jr., Nixon's vice presidential running mate in 1960, and Thomas Dudley Cabot, a former president of United Fruit Co., whose board included Dulles. Cabot presided over Gibraltar Steamship Co., a CIA front business during the Bay of Pigs.

The Paines met in Philadelphia when Ruth was active in a peace group that organized tours of Russians. Ruth had graduated from Antioch College in Ohio and went to Philadelphia for a job at a Quaker school. Michael was from the Philadelphia area, and they married in 1957, the same year Ruth started studying Russian. Michael had served in the U.S. Army from 1952 until 1960, with the last few years in the reserves.

They moved to Dallas when Michael found a position as a research engineer with Bell Helicopter, presumably being aided by the fact that his stepfather was the inventor of the Bell Helicopter. But in Dallas – probably the most conservative large city in the country at that time – they felt isolated as Northern liberals.

The Paines separated in 1962, and Michael moved into an apartment in Grand Prairie, not too far from their Irving house at 2515 W. Fifth Street. Ruth's loneliness grew. She was active in her church and choir, as well as the League of Women Voters, but that apparently wasn't enough.

When she met Marina at a party hosted by anti-communists, Ruth jumped at the chance to practice Russian with a native who spoke the language's modern style. "This was an opportunity for me to again practice in the language," she said. "I was interested in getting to know [Marina]." [113]

But Ruth didn't gain a good first impression of Lee, who spoke about returning to Russia since he had lost his Jaggars position due to his "record as a troublemaker" and "communistic tendencies." He was having trouble finding employment. So Ruth offered Marina and her daughter the opportunity to stay in the house she shared with her two kids and sometimes Michael. "If [Oswald] thought he couldn't support [Marina]....I simply wanted to say there was an alternative to her going back [to the Soviet Union]," she said. [114]

Michael Paine found Oswald to be "rigid" and "extremely bitter," someone who "couldn't believe there was much goodwill in people." But Oswald praised JFK, Paine said. During an American Civil Liberties Union meeting to which Paine took Oswald, the latter man said he thought Kennedy was "doing quite a good job in civil rights," Paine said. [115]

While Ruth was a Quaker, Michael attended a Unitarian church in a wealthy Dallas suburb and spent several Sunday afternoons in the spring of 1963 at Luby's cafeteria near SMU. He debated students about issues such as Cuba, disagreeing with the official hard line of the federal government. He also supported improving relations with Eastern European countries. [116]

Though on the liberal side, Paine was open enough to attend meetings that involved many conservatives. He even went to a John Birch Society meeting on the same evening that UN Ambassador Stevenson was rudely treated. The meeting was more of an introductory one that was sparsely attended; most Birchers "were down spitting on Stevenson," Paine noted. Reaching out to the other side was important, Paine said, because he "was interested in seeing more communication between the right and the left.... I wanted to be able to speak their language and be familiar with their feelings and attitudes." [117]

Soon after Marina and June moved into the Paine home in April 1963, Marina said she suggested that her husband look for work in New Orleans since he had relatives there. Oswald took off again, living with his Marcello-connected uncle for a few weeks until his family moved to the Big Easy.

Oswald in dark glasses poses with fellow workers in Minsk, Russia. FBI Item D33-40, Warren Commission Exhibit No. 2625. [Courtesy of U.S. National Archives]

Oswald holds a rifle and communist newspapers in 1963. Oswald claimed the photo superimposed his head on this body. Commission Exhibit No. 134. [Courtesy of U.S. National Archives]

Chapter Six

New Orleans Connections

One of [Guy] Banister's tasks that summer of 1963 was the sheep dipping of Lee Oswald to make him appear to be a dedicated communist. This sheep dipping succeeded exactly as planned.
– JIM GARRISON, 1988

Less than a month after moving to New Orleans, Lee Harvey Oswald found work at the William B. Reily & Co. coffee facility. The coffee company was located near Lafayette Square, the city's second oldest park named after the French general who fought with George Washington & Co. during the Revolutionary War. Long the center of New Orleans' intelligence community, the square contained offices of the Secret Service and Naval Intelligence in a federal building. CIA and FBI offices were also nearby.

Reily worked for the CIA for "years," according to CIA contractor Gerald Patrick Hemming. He was a strong supporter of anti-Castro groups, such as the CIA-sponsored Cuban Revolutionary Council [CRC]. [1]

The way Oswald obtained the job was suspect. Anti-Castro advocates might have been working to set up Oswald since 1961, District Attorney Jim Garrison said. Three months before the Bay of Pigs invasion, a Latin man with a distinctive scar over his left eye accompanied a young white man who gave his name as "Oswald" to the Bolton Ford dealership in New Orleans. They claimed to represent an anti-Castro group called Friends of Democratic Cuba and inquired about purchasing ten Ford pickup trucks, presumably to use in the invasion.

Two years later, the same Latin man with the scar would be present during pro-Castro leafleting actions Oswald conducted. He was likely a bodyguard in case the crowd became overly violent, Garrison said. [2]

In the same vein, someone could have impersonated Oswald in applying for other jobs before he obtained the Reily one. Whoever applied put down a different height than Oswald's correct one, Garrison noted.

Garrison suspected Kerry Thornley, a fellow Marine with Oswald, might have been impersonating him. Thornley admitted to meeting Banister and Ferrie while living in New Orleans in the early 1960s. Some claimed to have seen Thornley with Oswald in 1963, which Thornley denied. Thornley "bore a striking resemblance" to Oswald, said Garrison. [3]

When questioned by the Warren Commission, Thornley said Oswald was shorter than him, estimating his height at 5-foot-5. Oswald was actually 5-foot-11, an inch taller than Thornley. Garrison wondered if Thornley wanted to divert suspicions that he had impersonated Oswald by wrongly claiming there was a significant height difference. He also wondered if Thornley had impersonated Oswald to model the famous *Life* magazine photos, which were found in the Paines' garage. Adding fuel to speculation, Thornley, who later became a counterculture writer and befriended Roselli, wrote a novel based on Oswald's defection to Russia that he finished several months before the assassination. [4]

William Guy Banister was a key suspect for organizing a clandestine operation. The Louisiana-born Banister joined the FBI in 1934, eventually rising through the ranks to head the Chicago office. He became a staunch Hoover ally and anti-communist, helping with right-wing groups like the John Birch Society and Louisiana Committee on Un-American Activities. Leaving the FBI in 1954, Banister was hired as a deputy superintendent of the New Orleans Police Department, where he developed a network of informants on the activities of alleged communists on college campuses.

Forced to leave the police department after pulling a gun on a waiter, Banister started his detective agency in 1957, moving the office in 1960 to Lafayette Square near Reily & Co. He reportedly dealt weapons for the Bay of Pigs invasion and continued to supply anti-Castro groups that worked out of the same building at 544 Camp Street. Banister was listed as an incorporator for the Friends of Democratic Cuba that had impersonated Oswald in 1961. He had ties to virtually every group associated with the case, including the CIA, Cubans, John Birchers, Klansmen, military intelligence, Mafia, and FBI.

Since 1962, Ferrie, the expert pilot with ties to the CIA, mob, and anti-Castro Cubans who Oswald first met as a teen in the Civil Air Patrol, was seen with Banister in his Lafayette Square office. Cubans were often there, with anti-Castro groups working out of the same building that Banister used.

Oswald had use of one of Banister's offices for his pro-Castro activities, Garrison said. After Banister's death in 1964, family members would recover some of Oswald's pro-Castro leaflets in Banister's office. Federal agents would take Banister's files, though they would leave index cards on topics such as FPCC, civil rights programs, and Latin America. That raised some suspicions. "Oswald had not been a communist or Marxist of any kind," Garrison wrote. "What appeared to be considerably more probable was that Guy Banister – or someone associated with him – had been using Oswald as an agent provocateur." [5]

The CIA-backed Cuban Democratic Revolutionary Front, which had a unit that was involved in the Bay of Pigs invasion before becoming part of the CRC, opened an office at 544 Camp Street in 1961. Cuban exile Sergio Arcacha Smith headed the New Orleans office until he moved to Tampa in 1962. Smith met with Banister and Ferrie to discuss anti-Castro activities, with the latter men being open to help train exiles. But after a falling out, Smith would move, eventually settling in Houston in 1963.

Seeking communist credentials

A couple days after starting work as a machine greaser at the coffee plant, Oswald was joined by Marina and June. They argued over whether she should return to Russia and other matters. Oswald continued to practice shooting with his rifle and talked about somehow traveling to Cuba to perhaps become an advisor of Castro's, Marina said. Again, some suspected the effort was a ruse.

He did not talk negatively about JFK during this time. "I cannot conclude that he was against the president," Marina said. [6]

Seeking credentials to improve his chances of obtaining a Cuban visa, Oswald started a New Orleans chapter of the left-leaning Fair Play for Cuba Committee, probably under the urgings of Banister. The activist group began in New York in 1960 to support Castro's Cuban revolution. Among the early notable supporters of this group were writers Mailer and Truman Capote and historian William Williams. But by 1963, support for FPCC had dwindled, and some suspected the group was little more than a CIA-funded front organization.

Oswald wrote the national FPCC organization to request a charter and seek advice. National Director Vincent Lee suggested that Oswald rent a post office box, rather than open an office, noting that there was a "violent opposition." [7]

Oswald opened a box, putting down "A.J. Hidell" among the names. Soon after civil rights leader Medgar Evans was assassinated at his Jackson, Miss., home in mid-June, Oswald started the first of several actions.

During a leaflet distribution at a wharf where a U.S. Navy aircraft carrier docked, a police officer told Oswald that he would need to obtain permission from the port's board to continue. Oswald questioned why he needed anyone's permission since he was on public property, and the officer threatened to arrest him. He left.

In late June, Oswald offered to go to Russia with his family. Marina wrote a Soviet Embassy official, requesting that they be allowed to return to Russia. She cited her husband's difficulty in maintaining employment and her "homesickness." Pregnant with their second child, she said she wanted to have their daughter in the USSR. "Make us happy again, help us to return to that which we lost because of our foolishness," Marina wrote. [8]

Right wing or left wing?

Banister, who worked with the Office of Naval Intelligence during World War II and had many CIA contacts, was not the only right-wing advocate with whom Oswald associated during that summer. He reunited with Ferrie, who suffered from alopecia praecox, a rare disease that left him with no body hair. Ferrie sometimes wore brightly-colored wigs and painted-on eyebrows. He was easy to spot and hard to forget.

Numerous people reported they saw Ferrie with a man who looked like Oswald that summer, including in Banister's office and at a camp near Lake Pontchartrain on land owned by Mafia-connected William McLaney. There, Ferrie led the training of anti-Castro Cubans and right-wing Minutemen for Operation Mongoose campaigns.

When the FBI raided a cottage near that camp in July, Banister, who helped finance the camp, suspected Oswald was the informant. The FBI seized dynamite, bomb casings, and napalm materials that the owners planned to use to blow up oil refineries in Cuba. [9]

That raid might have been when Banister, Ferrie, and others moved from trying to kill Castro to going after JFK, Garrison said. Oswald, who maintained CIA contacts after returning from the Soviet Union, then stepped up his campaign to publicly portray himself as a Marxist, Garrison noted. [10]

For leafleting actions, Oswald was even allowed to hire young men from an employment agency to help him. Charles Steele Jr. told Garrison that Oswald paid him $2 an hour to distribute the pro-Castro flyers until media representatives left. Then, the demonstrations suddenly dissipated.

"This recruitment method was highly improbable for a true Marxist group," Garrison wrote. "Most such groups had members to do their leafleting but almost no money. Oswald's Fair Play for Cuba Committee, by contrast, had no apparent members other than himself but enough money that it could hire unemployed people." [11]

Further clouding those demonstrations, Oswald even employed a "fanatic anti-Castro Cuban exile" to help him pass out the pro-Castro leaflets, Garrison noted. He also used the address of the building that housed Banister's office, 544 Camp Street, on flyers at least initially. Banister's office actually used a side entrance of the building, which was demolished in the early 1970s for part of a federal government complex, at 531 Lafayette Street.

"Somebody must have pointed out to Oswald shortly afterward that he was endangering his cover by using this address, because he subsequently changed it to 4907 Magazine Street," Garrison said. [12]

Oswald played the right-wing side by offering to help anti-Castro Cuban activist Carlos Bringuier in early August, a ploy that may have been an attempt to infiltrate the Directorio Revolucionario Estudiantil. The organization formed in 1954 as a Catholic student group opposed to dictator Batista but started opposing Castro after he made overtures to the Soviets. The DRE received funds of $25,000 a month in 1963 under a CIA program run by George Joannides, who headed the agency's anti-Castro psychological warfare operations. [13]

A few days later, Bringuier and some other DRE members saw Oswald handing out FPCC handbills and confronted him. They were both arrested following a scuffle.

So who bailed out Oswald? Emile Bruneau, a state boxing commissioner who had ties to mob boss Marcello. While in custody, the supposed Marxist Oswald asked to speak with an FBI agent and met with John Quigley. The agent burned his notes of the conversation in violation of normal FBI procedure. That was another incident that made Garrison suspect that Oswald was an FBI informant along with an intelligence asset. [14]

Soon after the scuffle, Oswald debated Bringuier and another right-wing activist, Ed Butler, on a radio program hosted by William Stuckey. During a taped portion, Stuckey, who considered Oswald "intelligent" though misguided, stuck to talking about Cuba. But on the live segment, he surprised Oswald by stacking the deck against him in a three-on-one forum. Oswald held his own, even when his opponents changed the topic from Cuba to the Soviet Union and brought up his Russian defection.

The program effectively killed the city's FPCC chapter, which might have been fine with Banister, who just wanted to publicly portray Oswald as a Marxist. "After that program, the Fair Play for Cuba Committee, if there ever was one in New Orleans, had no future there," Stuckey said. Oswald's FPCC chapter had not attracted any members, though he sent honorary membership cards to Communist Party leaders. By December 1963, the national FPCC would disband. [15]

Involvement in bioweapon project?

Judyth Vary Baker also worked at the Reily coffee operation that summer, according to pay stubs and other documents. Baker, then age 20, and Oswald, 23, bonded to the point that a more intimate relationship developed. Witnesses saw her and Oswald together, with one couple going on double dates with them, according to researcher James Fetzer. [16]

Baker was in New Orleans that summer not to pursue a coffee career, but one in cancer research. While attending Manatee High School in Indiana, she presented her research into seawater composition and lung cancer at international science fairs. She attracted the attention of prominent researchers, including Nobel Prize winners Harold Urey and Robert Robinson. Dr. Alton Ochsner, who founded the Ochsner Clinic in New Orleans in 1942 that became a leader in linking smoking to cancer, offered her a summer internship in 1963 to work with noted cancer specialist Mary Stults Sherman.

Sherman was involved in carrying out secret research into developing a vaccine to prevent a cancer epidemic caused by a contaminated polio vaccine. Her work involved using a linear particle accelerator, a device that can create tumor-destroying beams to fight cancer that was in its early stages in the 1960s. But instead of using the accelerator to combat cancer, certain government officials "weaponized" the program starting in 1963 and sought to employ the device as a bioweapon to induce Castro with a form of lung cancer, Baker charged. [17]

Ochsner, whose clinic grew into the Ochsner Health System, had deep ties to the far right. He knew Murchison, Nicaraguan dictator Anastasio Somoza, and segregationist Louisiana Rep. F. Edward Hebert. He made more than 100 trips to Latin America and founded the Information Council of the Americas. The anti-communist group produced a film on Castro called *Hitler in Havana* and shadowed Oswald as he handed out leaflets and spoke on a radio program. Ochsner strongly opposed civil rights legislation, accusing JFK and RFK in a letter to Louisiana Sen. Allen Ellender of wanting a "virtual dictatorship." [18]

Ochsner secretly directed the anti-Castro bioweapon project, which had funding from the CIA, Baker said. A "secret cancer" lab for the project was run by Ferrie, whose apartment was full of hundreds of mice being used for cancer experiments, wrote Edward Haslam, an advertising executive whose father worked with Sherman. Ferrie, who also dabbled in hypnotism, Catholic theology, and weapons mechanics, was reportedly inducing cancer in the mice, injecting them with monkey viruses that could cause other diseases. [19]

Oswald became drawn into the bioweapon project to inform his government sources, Baker said, though his primary job in New Orleans was to identify pro-Castro spies. His activities with the FPCC were designed to "make him look like a harmless pro-Castro fool" so he could learn useful information to relay to government intelligence agencies, she claimed. While working at Reily, he would slip away to Ferrie's apartment and other places to help this effort, Baker said. [20]

Tenants who lived in the same apartment complex as Sherman said they saw Oswald enter a unit next to Sherman's several times. Oswald even asked one tenant where that unit's occupant, Juan Valdez, was. When he was there, the toilet flushed a lot of times, a witness said. [21]

Baker said the research was working. At one point, someone burglarized Sherman's apartment and took expensive medical equipment. [22]

Oswald was fired from Reily on July 19, reportedly for being absent too much. Within a few weeks, Baker, who said her job at Reily provided cover for both Oswald and her activities with the secret bioweapon project, was forced out as well. Within a few weeks of them leaving the coffee company, anyone who had a connection with Oswald left. Baker said she would object to using prisoners to test the bioweapon and be removed from working on that project shortly before Kennedy and Oswald's deaths. [23]

After those killings, little more would be heard about the anti-Castro bioweapon project. In July 1964, on the same day members of the Warren Commission would arrive in New Orleans to interview witnesses, Sherman would die mysteriously at the age of 51. Her body would be found in her apartment stabbed, mutilated, and burned. Her right arm would be completely incinerated, with some saying the damage didn't look like it was caused by fire. An autopsy would report her death as a murder. [24]

Aaron Kohn, managing director of the Metropolitan Crime Commission of New Orleans, would inform police that the day after Sherman's body was found, a woman called saying she worked at the same clinic with Sherman. The woman said that Sherman was the "second one of my friends here at Ochsner [Foundation] who has been mysteriously killed in the past year." Sherman knew about an alleged Marcello-affiliated, drug-trafficking ring done through the clinic, Kohn wrote.

In 1971, researcher Haslam would try to get a district attorney's office investigator he knew to obtain a police report of Sherman's murder. The investigator said he could not get it and took "flack" just for asking. The case would remain unsolved, as of 2022. [25]

Clay Shaw: CIA asset?

Louisiana-born Clay Shaw was another New Orleans figure tied to both Ochsner and Oswald. Publicly, Shaw helped found and directed the New Orleans International Trade Mart, which facilitated the sale of imported goods. Exhibiting polished manners with the air of nobility, he was active in civic affairs, particularly in the preservation of historic buildings in the French Quarter.

Behind the scenes, the World War II Army officer operated in some spooky circles, Garrison said. He used an alias, "Clay Bertrand" or sometimes "Clem Bertrand." When Charles Cabell spoke before the International Relations Association of New Orleans in 1961, who introduced the CIA's former second-in-command whom JFK ousted? None other than Shaw.

In July 1963, Shaw met a man who appeared to be Oswald at the seawall at Lake Pontchartrain and gave him what "looked like a roll of money," said witness Vernon Bundy. The African-American inmate at New Orleans Parish prison was there "to get a [heroin] fix," which would become a fairly easy detail used by Shaw's defense team to discredit Bundy. Garrison would argue that even heroin addicts could tell the truth at any given time, without much sympathy. [26]

In early September 1963, a black Cadillac appeared in the small town of Clinton as the Congress for Racial Equality sponsored an African-American voter registration driver. Many waiting in line said they saw a man who looked like Oswald emerge from the car and stand in line to register. He made a memorable impression since he was the only white person in the line and not an area resident. When it came his time to register, he gave his name as "Lee Harvey Oswald." [27]

Witnesses said the Cadillac's driver looked like Shaw. They identified another passenger, who donned a wig and painted eyebrows, as Ferrie. Shaw would later claim under oath that he did not know Oswald or Ferrie and had not been to Clinton. But Clinton town marshal John Manchester would tell the House Assassinations Committee that he approached the black Cadillac that day and instructed the driver to identify himself and produce his driver's license. The driver gave his name as "Clay Shaw from the International Trade Mart" and produced a driver's license that matched, according to documents released through the 1992 President John F. Kennedy Assassination Records Collection Act. [28]

Moreover, Sergio Smith would later pass a polygraph exam in which he stated that he had met Shaw, as well as Ferrie and Banister, to discuss supporting his group's anti-Castro activities. Ferrie and Banister had reacted positively, but Shaw had not, Smith said. [29]

Shaw was there to help Oswald get a job at a mental hospital in the nearby town of Jackson as part of building Oswald's assassin profile, according to Garrison. Shaw thought that Oswald registering to vote in that county could improve his chances of getting the job, Garrison believed.

Others wondered why registering to vote would help someone get a job and thought their venture into Clinton could help discredit a civil rights organization or cover up what they were really up to in Jackson. Baker postulated that Shaw, Ferrie, and Oswald were actually at the mental hospital to check on the bioweapon project.

'A triangulation of crossfire'

In September, longtime Ferrie friend and insurance salesman Perry Russo said he met with Shaw, Ferrie, and Oswald at Ferrie's apartment. Shaw used the name, "Clem Bertrand," while Oswald was introduced as "Leon," according to Garrison.

The men discussed assassinating Kennedy in a "triangulation of crossfire with at least two gunmen, but preferably three, shooting at the same time," Garrison said. "One of the gunmen, it was indicated, might have to be sacrificed as a scapegoat or patsy to allow the other participants time to make their escape. No one indicated to Oswald at the meeting that he was going to be the scapegoat, and there was no indication of any awareness on his part of such an eventuality."

They also discussed escape plans, such as flying to other countries. Shaw and Ferrie said they should make sure they were not at the assassination scene and were visible to people, Garrison said. Shaw said he would travel to the West coast, while Ferrie stated he would be in Hammond, La. That would be pretty much where they ended up on November 22. [30]

During the Garrison trial, Shaw would deny under oath that he had anything to do with the assassination, or that he worked for the CIA. However, a CIA document later released showed he was a "highly paid" CIA contract source or asset. And CIA officers Victor Marchetti and Richard Helms both indicated that Shaw had worked for the agency. [31]

Moreover, Shaw's address book contained a listing for "Lee Odom, P.O. Box 19106, Dallas, Texas." That same post office box number appeared in Oswald's address book. [32]

After a jury acquitted Shaw in 1969, Garrison charged Shaw with perjury. But the federal government intervened and dismissed the perjury charges in 1971. "Had Jim Garrison had access to the document stating that Clay Shaw was 'a highly paid CIA contract source,' he could have convicted Clay Shaw of perjury on the spot," noted Temple University professor Joan Mellen. [33]

Ruby summoned to New Orleans by Marcello

Oswald was not the only key JFK killing figure who visited New Orleans in the summer of 1963.

By then, Jack Ruby was in dire straits financially. He owed the IRS as much as $60,000, and the federal agency filed tax liens against him. [34]

To help pay that debt, Ruby skimmed money from the Carousel Club that he operated and Marcello secretly owned in downtown Dallas, the mob boss believed. That's why Marcello summoned Ruby to his 6,400-acre Churchill Farms compound outside New Orleans in June. The land contained swamps where Marcello reportedly deposited the bodies of people who he thought crossed him.

Marcello asked Ruby whether he was skimming profits off the Carousel Club. Ruby reportedly begged for his life and the lives of family members, and a deal was hatched. The bottom line was that Ruby owed Marcello a big favor. [35]

Ruby had a lifetime of associations with mafiosos. Growing up in Chicago, Ruby was "a runner for Al Capone. He was a gopher," Blakey said. "He was violently connected with a mob-dominated union. He was connected to Zooky the Bookie. The mob took out Zooky the Bookie because they wanted to take over his business, and they told Ruby to leave town and Ruby left." [36]

Ruby claimed he had no contact with "persons of notorious backgrounds" since his Chicago days. But the evidence of Ruby's continued Mafia involvement in Dallas included a statement by Luis Kutner, a lawyer and staff member of Sen. Estes Kefauver's committee investigating organized crime in 1950 and 1951. Kutner said that Ruby arrived in Dallas in 1947 from Chicago as a "syndicate lieutenant" who would "serve as a liaison" for Chicago mobsters. [37]

Ruby opened the Silver Spur Club in Dallas, which Dallas Police Lt. George Butler told the Kefauver committee was a hangout for the Chicago mob when they tried to bribe local authorities. Marcello claimed to have set up Ruby in the bar business. Bobby Gene Moore, a piano player for another nightclub operated by Ruby called the Vegas Club, told the FBI that Ruby was a "frequent visitor and associate" of alleged Dallas mob boss Joseph Civello after moving to

Dallas. Moore said Ruby frequented a meat shop run by the Civello family on Ross Avenue near downtown where Moore worked, as well as a nearby liquor store on Ross Avenue that fronted as a bookie joint. [38]

One of Ruby's "closest friends" was Lewis McWillie, who moved from Dallas to Cuba in 1958 to work in gambling casinos there until 1960, according to the House Assassinations Committee. Law enforcement files showed McWillie had ties to Trafficante and other mob bosses. The committee also found "circumstantial evidence" that Ruby himself met with Trafficante in Cuba in 1959. Others say Ruby paid off financial debts to Trafficante and other mafiosos by running guns to Cuba. Ruby associate James Beaird told the FBI that Ruby ran guns to Castro guerillas as early as 1957, saying he did it "for the money." Ruby reportedly switched sides in 1959 after Castro started throwing Mafia casinos out of Cuba, sending some guns to McWillie there. [39]

In Dallas, Ruby reported to Marcello associate Civello on a weekly basis about loan sharking and related matters, author Mario Machi wrote. In 1957, Civello was among attendees of an infamous meeting of mobsters in Apalachin, N.Y., and was indicted for conspiracy and perjury in 1960. He and 19 other mobsters were sentenced to five years in prison, but an appeals court overturned the convictions.

Dallas Police Det. G.D. Gandy reported that in 1957 he observed Ruby meet with McWillie, Johnny Ross Patrono, and other alleged mafiosos in Joseph Campisi's Egyptian Restaurant on Mockingbird Lane in Dallas. Campisi had met Ruby in 1947 at a downtown bar, shortly after Ruby moved from Chicago. Campisi and his wife attended Ruby's clubs a few times, including one where he emceed an amateur show involving unpaid women who wanted to try stripping. Ruby "was funny, and I enjoyed him because he was a little dizzy," Campisi said. Ruby punched guests who were too loud and drunk, and got in fights outside the club, he said. Campisi denied Ruby was a friend, saying that he had only been at his house once to eat dinner. [40]

Ruby's clubs were not known to be classy. Rival Abe Weinstein ran the most reputable burlesque joint, the Colony Club, which was near Ruby's Carousel Club, Campisi said. A longtime family friend and business associate of Civello, Campisi said he never discussed the 1957 indictment. Campisi also knew New Orleans mob boss Marcello and his brothers, Joe and Vincent, but said he did not have business dealings with them.

Ruby tried to beef up his business and influence by befriending police, giving them free drinks and other favors. Numerous officers frequented his clubs. While he would be arrested nine times in Dallas before November 1963 and prior charges included hitting an off-duty officer with a gun, his stiffest conviction was only for a traffic summons. [41]

> 26 April 1957
>
> Lieutenant J.M. Souter
> Criminal Intelligence Section
> Special Service Bureau
> Dallas Police Department
>
> SUBJECT: Egyptian Lounge
> 5410 E. Mockingbird
>
> Sir:
>
> On 25 April 1957, this officer entered SUBJECT CAFE and observed MORTON KAUFMAN, JAMES CAMPISI, aka: Black Jimmie and JOHNNY ROSS PATRONO sitting in the office. A short time later, LEWIS JOE MARTIN; aka McWillie and JACK RUBY entered the office. McWillie and Ruby sat at a table and ordered food and Black Jimmie and an unknown male stated they were "going for a drive".
>
> Respectfully submitted,
>
> G.D. Gandy, Detective
> Criminal Intelligence Section

A Dallas Police detective monitored Jack Ruby, seeing him with several suspected Mafia members in Joseph Campisi's Egyptian Restaurant in Dallas in 1957. [Dallas Police Department intelligence report, March 9, 1978]

Contrary to some reports, Ruby was not a fan of the Kennedys, believing they were soft on communism, said Beverly Oliver Massegee, a close friend of Ruby's who sung at the Colony Club when she was only 17 in 1963. "He hated the Kennedys. He hated Jack. He hated Bobby," Massegee said. "And his exact words were, 'And I hate their so-and-so father even more.' So I knew everything wasn't exactly adding up in Dallas, but at 17, what could I do about it?" [42]

Carousel Club dancer Gail Raven confirmed that Ruby did not like the Kennedys, especially Robert. [43]

Massegee knew Ruby so well that she traveled out of town with him "on numerous occasions. I was his armpiece a lot of times," said Massegee, who fibbed about her age to work at the club. "It made him feel important to have a good-looking girl on his arm, as it does most men." [44]

Whether Ruby was actually a Mafia member or just knew mobsters was hard to figure, Massegee said. "Was he part of the Mafia or was he acquainted with the Mafia? I don't know," she said. "My suspicions tell me, yeah, probably he was pretty well involved in it." [45]

Nagell and the Cuban connection

Another group that Oswald cemented ties with in New Orleans was Cubans. Numerous people observed him meeting with Hispanic men who were either Cuban or Mexican.

Among those who said he saw Oswald meeting with Latinos was super spy Nagell, who author Dick Russell called "the man who knew too much." Born in Greenwich, N.Y., in 1930, Nagell joined the U.S. Army and fought in Korea, earning a Purple Heart and Bronze Star while rising to the rank of lieutenant. He became an intelligence officer in Korea and Japan, reportedly spying on Oswald for Army counterintelligence when they were both in Japan.

After leaving the Army in late 1959, Nagell worked as an investigator for government agencies in Los Angeles and began spying for the CIA in late 1962. He infiltrated the American Communist Party and Soviet intelligence, and distributed Marxist literature in Mexico. He would later say he was never a communist, that appearing to be a communist was part of his work. Reporting to Desmond FitzGerald, the CIA's head of Cuban operations, Nagell learned more about anti-Castro Cubans' plans against JFK and started informing the Soviets as well, Russell wrote. [46]

In July, Oswald started associating more with members of the violent anti-Castro group Alpha 66, Nagell reported. Alpha 66 formed in 1961 by Cuban exile Antonio Veciana and others at the direction of a CIA operative known as "Maurice Bishop." The House Assassinations Committee reported that Bishop was the alias of David Phillips, the CIA veteran who would be promoted to chief of Cuban operations by September 1963. Veciana, who would receive thousands of dollars from Phillips to work on plots to kill Castro and stage commando raids in Cuban waters, claimed that Oswald was present during one meeting he had with Phillips. [47]

By August, Nagell claimed he had infiltrated Alpha 66 and taped a meeting attended by Oswald and two Cubans known as "Angel" and "Arcacha." The latter man could have been Sergio Smith, the Banister associate. [48]

Upon learning that Alpha 66 members wanted to assassinate Kennedy and make it look like Castro ordered the hit, Nagell reported that development to KGB, CIA, and FBI contacts. Not wanting to be linked to an assassination of the U.S. leader, the Soviets supposedly ordered Nagell to convince Oswald he was being set up as a patsy or to kill him in Mexico City before an attempt on JFK could be executed.

"While both U.S. and Soviet intelligence agencies were aware of the conspiracy, it was the KGB – not the CIA or FBI – that attempted to prevent it," wrote Russell. "The Soviets, who had reached a growing accommodation with Kennedy after the 1962 Cuban Missile Crisis, were also afraid that the assassination would falsely be blamed upon them or the Cubans." [49]

Nagell said he personally met Oswald in September in New Orleans and warned him that he was being set up as a "patsy" in an assassination plot by the anti-Castro Cubans and other "fascist elements." When Oswald declined to remove himself from the plot, the KGB ordered Nagell to kill him, while the CIA cut off Nagell, he said. [50]

If he killed Oswald, Nagell feared the CIA would view him as a traitor by taking orders from the KGB. He decided to send the FBI's Hoover a registered letter, warning of an attempt on JFK's life in Washington, D.C., planned for late September. At the same time, Oswald wrote the U.S. Communist Party and Socialist Workers Party, saying he was moving to the D.C. area in October. Oswald asked party leaders for contacts, allegedly under the recommendation of Banister. [51]

On September 20, Nagell, fearing he might be set up himself as a JFK killing conspirator, walked into an El Paso bank and fired two shots into a wall. Then he waited to be arrested. "I would rather be arrested than commit murder and treason," he told the FBI. He was convicted and served four-and-a-half years in prison. [52]

After Nagell's arrest and letter to Hoover, Oswald stopped trying to relocate to the D.C. area, focusing on going to Cuba. "Nagell, by his shots in the bank, had given the CIA and FBI public notice that, unlike Oswald, he refused to be a pawn in the plot," noted author James Douglass. "Although the whistle Nagell blew to Hoover did not save Kennedy's life, it may have been just loud enough with his bank caper to set back the plot two months." [53]

But Nagell realized that he failed, ultimately, to save JFK's life, even though he helped prolong it. "I was in a quandary in September '63. I didn't know what to do," Nagell said. "What did I accomplish? Not a goddamned thing." [54]

Paine is back

The few weeks Ruth Paine spent with Marina and June the previous spring made enough of an impression that she drove hundreds of miles out of her way to stop in New Orleans on September 20 on the way back from visiting relatives in the Midwest and Mid-Atlantic regions. Ruth and Marina had continued to correspond by letters, with Marina mentioning her continued arguments with Lee. Her husband would not be satisfied living anywhere, perhaps not even on the moon, Marina said.

By July, Ruth had extended an invitation for Marina and June to stay with her in Irving. "If Lee doesn't wish to live with you anymore, and prefers that you go to the Soviet Union, think about the possibility of living with me," Paine wrote. "I have long received [financial support] from my parents. I lived 'dependent' a long time. I would be happy to be an aunt to you." [55]

Ruth, who had just met Marina a few months before, insisted her interest was for friendship only. She stated that her belief that "it would be better" for Lee and Marina to not live together if they did not "receive happiness" was sincere.

"I enjoyed [Marina's] company," Ruth said. "Being able to talk Russian with her added a wider dimension to my rather small and boring life as a young mother." [56]

But was that all there was to this relationship? There were other Russians in Dallas with whom Ruth could have honed her language skills. Yet, she kept writing Marina, putting thoughts in her head to separate from her husband. It was odd, to say the least, that a separated woman with two young kids of her own would expose her family to the potential problems associated with letting a Russian émigré into their home less than a year after the Cuban Missile Crisis during the depths of the Cold War. Quakers believe in the concept of providing sanctuary to refugees and others in need, but what Ruth was doing with Marina seemed like going beyond that.

Was Ruth doing this as part of her payback to her CIA-connected family who had, as she told Marina, long financially supported her? Or perhaps as payback to some CIA contacts she had made? William Avery Hyde, her father who lived in Ohio in 1963 and had divorced Ruth's mother in 1961, told FBI agents that he had seen her daughter over Labor Day weekend at a relative's home in Pennsylvania. They had discussed the Oswalds, and Ruth "expressed concern" about Marina, discussing how she should move back in with her to have her child.

"William Hyde could not explain why his daughter and Marina Oswald were so closely attached, except that his daughter was interested in studying the Russian language," FBI agents reported. "He said he knew of no subversive connections Marina Oswald may have had." [57]

Ruth also visited her sister, Sylvia Hoke, in September at their home in the Washington, D.C., area. In addition, she stopped by the Ohio home of her brother, Carl Hyde. Ruth indicated she was leaving for New Orleans to "invite [Marina] to stay with her in her home," Hyde told FBI agents. Ruth had told her brother that Lee Oswald was a "communist" and Marina "did not share her husband's views." Ruth also said Oswald had "not allowed" Marina to learn English, and they were having marital difficulties. [58]

While it's hard to tie the aims of the CIA with that of Quakerism and peace organizations that Ruth supported, family bonds are often stronger than principles or beliefs. Being an informal CIA asset and "handler" of Marina, who monitored and tried to guide her, much the same way de Mohrenschildt and others did Oswald, could be accomplished under the guise of friendship. That summer, Ruth taught a class in Russian at St. Mark's School but attracted only one student, William Hootkins, who went on to act in movies such as *Star Wars* and *Raiders of the Lost Ark*. Her husband rented an apartment on his own, so they needed income from other sources.

Whatever the case, Oswald greeted Ruth more warmly than she expected on her September visit to New Orleans. He had allegedly made up his mind to move to Cuba, and Ruth's offer to take in his family and oversee the birth of another child fit in well with those plans. While Ruth and Marina visited the French Quarter with their kids, Oswald packed their belongings. The items he placed in her car included his rifle carefully wrapped in a blanket.

When they left, Lee warned Marina not to tell Ruth about his plans to enter Cuba. As far as Ruth knew, he was traveling to Houston in search of work.

Mexico bound

Oswald reportedly wasted little time boarding a bus for Laredo. He continued on to Mexico City, arriving on September 27, according to the FBI's Hoover and the Warren Commission.

After checking into a hotel, the story goes that he visited the Cuban Embassy to try to obtain a visa. Speaking to Silvia Duran, he explained how he just wanted a two-week transit visa and would continue to the USSR. He showed documents on how he had started the FPCC chapter and more as proof of him being "a friend of Cuba."

An official told Oswald he could expedite the process by obtaining a Russian visa; otherwise the process could take several weeks. So Oswald tried the Soviet Embassy, meeting with three consular officials who also worked for the KGB. Oswald complained about the FBI harassing him, saying he wanted to visit Cuba and then permanently remain in Soviet Union. He showed his documents.

Another official told him it would take at least four months to get a visa, and such cases were usually handled in the country where the applicants lived. "This won't do for me!" Oswald yelled, according to an account by a Soviet KGB officer. "For me, it's all going to end in tragedy!" [59]

Oswald returned to the Cuban Embassy, claiming the Soviets had promised to grant him a visa. Duran called a Soviet official to find out that wasn't quite accurate. Oswald returned to the Soviet Embassy the following day and said he dreamed of returning to Russia and living quietly with his family. At one point, he referred to being persecuted by the FBI and sobbed, "I'm afraid they'll kill me. Let me in!" [60]

Oswald then said he was even being followed in Mexico City and pulled out a revolver. "This is what I must now carry to protect my life," he stated. A Soviet official removed the bullets from the gun and handed it to another officer, who placed it back on the table. [61]

Eventually, Oswald calmed down, as officials gave him forms to fill out. He took back his gun and bullets, then walked out dejectedly. As he trudged out, a Soviet official heard him repeat that he feared for his life. "But if they don't leave me alone, I'm going to defend myself," he vowed. [62]

The Mexico City trip was part of crafting Oswald's image as a Marxist, Garrison said. But that plan was frustrated when Soviet and Cuban officials apparently thought Oswald was a U.S. intelligence agent, Garrison believed. Oswald likely thought he was part of a team that was going to kill Castro since he focused on getting to Cuba, while Oswald's government monitors wanted to paint him as a Castro agent to further doom the Cuban leader, according to Canfield and Weberman. [63]

After trying again unsuccessfully with the Cuban Embassy, Oswald took in a bullfight and saw the sights. Some claimed he received money from contacts supposedly to kill Castro while in Mexico City. Perhaps operatives such as Phillips and David Morales worked to set him up to make it appear he was plotting against Castro, Kennedy or both, others said. Perhaps he really did shoot at Kennedy as a way of "defending" himself when he thought there was no real way out, some theorized. [64]

Phillips denied plotting against Kennedy to the day he died of cancer in 1988. But in an unpublished novel, Phillips wrote about a CIA officer who was one of Oswald's handlers. The character states, "We gave [Oswald] the mission of killing Fidel Castro in Cuba.... I don't know why he killed Kennedy. But I do know he used precisely the plan we had devised against Castro." [65]

Oswald himself told Dallas police he went to Mexico to get a visa to "go to Russia by way of Cuba. They told me to come back in 30 days." Was an Oswald double involved to make him look more unstable than he was, or set him up? Duran later stated that the man who visited was blond and much shorter than Oswald. Cuban Consul Eusebio Azcue Lopez testified that the man he met was also blond. [66]

Hoover would admit to LBJ that photos the CIA used to attempt to prove Oswald visited the embassies there appeared fake. Hoover would add that Oswald – or someone impersonating Oswald might have received $6,500 from the Cuban Embassy when he was in Mexico. "It appears that there is a second person who was at the Soviet Embassy," Hoover said. Was Hoover trying to tie Castro and the Soviets to the assassination, or sound an alarm about another suspect? [67]

Return to Dallas

Upon failing to receive a visa to Cuba, Oswald returned to Dallas, telling Marina that the Soviet and Cuban embassies were "too bureaucratic." A typesetting job he had applied for and made a good impression during the interview was derailed by a bad reference from Jaggars-Chiles. A landlady told him to move for no apparent reason.

Thinking the FBI or someone was purposely dogging him, Oswald used the alias, "O.H. Lee," to rent a room on North Beckley in Oak Cliff. Marina and June continued to stay with Ruth, where it was more comfortable for the birth of their second daughter.

Oswald, who visited his family on weekends, "began to treat me better," Marina said. Even Ruth took more of a liking to him. Oswald was "really rather ordinary, not an ogre that was out to leave his wife, and be harsh and hostile to all that he knew," Ruth said. [68]

Ruth's warmer feelings toward Oswald developed to the point she helped him find work. Linnie Mae Randle, a neighbor of Ruth's, had a brother who worked at the book depository and Ruth said she had suggested that Oswald apply for an opening there. Paine called the depository to inquire for Oswald, and someone there said to have him come in the next day for an interview. [69]

But Ruth's statement was suspicious since Randle testified that she didn't know there was a job opening over at the TSBD. She had mentioned the TSBD as one of "several places that [Oswald] might go to look for work." [70]

Another suspicious move was that a Texas Employment Commission employee contacted the Paine home to refer Oswald to a better paying job as a cargo handler at Trans Texas Airways. But Ruth told him that Oswald was working elsewhere. At first, Paine told the Warren Commission that she didn't recall the other job, then said Oswald found out the job had been filled. [71]

At any rate, Oswald was immediately hired on October 16, and some suspected that his supervisor, William Shelley, worked for an intelligence agency. Byrd, who owned the TSBD from the 1930s until the 1970s, was also believed to have intelligence ties. His cousin was famed polar explorer Admiral Richard E. Byrd Jr., who in the 1950s was honorary chairman of a CIA front organization, the International Rescue Committee. His brother, U.S. Sen. Harry F. Byrd, was a far-right leader and a vocal proponent of segregation.

In November 1963, Byrd would leave for a long African hunting trip. He would not return until the following month, and some suspected he remained so long to avoid speculation about a possible role in the assassination. In the realm between coincidence and conspiracy that afflicts so many aspects of this case, Byrd had helped found the Civil Air Patrol, the same organization that Ferrie and Oswald once joined. [72]

So, once again, Oswald was not joining an ordinary employer.

Threatening the FBI

By late October, the Oswalds had an addition to their family, Rachel. But rather than embrace the expanding family and find a home large enough for all, Oswald rented a lone room in the Oak Cliff neighborhood of Dallas. He said the reason was to be closer to work, but the room was still two miles away from the TSBD. So Marina and their daughters continued to stay with Ruth.

In early November, Ruth said FBI agent James Hosty Jr. interviewed her and Marina twice. Among the information Hosty sought was where Oswald lived and worked. In addition, Hosty said he had a "counter-espionage concern….Could either of the Oswalds be Soviet intelligence agents?" [73]

Feeling overwhelmed and frustrated, Oswald visited the Dallas FBI office around November 12. He asked secretary Nannie Lee Fenner if Hosty was there.

After she checked and told him he was not, Oswald left a short letter in an envelope addressed to Hosty.

Fenner opened the envelope and stated in a sworn statement that the note said something like: "Let this be a warning. I will blow up the FBI and the Dallas Police Department if you don't stop bothering my wife. Signed, Lee Harvey Oswald." [74]

Thinking the note could be serious, Fenner showed it to Kyle Clark, assistant special agent in charge. "It is just a nut," Clark responded, telling her to give it to Hosty.

Fenner did after showing the note to a few others in the office. Hosty commented "to the effect that Oswald was a nut." Hosty would say that the note didn't contain an explicit threat, as Fenner believed, and swear in an affidavit that he "never had any information indicating potential violence on the part of Lee Harvey Oswald." [75]

Hosty would write that the letter said, in effect, "If you want to talk to me, you should talk to me to my face. Stop harassing my wife, and stop trying to ask her about me. You have no right to harass her." He would claim the letter was not signed and might have come from a "radical right-winger." [76]

However, the same day Oswald was arrested, Hosty reportedly told Dallas police officers, "We knew that Lee Harvey Oswald was capable of assassinating the president of the United States, but we didn't dream he would do it." Hosty would deny making such a statement, which was written in a memo by Dallas Police Lt. Jack Revill. [77]

Many would wonder why the FBI did not alert the Dallas police or Secret Service to watch Oswald on November 22, or why FBI agents themselves didn't watch him that day. Hosty would tell the Warren Commission he didn't alert Dallas police or the Secret Service about Oswald before the assassination because he "was a security risk of a sort, but not the type of person who would engage in violence." [78]

Aynesworth would write in The Dallas Morning News that Police Chief Jesse Curry privately told friends, "If we had known that a defector or a communist was anywhere in this town, let alone on the parade route, we would have been sitting on his lap, you can bet on that." [79]

Oswald worked in a coffee business believed to have CIA ties near New Orleans' Lafayette Square in 1963. A federal building on the south side of the square, at far right, contained offices of the Secret Service and Naval Intelligence back then. CIA and FBI offices were also nearby. The white building behind the Lafayette Square sign housed federal courts in the early 1960s and later became the home of the Fifth Circuit Court of Appeals. Just left of that court building was the Newman Building at 544 Camp Street, where Oswald, David Ferrie, and Cubans were believed by some to have met with Guy Banister in his office. The Newman Building was torn down in the 1970s to expand a federal complex. So a few months before JFK's assassination, Oswald worked and hung out in the heart of New Orleans' intelligence community. [Shay photo]

Now part of the Hale Boggs Federal Building, the Newman Building stood here at Camp and Lafayette streets. The Reily Coffee Co., where Oswald worked, was a couple of blocks southeast of here on Magazine Street. Banister entered the Newman Building from the Lafayette Street entrance to get to his office. The 544 Camp Street address, which was found stamped on Fair Play for Cuba Committee leaflets distributed by Oswald, was a separate entrance in the same building that led to the second floor. Anti-Castro Cuban groups also had offices in the building in the early 1960s. The Newman Building was demolished in the early 1970s to make way for an expansion of the federal complex that was named after Boggs. [Shay photo]

Chapter Seven

Multiple Threats

Dear Sir: Your letter of February 11th has been received. In response to your request, I am enclosing a copy of my speech, "Time for Decision"; however, I would prefer that you not reprint this for your own use. Very truly yours, John Edgar Hoover
– **HOOVER**, letter to JFK killing suspect **Thomas Vallee**, February 15, 1968

Throughout the last few months of John F. Kennedy's life, threats and warning signs intensified. The more he tried to de-escalate U.S. involvement in the Vietnam War, support civil rights, improve relations with the Soviet Union and Cuba, and help lower-income people, the more he enraged far right-wing types.

While the horrible deed eventually happened in Dallas, forever staining that city, what is often lost in this tragedy is that it could easily have occurred in several other cities, including Chicago, Miami, and Tampa.

Alpha 66, the anti-Castro paramilitary group, reportedly planned several assassination attempts on Kennedy during the president's final year. In December 1962, JFK addressed more than 1,000 Cuban exiles and a crowd of some 40,000 attendees at the Orange Bowl in Miami. He told the large gathering that a flag presented to him by leaders of the Bay of Pigs invasion would "be returned to this brigade in a free Havana."

Some Kennedy aides objected to the president delivering such a message to the crowd, saying it would build up false expectations that the U.S. would support another invasion. JFK reportedly agreed not to speak at the event, but then brigade leaders such as San Roman personally invited him to do so. So he changed his mind.

By that time, many in the anti-Castro Cuban community had heard about Kennedy's pledge not to invade Cuba again that he made to help end the Cuban Missile Crisis. Miami police and Secret Service agents received tips about some Cubans talking about setting off a bomb when JFK spoke in that stadium. Authorities questioned enough people beforehand to stop such an event from occurring. [1]

However, that wasn't the end of such conspiratorial talk. Not by a long shot. Within the Secret Service during the chaotic months leading up to November 22, "rumors were flying about threats on the president's life," wrote Agent Bolden, who had become a family friend of the Kennedys.

"Reports had circulated in the agency about Cuban dissidents and right-wing southerners who were stalking [Kennedy] and plotting his assassination," wrote Bolden, who worked in the Chicago office in 1963. "Each weekly meeting brought information about some new organized group with a plot of its own." [2]

Klan leader exposes convention of JFK foes

If there was one event in 1963 that galvanized the anti-Kennedy forces, it was likely the Congress of Freedom in New Orleans in April, an annual convention of those who were to the right of the far right. Gen. Walker and Lt. Gen. Pedro del Valle, a founder of the minuteman group Defenders of the American Constitution, were among the meeting's speakers. Del Valle and Walker had discussed assassinating certain "enemies" in top government and business positions as early as 1962, author Jeffrey H. Caufield wrote. [3]

William "Willie" Somersett, a long-time Florida Klan leader who became a government informant in 1949, said speakers there called for a broad-based assassination campaign against not just political leaders they considered pro-communist, but those in business and international relations. Most stopped short of openly mentioning a specific plot against Kennedy. [4]

Somersett, who rose to national Klan leadership positions, knew better than most what they meant and how serious they were. As a Klan leader, he agreed with many right-wing causes, such as segregation and opposing Kennedy's perceived push to sell out his country to the Soviets and United Nations-supporting liberals. But he might not have been a hardcore racist; in 1964, he would try to stop race discrimination among hiring of mechanics in Miami. [5]

Moreover, Somersett did not support Klan violence, believing there were legal ways to advance the Klan agenda without resorting to lynchings, shootings, and bombings. But he needed to make a living. Organizing for a labor union on a part-time basis didn't pay many bills. As a longtime member of far-right groups and an imposing man whose nickname among authorities was "88" since he reminded them of an Oldsmobile 88, Somersett could gain the confidence of KKK leaders like Joseph A. Milteer. Somersett and Milteer developed a fairly close relationship, with Milteer representing the Dixie Klan faction and far-right Constitution Party that was a front for a violent undercover group.

Somersett fed the FBI information even as he became adjutant to the National Grand Council of Klans, a position that afforded him extensive travel opportunities to KKK meetings. Through that position, he had helped authorities stop plots against not just Kennedy but King Jr. and others. The risks were great; if fellow Klan members discovered his role, he faced retaliation that included death. The FBI even dropped him as an informant in 1961 after agents feared he was compromised, but Somersett went to work for Miami police and still fed the FBI tidbits for free. Perhaps there was something that drove Somersett beyond money.

"Through the years, Somersett had been associated with right-wing politics, but he disliked groups pressing for violence," journalist Dan Christensen wrote. "Why he became an informer is uncertain. Money? Honor? Patriotism? It could just have been his job." [6]

After Somersett informed the FBI of plots discussed at the COF meeting in New Orleans, agents interrogated enough suspects who spoke there to cool much of the assassination talk. But some began to discuss a more specific plan targeting Kennedy, Somersett said.

Gunman in Nashville

In May, Kennedy became the first president to visit Nashville, Tenn., since FDR in the 1930s, commemorating Vanderbilt University's 90th anniversary and the construction of a dam. He rode in an open 1962 Lincoln Continental convertible along crowded downtown streets. The previous day, newspapers had printed the motorcade's route.

What would happen in Dallas a few months later could have occurred in Tennessee's capital, some said. As Klansmen and Cubans stalked Kennedy, he told a crowd of about 30,000 at a football stadium on the Vanderbilt campus that "educated men and women" should "reject the temptations of prejudice and violence" and "reaffirm the values of freedom and law on which our society depends." Every person was "entitled to be regarded with decency and treated with dignity," JFK stated. Some of the first civil rights lunch counter sit-ins had successfully integrated Nashville facilities in 1960. By 1963, the focus of the civil rights movement was more on Mississippi and Alabama.

People who rushed the stage to gain a closer look were friendly, though one account reported that Kennedy was momentarily startled by the sound of a falling water jug. Others were not so friendly.

After a lunch at the governor's mansion, Kennedy was driven to Overton High School to board an Army helicopter that would take him to another stop in

Alabama. As Kennedy left his vehicle and was about to board the helicopter, a man approached, carrying a gun underneath a sack, according to a 1992 article in the Nashville Banner. Secret Service agents spied the man's suspicious baggage before he could get too close to the president and grabbed him. [7]

The matter was kept quiet to supposedly not encourage similar incidents. Details about the man and what happened to him have remained a mystery, to the point that articles reliving JFK's 1963 visit to Nashville decades later did not include anything about the gunman.

But a Secret Service report would reveal that Thomas Vallee, a potential suspect in the 1963 Chicago plot, had lived in the small town of Rogersville, Tenn., until June 1963, when he moved to Chicago. Vallee was in Knoxville, which is about 180 miles from Nashville, on May 25 when he was arrested for driving while intoxicated. Vallee would return to Tennessee in early 1964 before later moving to New York, Ohio, and back to Chicago, authorities said. [8]

Threats in Ireland, LA

Threats that weren't nearly as serious as a gunman approaching the president didn't let up. No matter how small, Secret Service agents had to check them out.

Before a June 1963 trip to Ireland, agents were alerted to two phone threats saying JFK would be killed on that trip. One specifically said a man with a rifle would shoot at his motorcade from a building above. Extra precautions were taken, such as agents carrying guns despite that violating Irish law. [9]

That same month, Kennedy attended a Los Angeles screening of the movie, *PT-109*, a film in which Cliff Robertson depicted JFK's World War II heroics. In an unusual step, Kennedy was allowed to choose the actor who portrayed him, but his first choice, Warren Beatty, declined due to not liking the script. While there were no direct threats as Kennedy viewed the film, Nagell reported that some Alpha 66 members planned to target him during that Los Angeles visit.

Vaughn Marlowe, the executive officer of the Los Angeles chapter of the Fair Play for Cuba Committee, was being set up as a patsy, Nagell claimed. Marlowe not only worked for the FPCC, but he supported the Socialist Workers Party and was publicly critical of JFK. He also happened to be a sharpshooter while in the U.S. Army as a Korean War veteran. Like Oswald, he sometimes used a pseudonym and had visited the Cuban Embassy in Mexico City. [10]

Marlowe would tell author Russell that he joked that Nagell or someone he worked with was trying to recruit him to "be Oswald." He was aware of being under surveillance by Nagell, who wasn't trying to recruit him as much as warn him about a possible Alpha 66 plot. Nothing came of that potential threat, though some said it could have been one of several dry runs. [11]

In July, James A. Hawkins, a 22-year old unemployed man from Richmond, Va., criticized JFK's civil rights efforts in front of a gas station attendant in Laurel, Md. Then, he stated that he was going to Washington "to blow up the White House and kill the president." The attendant called police, who searched Hawkins' bag and did not find any weapons. Hawkins headed south to Mobile, Ala., where he was arrested by Secret Service agents and claimed to be joking about the threat. [12]

But Hawkins had also boasted to some people in Maryland that he was going to New Orleans to "attend a meeting which would lead to the assassination of John F. Kennedy," a Mobile police sergeant later told New Orleans Assistant DA Andrew Sciambra. [13]

In September, Nagell told his government contacts that Kennedy could be targeted in Washington, D.C., later that month or in early October. From New Orleans, Oswald had been writing left-wing officials saying he was moving to the D.C. area in October. There was also the strange matter about Oswald's name written on the registry of a restaurant in Wisconsin a week before Kennedy was to speak in that state in September. Some wondered if that was to show he was stalking JFK, or was even another attempted plot. [14]

From Indiana to Texas, killing talk intensifies

As late November neared, the killing talk ratcheted up a few notches. In September, John Richard Salisbury, an engineer with Brown & Root construction firm in Houston, visited a relative, Robert Norris, employed by Hunt Oil Co. in Dallas. Norris supposedly said JFK will "get shot or killed," if he visited Texas, according to Salisbury. [15]

During a John Birch Society meeting in a Dallas suburb that same month, Castellanos, the anti-Castro activist who tried to join the Bay of Pigs in 1961, vowed that he and others would give JFK "the works when he gets in Dallas." Two other Cuban exiles, Ed Hughes and Francisco Leyba, spoke at the meeting. [16]

In October, Army private Eugene B. Dinkin, a telegraph code breaker stationed in Europe, wrote Robert Kennedy that "an attempt to assassinate the President would occur on November 28th; that if it were to succeed, blame would be placed upon a communist or a Negro, who would be designated the assassin." Dinkin added that the conspiracy "was being engineered by the military," and "a military coup might ensue." He based such conclusions on studies of military newspapers in which he suspected a bias to portray JFK as a communist sympathizer. [17]

When he got no response from RFK, Dinkin told a newspaper editor in Geneva, Switzerland, and the editor of Overseas Weekly in Germany about his plot suspicions. He would be transported to a psychiatric hospital in France, then to Walter Reed Hospital in Washington, D.C.

At a Constitution Party convention in Indianapolis in mid-October, more speakers targeted JFK. In addition, Milteer reportedly offered to have a member of the Student Non-Violent Coordinating Committee in Atlanta killed. [18]

In Maryland, a delegate to Republican Barry Goldwater told CIA employee Ruth Taden that a former CIA courier in West Virginia said before the assassination that Kennedy and his presumed assassin would both soon be killed, according to a CIA document that was declassified and released in 2021. The delegate, identified only as Mrs. Sherwood, said in 1964 that the courier had "disappeared from sight," according to Taden, who could not be located. [19]

Around November 1, mattress company representative Delbert Lekiartin told FBI agents that furniture representative Louis L. Springfield said that if Kennedy came to Dallas, he "would, could, or might be shot." Springfield had said "it would be very easy to do so that someone could shoot the president from an overpass and could conceal himself behind the abutments on the overpass." [20]

Springfield also said it "would be quite easy" to obtain a gun or rifle from a mail-order house, according to Lekiartin. That was a specific detail that authorities attributed to Oswald. The remarks were made at the Dallas Trade Mart on Stemmons Freeway where both companies did business. [21]

Springfield, a Marine reserves sergeant and intelligence chief at the former Naval Air Station in Grand Prairie, admitted to an FBI agent that men at the unit "frequently" discussed how JFK should be killed, but their remarks were "in jest." He clarified that he never said JFK would be killed for sure in Dallas, but that it was possible based on "the feelings of individuals he knew and the comments some of them made."

He added that he "probably" said that whoever shot Kennedy deserved a medal, but he denied making the remarks about the mail-order rifle. The base would be decommissioned, becoming the Grand Prairie Armed Forces Reserve Complex.

Ted Marscico, also of the mattress company, confirmed Lekiartin's account, including the part about the mail-order rifle. He added that he tried to turn the conversation into a more light-hearted one, but Springfield would maintain seriously that JFK "would be shot." [22]

```
                              SECRET

                                              DD/S&T 1543/64
                                              18 May 1964

         MEMORANDUM FOR:  Deputy Director Security

         SUBJECT       :  TADEN, Mrs. Ruth
                          # 58479

              1. Subject is a staff employee of OEL. She advised
         the undersigned on the morning of 18 May 1964 of statements
         made to her on Thursday evening 14 May, which associated
         the CIA with the assassination of President Kennedy. She
         wanted a report of the conversation made known to the Office
         of Security.

              2. Mrs. Taden indicated that she resided in Prince
         Georges County, Maryland, and several months previously had
         registered as a Republican in order to vote in the up-coming
         primary elections. This past Thursday night a Mrs. Sherwood
         telephoned Mrs. Taden indicating she was one of the Delegates
         on the Republican ballot and was supporting Senator Barry
         Goldwater. Mrs. Taden told Mrs. Sherwood that she had not
         decided which candidate to support, and that although she had
         registered Republican she held a deep respect for the late
         President Kennedy. Mrs. Sherwood then made some disparaging
         remarks about the late President Kennedy. She also furnished
         specific information regarding what she described as a
         reliable prediction, made prior to November 1963, that
         President Kennedy would be assassinated.

              3. Mrs. Sherwood indicated that an acquaintance in West
         Virginia, who said he was a former CIA courier, had told her
         prior to the assassination of President Kennedy that President
         Kennedy would be assassinated and that the assassin in turn
         would also be killed. Mrs. Sherwood further advised, according
         to Mrs. Taden, that her attempts to locate this person in
         West Virginia, after the assassination, were not successful.
         Apparently, in Mrs. Sherwood's words, this person "just dis-
         appeared from sight", following the assassination of President
         Kennedy.

         Document Number 1280-466B
         for FOIA Review on  FEB 1977
                                       SECRET
```

This 1964 CIA document, declassified and released in 2021, outlines a prior warning of Kennedy and his presumed assassin being killed. [U.S. National Archives]

Russell McLarry, who worked near the Dallas Trade Mart, reportedly told two women he would shoot JFK when he got there. Secret Service would arrest him shortly after the assassination, and he would say he was "glad" JFK was killed. But once hauled before a grand jury, McLarry would insist he was joking and not be indicted.

A man in Mexico in mid-November told the FBI of a plot to kill JFK. He said he was a Klan member and had heard that a group related to the far-right National States' Rights Party planned to assassinate Kennedy and others. [23]

A Dallas bar operator said he heard there was a $100,000 offer being circulated in various right-wing political circles to kill JFK. Besides such offers, betting was big. After Kennedy was killed, a service station manager in Grants, N.M., would say that someone showed him $8,000 that he had won in a bet about when Kennedy would die. [24]

In Chicago, employees of the Cokesbury bookstore reported customers who either knew something or were psychic. A man in his 40s asked on November 21 about a certain book on JFK, then said he "was dead or would be dead." About a month earlier, a different man asked about books on ESP and outer space, then said Kennedy would soon die.

White House cancels Chicago trip amid plot

The most established plot besides the one in Dallas centered on Chicago. On November 2, JFK planned to visit the Windy City, riding in a motorcade to view the Army-Air Force football game at Soldier Field. After flying to O'Hare Airport, Kennedy would depart in a limousine along the Northwest Expressway, exiting at Jackson Boulevard to pass through warehouses and crowds lined on sidewalks to the stadium. The motorcade would have to make at least one sharp 90-degree turn that would slow it to almost a standstill, similar to what would occur in Dallas three weeks later.

Among those who worked in the buildings along that parade route was Thomas Arthur Vallee. Born in Chicago, the 29-year-old former Marine had moved from an east Tennessee town in June to start a job as a lithographer apprentice at IPP Litho-Plate, 625 W. Jackson. Vallee shared other similarities with Oswald besides landing work along a future Kennedy parade route. He enlisted in the Marines when he was just 16 and served three years, before taking a break and re-enlisting for a year. He had been stationed at a U-2 base, Camp Otsu in Japan. Vallee was hospitalized at least twice, once during an auto accident in which his father died, and another due to a mortar shell exploding near him in Korea, according to an FBI report. Both parents were deceased, as of 1963, though a sister lived in Chicago.

Like Oswald, who served at Camp Atsugi in Japan, Vallee had apparently been recruited by CIA agents to perform discreet assignments. But instead of defecting to Russia, Vallee trained anti-Castro Cubans on Long Island. Both owned rifles and were loners, basically "perfect for a frame-up," wrote author Edwin Black. [25]

Vallee had been honorably discharged from the Marines in 1956 after being diagnosed by military doctors as schizophrenic and paranoid, which was later changed to passive aggressive. A John Birch Society member who claimed to be an expert marksman, he was "outspokenly opposed to President Kennedy's foreign policy," according to the House Assassinations Committee. He regularly stated anti-Kennedy remarks in public that some took as threats, to the point a Chicago police lieutenant warned him against doing that in a cafeteria. [26]

While Vallee talked openly against Kennedy, others planned sinister action. On October 30, an FBI agent in D.C. phoned the Chicago office of the Secret Service to relay a tip from an informant about a four-man team that would allegedly target JFK as he rode to Soldier Field. The men were paramilitary "fanatics" who owned rifles with telescopic sights, according to the tip from an informant known only as "Lee." Some thought the informant could have been Oswald or a government agent who monitored him. At least one of the suspects had a "Spanish-sounding name" and might have been Cuban, Secret Service Agent Bolden would tell the House Assassinations Committee. [27]

The following day, a woman phoned Chicago police to report that four men had arrived from outside the city and she observed rifles in a room they rented from her near the Northwest Expressway. Maurice Martineau, the Chicago special agent in charge, ordered a 24-hour surveillance of the suspects. Agents detained two men on November 1, though records could not be found if they discovered weapons in their possession. They could not locate the two other suspects. [28]

Other Secret Service agents targeted Vallee, discovering two rifles, a handgun, and 2,500 rounds of ammunition in his small apartment. A person who had such weapons and ammo making public threats against the president was not then considered a crime in itself, but authorities started watching Vallee more closely on November 1. Around 9 a.m. on November 2, just two hours before JFK was due to arrive, two Chicago police officers stopped Vallee after he made a turn without a signal near Wrigley Field. The white Ford Falcon he drove had New York license plates, as apparently he hadn't lived in Tennessee long after moving there from Long Island.

Police didn't find guns but discovered a hunting knife on the front seat and 750 rounds of ammo in the trunk. They took Vallee in for questioning, while other officers drove to his residence to seize the weapons. Vallee would make more anti-Kennedy remarks to police but deny that he planned to shoot him. [29]

At the same time, Kennedy received word in D.C. that corrupt South Vietnam President Ngo Dinh Diem had been assassinated after a CIA-supported coup overtook the presidential palace. JFK, who some claimed was about to announce that U.S. troops would be withdrawn from Vietnam, still made plans to fly to Chicago. Aides planned to build a special communications station under Soldier Field stands to keep Kennedy on top of the news from Vietnam. But by 10:15 a.m., with two potential snipers still at large on the streets of Chicago, Kennedy's security team had convinced him to cancel the trip. Officials cited the diplomatic crisis in Vietnam as the reason. But Agent Bolden said the decision was made after Agent Martineau called the White House and recommended that the trip be canceled. [30]

Vallee and the two assassination-team suspects were soon released. Vallee would be found guilty of a weapons charge but only given probation. No charges would be filed against the other suspects, and their names were not released. In 1968, Vallee would write to none other than J. Edgar Hoover from a Columbus, Ohio, address. He would request a copy of his speech when Hoover received the Sword of Loyola award from the Chicago university in 1964. Vallee, whose medical issues affected his writing, erratically misspelled several words, such as spelling sword "soward." He asked for permission to print a "few hundred coppies [sic] for my own use" and for any other statements on crime and "communist Subversion" in the U.S.

A few months before MLK and RFK would be assassinated, Hoover quickly and politely sent Vallee, a possible suspect in JFK's killing, a written response. The letter calls Vallee "sir" and notes that a copy of Hoover's speech was enclosed. But Hoover requested that Vallee "not reprint this for your own use." A typewritten note written by someone at the FBI attached to the bottom of the letter confirmed that Vallee was arrested on November 2, 1963, due to Secret Service concerns that he "might cause trouble during President Kennedy's visit to Chicago." So the FBI confirmed existence of a plot going on in Chicago to the extent that at least one suspect had been arrested three weeks before Kennedy died. [31]

Perhaps Vallee was writing Hoover to gain some protection if he got in legal trouble again. But why would Hoover respond positively to a potential suspect in JFK's killing around the same time that King and RFK became bigger targets? It was not clear when the FBI note on Vallee's arrest was attached, but Hoover, as head lawman, should have been aware of an arrest in such a major case.

In 1974, the FBI would report that it tried, and failed, to match Vallee's photo with some suspects detained by Dallas police in 1963, so he remained a person of interest for years. Two others who some thought had been detained in Dallas that day with Vallee included Watergate burglars Hunt and Sturgis.

Vallee would pass away in 1988 at age 54 in Chicago, never called by investigating committees. [32]

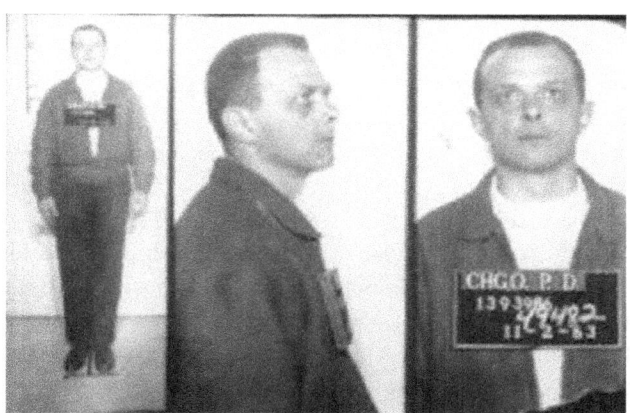

Thomas Arthur Vallee was arrested in Chicago on November 2, 1963, shortly before Kennedy was scheduled to visit. He was found with weapons and ammunition, and four others were suspected of a plot to shoot JFK that day. Below, FBI Director J. Edgar Hoover answers Vallee's letter in 1968. [U.S. National Archives]

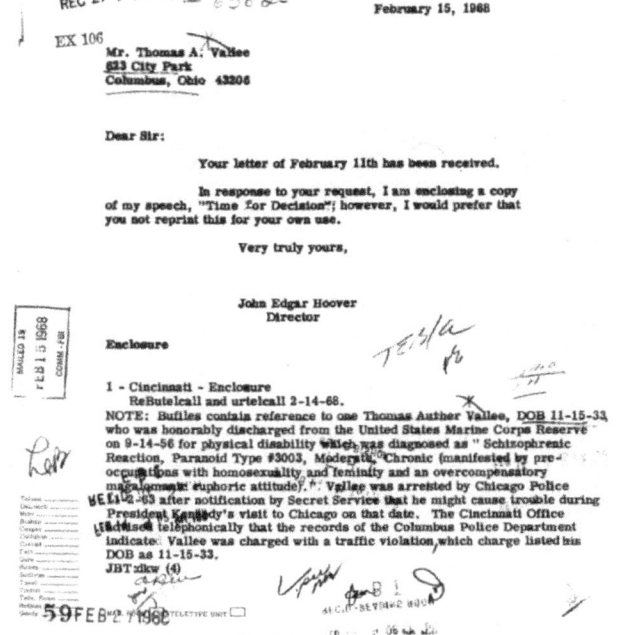

The House Assassinations Committee would scold the Warren Commission for not more thoroughly investigating Vallee, then not look into the matter itself and conclude it was unable to "determine specifically" why JFK's 1963 trip to Chicago was canceled. Bolden would tell a Chicago TV station that Kennedy's life being in "such severe danger" was the reason. "I think there would have been an attempt," Bolden said. "I think it would've been successful."

Less than a week before JFK's death, Bolden would be suddenly ordered to report to Washington, D.C., where the IRS offered him an undercover position for an investigation of Congressional aides. That would require his old identity – even his birth certificate – to be erased, which raised his suspicions about being "disappeared." Bolden declined the position, to the anger of superiors, and returned to Chicago fearful that JFK was about to be killed. [33]

Six days after Kennedy was assassinated, the Chicago City Council would vote to rename the Northwest Expressway – which Kennedy had been scheduled to travel upon earlier that month – John F. Kennedy Expressway. Unlike in Dallas, police and Secret Service in Chicago had detained enough suspects to convince JFK not to visit and thwart the plot. But just barely.

Foiling the Florida plot

As Kennedy prepared for a visit to Florida, the Secret Service issued a memo on November 8 about a slender, white male, around age 20, threatening to kill JFK when he visited that state. "Subject stated he will use a gun, and if he couldn't get closer he would find another way," the memo stated, according to a short Tampa Tribune article that would be published without a byline the day after Kennedy was killed. [34]

At least two other people made threats against JFK, and Tampa authorities located and arrested one, Police Chief J.P. Mullins said in the article. He would remain in custody at least until November 23.

On November 9, Miami police convinced Klan informant Somersett to secretly tape record a conversation with KKK leader Milteer at Somersett's apartment. On tape, Milteer claimed there was a plot to assassinate JFK still in the works. He refrained from saying he was involved himself.

In the recording, Milteer and Somersett discussed JFK's planned appearances on November 18 in Tampa and Miami. At one point, Somersett asked, "How in the hell do you figure would be the best way to get [Kennedy]?"

Milteer replied, "From an office building with a high-powered rifle."

"You think [Kennedy] knows he is a marked man?" queried Somersett.

"Sure he does."

"They are really going to try to kill him?"

"Oh, yeah. It is in the working," Milteer said. 35

Milteer identified Jack William Brown, who led the Dixie Klan in Chattanooga, Tenn., as someone who was "just as likely to get [JFK] as anybody." Brown was suspected of bombing several homes of African-Americans in the Chattanooga area in the 1960s. He had supposedly stalked Martin Luther King "for miles and miles, and couldn't get close enough to him," Milteer said. 36

The Klan leader speculated that Brown could have been involved in the bombing of a Birmingham, Ala., church on September 15 in which four young African-American girls were killed and as many as 22 other people injured. Three other Klansmen would be convicted for that horrendous crime and sentenced to life in prison.

Miami police provided a transcript of the recording to Secret Service agents on November 12. The Secret Service and FBI opened files on the matter and conducted a superficial investigation of Milteer. 37

The Tampa situation was complicated by other reported threats. About a month earlier, legal secretary Geraldine Heavner was having lunch in a Tampa drugstore when a Cuban man sat down beside her. At one point, the man told Heavner that Kennedy was "going to be shot in an open car," she reported.

Wayne Gainey, a psychiatric outpatient in Tampa, claimed that Klan members urged him to attempt to kill JFK. His parents assured police they would watch him, and an agent would monitor the house during Kennedy's visit. John William Warrington, another mental patient, claimed to want to kill JFK because of his association with King. He wrote threatening letters shortly before Kennedy's visit and was arrested. 42

Tampa landlord Diane Grybek said tenant Henry Edward Scott, or Enrico Aaron de Dusseldorf, told her he was aware of a plot to assassinate JFK in Tampa. Scott, a tax cab driver who went by "Rico," was an El Salvador native who had relatives in Cuba. But when FBI agents interviewed Scott, he denied saying he knew of a plot, only that it would have been easy to accomplish in Tampa had someone tried. Scott claimed to have arranged gun sales on behalf of anti-Castro Cubans that were shipped through New Orleans and Central America. FBI agents found a slip of paper on him with the name of Raymond Harrell of Dallas. Harrell told agents he only knew Scott from being driven in his cab in Laredo, Tx. 38

Kennedy was preoccupied with the weight of international and domestic issues to worry much about personal threats. After delivering a speech to the

AFL-CIO convention in New York City on November 15, Kennedy flew to Palm Beach to relax. He toured Cape Canaveral on November 16 and worked on speeches that he planned to give in Tampa and Miami on November 18.

In Tampa, Secret Service and FBI took few chances in preparing for Kennedy's arrival. Advance security teams started working on the scene by November 11. Scores of police and agents searched the buildings along the motorcade route for signs of trouble. Kennedy was briefed about the threat, meeting with high-ranking military officers at MacDill Air Force Base around noon on November 18. After a luncheon, he took a helicopter to Al Lopez Field, a minor league baseball stadium that would be razed in 1989 and eventually become the home of the Tampa Bay Buccaneers. He briefly addressed about 10,000 people, commenting that Cuban exiles had shouldered a "heavy burden" during the missile crisis and thanking workers who had lost jobs due to the embargo on Cuban tobacco done to isolate Castro. The business crowd at the Fort Homer Hesterly Armory didn't much like his defense of tax and economic policies, though the steelworkers at the International Inn were more open to his remarks. [39]

Then came the more nerve-wracking motorcade that wound through downtown streets lined with cheering crowds and potential gunmen in offices above. Several hundred police from Tampa and surrounding areas manned the streets. Officers with rifles stood watch along overpasses and other potential dangerous locations. There were even more "characters" for Secret Service and police to worry about during that motorcade through Tampa than Dallas, Agent Gerald Blaine told researcher Vince Palamara. "We did a lot of work on that," said Blaine, who rode in a lead car with Chief Mullins. [40]

Mafia boss Trafficante was reportedly involved in planning the Tampa plot, but he aborted the mission after observing the stepped-up security, according to authors Lamar Waldron and Thom Hartman. Gunmen had planned to fire upon Kennedy's motorcade as it made a slow turn in front of the Floridan Palace Hotel in the downtown area, they wrote. [41]

Despite the beefed-up security, most authorities would not learn much about Gilberto Policarpo Lopez until he made a suspicious trip from Texas into Mexico and then took a plane to Cuba shortly after the assassination. Then, the CIA would be intently interested in him, according to government documents.

Lopez was born in Cuba but emigrated to Florida when he was 20 in 1960 to avoid service in the Cuban military. A cousin and Lopez's wife told the FBI that Lopez was pro-Castro and had a brother in the Cuban army. He married an American woman in 1962, living in Key West, where he worked for Pepsi-Cola and a bakery. They moved to Tampa in June 1963, where Lopez started working for a local construction company about the same time Oswald and Vallee obtained new jobs in Dallas and Chicago, respectively. In August, Lopez's wife returned to Key West due to marital problems, the Church Committee reported, while Lopez remained in Tampa. [42]

On November 17, Lopez attended a meeting of the Fair Play for Cuba Committee in Tampa, according to the committee. Members showed photographic slides of Cuba on a projector. He was reportedly waiting on a phone call from Cuba to get the "go ahead order" to return there. [43]

Lopez would remain in Tampa until at least November 20 when he received a Mexican tourist card from the consulate there. After receiving $190 from the Tampa FPCC chapter, Lopez would travel from Texas into Mexico on November 23, crossing the border at Nuevo Laredo by auto and arriving in Mexico City by November 25, according to the House Assassinations Committee. He would check into the Roosevelt Hotel, then take a regular flight to Cuba on November 27, apparently with a courtesy visa, and be the only passenger with nine crew members. Mexican authorities would for some reason take a picture of Lopez, wearing dark sunglasses, at the airport. The route would be similar to one Oswald reportedly attempted to take right after Kennedy's assassination. Lopez would make it; Oswald, who failed to obtain a Cuban and Soviet visa two months before, would not. [44]

After the killing, the CIA and other government agencies would be highly interested in Lopez. In early December, the CIA would issue a request for "urgent traces" of Lopez, noting that a source indicated that the "timing and circumstances" surrounding his travel were "suspicious." His wife would receive a letter saying he had made it to Cuba and another later reporting that he was working as an elevator operator in Havana. [45]

The CIA would not tell the Warren Commission about Lopez's sudden trip. Moreover, the Warren Commission would only make one request to the CIA for information on matters related to Cuba, and that would be on Ruby's alleged visit there in 1959, the Church Committee reported. In 1975, the CIA would classify Lopez's file as one to not destroy because he was still "a subject of possible interest in the assassination investigation." The House committee would conclude that Lopez was not connected with the assassination but did not investigate whether he was being set up as a patsy if the Tampa plot had worked.

After dealing with the Tampa threat, Kennedy flew to Miami to speak at the Inter-American Press Association dinner that evening, where he pledged that the U.S. would "not permit establishment of another Cuba in the Western Hemisphere." Some attendees urged Kennedy to take a stronger stand against Castro. Authorities had received a bomb threat and a warning about a gunman with a high-powered rifle there. Some 250 police officers were added to the security force. There was no motorcade through Miami. [46]

Some said Santiago Garriga, who started a FPCC chapter in Miami, was another potential patsy. He had met Cuban officials in Mexico City. He had a CIA pseudonym, AMKNOB-1, and could have been a double agent. He was suspected of selling false Cuban passports. "Garriga is the potential fall guy who is the most clearly linked with intelligence," wrote Paul Bleau, a business professor at St. Lawrence College in Canada. "Like Oswald and Nagell, he could be portrayed as a double agent by those who packaged them." [47]

Gilberto Policarpo Lopez attended a Fair Play for Cuba Committee meeting in Tampa the day before JFK visited that city. On November 23, he would cross the Texas border with Mexico and later board a plane for Cuba in Mexico City, taking a route similar to one that Oswald reportedly tried to take after JFK's assassination. [U.S. National Archives]

'On a time frame'

With attempts foiled in Chicago and Florida, anti-Kennedy forces focused on Dallas, according to reports. Somersett and cab driver Scott were among those who stated that some of the same conspirators of the Florida and Chicago plots moved on to Dallas.

The plotters knew they had to kill Kennedy before 1964 since that was an election year and media coverage, as well as general attention of the president, would increase sharply then, Marrs said. "They are on a time frame," Marrs noted. "They've got to get it done before the first of 1964. And the Texas trip was his last scheduled trip [of 1963]." [48]

Efforts to warn the Secret Service and other authorities in Dallas would, for whatever reasons, not work as well as they did in Chicago and Florida. The FBI curiously issued a "flash warning" to instruct authorities not to detain Oswald in the weeks before the assassination, Stone said, a charge the FBI denied.

A day before the assassination, anti-Castro Cuban exile and suspected gun runner Homer Echevarria discussed an arms sale, saying that his group had "plenty of money" to mount an operation against Castro and would do so as soon as "we or they take care of Kennedy," according to a declassified Secret Service report. The group, 30th of November, was financed by a Chicago-based coalition of anti-Castro organizations with reported ties to organized crime. Oswald had reportedly been contacted by groups backed by the coalition. [49]

Instead of telling the Secret Service in Dallas, Agent Martineau launched a local investigation that found that Echevarria worked as a Chicago bus driver and at one time was employed with a construction drilling business in Dallas. The Dallas Secret Service would not be warned. Echevarria would tell an agent five days after Kennedy was killed that JFK was a "rich man's son who did not give a damn about people," while Johnson was a "common person who would get things done." The FBI would soon take over the case, and Secret Service agents would be told to forget Echevarria existed.

Somersett said he sent copies of the Milteer tape to RFK, the FBI, and Secret Service well before November 22. He would charge Robert Kennedy with not performing his duties as attorney general by sending more FBI agents to Dallas to guard his brother. But it was not clear if RFK heard that tape. [50]

Numerous potential conspirators allegedly were in Dallas shortly before the assassination. Allen Dulles spoke at a meeting of the Dallas Council on World Affairs just five weeks before the assassination. CIA alleged assassin William Harvey, who had been shipped to Rome after his Cuban adventures, was seen on a plane to Dallas in early November, according to Talbot. [51]

Oswald, or someone who looked like him, was part of a group that drove to Dallas from Miami, along with Watergate burglar Sturgis and alleged CIA agent agent Marita Lorenz, the latter woman said in a sworn deposition. Lorenz stated she was not told it was an operation to assassinate Kennedy. She suspected they were going to raid an arsenal, and she left Dallas before the assassination.

Sturgis met in Dallas with fellow Watergate burglar Hunt and received an envelope full of cash, Lorenz said. The CIA would deny that Lorenz had been employed by the agency. Lorenz would make the statements as part of a libel lawsuit that Hunt filed against former CIA officer Victor Marchetti. A jury would find in 1985 that Marchetti did not libel Hunt when he wrote that the former CIA officer who helped plan the Bay of Pigs invasion was involved in the JFK assassination. Hunt would claim that he was at home cooking a meal with his family in the D.C. area that day. Saint John Hunt, his son who was in fifth grade in 1963, was sent home from school like most kids but would say he never saw his dad that day. His mom, who would die in a strange plane crash during the Watergate aftermath, would tell Saint John that his dad was on a "business trip to Dallas." [52]

Two days before the assassination, Rose Cheramie, who was born Melba Marcades, was thrown from a vehicle along a roadway about 150 miles northwest of New Orleans. She told authorities she had worked for Ruby and she was traveling with two men from Florida who were driving to Dallas to "kill Kennedy" when they threw her from the car. Louisiana State Police Lt. Francis Fruge informed Dallas Police Capt. Will Fritz about what Cheramie said, but he "wasn't interested." One of the men was identified by a witness as Sergio Smith, the anti-Castro leader who was living in Houston at the time. [53]

Plot organizers likely "flooded [Dallas] with so many characters with nefarious reputations because they thought, 'Well, if all these people get scooped up, it'll muddy the waters so much that they'll never straighten it out'," said Chauncey Holt, who claimed to work for both the Mafia and CIA.

Holt would be in Dallas that fateful day with other mobsters and deliver forged Secret Service documents and guns with silencers, he said. He was told it would only be "an incident" that could be blamed on Castro, not an assassination. [54]

There were likely "several conspiracies in place and active at the time of the assassination," noted author Robert Groden. "So many, in fact, that those peripherally involved in other plots probably do not know that theirs was not the one that succeeded." [55]

Holt further explained the "need to know" planning concept:

> If you try to inquire, just one time, if you show some curiosity, just one time, as to what is going on, then you won't be around. You'll either be dead, or you'll be ostracized. Not only is it isolation from top to bottom, but laterally as well. It operates not only at the higher ups, naturally they are interested in protecting themselves more than anyone else. These guys down here are protecting themselves, too.
>
> It's just another example of plausible deniability. I say, "Hey, give me a lie detector test!" If they ask, "Did you, were you there for the purpose of

assassinating Kennedy or engaging in an attempted assassination of Kennedy?" and in all honesty, we could say, "No, I wasn't." [56]

UN ambassador Stevenson, who was spat upon and hit in the head with a wooden sign during his Dallas visit on October 24, pleaded with JFK not to go to Texas. He was not the only one. A few days after the ugly Stevenson incident, Dallas resident Nelle M. Doyle wrote a letter to White House press secretary Pierre Salinger with a similar plea.

"This 'hoodlum mob' in Dallas is frenzied and infuriated that their attack on Ambassador Adlai Stevenson on the 24th backfired on them," Doyle wrote. "I have heard that some of them have said they 'have just started.' These people are crazy, or crazed, and I'm sure that we must realize that their actions in the future are unpredictable."

But Kennedy was adamant about needing to campaign in Texas, noting how close the state had been in the 1960 election. He wanted to see if a presidential visit could help mend a rift between the state's conservative Democratic wing led by LBJ and liberal side led by Yarborough.

Despite Kennedy's aides canceling the November 2 Chicago visit likely due to security concerns, Salinger wrote back to Doyle on November 8, "I think it would be a most unhappy thing if there were a city in the United States that the president could not visit." [57]

Ruby's heightened role

Meanwhile, Ruby's alleged promise to Marcello to get more involved in the plot seemingly took hold. Ruby traveled to Chicago before the assassination, when Walt Sheridan, an aide to Robert Kennedy, found evidence that a Hoffa associate gave Ruby a "bundle of money." Ruby's main job was to get a police officer to quickly kill Oswald or another patsy, some said. [58]

Phone calls Ruby made to mobsters, such as Marcello lieutenant Nofio Pecora and Hoffa lieutenant Robert Baker, increased in the months before November. The FBI also monitored two separate meetings between Ruby and Roselli in the two months preceding the assassination.

In addition, more people saw Ruby, who also lived in Oak Cliff near Oswald's room, with the alleged lone assassin during October and November. Some also saw Ruby with Dallas Police officer J.D. Tippit, who would be shot on the same day as Kennedy, as some say he was trying to arrest Oswald and others say he was trying to kill him.

Attorney Carroll Jarnagin said he overheard a conversation between Ruby and Oswald in the Carousel Club in early October. They were "talking about opening a drug franchise and killing Gov. Connally," said Jarnagin, who went to the club on behalf of a client. The Mafia "really wants to get" Robert Kennedy, Jarnagin claimed Ruby said. Oswald later said the way to get RFK was "to get his brother, " Jarnagin stated. After Kennedy was killed, the crime syndicate would "take over and profit from the drug industry," Jarnagin charged. "Hoover did not want to confront the drug trade because he knew [the Mafia] would kill a lot of agents." [59]

Jarnagin reported what he overheard to Dallas police and the FBI. He said he was interviewed by two FBI agents, and one believed him while the other "thought I had been hallucinating." He would reportedly fail a polygraph exam in 1964, but he would continue to say his account was true. In a 1988 interview, Jarnagin would say there had been two attempts on his life, and he was reluctant to give his phone number. He would pass away of cancer in 1998.

Then in early November, Beverly Massegee said Ruby introduced her to Oswald as "a friend with the CIA." "How well they knew each other, I don't know, but I know they were definitely friends," Massegee said. "[Oswald] looked like he wasn't in a particularly good mood. He wasn't good looking. He didn't have any money so I didn't have anything to say to him. I was pretty much a snot back then."

Though the meeting was brief, Massegee said she had no doubt that the man she met was Oswald, which has been disputed. "The same man that [Ruby] killed in the basement of the police station is the same man he introduced me to," she said, adding that she saw Oswald, or someone impersonating him, in Ruby's club at least four times. She said she had heard speculation about Oswald imposters and did not know if the man could be a "double." [60]

One time, Oswald stood up as Wally Weston, a comedian at the Carousel, performed and loudly said he thought he was "a communist," Massegee said. Weston jumped off the stage and punched Oswald in the mouth, she said. Oswald fell back, and Ruby grabbed him, saying, "You ----, I told you not to come in this club again." Others, including a mentalist who went by the stage name Bill Demar, placed Oswald in the club. [61]

Someone who Massegee identified as Ferrie pulled a gun on another night, and Ruby grabbed the weapon. "As I look back, there [were] a lot of nerves crackling that last week," Massegee said. [62]

Several witnesses told Pulte and fellow researcher J.G. Lowrey that Ruby and Oswald met together at the home of oil industry lawyer Dick Loomis. He lived on East 10th Street, close to Oswald's room and about a block from where

Officer Tippit would be killed. Loomis' father was a prominent attorney whose office was in the same building as Lamar Hunt's. [63]

At one time, neighbors observed Ruby, Oswald, and Loomis sitting on the hood of a car in front of Loomis' house, drinking beer and throwing the cans into the street. Classical piano instructor Myrtle McKay, the aunt of Loomis who lived on the same block, became angry that the men were drinking in the open and littering the neighborhood with cans, according to her friends.

"The McKays never wanted to talk about any of it," Ruth Rydell, a friend of Myrtle, said. "They tried to forget about it." [64]

Mack Pate, who owned an auto shop close to Oswald and Ruby's residences in the early 1960s, said a representative of Kirby's Pig Stand in that neighborhood told him Ruby, Oswald, and Tippit ate there together "a number" of times. The Pig Stand was billed as the nation's first drive-in restaurant, dating to 1921. Pate said others told him they had seen Ruby and Oswald together. [65]

In addition, Ruby and a man who looked like Oswald visited a Dallas electronics store in early November. They discussed buying and selling electronic equipment, store employees said. [66]

Esther Ann Mash, a waitress at the Carousel Club who went with Ruby to gambling houses at times, put Ruby and Oswald together even earlier. In April 1963, she said she observed Ruby, Oswald, and "men who looked like what gangsters would look like in my mind" together in the club. The "gangster" types were older and balding, with one wearing a felt hat, she said. Oswald stood out as smaller than the others and drank beer, not mixed drinks like the huskier men, she said. The men were "talking around Oswald," she said. [67]

"Jack asked me not to listen in on their conversation, but after they were drinking for awhile, they didn't stop talking when I approached," Mash said. "I knew Jack was in the Mafia. I got the impression that they were definitely plotting to kill someone." [68]

Oswald double?

The plotters knew they had to create a profile to make Oswald appear to be someone who could assassinate the president. Besides having him apparently take a shot at Walker, fight anti-Castro activists, apparently stalk JFK, and try to get visas to Cuba and Russia, Oswald – or someone who looked like him – took several provocative actions in the Dallas area in the two months leading up to the killing.

Between September 25 and October 5 alone, witnesses said they saw men who looked like Oswald at the same time in several cities, including Dallas, Houston, New Orleans, Mexico City, and Alice, Tx. "What is obvious from the multiple, concurrent Oswald sightings is the unseen hand of covert operations," wrote authors James DiEugenio and Lisa Pease. "They were very, very similar – but different people." [69]

Witnesses reported the incidents at a couple gun shops, car dealership, rifle range, and the former Redbird Airport. One cited by Malcolm Price Jr. at the Sports Drome Rifle Range in Dallas occurred in late September when the Warren Commission claimed Oswald was in Mexico. The man at the rifle range was alone and drove a car – the real Oswald was not known to drive. He hit not only his target's bulls-eye but those of nearby targets. [70]

Marina said that FBI agents took her to a store in Fort Worth where Oswald supposedly bought a gun. Someone told her a woman who looked like Marina wearing a maternity outfit similar to one she had was with him. "But I had never been there," Marina said. [71]

Then, a man who looked like Oswald test drove a car from the downtown Lincoln Mercury dealership, driving at a high rate of speed. He told the salesman he would soon have enough money to buy a car and might go back to the Soviet Union. He gave his name as "Lee Oswald." Again, the real Oswald supposedly did not drive.

About the same time, someone who looked like Oswald applied for a job at the Southland Hotel parking garage. He asked how high the building was and if it had a good view of downtown.

"We have a rifle with a scope, ammunition, target practice, a tall building from which to shoot the president and enough money within a few weeks to buy a new car," DiEugenio and Pease wrote. "The framing of 'Harvey Oswald' as the assassin was nearly complete." [72]

Around 10 a.m. on November 20, waitress Mary Dowling said someone who looked like Oswald complained about his food at the Dobbs House Restaurant. Officer Tippit also happened to be there.

A half-hour later, refrigeration mechanic Ralph Yates claimed he picked up a hitchhiker who looked like Oswald in Oak Cliff. The man carried a package he said contained "curtain rods," a similar statement Oswald would make to a co-worker who drove him to work on November 22. The hitchhiker even brought up whether Yates thought the president could be killed from a building with a rifle and showed him a photo of a man holding a rifle. [73]

Yates, who passed a lie detector test, dropped the man off near the Texas School Book Depository building. At the time, the real Oswald was supposed to be at work in the depository. [74]

The Odio incident

Silvia Odio, a young Cuban immigrant whose parents were active in an anti-Castro group and had been arrested for running guns, reported a remarkable meeting in late September.

Three strange men knocked on the door of her residence in the Crestwood Apartments in East Dallas. Two looked Cuban and spoke Spanish, telling Odio their names were Leopoldo and Angelo or Angel. They introduced the other white man to her as "Leon Oswald," who was "very much interested in the Cuban cause." [75]

Oswald didn't say much but maintained a "kind of funny smile," Odio said. She and her sister, Annie, later recognized him as the man police arrested for JFK's killing. The trio asked Odio to write letters to help them raise funds for an anti-Castro group. Either the next day or two days later, Leopoldo called Odio and told her Oswald said Kennedy "should have been assassinated after the Bay of Pigs" and that it was "easy to do it." [76]

The problem was some believed Oswald already had left for Mexico when the Odio meeting occurred. So who was this "Leon Oswald?" Odio was interviewed by the FBI and Warren Commission, and the commission requested that the FBI probe further into the Odio incident.

Agents would report they located Loran Hall in California, who would say he may have visited Odio with associates named Lawrence Howard and William Seymour. Hall would say Seymour resembled Oswald, and the commission would conclude before the FBI completed its investigation that Oswald was not at Odio's apartment and had left for Mexico on September 25. The commission would not address why the Cubans introduced the man to her as "Leon Oswald" or explain Leopoldo and Hall's phone calls.

The FBI would determine that Seymour was in Florida at the time. Hall would change his account to claim that a Cuban man named Celio Castro accompanied him and Howard to Dallas. But Castro would say he never met Odio, who would say she did not meet Castro, Hall, Seymour, or Howard. [77]

In addition, Hall "owed" the FBI a favor when he made his claims for helping him get released from jail on a drug charge in 1963, journalist Golz reported. [78]

"The Odio incident remains one of the lingering enigmas in the original assassination investigation," House Assassinations Committee investigator Gaeton Fonzi would state. "It appears that Silvia Odio's testimony is essentially credible. There is a strong probability that one of the men was or appeared to be Lee Harvey Oswald. No conclusion about the significance of that visit could be reached." [79]

Hall, an anti-communist mercenary who was involved in the Bay of Pigs, would tell the House Assassinations Committee that "almost every meeting that I ever went to [before the assassination] I heard somebody plotting or talking about [how] somebody should blow Kennedy's head off." He would say he was asked by right-wing activists working with CIA operatives to join the JFK conspiracy but refused.

Convoluted alliance

In Dallas, there was a convoluted alliance between Cubans, right-wing businessmen, mobsters, and the CIA who operated out of "safe" houses and apartments, according to Pulte.

Anti-Castro activist Rolando Masferrer coordinated a hit team with close assistance from Cuban Democratic Revolutionary Front leader Varona, some Cuban sources told Pulte. Relatives and associates of the two anti-Castro leaders lived in the same apartment complex as Odio. [80]

"To place Lee Harvey Oswald at the same apartment complex where members of the Masferrer and Varona families were living is to come dangerously close to discovering a major piece of the assassination puzzle," Pulte said. [81]

Oswald was also among the visitors to a home on Harlandale Avenue in the South Dallas neighborhood of East Oak Cliff, where anti-Castro activists would meet in the months before the JFK killing, according to a Dallas County Sheriff's Department report. The home was rented by Jorge Salazar, who Pulte said "distinguished himself in the eyes of his co-conspirators by his daring" and was a CIA asset. [82]

Oswald knew some of those Cubans at the Dallas house from when he was in New Orleans, Garrison said. The Cubans were possibly with the Freedom for Cuba Party, according to Dallas policeman Buddy Walthers. Oswald and Ferrie were members of that party, which appeared to be "a corruption of the anti-Castro Free Cuba Committee," Garrison said. [83]

Veciana, the co-founder of anti-Castro Alpha 66, met at the Harlandale house at least once, in April 1963, according to an FBI report. Veciana would tell the House Assassinations Committee that he met with Oswald and the CIA's Phillips in in Dallas. [84]

Oswald warns of 'Big Event?'

A few weeks before the assassination, Dallas police received a letter from an "A.J. Hidell" warning of an assassination plot against Kennedy, Marrs said. Hidell was among the aliases Oswald used. [85]

Then just five days before the assassination, William Walter, a security clerk in the FBI's New Orleans office, received a teletype from headquarters warning that a "militant revolutionary group" may attempt to assassinate Kennedy during his trip to Dallas. The message urged bureaus to "immediately contact all logical racial and hate group informants" to determine if there was any basis for the threat. [86]

Walter said he told his supervisor, who instructed him to inform agents who knew such informants. But none of those agents recalled hearing anything about the teletype after Kennedy was killed. Some said the original tip might have come from Oswald. [87]

Marrs also believed Oswald could have been the one who informed the FBI about the Chicago plot and stayed with the Dallas plot because he thought he could stop it. "I think Oswald tried to warn his [FBI and CIA] superiors that there was going to be the assassination attempt in Dallas," Marrs said. "But see, he never realized that he was whistleblowing and tipping off people who [could have been] behind it." [88]

A few weeks before the killing, Oswald called his alleged New Orleans girlfriend Baker. He mentioned a plot against JFK. Baker begged Oswald to get out.

He refused. "If I stay here, maybe I can prevent this," he allegedly told her.

Baker said Oswald told her that those involved in the plot called the operation the "Big Event." Howard Hunt would use the same term to son Saint John Hunt in 2003, saying that Sturgis called the JFK hit the "Big Event" in a 1963 Miami meeting, according to reports. [89]

Almost two months earlier, Oswald had begged Soviet officials in Mexico City for a visa, telling them his life was in danger. If Oswald did tip off the police and FBI through letters and calls, his place in history should be reconsidered, Marrs said. "I just think there is a lot of substance to it," he said.

"It flies directly in the face of everything we've been told about Lee Harvey Oswald, that he was a loner, pro-communist, blah, blah, blah. Oswald very possibly was not the heel in the assassination; he was the hero. He tried to stop it. And yet, for his trouble, they tagged him as the patsy." [90]

The day before

On November 21, 1963, John Guare was eight years away from seeing his first play, *The House of Blue Leaves*, become an award-winning production. He was worlds away from his New York home, drafted out of Yale's drama school to serve basic training at Lackland Air Force Base in San Antonio, Texas. Little had prepared him for the depths of racism and hatred he was to witness.

That day, Air Force One touched down at Lackland in the midst of Kennedy's Texas visit. With his fellow troops, Guare stood at attention and saluted the president and First Lady as they stepped out of the plane. While JFK and others spoke, their sergeant commanded the troops to be at ease. The comments from fellow airmen shocked Guare.

"We got to stand in this hot sun for a n----- lover?"

"He ain't my president."

"I'd like to show that wife of his what a man is." [91]

Kennedy received little better cooperation from LBJ and Yarborough, whose feud with conservative leaders like Johnson was so ugly that Yarborough refused to ride in the same car as LBJ in the San Antonio motorcade. The press had a field day. "Yarborough Snubs LBJ," the headline in *The Dallas Morning News* would read the next day.

As Kennedy toured Lackland and Brooks Air Force bases, another link to a sinister plot would soon be discovered and traced to that same city. On November 25, a rifle that could have been similar to the one that Oswald owned would be found in a hotel room in Terre Haute, Ind. Authorities would trace that weapon to Harry L. Power, a salesman from San Antonio and ex-Marine who checked into that hotel and apparently left behind the rifle, according to an FBI report. Frank Riddle, retired police chief of Terre Haute, would report that San Antonio authorities told him Power was an expert marksman and a Young Communist League member. The rifle would be confiscated and the Warren Commission informed, but nothing about Power or that gun would appear in the commission's report. [92]

The Secret Service would refer to the rifle as a 7.65-millimeter German Mauser, while Riddle indicated in an Associated Press article that it was a 6.5-millimeter Italian Mannlicher-Carcano. Curiously, Dallas authorities would also call the rifle confiscated in the Texas School Book Depository on November 22 a Mauser, before changing that to a Mannlicher-Carcano after it was found that the rifle Oswald had purchased through the mail a few months earlier was a Mannlicher-Carcano.

In Houston, JFK and LBJ reportedly exchanged heated, angry words. At a speech, several witnesses said they saw Kennedy's hands vibrating hard, a symptom of Addison's disease. Several people picketed Kennedy's visit to Houston. James Milton Parrott, a 24-year-old Air Force veteran and student who was in the Texas Young Republicans, was among them. Future President George H.W. Bush would tell an FBI agent that he heard Parrott speak about killing JFK. Parrott would deny he threatened Kennedy's life. [93]

JFK and Jackie would not arrive at their Fort Worth hotel until after midnight.

In Dallas, Beverly Massegee said she accompanied Jack Ruby and Chicago salesman Lawrence Meyers to Campisi's Restaurant that evening. Meyers had a son who worked in military intelligence and ended up in Mexico City as a "journalist" around the time Oswald was there.

Campisi's gave Ruby's party a pizza "on the house," and Ruby didn't pay for the dinner, putting it on a tab, she said. Ruby and Meyers retreated into Campisi's back office to talk and make phone calls, Massegee said. Joseph Campisi said he wasn't there, that his brother, Sam, managed the establishment on November 21. He added that he had not met Meyers before.

After leaving Campisi's, Massegee said they attended a party at the Cabana Motor Hotel. Among those staying at the Cabana that evening was Eugene Brading, a Mafia-affiliated convict who would be arrested the following day.

At one point, Ruby talked about wanting to start a nicer club in a better part of Dallas, Massegee said. She said he also referred to JFK as an "SOB." Ruby himself told FBI agents that he went to the restaurant with business partner Ralph Paul, never mentioning Meyers or the Cabana. Paul would tell an FBI agent a day after Ruby shot Oswald that he had not been with Ruby that evening and Ruby had never mentioned Oswald before. [94]

In Irving, Oswald took the unusual step of staying with his family on a weeknight, rather than remaining in his Oak Cliff room that was closer to work. A few days before, Ruth had tried to call Oswald's rooming house, and someone told her there was no Lee Oswald there. When Oswald called Marina the next day, she had asked him about that, and he admitted using an alias to rent the room. He didn't say anyone put him up to it. She had angrily scolded him for such "foolishness." [95]

Lee told Marina he came to Irving early because "he was lonely because he hadn't come the preceding weekend, and he wanted to make his peace with me," she said. He gave police a different reason, saying that Ruth planned a party for her kids on the weekend and he "didn't want to be around at such a time." [96]

Oswald was attentive, putting away diapers, playing with his daughters and neighborhood children. "He tried to start a conversation with me several times, but I would not answer," Marina said. [97]

Oswald suggested they move in together in Dallas, but Marina refused that offer, saying it would be better to save money on the present arrangements at least through the holidays. "Once again," Marina preferred her friends to her husband, Lee noted. Some thought Marina wanted to teach him a lesson about lying to her. [98]

Oswald then watched TV until about 9 p.m. when he went to bed. Marina didn't join him until about 11:30 p.m. and sensed he was still awake, brooding, thinking. "But I didn't talk to him," she said. [99]

Around 3 a.m., Marina put a foot on his leg in a playful gesture. He shoved her foot and pulled his leg away. *He's in a mean mood*, she thought. She left him alone. [100]

Oswald rented a room at this home in the Oak Cliff neighborhood of Dallas during his final six weeks. The house was near where Jack Ruby lived. In later years, the home was turned into a museum, similar to Ruth Paine's home in Irving where Marina Oswald stayed. [Shay photo]

Chapter Eight

The Sun Goes Out in Dallas

The lesson of Dallas was clear. If a president can be shot down with impunity at high noon in the sunny streets of an American city, then any kind of deceit is possible.

– **DAVID TALBOT**, *Brothers*, 2007

The crowd started growing two hours before dawn on November 22, 1963, at a parking lot across from the historic Hotel Texas in downtown Fort Worth. By daybreak, there were more than 5,000 people, many of them working-class union men, seeking a glimpse of the president who would address them from a flatbed truck. [1]

John F. Kennedy rose at 7:30 a.m. and prepared for another busy day on his whirlwind campaign through Texas. While dressing, he gazed out a window of their eighth-floor suite, pleased at the size of the crowd. "Isn't that terrific?" he motioned to Jackie. [2]

About 25 miles away, Oswald was already on his way to work. He had gazed lovingly at his young daughters and told Marina he left some money on the bureau, instructing her to buy clothes for her and their girls. He donned a Marine ring, gray jacket, and wrist bracelet inscribed with the name, "Lee." He left Marina almost $200. She would later notice he also left his wedding ring in a china cup on her dresser. [3]

Buell Wesley Frazier, who usually gave his school book depository co-worker a ride when he stayed in Irving, asked what was in a long, wrapped package that Oswald placed on the back seat of his 1954 Chevrolet Bel Air. "Curtain rods," Oswald replied, adding that he planned to hang some curtains in his Dallas room. Later, Oswald would claim it was his lunch. Frazier noted that the package wasn't long enough to hold a rifle, even a disassembled one. [4]

On the 20-minute drive, "Lee was just his typical old self," said Frazier, then 19. "He didn't talk much." At times, Oswald would speak about his girls. [5]

In another corner of Dallas, American flags were positioned upside down at the Turtle Creek home of Gen. Walker in apparent protest of Kennedy's visit.

Walker, however, was at some meetings in New Orleans and preparing to fly to Shreveport.

'Heading into nut country'

In homes across the Dallas region, subscribers to The Dallas Morning News opened the paper to see a full-page advertisement that sarcastically read in bold letters, "Welcome Mr. Kennedy to Dallas." In harsh terms, it accused the president of ignoring the Constitution and giving aid to communists.

H.L. Hunt's son, Nelson, and at least one crony – oilman and future Dallas Cowboys owner H.R. "Bum" Bright – reportedly helped finance the message. Joseph Grinnan, an oilman, local John Birch Society leader, and Hunt associate, spearheaded the ad idea with Larrie Schmidt, who had served in the Army under Walker and was one of the organizers of protests against Stevenson in October.

The real authors did not have the guts to put their own names on the ad. The missive was signed by "The American Fact-Finding Committee," which claimed to be "an unaffiliated and non-partisan group of citizens who wish truth." As chairman, it listed Bernard Weissman, a carpet salesman who had just moved to Dallas three weeks before and declined to officially join the Birchers due to members' anti-Semitism and extremism. [6]

In reality, the "unaffiliated" committee was just a few people, including Grinnan and Schmidt, who convinced Army buddy Weissman to move to Dallas, Weissman would tell the Warren Commission. Schmidt and Weissman wanted to infiltrate right-wing organizations and eventually control those groups with a better organization. Schmidt was making inroads with the Birchers and was named executive secretary of the Dallas chapter of Young Americans for Freedom. That group formed in 1960 at the home of writer William Buckley Jr., who some believed had CIA links. Ronald Reagan was among its national advisory board members.

"In the final tale, the John Birch Society printed that ad," Weissman said. [7]

Weissman, who also served under Walker but sought to distance himself from "radical" types, said he allowed his name to be used on the ad because he thought it would help found a "completely democratic type of organization" that was conservative but not against Jewish people, African-Americans, and Catholics. "I felt any recognition that came would then be in my favor because these organizations would have to back me personally as representing them." [8]

Weissman did not contribute money to the ad, which he said cost $1,462, or $13,433 in 2022 dollars. Nelson Hunt told FBI agents that he gave Grinnan between $200 and $300 for the ad, which he thought "was a criticism of

President Kennedy in a dignified way." Grinnan used language similar to Hunt, saying it was a "dignified way of protesting the policies" of JFK. [9]

Bright declined to tell agents how much he had contributed but said he also covered another man's contribution that he believed was a loan. Bright admitted someone read the ad's contents to him over the phone. Dallas insurance executive Edgar R. Crissey told FBI agents that he contributed $15 to the ad himself and solicited another $135 from some other people. At one point, Crissey termed the ad "ill-timed." [10]

The ad had been approved by Ted Dealey, the combative, far-right News publisher. In 1961, Dealey verbally attacked Kennedy at a White House event that included other publishers, calling him weak in dealing with the Soviet Union and Cuba. Kennedy had reportedly responded that he had "responsibility for the lives of 180 million Americans, which you have not." Wars were "easier to talk about" than to fight, and JFK was "just as tough" as Dealey, he said.

Dealey's son, Joe, president of the *News* who would eventually become publisher, had just returned from a trip and hadn't approved the ad. That fell on his father, whom the younger Dealey wasted little time calling. Running the ad on the day Kennedy visited Dallas was like "inviting someone to dinner and then throwing tapioca in his face," Joe Dealey charged. Ted Dealey defended his decision, saying the ad was no different from what the News editorial page contained. "The timing is bad," his son replied. The News had also run what historian William Manchester called "two abrasive stories" on its front page and a third inside, all of which angered Kennedy. [11]

The ad targeting Kennedy contrasted to what the Tampa Tribune ran on the day of Kennedy's visit there four days earlier. A conservative group financed a large ad that day, but it refrained from criticizing Kennedy, issuing a plea for an end to communist control in Cuba.

After giving his final speech at a formal breakfast in the Grand Ballroom of Hotel Texas, JFK retreated to his suite to prepare to leave for Dallas. Aide Kenneth O'Donnell showed him the News advertisement. His face became grave as he said, "Can you imagine a paper doing a thing like that?" Turning to Jackie, Kennedy stated, "We're heading into nut country today."

Then he paced and stopped before his wife. "You know, last night would have been a hell of a night to assassinate a president.....Suppose a man had a pistol in a briefcase." Kennedy even pointed his finger at a wall and faked like he was shooting a gun. Was he trying to provide comic relief? Was he at least semi-serious? "Then he could have dropped the gun and the briefcase and melted away in the crowd." [12]

Parade route changed?

Following the short flight from the former Carswell Air Force Base to Love Field, the presidential motorcade began to proceed. The News had published a small map that only showed the parade passing along Main Street to Stemmons Freeway and the Trade Mart, where Kennedy was scheduled to speak at a 12:30 p.m. luncheon. The competing Dallas Times Herald had run a more detailed description of the route, saying it would proceed along Main Street, zigzag to Elm Street at Houston Street, and then onto Stemmons Freeway. [13]

The zigzag was approved at the last minute by Mayor Cabell to allow the motorcade to get closer to the Texas School Book Depository and take a slow hairpin turn, some said. "There is no way that the presidential motorcade could have taken the peculiar and improper route it took through Dealey Plaza – which even contradicted the route published in the [News] – without the approval of the mayor," wrote author James Fetzer. William Mike Niebuhr, a plugged-in antique store owner who ran for Dallas City Council in 1977 and 1981, confirmed that Cabell approved the altered parade route. [14]

John and Jackie Kennedy sat on blue leather seats in the rear of the limousine, a blue, four-door 1961 Lincoln Continental convertible. The roof panel had been removed, supposedly at Kennedy's request, to allow better views between them and the crowd. Gov. Connally and wife Nellie sat on folded seats directly behind Secret Service agents William Greer, the driver, and Roy Kellerman. Agents followed them in a black 1956 Cadillac, scanning the crowd and buildings for signs of trouble. The Johnsons and other dignitaries followed in vehicles behind them.

The tens of thousands of people who lined the streets to greet the Kennedys were mostly smiling and cheering. Some waved Confederate flags and held protest signs, while supporters of Walker and John Birch Society members distributed leaflets saying JFK was "wanted for treason." But most people merely sought a glimpse of the attractive presidential couple.

As the procession weaved its way into downtown Dallas, some observed a contrast between the reactions to Kennedy from people lining the streets and the mostly businessmen who stood above them inside office buildings. People inside the offices – who included H.L. Hunt – stared down at them "rather stonily" when the vehicles slowly passed through the shadowy downtown streets, said U.S. Sen. Ralph Yarborough.

"They just stood there looking at the president. And they weren't saying anything," recalled Yarborough, who rode in the motorcade two cars behind JFK. "I'd look up there on the second, third floor. I'd see people through glass windows up there, standing back.... They'd be looking down at the president, it looked to me like, with positive hate. I saw them, and I grew apprehensive." [15]

Witnesses report men behind grassy knoll

Some three hours before Kennedy reached Dealey Plaza, electrical equipment worker Julius Hardie said he saw three men on the triple underpass. The wide railroad bridge just west of the depository building spanned three downtown traffic arteries – Elm, Main, and Commerce streets.

Two men carried "long guns," Hardie said. He told FBI agents but did not hear back. [16]

About 90 minutes later, Julia Ann Mercer said she saw a man who looked like Ruby in a green pickup truck parked on Elm Street just west of the triple underpass. Another man who resembled Oswald got out of the vehicle, pulled out what appeared to be a rifle case wrapped in paper from the pickup bed, and walked up the grassy knoll, she said. Mercer testified before the Warren Commission but said her comments were changed by the FBI. [17]

Others saw men carrying rifles in the area. Phillip Hathaway said he said a big blond-haired man dressed in a suit toting what looked like a rifle in a case as he walked towards Main Street on Akard Street shortly before noon. [18]

Lee Bowers Jr., a railroad supervisor stationed in a tower in the parking lot near the grassy knoll area, reported three suspicious cars that entered the lot within 20 minutes of the shooting. The driver of one appeared to be speaking into a walkie-talkie or microphone, Bowers said. All of the cars appeared to be slowly cruising through the lot as if they were staking out the area or looking for someone, he said. He also reported seeing two men behind the grassy knoll fence gazing towards the motorcade. [19]

Police identified the owner of one car seen leaving the parking lot as Harold Isaacs, who later suspiciously said he had the car crushed. [20]

About the same time, uniformed soldier Gordon Arnold attempted to set up a movie camera near the railroad bridge about the triple underpass. A man wearing a light-colored suit stopped his efforts, showing him an ID and saying he was with the Secret Service. He told Arnold to leave. Arnold walked a few steps in front of the fence to film the motorcade.

Four other people besides Arnold said they met men who displayed Secret Service credentials in that area around that time, according to Dallas Morning News reporter Golz. Among those were two Dallas Police officers, Joe Marshall Smith and Sgt. D.V. Harkness. Smith said one apparently phony agent had "dirty" hands or fingernails. None of the 28 Secret Service agents assigned to guard the motorcade was known to be on foot at the scene before or after the shooting, Golz reported. [21]

Sherry Fiester, a certified crime scene analyst who worked as a forensics detective for a Louisiana sheriff's department, would later conclude that the fatal shot came from a shooter standing on one of the bridges over Elm Street directly in front of Kennedy, after she analyzed the blood splatter evidence. Former Allegheny County, Pa., coroner Cyril Wecht would maintain as late as 2022 that the fatal shot came from the grassy knoll area. [22]

Arnold Rowland said he was standing on Houston Street when he saw two men through the windows of the sixth floor of the school book depository building about 15 minutes before the motorcade arrived. One had a rifle with a telescopic sight in the window closest to the grassy knoll, Rowland told the Warren Commission.

Another man, who Rowland thought was African American, was in the easternmost window where authorities believed Oswald fired, he said. Rowland said he thought they were Secret Service agents scouting out the crowd and didn't immediately report it. He said he lost sight of the man with the rifle but saw the African-American man in the window just before the motorcade appeared. It's possible he was seeing the black man in a fifth-floor window, as other witnesses did. [23]

Carolyn Walter, who worked in a factory in the nearby Dal-Tex Building, said she also saw two men in a corner upper-floor window of the depository building as the motorcade arrived. One held a rifle through an open window, and she thought he was "some kind of guard." [24]

Howard Brennan, a steamfitter for a construction company in his mid-40s, was situated at the southwest corner of Houston and Elm, directly across from the TSBD. He jumped on the top ledge of a retainer wall there and had a good view of that building. From that vantage point, he said he observed a white man in his early 30s, who was slender, neat, 5-foot-10, from 160 to 170 pounds, wearing light-colored clothes in the sixth-floor window closest to Houston Street.

This is what Brennan saw a few minutes before Kennedy's motorcade arrived at that corner:

> I observed quite a few people in different windows. In particular, I saw this one man on the sixth floor which left the window to my knowledge a couple of times..... At one time he came to the window, and he sat sideways on the window sill. That was previous to President Kennedy getting there. And I could see practically his whole body, from his hips up...

There was no other person on that floor that ever came to the window that I noticed. There were people on the next floor down, which is the fifth floor, colored guys. In particular, I only remember two that I identified. [25]

Meanwhile, two men standing near each other on the north side of Elm Street near the grassy knoll reacted strangely as the motorcade reached them. One pumped an umbrella he carried, while the other waved his right arm and appeared to speak into a walkie-talkie. The first man was the only person in the area with an open umbrella – the rain stopped well before noon and the sun shined so brightly that Jackie Kennedy complained about the heat. Many researchers believed the men were providing signals to assassins that more shots were needed to fatally hit JFK.

While most around these men would soon dive to the ground for cover, this pair would merely sit down on the curb. As many around them would scream and run, they would calmly walk away in opposite directions.

Dallas police, sheriff deputies told not to help

By the time the motorcade reached Dealey Plaza on the western edge of downtown, some in the Kennedy contingent thought they were in the clear. Deputy Sheriff Roger Craig observed the motorcade pass in front of him as he stood with other officers outside the sheriff's office on Houston Street. Craig felt a little helpless, remembering how Sheriff Bill Decker had ordered him and other deputies not to provide security to JFK's motorcade.

They had drilled hard in preparation to help before that day. Dallas Police Chief Jesse Curry also told officers to end their duty at Houston and Main streets, a block before the motorcade reached the killing zone. Curry claimed he was following Secret Service orders. [26]

As the presidential vehicle slowly turned onto Elm Street, Nellie Connally said to Kennedy, "Mr. President, you can't say that Dallas doesn't love you."

JFK smiled and replied, "No, you certainly can't." [27]

But just a few seconds later, at 12:29 p.m. Central Standard Time, gunshots destroyed those friendly sentiments and more. Agent Greer did not accelerate until the fatal shot to Kennedy's head some five seconds after the first shot, according to one film. Greer later admitted he "should have swerved the car." Agent Kellerman also failed to protect Kennedy.

"Kellerman and Greer were in a position to take swift evasive action, and for five terrible seconds they were immobilized," wrote Manchester. [28]

As Kennedy and Connally were shot, Jackie Kennedy climbed onto the back of the presidential car and retrieved a piece of her husband's skull. Agent Clint Hill, who was on a running board of the vehicle behind the Kennedys, jumped onto the car and shielded Jackie Kennedy with his body. He was among the few Secret Service agents to react quickly. Reports surfaced that numerous agents had stayed out drinking until the wee morning hours at The Cellar in Fort Worth.

Two Dallas police motorcycle officers riding to the left rear of the presidential limousine were splattered with blood and brain matter. That and other aspects, including the piece of skull Jackie retrieved from the back of the car, led some researchers to conclude the fatal shot came from in front of the vehicle, not from the sixth floor of the depository building as claimed by the Warren Commission.

However, one officer, Bobby Hargis, said the brain matter could have been lifted in the air from a shot from behind, and he rode into it. Similarly, the skull piece could have lifted and settled behind Kennedy as the car moved forward. However, Greer had hit the brakes, and the vehicle was at a virtual stop. [29]

Once he realized what happened, Greer accelerated, driving quickly to Parkland Memorial Hospital about three-and-a-half miles away. Doctors and nurses greeted the blood-stained limousine, with Secret Service taking Gov. Connally out first to provide more room to remove Kennedy. Jackie remained hovered over her husband, her pink suit so blood stained that doctors thought at first that she had been shot. Agent Hill had covered them both. As he helped Jackie out of the car, she said, "They murdered my husband." Hill put his coat over Kennedy's face and shoulders as agents lifted him onto a stretcher.

Some tried to convince Jackie to immediately change clothes, but she refused, saying she wanted people to see what "they" had done. Secret Service agents immediately washed the presidential limousine, despite the vehicle being part of a crime scene. After a medical student noted that there was what looked like a small bullet hole in the windshield, a Secret Service agent drove the vehicle away. Kennedy would soon be pronounced dead, as doctors could do little to save him. The windshield of the 1961 Lincoln would be removed, with officials saying there was no bullet hole, only cracks. [30]

Rifle protruding from sixth-floor window

As Kennedy passed by Brennan, the latter man said he heard a "crack that I positively thought was a backfire....of a motorcycle." He also thought someone could be tossing firecrackers from the TSBD so he looked up:

This man that I saw previous was aiming for his last shot. Well, as it appeared to me, he was standing up and resting against the left window sill, with gun shouldered to his right shoulder, holding the gun with his left hand and taking positive aim, and fired his last shot. As I calculate a couple of seconds. He drew the gun back from the window as though he was drawing it back to his side and maybe paused for another second as though to assure his self that he hit his mark, and then he disappeared. [31]

The man used "some type of a high-powered rifle," but Brennan did not see a scope. He was pointing the gun towards Kennedy, Brennan said. [32]

Elizabeth Cabell was in the motorcade with her mayor husband three or four cars behind Kennedy. As the first shot rang out, her vehicle was in the process of turning onto Elm from Houston. "I was directly facing [the TSBD building]," Cabell said. "I heard the shot, and without having to turn my head, I jerked my head up..... I heard the direction from which the shot came, and I just jerked my head up.... I saw a projection out of one of those windows... on the top floor." [33]

Cabell turned to her husband and was about to say, "Earle, it is a shot." But before she could say anything, he exclaimed, "Oh, no!" Other shots rang out.

As a staff photographer for the Dallas Times Herald, Bob Jackson was in the motorcade five or six vehicles behind Kennedy. Several other photojournalists were in the car, including Tom Dillard with The Dallas Morning News, and Malcolm Couch, a part-time news camera operator with WFAA-TV.

As their vehicle crept along Houston Street some 15 feet from Main Street, they heard what sounded like an explosion. "My God, they've thrown a torpedo!" Dillard yelled.

When two more loud sounds followed, he realized it wasn't a torpedo. "It's heavy rifle fire," Dillard stated. [34]

Jackson looked all around, fixing his eyes on the TSBD directly in front of him. He noticed two black men in a window looking above them as if trying to discover the source of the gunshots, so his eyes continued gazing upward. He stopped, shocked. "There is the gun!" Jackson exclaimed.

"Where?" someone asked.

"It came from that window!" Jackson said, pointing towards the sixth-floor window. [35]

Couch glanced up to the window. He, too, observed about one foot of a rifle barrel. "I saw no one in the window – just a quick one-second glance at the barrel," he said. Dillard looked, too, and didn't see a gun barrel. [36]

Jackson observed about nine inches of the rifle's stock and a foot of the barrel. As he kept his eyes on the window the same one from which the Warren Commission claimed Oswald fired – someone drew the barrel "fairly slowly back into the building." But he never saw a person there, not even "a form." [37]

Soldier feels shots pass by him

While numerous witnesses in the motorcade trailing Kennedy thought the shots came from behind him, many stationed near the grassy knoll had a different viewpoint.

As he filmed the motorcade, Arnold, the soldier who was told to move by a fake Secret Service agent, felt a bullet pass mere inches over his left shoulder. He stood about three feet from the grassy knoll fence. "I had just gotten out of basic training," he said. "In my mind, live ammunition was being fired. It was being fired over my head." [38]

Arnold's military training took over, and he hit the ground. He felt a second shot, then someone kicked him and told him to get up. Two men dressed as police – he said one was crying and waving a shotgun – demanded his film. He gave them the film and did not report the incident to authorities since there "were a lot of people making claims about pictures and stuff, and they were dying sort of peculiarly." [39]

Sam Holland, a railroad company supervisor standing on top of the triple underpass, said there were two police officers and a plainclothes detective or FBI agent working in the area to keep people away from the bridge.

Arnold was not the only one whose film was confiscated. Sticking to a vow to witness the presidential motorcade, Beverly Oliver Massegee found a spot on the south side of Elm Street that was uncrowded. She said she filmed the assassination with a motion camera from the opposite direction of clothier Abraham Zapruder, who was stationed on a concrete block in the grassy knoll.

Massegee said she started filming well before the motorcade reached her and kept the camera steady, even when she heard shots fired. Photos in her 1994 book, *Nightmare in Dallas*, show Massegee continuing to stand and film as nearby witnesses ducked for cover. Despite being a clear witness, she said no one questioned her, and she kept a low profile as the famed "Babushka Lady." Critics of her account claimed the Babushka Lady appeared older and heavier in photos than Massegee was in 1963 and disputed other statements she made. [40]

Two men who claimed they were FBI agents would wait for her at work a couple days later and take her film, she said. They would not return the film as promised, she said. [41]

A few feet away from Massegee, Mary Moorman took photographs of the motorcade with her Polaroid camera. She handed the photos to her friend, Jean Hill, who placed them in a coat pocket. Moorman and Hill would be questioned at the Dallas sheriff's offices, and their photos would be taken by federal authorities.

Some photos would eventually be returned, but two would have the backgrounds destroyed. Moorman would sell at least one to media organizations for $600. Some believed that photo shows a gunman firing from behind the grassy knoll fence. [42]

An enlargement of another photo of the TSBD taken some 15 seconds after Kennedy was struck in the head shows the face of a man in the far west window on the sixth floor, said Groden, who believed that Connally was shot in the back from that point. [43]

Zapruder, whose film has been used to both support and debunk claims that Kennedy was hit from the front, also would have his famous short movie confiscated. But unlike most others, he would be paid for it. Life magazine, whose publisher had links to the CIA, would pay him more than $150,000, according to a contract. [44]

Smoke in grassy knoll area, man running away

Hill, standing on the south side of Elm Street, reported seeing a man "fire from behind the wooden fence" of the knoll and a "puff of smoke." She also observed a man walk hurriedly in front of the TSBD towards the parking lot behind the grassy knoll as most other people froze with shock. She would claim that man resembled Ruby. [45]

Hill was among those who ran up the knoll during those chaotic moments after the shooting. She was stopped in the parking lot by a man in a suit who showed her what he claimed was Secret Service credentials. She lost sight of the man running by the railroad tracks at the triple underpass bridge. [46]

The man running away could have been the same one who Dallas Police officer Tom Tilson Jr. chased. Tilson had a day off and was driving with a daughter in his car to pick up another daughter watching the downtown motorcade. He drove east on Commerce, and as he passed under Stemmons, Tilson said he spied a man running from the scene down a grassy slope just west of the triple underpass. He observed the man throw something in the back seat of a car parked on the grass just off Elm Street and hurry into the driver's seat.

As the black vehicle zoomed off, Tilson took chase. He obtained the license plate and saw that the stocky driver was wearing the kind of old dark suit that Ruby often wore. "If that wasn't Jack Ruby, it was someone who was his twin brother," Tilson said. [47]

Tilson phoned in the information to the police homicide unit but was not contacted. He threw away the piece of paper with the car's license plate number and only found out much later that the unit ignored his lead. "They didn't want to have to look for anyone else," Tilson noted. "They wanted to clear up the case." [48]

Holland, the railroad supervisor on the triple underpass bridge, also reported seeing a "puff of smoke" near the trees around the grassy knoll fence. He said there was "no doubt" the fatal shot came from behind that picket fence and counted four shots in all. Other railroad workers standing on the triple underpass also reported seeing smoke near the trees. One observed footprints in the mud by the fence. [49]

Others who stood on the north side of Elm Street in front of the grassy knoll, such as Bill Newman and journalist Cheryl McKinnon, reported that shots seemed to come from behind the knoll. "The only thing I am absolutely sure of today is that at least two of the shots fired that day in Dealey Plaza came from behind where I stood on the knoll, not from the book depository," McKinnon would write. [50]

JFK aides and World War II veterans Kenneth O'Donnell and Dave Powers, who were in the car directly behind the president, both told FBI agents they heard at least two shots come from the knoll. Then, Eddie Younger told Pulte that his grandfather, an Apache Indian who was standing on Elm Street when the shooting started, saw a "flash of light" from a manhole on Elm. [51]

To prove that someone could have escaped through an Elm Street drainage ditch, newspaper publisher and researcher Penn Jones Jr. would crawl through that drain all the way to the old Dallas jail. He would make it, but the journey "wore out the knees of my britches," Jones said. [52]

The deaf-mute Ed Hoffman indicated that he observed a man throw a rifle to another as he stood on the shoulder of Stemmons Freeway near Elm Street about 200 yards west of the lot behind the knoll. While Hoffman could not hear, his gift of sight was acute. A man in a dark suit carried a rifle near the fence and threw it to another man wearing coveralls and a railroad worker's hat, Hoffman said. That man disassembled the rifle and placed it in a bag, before walking north along the tracks. The other man ran back to the picket fence and slowed to walk calmly as if nothing had occurred, Hoffman said. [53]

Moments later, Hoffman saw Kennedy's car and noticed the blood, realizing something horrible had occurred. He attempted to tell authorities through gestures, but no one took him seriously. [54]

Michael Brownlow, who was with his grandmother as a boy standing on Houston Street near the fateful turn by the depository building on Elm Street, said he heard as many as four shots ring out. He observed people running up the grassy knoll and assumed someone fired on the motorcade from there.

Brownlow became an ardent student of the killing and regularly spoke at the grassy knoll to tourists and others about what occurred. "The shot that hit President Kennedy in the throat and the shot that hit him in the temple both came from behind the fence of the grassy knoll," Brownlow said during an interview. [55]

Deputy Craig and the Rambler

In the chaos that ensued immediately after the shooting, Sheriff Decker and Chief Curry forgot about federal officials' request not to help and ordered their officers to run to the area behind the grassy knoll. Deputy Craig followed another officer up the grassy knoll behind a picket fence, where he observed "complete confusion and hysteria." He detained a woman who tried to drive away, turning him over to another deputy sheriff, C.I. Lewis, who then lost her.

Reported Craig:

> Had I known then what I know now, I would have personally questioned the woman and impounded and searched her car. I had no way of knowing that an officer, with whom I had worked for four years, was capable of losing a 30-year-old woman and a 3,000-lb. automobile. To this day, Officer Lewis does not know who she was, where she came from or what happened to her. [56]

As he spoke with one person, he suddenly observed a 20-something white man running down the grassy knoll near the depository building. A light-colored Rambler station wagon driven by a darker-skinned man stopped on Elm Street and picked up the man before Craig could cross the street through the traffic and stop them. [57]

The man running "looked like he was in an awful hurry," Craig told the Warren Commission. At the police station later, Craig identified Oswald as the man running down the grassy knoll into the Rambler. [58]

Other witnesses saw a man run out of the depository building into a Rambler. "If it wasn't Oswald, it was his identical twin," Helen Forrest said. Before the Rambler picked up the man near the depository, it picked up a "heavy set" man that Richard Carr previously witnessed looking out of a sixth-floor window of the depository building. After hearing gunshots, Carr said he saw the man walk quickly down Houston Street and get in the Rambler on Record Street. [59]

Some researchers believed the Rambler could have been owned by Ruth Paine, but others said she owned a similar-looking Chevy station wagon. Later when Craig identified him, Oswald would seem to confirm leaving in a station wagon, which he said "belongs to Mrs. Paine. Don't try to drag her into this." A short while later, Oswald would say he left the TSBD by catching a bus. [60]

In 1989, researcher Richard Bartholomew would notice a 1959 Rambler station wagon parked on the campus of the University of Texas at Austin. The vehicle contained at least two Esquire magazines published in 1963 on its rear seat. In the early 1960s, it was owned by Cecil Bernard Smith, an LBJ friend who opened Austin's first Volkswagen dealership. Smith donated land to the university to endow five chairs in Mexican and Latin American studies and was known to be an extreme right-winger, Bartholomew said. [61]

Some bullets miss their marks

At least two and probably four shots fired at the motorcade missed their target, said Groden, who would become a photographic consultant for the House Assassinations Committee. Bystander James Tague, who stood on a median between Main and Commerce streets at the triple underpass, was struck by curb pieces or fragments from a stray bullet after he ducked behind the underpass' corner. A stray bullet pierced the south curb of the street there.

That was a different bullet than the three outlined in the Warren Report, proving a conspiracy, Groden would say in 2016 in Dealey Plaza. The FBI confirmed the bullet was different by removing the curb and testing it for metal traces, he said. Investigators did not find any traces of copper – the three bullets that the Warren Commission said were fired by Oswald were all copper-jacketed. [62]

Another stray bullet struck the south curb of Elm Street near a manhole cover and was retrieved by a man who claimed to be an FBI agent in the nearby grass, Groden said. The bullet, which was not placed among evidence, lined up with the Dallas County Records Building diagonally across Houston and Elm streets from the TSBD structure. A 30.06 shell would be found on the Records Building rooftop in 1975. [63]

A section of the north sidewalk along Elm Street was also likely hit, and some witnesses said they saw a bullet strike the middle of Elm Street. In addition, the presidential limousine was struck on the metal frame above the windshield, and the windshield itself suffered damage from a bullet fragment, Groden said. [64]

Groden pinpointed likely firing points as behind the grassy knoll stockade fence and wall, the west and east windows of the sixth floor of the former TSBD building, a second-floor closet window of the Dal-Tex Building across Houston Street from the TSBD, and the Dallas County Records Building rooftop. [65]

Where was Oswald during shooting?

At about 11:40 a.m., Oswald was seen by coworkers on the sixth floor of the depository building near the windows. He remained on the sixth floor while the others descended by elevator to the second floor for lunch. Oswald stayed there to shoot at Kennedy from his "sniper's nest," according to the Warren Commission.

But Bonnie Ray Williams, one of the depository workers laying new plywood on the sixth floor that day, returned to the sixth floor because he thought coworkers planned to watch the presidential motorcade from there. He said he didn't see anyone else on the floor, ate his lunch alone, and left around 12:20 p.m. He joined two coworkers, Harold Norman and James Jarman, on the fifth floor to watch the parade. [66]

When shooting broke out at 12:29 p.m., Williams thought at least one shot came from above them. Norman added he heard three shots, shell hulls hitting the floor and someone working a bolt on a rifle above them. Jarman said he heard shots but didn't hear shells fall or a rifle bolt. [67]

Oswald claimed that he went down to eat lunch in the first-floor breakroom, which had a pay phone where he apparently waited. Then he walked up to the second-floor lunchroom and purchased a Coke. Carolyn Arnold, secretary to the depository's vice president, said she saw Oswald alone in the second-floor lunchroom around 12:15 p.m. [68]

No one observed Oswald on the sixth floor shooting at JFK with a rifle, although Brennan said he saw a man with a rifle matching Oswald's general description. As JFK was shot, police Officer Marrion Baker said he felt someone was firing from either the TSBD or Dal-Tex Building when "all these pigeons began to fly up." He parked his motorcycle nearby and ran into the TSBD building. [69]

He saw some people in the lobby. "Where are the stairs or elevator?" Baker asked.

Roy Truly, superintendent of the building, spoke up. "Follow me, officer, and I will show you." They ran back to the elevator, and Truly cried out for the elevator, which wasn't coming down. "Let's take the stairs," Baker said, drawing his gun.

As they reached the second floor, Baker observed a man walking away from him in the lunchroom. "Come here!" Baker yelled.

The man walked back towards Baker, who asked Truly, "Do you know this man? Does he work here?"

"Yes, he works here," Truly answered. The man did not seem out of breath. Baker and Truly continued running up the stairs. The man, who Baker later identified as Oswald, walked away. [70]

Some employees who were taking the back stairs, including Dorothy Garner, said they did not encounter Oswald racing down the stairs in the two minutes after the shooting. Truly said he could not have taken the elevator down, that it was occupied. Photographs taken just before and after the shooting led the House Assassinations Committee to conclude that there was an "apparent rearranging of boxes" around the sixth-floor "sniper's nest" within two minutes of the last shot. [71]

Getaway plan: Wait for a bus

As Baker continued up the steps, Oswald left the building by 12:33 p.m. The president's alleged lone assassin did not have a getaway plan beyond waiting for a bus, according to the Warren Commission. At the same time, Craig and others reported they saw a man who looked like Oswald climb into a car on Elm Street.

The Warren Commission traced Oswald's escape route to leaving the bus at 12:44 p.m. when it became bogged down in traffic and hopping on another to the bus station. Then Oswald caught a cab to his Oak Cliff boarding house room, the commission's report said. Around 1 p.m., Oswald retrieved his pistol and left to apparently rendezvous with some co-conspirators at the nearby Texas Theatre.

The historic theater "was the second point of call," said Massegee. "If anything goes wrong, we meet here. He got met all right." [72]

Oswald thought there was just going to be an attempt on JFK and then blame it on Castro so more officials would be willing to go after the Cuban leader, Massegee said. "I don't think that he ever really realized that it was really going to happen. I think he was in shock like everybody else. That's why he ran like he did and went to the Texas Theatre." [73]

Tippit: Conspirator or sacrifice?

While walking or running to the movie house, Oswald apparently was stopped by Officer Tippit. Some believed the Dallas patrolman had been instructed by Ruby to provoke Oswald and shoot him so he wouldn't talk about what he knew. But Tippit thought Oswald would be unarmed, as he was not thought to have a gun in his boarding house room. [74]

Others thought Tippit was a sacrifice, providing conspirators a reason for tying Oswald to JFK's assassination. "Tippit had to die because they needed another killing in order to get more evidence against the patsy [Oswald]," Staffan H. Westerberg and Pete Engwall wrote. [75]

At any rate, the bottom line was that Tippit, who some claimed to have seen eating at a restaurant with Ruby and Oswald and in the Carousel Club with Ruby before that day, ended up dead close to the rooming house where Oswald lived. Police had a reason to arrest Oswald and tie him to Kennedy's death. And the Warren Commission had its lone killer.

Fifteen minutes after Kennedy was shot, witnesses said they observed Tippit in his patrol car at a gas station on Zang Boulevard near Oswald's rooming house, watching cars drive over the Houston Street viaduct. A few minutes later, he zoomed down a street, telling a dispatcher he was at a different location.

Around 1 p.m., Tippit ran into the Top Ten Record Shop on West Jefferson Boulevard, an institution that attracted everyone from well-known musicians to Oswald and Ruby. He tried to call someone on the pay phone but didn't get an answer. He ran back to his car, drove off, and stopped a vehicle driven by James Andrews. He checked the front and back seats, then drove off.

Between 12:45 p.m. and 1:08 p.m., there were three calls by police dispatchers to him "for no apparent reason, at a time of unparalleled traffic on the police radio," noted researcher Lowrey. [76]

Between 1:06 p.m. and 1:15 p.m., Tippit was shot near the corner of East Tenth Street and Patton Avenue, according to witnesses. Several witnesses said Oswald fired the shots and then fled. Others could not identify Oswald as the shooter, saying the man they saw was short and stocky. At least one witness said there was a second man involved in the shooting.

Tippit had four bullets in him, three manufactured by Winchester and one by Remington-Peters. That indicated that two different shooters likely fired at Tippit, Garrison said. But others said that was not really unusual, and the shells found at the scene matched Oswald's revolver. However, the FBI could not conclude that any of the bullets in Tippit were fired from Oswald's gun.

Meanwhile, Oswald was observed by his landlord, Earlene Roberts, leaving the house a few minutes after 1 p.m. That was about a mile from where Tippit was shot. Even if Tippit was shot as late as 1:15 p.m., Oswald did not have time to get to the scene unless someone drove him there, many researchers contend.

"The Warren Commission simply ignored these time anomalies," Garrison wrote. [77]

Were two men arrested in Texas Theatre?

As police swarmed on the scene, shoe store manager Johnny Brewer noticed a man duck into his outside doorway when he heard sirens about 1:35 p.m. The man continued to the Texas Theatre, where Brewer lost sight of him. He hurried over there and asked a ticket seller if she had recently sold a ticket.

When hearing that she hadn't, Brewer walked into the theater, where concession stand operator W.H. Burroughs said he had heard doors open but not observed anyone enter the lobby. They checked the balcony but did not find the man Brewer saw.

By that time, police entered the theater and turned on the lights to search the premises. Officer M.N. McDonald said a man near the front told him that a suspicious man sat towards the rear of the theater. McDonald soon made it to Oswald's row with other officers converging there. Oswald suddenly stood up. McDonald claimed Oswald said either, "This is it," or "Well, it's all over now." But other officers there did not hear Oswald say anything. [78]

Oswald then punched the officer in the face, according to McDonald. The two men wrestled for Oswald's weapon. McDonald heard the gun's hammer click but not fire, perhaps because he had blocked the weapon's hammer with his hand.

McDonald subdued Oswald, and other officers converged on the suspect. "I don't know why you are treating me like this," Oswald said as he was escorted out the front. "The only thing I have done is carry a pistol into a movie....I want a lawyer. I am not resisting arrest." [79]

As Brewer watched, he said he heard one officer say, "Kill the president, will you?" Some wondered how the officer already knew Oswald was an assassination suspect. A theater patron said he observed a man in the back watching the scene who looked like Ruby. [80]

Another patron, Jack Davis, said that shortly after the movie began at 1 p.m., a man sat down in the seat next to him. Davis thought that was odd because the theater was almost empty with maybe 20 people in it. The man didn't say anything but quickly rose and sat next to another patron as if he was trying to rendezvous with a contact he hadn't met before.

The strange man, who Davis later identified as Oswald, then went to the lobby and returned to the theater a few minutes later. Burroughs also said a man who looked like Oswald entered the theater shortly after 1 p.m. Could that have been the man Deputy Craig and others saw get into the Rambler? [81]

As Oswald was escorted out the front of the Texas Theatre, Burroughs and hobby store owner Bernard Haire said they saw Dallas police arrest another man who resembled Oswald a few minutes later. But in the second instance, police took the man out back, put him in a patrol car, and apparently let him go after driving a short distance. There was no record of two arrests at the theater that day. [82]

Just 45 minutes after Oswald was arrested and taken downtown, mechanic T.F. White said he saw a man who looked like Oswald sitting in a vehicle in the parking lot of an Oak Cliff El Chico restaurant. He wrote down the car's license plate number, which turned out to be owned by Carl Mather, a close friend of Tippit who worked for Collins Radio, a communications company that contracted with the CIA. [83]

Oswald's possessions include government ID

On the drive downtown to police headquarters, Oswald continued to lobby for his "rights." "What is this all about?" he asked. Told that a police officer was shot, he expressed surprise. "A police officer has been killed?" [84]

At the station, authorities found several identification cards on the only suspect in which they were really interested. One card read, "Lee Harvey Oswald," while another contained the alias, "Alek Hidell." Oswald also possessed a U.S. Department of Defense ID badge similar to the one U-2 pilot Powers carried. [85]

In addition, police found on Oswald a piece of paper with a list of schools he had attended and military bases where he was stationed, Marrs said. "It was very deliberately planned," he said. [86]

Less than two hours after the assassination, well before Oswald was charged, Hoover told Robert Kennedy that he "thought we had the man who killed the president." He described Oswald as pro-communist and a "mean-minded individual in the category of a nut." [87]

Despite Oswald never confessing and not knowing all the facts, Mayor Cabell immediately called the assassination "the irrational act of a single man." Most other political leaders, as well as the major media, soon followed suit. [88]

"They had the cover story all laid out and smeared [Oswald]," Marrs said. "Hoover had the whole rundown on him right away." [89]

Hal Hendrix of the Miami News, who Carl Bernstein wrote was "extremely helpful" in feeding the CIA information about anti-Castro Cubans, had more detailed background information on Oswald than most right after he was arrested. Some claimed Hendrix could have obtained the information from a TV broadcast of Oswald's New Orleans radio station debate and not the CIA. But the Senate Subcommittee on Multinational Corporations would report in 1973 that Hendrix was used by the CIA during the late 1950s and early 1960s to write "black propaganda" against Castro. Hendrix would deny being a CIA informant in testimony before the subcommittee but later plead guilty to lying under oath. He would be only fined $100 in return for cooperating in an investigation of ITT and CIA officials. [90]

One who didn't immediately leap to conclusions was Dallas District Attorney Henry Wade, who told a News reporter that "preliminary reports indicated more than one person was involved in the shooting" of Kennedy. But after that story was published, LBJ aide Cliff Carter reportedly would tell Wade that bringing up a possible conspiracy would "hurt foreign relations." Wade fell in line. [91]

During initial interrogation with Dallas Capt. Fritz and others, Oswald answered queries on his background. He said he worked in a factory in Russia and "liked everything over there except the weather." [92]

A composed 'young punk'

Oswald seemed calm, composed, almost reveling in the attention. Besides Fritz, questioners included FBI agents Hosty and James W. Bookhout, Secret Service agents Forrest Sorrels and Thomas J. Kelley, and other Dallas police officers. More than 25 different persons, including a postal inspector and U.S.

marshal, participated in or were present at some point during interrogations, according to the Warren Report.

Upon recognizing Hosty, Oswald said he didn't "appreciate" Hosty going to his home and questioning his wife when he was not there. The FBI agent "practically told [Marina] she would have to go back to Russia," he accused. Hosty would write that Oswald seemed like "a young punk. He was sitting there with a wise-ass smirk, the kind you wanted to slap off his face.... His hands were cuffed behind his back, but even so, he was trying to sit nonchalantly, cocky and self-assured, in the straight-backed wooden chair."

At times, some interrogators changed their minds about how they viewed Oswald, apparently trying to get their conclusions to match. For example, Bookhout said Oswald gave "an emphatic denial" of being involved with JFK's assassination and Tippit's killing. But when told by commission assistant counsel Samuel Stern that Hosty described Oswald as "frantically" denying involvement, Bookhout would agree that "probably" described it. Hosty would say "emphatically" was a better way to describe Oswald's denial. [94]

Oswald said the only rifle he saw at work was displayed by supervisor Roy Truly two days before, and he claimed to not have owned a rifle. He stated he left work because he "figured there would be no work performed that afternoon.... I changed my clothing and went to a movie." He carried a pistol "because I felt like it..... You know how boys do when they have a gun, they carry it." [95]

Oswald was taken to the police basement for the first lineup around 4 p.m. He protested that he stood out too much since he was wearing different clothes than others in the lineup and they were significantly younger. Interrogators asked some strange questions, such as if Oswald believed in "a deity." He replied, "I don't care to discuss that." When asked if he had read the Bible, Oswald said it was "fair reading, but not very interesting. As a matter of fact, I am a student of philosophy, and I don't consider the Bible as even a reasonable or intelligent philosophy." [96]

At another lineup that evening, which Oswald again thought was unfair, he yelled to reporters, "I didn't shoot anyone!" He later yelled, "I am only a patsy!" He was formally arraigned for the murder of Tippit around 7 p.m. [97]

A couple hours later, police administered a paraffin test to see if it proved Oswald fired a rifle or pistol. The test showed Oswald positive for nitrates on both hands, but not his right cheek, which Garrison said proved he didn't fire a rifle when Kennedy was shot. "It was impossible for him to have fired a rifle," Garrison said. Someone can get nitrates on their hands from smoking a cigarette or moving crates in a room that was recently painted, he said. [98]

Dallas police were filmed carrying a rifle out of the depository building. Seymour Weitzman, a deputy constable and weapons expert, said in a sworn affidavit that a 7.65-millimeter German Mauser had been found. District Attorney Wade called the rifle a Mauser before later changing his statement to say it was really an Italian Mannlicher-Carcano. [99]

Officers also found three rifle cartridges on the sixth floor "laying in such a way that they looked as though they had been carefully and deliberately placed there," wrote Craig, who also said a Mauser was discovered. Weitzman would change his recollection to agree it was a Carcano, while Craig would not. [100]

At a late-night press conference, Wade claimed the paraffin test showed Oswald recently fired a gun. When a reporter asked if it proved he fired a rifle, Wade just answered, "A gun." [101]

In a weird twist, Oswald appeared at the conference and answered some questions. When a newsman asked if he killed Kennedy, Oswald replied, "No. I have not been charged with that. In fact, nobody has said that to me, yet. I did not shoot anyone." [102]

Around 1:30 a.m. November 23, Oswald was charged with murdering JFK. He asked again for legal representation. No one stepped up to help him.

'Tramps' arrested

Oswald was not the only one arrested or detained in connection with Kennedy's slaying that day. Newspaper reports stated that as many as a dozen people were taken into custody around Dealey Plaza right after the shooting. One was Brading at the Dal-Tex Building, who told police he was in Dallas on oil business and went into the building to make a phone call.

In addition, two people were arrested in Fort Worth and one in New Orleans. Most, including Brading, were released once Oswald was arrested. [103]

Some famous photographs showed three "tramps" walking without being handcuffed with uniformed officers in front and behind them. Their clothing appeared shabby but clean, and their shoes did not look worn. The officers were carrying rifles but appeared rather casual like they were escorting some petty thieves, not potential assassins.

While some speculated the "tramps" were CIA operative Chauncey Holt, Watergate burglars Hunt and Sturgis, or Chicago arrestee Vallee, Dallas police would release a statement in 1989 claiming they were mere vagrants. Police would identify them as Gus W. Abrams, 53; Harold Doyle, 32, of Red Jacket, W.V.; and John Forrester Gedney, 38. "They are passing through town," according to a police report. "They have no means of support." The men would be released on November 26, 1963. [104]

Doyle and Gedley confirmed they were two of the "tramps," while the sister of Abrams identified him as the third, some researchers said. Others said those homeless men were not the same "tramps" arrested and photographed. [105]

Holt later claimed to be part of the plot, stationed in that parking lot behind the knoll. He didn't expect to hear actual shooting, as he thought it would be a backfire or an incident they could blame on Castro supporters. So when shooting started, Holt was as shocked as anyone. *We had gotten ourselves into something that is way over our heads,* he thought. Along with others, Holt hid in a railroad car until police found them. The FBI let him and others go, he said. [106]

Other nefarious characters would claim to have been in that area. Mob and CIA operative James Files would admit that he fired a rifle from behind the knoll. His partner that day was mobster Charles Nicoletti, Files would say. Television producer Robert Vernon would claim that teeth marks on a cartridge shell jacket found on the grassy knoll matched Files, who was known to chew on spent shells. [107]

Some, like Brownlow and author Jerome Kroth, believed Files' account to be credible. But the FBI would discount Files' alleged involvement. Files would be imprisoned for the 1991 attempted murders of two Illinois police officers and paroled in 2016.

Others would accuse Charles Harrelson, the estranged father of actor Woody Harrelson, of firing at least one shot at Kennedy. Harrelson would be convicted of killing Judge John Wood Jr. and die of a heart attack in prison in 2007.

At 2:19 p.m. on November 22, some Dallas police officers were dispatched to a triplex at 5818 Belmont Avenue in East Dallas to check on a report of a man seen getting out of a light green car with a rifle. Another car parked there belonged to George T. Hunsaker, who was related to Ruby associate Clifford Hunsaker. [108]

The triplex was believed to be managed by Stanley Skotnicki, who bought the residence in 1967 and had a business associate, John Grizzaffi, who had ties to reputed mafioso Civello, Pulte said. Skotnicki's first wife, Katja, was a close friend of Marina Oswald. [109]

Donald Wayne House was arrested in Fort Worth for suspicion of being involved. He said he tried to visit Army buddy Randall Hunsaker and went to the motorcade when he couldn't find Hunsaker. He would soon be released.

Some of the incidents could have been phony ones to divert authorities' attention away from the real killers, a common tactic in a CIA operation. Anti-Castro operative Masferrer led "at least two dozen diversions" that were executed on November 22 in Dallas, Pulte said. Those incidents included calls to police about bogus events supposedly related to the killing and a fight reported near the murder of Tippit. [110]

CIA cargo plane picks up men in Dallas

Some odd aviation activity occurred in the Dallas area shortly after JFK died. At about 1 p.m. at the private Redbird Airport about six miles south of the Texas Theatre, some nearby residents complained of a small plane revving its engines while parked at the end of the airstrip on some grass for about an hour before it finally took off.

Air traffic controller Louis Gaudin reported seeing three men in business suits board a small aircraft about 2 p.m. and head north. The plane returned with only two occupants and was met by a Dallas police officer. [111]

Then around 3:30 p.m., a CIA cargo plane with no military markings – just a brown egg-shaped earth – stopped in a sandy area near the Trinity River in southeast Dallas, according to U.S. Air Force Sgt. Robert G. Vinson. As a passenger on the plane, Vinson observed two men run on board. [112]

Vinson happened to board that plane from Andrews Air Force Base near Washington, D.C., since it was the only aircraft from that base heading in the direction of his Colorado home that day. Vinson said the bigger man looked Latino, while the smaller one resembled Oswald. The plane took off and landed at Roswell Air Force Base in New Mexico. The pilots and two men ran off the plane without saying a word to Vinson, who could not leave to catch a bus home for a few more hours because the base had suddenly been placed on alert after the CIA plane landed. [113]

Marcello pilot Ferrie also made a sudden trip, but not by plane, according to Garrison. With two young companions, Ferrie drove almost 400 miles through a storm to Houston on November 22. At Houston's Winterland Ice Skating Rink, Ferrie loudly introduced himself to the manager, but he never skated. As his two companions hit the ice, Ferrie stood by a pay phone and answered some calls. [114]

Ferrie was "supposed to have been the getaway pilot in the assassination," said New Orleans private eye Jack Martin, who worked at times for Banister. However, Ferrie told FBI agents that he didn't leave New Orleans until 9 p.m. November 22 and checked into a Texas motel early on November 23. Then the group went to Winterland on November 23. [115]

Garrison suspected Ferrie was lying. On November 22, he had sent some investigators to Ferrie's apartment, who found rifles, ammunition, and a large map of Cuba on the wall. Two young men there told investigators that Ferrie had left for Texas about an hour after the assassination. Garrison's investigators would not find him until November 25, when they took him in for questioning. [116]

Ferrie would maintain that the trip was simply to go ice skating, but Garrison would discover Ferrie traveled to a Galveston motel where Ruby called the night before he shot Oswald. Garrison had Ferrie arrested, but the FBI would conclude he had nothing to do with the assassination and soon let him go. About the same time, Judyth Baker said she received a call from Ferrie, who told her that Ruby was forced to kill Oswald or be murdered himself. Ferrie also said that he would not be contacting her again and suggested that she move away and not say anything about what she had done with the anti-Castro bioweapon project. She would remain silent for some 35 years before speaking and writing about her time with Oswald. [117]

Ruth, Marina differ on reactions

After hearing of the assassination on television, Ruth said she cried immediately but Marina did not – she went out and hung up clothes. But in another instance of conflicting testimony involving Ruth, Marina testified that she did immediately go to her room and cry. [118]

Then there was the phone call from Michael. About 30 minutes after Kennedy was shot and well before Oswald was arrested, Michael called Ruth and said he "felt sure Lee Harvey Oswald had killed the president but was not responsible." He added, "We both know who is responsible," according to an FBI report. When questioned about the phone call by the Warren Commission, Michael would deny making such a statement. [119]

Police soon arrived to search the Paine's home, finding that Oswald's rifle was gone. They also discovered some peculiar items, including a Minox spy camera. Ruth and Michael Paine said they were unaware that Oswald stored a rifle in their garage. Michael said he moved the package, which he thought was camping equipment, several times but never opened it. [120]

Authorities also found several metal file cabinets that appeared to contain "names and activities of Cuban sympathizers," reported Dallas Deputy Sheriff Buddy Walther. The cabinets were not entered into evidence as belonging to Oswald, and they would disappear. Some would wonder if they were owned by the Paines to plant them as belonging to Oswald. [121]

Marguerite said she heard that her son was a suspect via a radio broadcast as she drove to work. She returned home, called Robert Oswald, and hurried to Dallas police headquarters where Oswald was being held.

After meeting Marina and the Paines there, they were not allowed to see Oswald. They returned to the Paines' home, where some reporters for Life magazine showed up. Marguerite wanted the magazine to pay her to talk since she was "penniless," but the Life reporter offered only expenses. They ended up moving to the Adolphus Hotel in downtown Dallas.

Gleeful for death

After the assassination, most of Kennedy's mob-connected enemies didn't try to contain their glee. Hoffa reportedly heard the news at a restaurant in Miami and immediately climbed on the table and shouted in joy. He yelled at a secretary who cried and would be angry that some Teamsters employees sent condolences to Jackie Kennedy. [122]

Hoffa reportedly said, "I told you they could do it. I'll never forget what Carlos and Santo did for me." [123]

Trafficante toasted Kennedy's death at the International Inn in Tampa, where JFK had delivered a speech to a crowd that included many United Steelworkers members four days earlier. Marcello also celebrated.

FBI wiretaps caught some disappointment that RFK wasn't assassinated. "They killed the good one," lamented northeastern Pennsylvania mob boss Russell Bufalino. [124]

Another said LBJ would be "good for America." Still another Mafia don predicted the FBI would "be like it was five years ago. We'll open up the whole town." [125]

At the Murchison family mansion in Dallas, champagne and caviar flowed for an entire week, said May Newman, a seamstress for Virginia Murchison. She described the mood at that mansion as "very joyous and happy. I was the only one in that household at that time that felt any grief for his assassination." [126]

Clint Murchison Jr., the son who owned the Dallas Cowboys, had been stopped on November 22 by Dallas police, and two rifles were found in the trunk of his car, according to producer and actor Caruth Clark Byrd, son of Murchison friend D. Harold Byrd. Murchison claimed the rifles were for hunting and was not detained. [127]

H.L. Hunt was reportedly flown out of Dallas a day or so after the assassination to stay at a D.C. hotel for at least a week.

Klan leader Milteer, who accurately predicted the killing and some say was photographed in Dealey Plaza that day, was "very jubilant" about Kennedy dying, Willie Somersett said. "Everything ran true to form," he told Somersett, who met Milteer in Jacksonville, Fla, on November 23 before they drove to Columbia, S.C. "I guess you thought I was kidding you when I said [Kennedy] would be killed from a window with a high-powered rifle. I don't do any guessing." [128]

After apparently making a long-distance call the following day, Milteer told Somersett that Oswald "will not say anything," and that "the right wing had no worry whatsoever" about being blamed. Money had been "furnished to the right people to do the right job without throwing anything onto the patriots," Milteer said. [129]

Milteer also said he was putting out propaganda fliers that would blame Kennedy's death on Jewish people so they would be targeted. A rough draft read in part, "You Jews killed the president. We're going to kill you. – The International Underground."

On November 24, some other Klan leaders showed up at their South Carolina hotel room. One thought assassinating the president made the U.S. look bad worldwide, saying, "It wouldn't have been so bad if it was Martin Luther King."

Milteer reportedly responded that Kennedy needed to be killed, and if King had been targeted, the "Jews" would simply find another "race agitator." [130]

Some students cheered the news of JFK's death. John Albach "walked out of school after a third of his math class at Bryan Adams High [in East Dallas] cheered after hearing of the assassination on the loudspeaker," wrote columnist Molly Ivins. Some claimed they cheered the news they would be let out of school, "but they cheered in Mrs. Schulke's world history class at Highland Park [Middle School], even though she asked them to stop," Ivins noted. [131]

As a five-year-old, William Bogy observed Kennedy ride by in a motorcade about 15 feet away in San Antonio. His joy soon turned to bewilderment. "What I remember the most were kids at school whose parents were glad Kennedy was dead," Bogy said. In Dallas, grown men cheered and threw their hats in the air. But that hateful reaction wasn't confined to Texas; students also applauded the news in Mississippi, Alabama, and other states. In Oklahoma City, a physician told a visitor, "Good, I hope they got Jackie." [132]

Perhaps those responses were in the minority. People posting their remembrances on a BBC site told tales of real grief. A U.S. Air Force soldier stationed in Turkey "wanted to punch" a sergeant who was smiling that day. "People were crying," recalled a Dallas college student.

"Every adult I encountered for days was grim," wrote a man in Waco, Texas. A student in Washington state observed her teacher cry. Students at a South Dakota Catholic school got on their knees to pray. "I had my hands over my head, tears rolling down my cheeks and my heart was overwhelmed with grief," said a man from Sierra Leone. [133]

At Lackland Air Force Base in San Antonio, Guare watched an officer get out of a car. He called the troops to attention. "Gentlemen, the president of the United States has been shot," he said.

Guare, the only airman there from the East and one of the few to graduate from college, stepped forward. "What!" he gasped.

"Back in line, soldier," the officer commanded. "What is he? A personal friend of yours?"

"Yes," Guare replied. "I don't know him, but he is my friend."

As the airmen gathered around the officer's car, listening to radio reports, some troops made bets on what time Kennedy would die. "Come on, you fucker, die," some said.

"He's our commander in chief," Guare said.

"Yours. Not mine."

When the radio announcer reported that Kennedy died, many troops cheered. They had the day off. Some lit firecrackers. "That shows what we do to n----- lovers!" at least one said.

"I have never felt so isolated in my life as I did that day," Guare would later write. [134]

Cabell hosts celebratory party, Dulles hunkers down

At the Washington, D.C., home of Charles Cabell, the former CIA deputy director reportedly toasted Kennedy's death with high-ranking military officials in a celebratory party on November 24. Dallas Police Lt. Revill was there as a personal guard for Mayor Cabell, who flew to D.C. to attend JFK's funeral and burial at Arlington Cemetery. Revill told a friend he was repulsed by the scene and sought refuge in a guest bedroom. [135]

Allen Dulles acted like he was still the CIA director. On November 22, he journeyed to a remote CIA facility in Northern Virginia called "The Farm," which was used as an alternate command post. "That whole fateful weekend, [Dulles was] hunkered down in a CIA command post," author David Talbot said. "There are many odd circumstances like this." [136]

While most officials mourned at least in public, LBJ seemed less shocked than most. He demanded that he be sworn in as president immediately in Dallas, although Kennedy's aides wanted to leave as soon as possible. LBJ claimed Robert Kennedy recommended that he take the oath in Dallas, which RFK denied. [137]

Nixon, who had lost the 1962 California gubernatorial race and joined a New York law firm, happened to be in Dallas the day Kennedy died, addressing a soft drink bottlers convention. He had left Dallas a few hours before the shooting. Upon hearing the news, Nixon's main initial concern was that the crime would not be linked to a "right-winger," according to former aide Stephen Hess. One of the first people Nixon called was Hoover, who assured him that "somebody with a Cuban connection" was responsible. The next morning, Hess found numerous Republican operatives in Nixon's apartment discussing their next political moves. [138]

The afternoon that JFK died, Banister and Jack Martin drank heavily at a New Orleans bar. Returning to their office, they argued over whether Martin went through Banister's private files. Martin said he became angry, telling Banister that he "remembered the people," including Oswald and Ferrie, who hung around the office that summer. Banister pistol whipped Martin, who had to be treated at a hospital. [139]

Clay Shaw left New Orleans for the West on November 15, supposedly to make a speech. He did not return until after November 22. The travel agency that arranged Shaw's trip was located at the Trade Mart where he worked and happened to be the same one that arranged for Oswald to go to Russia in 1959, Garrison said. [140]

'Well, it's over'

Late that evening, William Anderson, who was renting a room in a South Dallas house, said he heard men's voices outside his window discussing something. He said one clearly stated, "Well, it's over." His companion told the first man to keep quiet.

A few days before the killing, reputed Mafia affiliate Dudley H. McFadin and associate Tommy Johnson had rented a cottage in the back of that house. The men had acted suspiciously, always backing their cars in to park and leaving at all hours of the night. They claimed to be working on November 22 and not in downtown Dallas.

Anderson and the landlord, Myrtle Rogers, went to the cottage a couple days later and found some rifle shells. McFadin claimed the shells were from a deer hunting trip, while he said Johnson had left the cottage with a nervous breakdown over his marital troubles and was in a mental institution. [141]

McFadin told the FBI that both he and Johnson were having marital difficulties at the same time, so they rented the cottage to take a break. The cottage happened to be near the home on Harlandale believed to be a center of anti-Castro activity. [142]

McFadin lived on Rosebud Drive in Irving, the same street where Oswald's TSBD supervisor, William Shelley, moved a few years later. It was also not far from where the Paines and Oswalds lived.

'Brother, you won't find anything there'

On November 23, Marina, her daughters, and Marguerite went to the police station to visit Oswald. They entered an enclosed room with a glass wall about 1 p.m. and took turns picking up the phone to speak to him. "He tried to console me that I should not worry," Marina said. "He spoke of some friends who would supposedly help him." [143]

Marina told her husband that police had searched for his rifle at the Paine's house, finding one in the TSBD building. She didn't openly accuse him but got the feeling that he was guilty:

> I couldn't accuse him – after all, he was my husband.... But I could see by his eyes that he was guilty [of something]. Rather, he tried to appear to be brave. However, by his eyes, I could tell that he was afraid. This was just a feeling. It is hard to describe. He said goodbye to me with his eyes. I knew that. He said that everything would turn out well, but he did not believe it himself.... I didn't see him again. [144]

Oswald told his mother that his bruises and black eyes were due to "a scuffle" at the Texas Theatre. "Everything is fine," he said.

Around 3:30 p.m., Robert visited his brother. They engaged in some small talk, then Robert looked harder at Oswald. "Lee, what the Sam Hill is going on?"

"I don't know," Oswald answered, barely returning his gaze.

Robert's eyes became wider, his voice louder. "You don't know? Look, they've got your pistol. They've got your rifle. They've got you charged with shooting the president and a police officer. And you tell me you don't know? I want to know just what's going on."

Oswald stiffened. "I just don't know what they're talking about," he said firmly. "Don't believe all this so-called evidence."

Robert studied his brother's face, trying to unearth answers in his eyes. Oswald noticed his stare. "Brother," Lee replied quietly, "you won't find anything there." [145]

When Robert stated that he didn't believe the Paines were friends of Lee's, he replied, "Yes, they are." [146]

Calling military counterintelligence officer

At some time on November 23, Oswald supposedly called John Hurt, a former U.S. Army counterintelligence officer who could have worked for the CIA. Some theorized that Oswald sought help to verify his background in intelligence to authorities. [147]

Late that night, Bolden, as the Chicago office's night duty agent, received a call from Agent Sorrels, who oversaw the Dallas Secret Service office. Sorrels said Oswald had mentioned John Hurt or Hurd as a possible contact. He wanted "every agent" to be assigned to help track him down. Agents did so the next day, but Bolden heard nothing about the search. [148]

Oswald knew he would need help, and he expected others to step in to do so. New Orleans attorney Dean Andrews Jr. told the Warren Commission that a "Clay Bertrand" – believed to be Shaw – called him on either November 22 or 23 to ask that he represent Oswald. Andrews was sick with pneumonia in the hospital but told Bertrand that he would "find somebody that could." Andrews later claimed someone else called him to ask about him representing Oswald, but it was not Bertrand, who he had worked for previously. [149]

When a lawyer didn't seem to materialize, Oswald phoned Ruth about 4 p.m. on November 23 and asked her to call John Abt, chief counsel of the Communist Party, to see if he would take the case.

"He sounded to me almost as if nothing out of the ordinary had happened," Ruth said of Oswald. "He expressed gratitude to me. I felt, but did not express, considerable irritation at his seeming to be so apart from the situation, so presuming of his own innocence... I was quite stunned that he called at all or that he thought he could ask anything of me – appalled, really." Still, Ruth tried unsuccessfully to reach Abt, who would say that he doubted that he would have taken the case. [150]

Oswald talked with H. Louis Nichols, president of the Dallas Bar Association. He asked Nichols if he knew Abt or any lawyers with the ACLU. Nichols offered to help find someone, but Oswald told him to return the following week to check if he had found anyone. [151]

In another session, police showed Oswald the famous photo of him holding a rifle that would run on the cover of Life in a few months. Oswald said he understood photography "real well" and his face had been superimposed on the shot. "That picture is not mine, but the face is mine," he said. [152]

Oswald then called Ruth again and wanted to speak to Marina. "He felt irritated at not having been able to reach her," Ruth said. "He thought she should be at my house." [153]

Both Robert and Marguerite were suspicious of the Paines, perhaps not trusting their background. They convinced Marina not to return there that evening. Marguerite said Ruth had Marina there to babysit her two kids, "so actually she wasn't doing my son or Marina the favor that she claims she was doing."

Robert said there was something he didn't like about Michael Paine in particular. He suspected the Paines were "somehow involved in this affair." [154]

Ruby stalks Oswald, Hunt aide surveys police HQ

Following the assassination, Jack Ruby seemed to be everywhere. Witnesses claimed to see him at The Dallas Morning News offices, at the scenes of Kennedy's killing and Oswald's arrest, at police headquarters, at his synagogue, telling friends such as Dallas Officer Harry Olsen that it was "too bad that a peon" like Oswald "could do something like that." [155]

Since multiple officers and television cameras placed him at police headquarters, it's a safe bet he was, indeed, there. Somehow, Ruby was able to make his way into the area where Oswald was interrogated several times over the following two days. One way he maintained his position in the station was by serving as an informal guide for the vast number of out-of-town media members. He pointed out who key officials were and even helped get some interviews.

"Hey, Jack, what are you doing here?" a Dallas detective asked him at one point during the hectic assassination evening.

"I am helping all these fellows," Ruby replied, pointing to the reporters around him. [156]

At about 11:05 p.m. on November 22, Dallas Lt. John W. Finley was surprised to see Ruby walking down a hallway of the Homicide Bureau office giving sandwiches to officers. Ruby worked his way through the unguarded door of the office where Oswald was being interrogated, giving sandwiches to officers in the room. [157]

At one point, Ruby came within five feet of Oswald and remained in there for at least five minutes, Finley told Pulte. "Ruby's behavior may have been an attempt to find out what Oswald said to the interrogators about the possible role of others in a conspiracy to assassinate Kennedy," Pulte wrote. [158]

When Oswald was brought out for his midnight press conference, among those he walked past was Ruby. District Attorney Wade at one point stated that Oswald had been associated with the anti-Castro "Free Cuba Committee." Ruby knew Oswald's background well enough to shout out, "Henry, that's the [pro-Castro] Fair Play for Cuba Committee!" [159]

After that conference, CBS News correspondent Ike Pappas described Oswald in his notes as "a cool customer." Pappas detected a "slight Spanish accent," as he wrote that the "message" of Oswald being charged with JFK's assassination didn't appear to immediately get through to him. "He told us all this morning that he didn't kill the president," Pappas wrote. Oswald said he was "waiting for someone to come forward to give me…legal assistance." [160]

In the wee hours of November 23, Ruby woke up his roommate, George Senator, and called his handyman. He drove them to a billboard along a roadway that read, "Impeach Earl Warren." The chief justice, a Republican, was hated by some in Dallas almost as much as Kennedy for decisions such as outlawing segregation and formal prayers in public schools. Ruby photographed the billboard for some odd reason.

Ruby returned to police headquarters later that afternoon, appearing to look for an ideal way to get at Oswald. He phoned a local radio station to see if anyone knew when Oswald would be transferred to the county jail. In the wee hours of November 24, the Dallas FBI office and sheriff's office each received calls from a man saying that a committee had decided to "kill the man that killed the president," according to the Warren Commission. A Dallas police lieutenant recognized the man's voice as Ruby's. [161]

Hunt aide John Curington was another unauthorized visitor to police headquarters. He said Hunt asked him to go to the Dallas police station and see what kind of security police had on Oswald. Curington said he entered the police station three times on November 23 without trouble. He even rode on an elevator that contained none other than Oswald and Capt. Fritz. [162]

Curington reported that night about the lax security, and Hunt left Dallas for D.C. before Ruby would shoot Oswald. He would not return for at least a week. [163]

An 'emotional feeling'

Ruby arose on November 24 and claimed to have read in the papers that Jackie Kennedy may have to come back to Dallas for Oswald's trial.

"Suddenly the feeling, the emotional feeling came within me that someone owed this debt to our beloved president to save [his wife] the ordeal of coming back," Ruby claimed to the Warren Commission. "I don't know why that came through my mind." [164]

Many didn't buy that explanation by the nightclub operator. "You can't tell me a guy who's running a strip joint and beating up women is worried that [Jackie Kennedy will] have to come back to Texas for a trial," Chauncey Holt noted. [165]

The House Assassinations Committee didn't buy it, reporting that Ruby wrote a note to attorney Joseph Tonahill claiming that his first lawyer, Tom Howard, "told me to say that I shot Oswald so that Caroline and Mrs. Kennedy wouldn't have to come to Dallas to testify." [166]

Some journalists saw Ruby at the police station that morning, checking to see if Oswald had been transferred. He was supposed to be moved at 10 a.m., but that was delayed for some reason by more than an hour. Some believed the delay was to allow Ruby access to Oswald. Others said it was to wait for more media to show up. Oswald added to the delay by asking to change clothes.

In his final interrogation session that morning, Oswald said he had never intended to organize a Fair Play for Cuba Committee branch in Dallas since he "was too busy trying to get a job." A map police found in his room marked with an X near his worksite was to show where to go for his job interview there. "I have to walk from where I am going most of the time," he said. "I would put these markings on this map so I could plan my itinerary around with less walking." [167]

After sending a money order to an employee at a nearby Western Union outlet, Ruby said he suddenly decided to walk down the police ramp around 11:20 a.m. to where Oswald was being transferred. "I didn't sneak in," he said. "I walked down those few steps… There was no one near me when I walked down that ramp." [168]

Finley disputed that Ruby entered the police basement through the ramp, saying he thought he entered from the alley door. That door was usually locked, requiring someone from the inside to open it, but it could have been propped open, Finley said. 169

The House Assassinations Committee concluded that Ruby had help reaching Oswald, "even though the assistance may have been provided with no knowledge of Ruby's intentions." There were unlocked doors and a lack of guards along the stairway, the committee reported.

Ruby's lawyer Howard entered the station as Oswald was led off the elevator. Howard waved at a detective as he went back outside, saying, "That's all I wanted to see." 170

Upon seeing Oswald, Ruby said he became "carried away emotionally. I had the gun in my right hip pocket, and impulsively, if that is the correct word here, I saw him. And that is all I can say. And I didn't care what happened to me." 171

Thrusting his pistol into Oswald's ribs, Ruby pulled the trigger. "You killed my president, you rat!" he snarled.

Shocked police wrestled the gun from Ruby and pinned him to the floor. "I am Jack Ruby," he stated. "You all know me." 172

Dallas police did not make a move to stop Ruby beforehand, according to photographs, Hoover said. "Neither officer on either side made any effort to grab [Ruby] not until after the pistol was fired," he wrote. Police Chief Curry said he moved Oswald during daylight hours at the requests of television journalists who said Oswald would be filmed clearer in daylight, according to Hoover. But others said Curry really wanted to transfer Oswald secretly. Mayor Cabell ordered Chief Curry to move Oswald in front of the media, said Niebuhr, a strong ally of long-time Dallas County Commissioner John Wiley Price. 173

As Oswald was rushed to Parkland Hospital, Ruby told police at the station that he hadn't planned the hit. "It was one chance in a million," Ruby said. "I guess I just had to show the world that a Jew has guts." Oswald was pronounced dead at 1:07 p.m. 174

Though Ruby would tell the Warren Commission that he did not speak with Mafia affiliates before the shooting, phone records lent a different story. Ruby would write letters while jailed alluding to a deep conspiracy, with LBJ the major player. He would tell a psychiatrist that he was "framed to kill Oswald." 175

Joseph Campisi, who denied being involved in organized crime despite Ruby and others tied to the Mafia frequenting his establishment, paid Ruby a visit in jail shortly after he shot Oswald. Ruby wanted to know "how the people on the street, his friends, thought about what he did," Campisi said. He told him, "They don't think nothing." Ruby cried at one point, seemingly feeling sorry for himself, but never talked about politics or why he shot Oswald. Just before they left, Ruby asked Campisi to tell jewelry salesman Milton Joseph, who first introduced Ruby to Campisi, that he was still banned from his club. Joseph and Ruby had a long-time falling out and weren't speaking. "We thought that was funny," Campisi said.

While prosecutor Bill Alexander and others would say Ruby was not in the Mafia, some Carousel Club employees believed he was acting on orders. Ruby "had no choice" but to kill Oswald, dancer Gail Raven said. "Jack had bosses, just like everyone else." [176]

When former Carousel waitress Mash observed Ruby shoot Oswald on live television, she "knew then he had done it to silence him." Mash had moved away from Dallas by then. [177]

'He cry'

As Lee was shot, Marina and Marguerite had the television off in their room at the Executive Inn near Love Field, where Secret Service had moved them since it wasn't near as busy as the Adolphus. So they did not know anything as Robert arrived and "frantically" told them to pack.

Secret Service agents swarmed around the hotel. In the car, a Secret Service agent said he would take them to Robert's in-laws some 45 miles away. Marguerite bristled and said she wanted to be near her son. "For security reasons, this is the best place," the agent said.

"Security reasons?" Marguerite cried. "I am not going out in this little country town."

The agents decided to take them to Irving, stopping at the police chief's home. They noticed a lot of cars there. An agent admitted that Lee was shot.

"How badly?" Marguerite asked.

"In the shoulder," he fibbed.

As Marina went inside the chief's home to call Ruth to obtain diapers and other items, Marguerite heard something said over the radio. "Do not repeat," the agent said.

She knew. "My son is gone, isn't he?" He didn't answer. "Answer me. I want to know. If my son is gone, I want to meditate."

Finally, the agent replied, "Yes, Mrs. Oswald, your son has just expired." [178]

Crying, Marguerite went into the home to tell Marina. Marguerite suddenly stopped bawling. "I want to see Lee," she stated.

Marina added, "I want to see Lee, too."

The police chief said it would be better to wait until he was at the funeral home, but they were insistent. On the drive to Parkland Hospital, an agent tried to get them to reconsider "for security reasons."

"Even though I am poor, I have as much right as any other human being," Marguerite argued. "Mrs. Kennedy was escorted to the hospital to see her husband. And I insist upon being escorted [with] enough security to take me to the hospital to see my son." [179]

At Parkland, they were escorted upstairs. Lee's body was on a firm operating room table. The room was full of police guarding the body.

Marina went up to his lifeless body first, opening his eyelids. "He cry," she told a doctor. "His eye wet." [180]

Marguerite said she didn't touch her son's body but wanted to "make sure it was my son." After she was satisfied, she told officers at the hospital, "I think some day you will hang your heads in shame. I happen to know, and know some facts, that maybe this is the unsung hero of this episode." [181]

Michael Brownlow was an eyewitnesses as a boy standing on Houston Street near Kennedy's vehicle as shots rang out. He is among those who believe there was at least one other shooter from behind the grassy knoll, not far from where he is standing. [Shay photo]

Dealey Plaza photographed from above on November 25, 1963. [Squire Haskins Photography, courtesy of Dallas Remembers 20th Anniversary Celebration Committee, 1983]

Chapter Nine

The Fix Is In

We are supposed to be closing doors, not opening them.
— **J. LEE RANKIN**, Warren Commission lawyer, 1964

In the early morning hours of November 23, 1963, James J. Humes washed the blood of the nation's 35th president off his hands. He had just played a key role in probably the most controversial autopsy in modern U.S. history at Bethesda Naval Hospital, a few miles north of the White House.

But the director of laboratories of the National Medical School in Bethesda couldn't just wash Kennedy's blood off notes he and others took of the proceedings. Stunningly, he carted those documents to his nearby home, hand-copied them onto other pieces of paper, and threw the original notes and his first autopsy report draft into the fireplace. They were stained with the fallen president's blood, and Humes claimed he didn't want to see those in the hands of "some sensation seeker." [1]

"When I noticed that these bloodstains were on this document that I had prepared, I said nobody's going to ever get these documents," Humes would say in a sworn deposition in 1996 before the Assassination Records Review Board. [2]

Like many aspects of this assassination, there was a more sinister side to Humes' destruction of evidence. James Morningstar Young, a White House physician who was present at the autopsy, would say in an interview with Navy historians in 2001 that Humes was ordered to destroy the notes by Rear Adm. George Burkley, who attended the autopsy as Kennedy's personal physician. Burkley ordered them destroyed "at the request" of Robert Kennedy, Young would say. [3]

RFK was concerned about people knowing that his brother had Addison's disease, according to Young:

> It's terribly unfortunate that Dr. Burkley actually gave an order to Jim Humes sometime later at the request of Robert Kennedy, I believe, that all of the autopsy notes that he had taken should be destroyed. Which apparently he did, Jim Humes, which is a tragedy because I think that it's too bad, only to go ahead and keep the lid on the fact that President Kennedy really did have

Addison's disease. And on autopsy, he had no evidence of any adrenal glands at all. None. They couldn't find any piece [of the adrenal glands] at all. [4]

Others believed there was a deeper motive behind the destruction of notes, claiming that the autopsy was ultimately commanded by high-level military officials who wanted to make sure there was little doubt in the official records that the shots that killed Kennedy appeared to come only from where Oswald supposedly was on the sixth floor of the TSBD. Adm. Burkley, who had been in the motorcade in Dallas, at Parkland Memorial Hospital as Kennedy died, and at the Bethesda autopsy, would not be asked whether he gave such an order before he passed away in 1991. He would eventually believe that Oswald did not act alone, some said. [5]

Other doctors present at JFK's autopsy, including Bethesda Naval chief pathologist J. Thornton Boswell, Walter Reed Medical Center pathologist Pierre A. Finck, and pathologist Robert Karnei, took notes. While some of those documents were eventually admitted as ARRB exhibits, Boswell would tell the federal agency that he gave his notes to Humes, who destroyed them because "he didn't want this material in a museum barn out on [Route] 66." [6]

Humes would ask Boswell not to say anything about whether JFK had Addison's disease to any investigations before 1994, saying that Humes had promised Burkley to keep that under wraps. Humes would say in 1996 that he only burned notes, before admitting he also burned a draft report. [7]

Finck's notes were also missing, and Humes could have destroyed those, said Gary L. Aguilar, a California ophthalmologist who lectured on the medical evidence of the assassination. Kennedy's autopsy was riddled with other mistakes and misrepresentations, he said. One problem was that Humes and Boswell did not have specialties in forensic autopsies, while Finck had not done a hands-on autopsy in several years, he said.

"They were in way over their heads," said Aguilar, a board member of the Assassination Archives and Research Center, which preserved documents on political assassinations. "They were basically honorable men who had to follow orders, or they would jeopardize their careers if they did not." [8]

'Jaw-dropping'

The autopsy note-burning controversy would be relatively minute among the shocking events that transpired in the aftermath of Kennedy's death. But the scandal provided another example of government officials and physicians caught lying. If those handling the investigation of JFK's death could be caught apparently covering up a smaller lie, that lent more credence to what many believed was the concealment of larger truths.

"Dr. Humes may have had his reasons for burning the original autopsy notes," said Philip Shenon, a former New York Times journalist and author of *A Cruel and Shocking Act: The Secret History of the Kennedy Assassination*. "But it was still jaw-dropping to discover what he did." [9]

Aguilar and researcher Kathy Cunningham called Humes' explanation for destroying notes "dubious at best," noting that Humes – or someone – preserved some other blood-stained notes. Humes' note burning "would have been medico legally frowned upon had it occurred in a civilian autopsy of even the most undistinguished murder victim," they wrote. [10]

The ARRB board would add in a report that Humes "finally acknowledged under persistent questioning – in testimony that appears to differ from what he told the Warren Commission – that he had destroyed both his notes taken at the autopsy and the first draft of the autopsy report." [11]

In explaining his view of why Humes burned notes in a 1966 U.S. News & World Report interview, former Warren Commission assistant counsel and Pennsylvania Sen. Arlen Specter would not mention Humes' concerns about profiteers:

> [Humes] had never performed an autopsy on a president, and he was using his best judgment under the circumstances, never dreaming that loose, handwritten notes would become a subject of some concern.
>
> That matter was of concern immediately to his superiors, and he was questioned on it. He made a formal report on it, and he explained his reasons fully before the commission. [12]

The autopsy was one of the most important facets of the assassination's investigation since it provided physical evidence to help determine where bullets exited and entered Kennedy, how many there were, and if there was more than one assassin. The problem was, like much of the case, there was little agreement on basic facts even decades after the assassination.

James Curtis Jenkins, a Naval medical technician assisting pathologists during Kennedy's autopsy, said during a Dallas conference organized by JFK Lancer Productions and Publications that he observed a large posterior hole in Kennedy's head, as well as a small hole in the right temporal bone, just above the right ear. He recalled that Finck also saw the smaller hole and speculated that a bullet might have caused this hole, according to notes taken at the conference. Jenkins said that about one-third of Kennedy's brain mass was missing, and the brain appeared to have been removed before the autopsy. [13]

The hole above the ear was "entirely consistent with an entry wound, and inconsistent with a bullet exit wound," wrote Douglas P. Horne, a Naval officer and former chief analyst of military records for the ARRB. Horne added:

> Jenkins' bullet entry site supports a shot from the right front that would have caused the huge blowout in the right rear posterior skull, the large avulsed wound seen by all the Parkland witnesses. This was the large defect, devoid of scalp and skull, that neurosurgeon Kemp Clark at Parkland described as a probable "tangential wound" at the Parkland press conference the afternoon of the assassination....
>
> Jenkins' bullet hole is consistent with the same-day testimony of Bill Newman, who thought he saw part of President Kennedy's ear "blown off" – presumably Newman saw a bone fragment exit this area immediately after the bullet's impact. Jenkins' bullet entry site is also consistent with the wound diagram of the side of the head (a lateral view) made by Tom Robinson in 1996 for the ARRB. [14]

In testimony before the Warren Commission in 1964 and House Select Committee on Assassinations in 1977, Humes would say he believed only two gunshots struck Kennedy and both came from behind. But when asked by the House Assassinations Committee if he could say the shots came from above JFK, Humes would not be sure. "I think behind is probably the most one can say from the anatomical findings," Humes would testify in 1977. [15]

Burkley initially told the pathologists that they needed to find the bullet "to complete the case," Boswell would say. After they determined there were only bullet fragments inside Kennedy, they continued with the autopsy. [16]

The autopsy room included a closed-circuit television camera so audiences across the street at the National Institutes of Health could observe the proceedings. But no one switched on that camera for the Kennedy autopsy. Humes would say he wished that had occurred to help end speculation. [17]

What happened to JFK's brain?

The issue of what ultimately happened to the remains of Kennedy's brain was another mystery. Humes and Boswell would tell the assassinations review board that they placed the remains of the brain in a stainless-steel container during the autopsy and then examined it two or three days later. Humes would add that he gave the brain remains to Adm. Burkley and did not see them again.

The remains reportedly would be taken from the White House to the National Archives in 1965, according to the House Assassinations Committee, then turn up missing in 1966. Robert Kennedy "most likely acquired possession of, or at least personal control over, these materials," the panel would report. [18]

Cyril Wecht would discover in 1972 that Kennedy's brain matter was missing when he examined evidence at the National Archives. The remains of JFK's brain would remain a mystery, as of early 2022.

Researcher David Lifton believed that Kennedy's body was altered between leaving Dallas and arriving in Bethesda.

"When the body arrived at Bethesda, two FBI agents were present, and they wrote in their report that it was 'apparent' that there had been 'surgery of the head area, namely, in the top of the skull'," Lifton said. "The kind of 'surgery' we are talking about is not the normal life-saving craniotomy, but a pathological craniotomy, the procedure done at an autopsy to remove the top of the skullcap to provide access to the brain." [19]

As aides loaded Kennedy's casket into a Navy ambulance after Air Force One landed at Andrews Air Force Base near D.C., the casket slipped and a handle broke off, said Young, the White House physician. "Lo and behold, when he got to Bethesda, they had a different coffin and they had him in a body bag," Young said. "They had to change coffins before they took him out to Bethesda. So they changed the coffin to get one that did not have a broken handle on it, and apparently put him in a body bag." [20]

Humes would write in a 1992 Journal of the American Medical Association article that "there was no body bag anywhere near the scene." He would add that there was not any interference during the autopsy from military officials or anyone else, while admitting to only one error:

> If we made a mistake, it was in not calling Dallas before we started the autopsy. Our information from Parkland Hospital in Dallas before we started the autopsy was zero. If only we had seen the president's clothes, tracking the second bullet would have been a piece of cake, but we didn't have the clothes. In hindsight, we could have saved ourselves a lot of trouble if we had known that the doctors at Parkland performed a tracheostomy in an attempt to save the president's life and that this procedure obliterated the exit wound of the bullet that entered at the base of the neck. [21]

'Public must be satisfied Oswald was the assassin'

If it was up to LBJ, there would not have even been a Warren Commission. Johnson favored just letting Hoover – whom LBJ called "my brother and personal friend" during a phone call a week after Kennedy died   oversee the federal investigation and report. LBJ wanted another close associate, Texas Attorney General Waggoner Carr, to handle local details in an inquiry.

Hoover sought a rushed investigation that named Oswald as the lone assassin. Shortly after JFK was killed, Hoover told LBJ it would be "very, very bad to have a rash of investigations." FBI agents working on the case almost 24 hours a day would not interview key informants and suspects, such as Vallee, Marcello, Banister, and Ferrie. Hoover's office reportedly nixed an agent interviewing John Wilson Hudson, an alleged intelligence agent and mercenary who was arrested in Cuba in 1959 and might have seen Ruby bringing meals in prison to a mafioso, according to government documents. The British-born Hudson sometimes went by Carl John Wilson or John Wilson Carlos.

On November 24 – the day Oswald was killed – Hoover called White House aide Walter Jenkins to lobby for "having something issued so we can convince the public that Oswald is the real assassin." The following day, U.S. Deputy Attorney General Nicholas Katzenbach wrote LBJ aide Bill Moyers a memo. It seemed to be a direct call to whitewash any real investigation. However, Katzenbach would tell the House Assassinations Committee that he merely sought to head off unwarranted speculation, "that the quicker some information could be made available that went beyond what the press was able to uncover and what the press was able to speculate about was desirable." [22]

Unlike LBJ, Katzenbach seemed willing to accept a commission. But Katzenbach's actual memo was written in almost sinister terms:

> The public must be satisfied that Oswald was the assassin; that he did not have confederates who are still at large; and that the evidence was such that he would have been convicted at trial.
>
> Speculation about Oswald's motivation ought to be cut off, and we should have some basis for rebutting thought that this was a communist conspiracy or (as the Iron Curtain press is saying) a right-wing conspiracy to blame it on the communists. Unfortunately the facts on Oswald seem about too pat – too obvious (Marxist, Cuba, Russian wife, etc.). The Dallas police have put out statements on the communist conspiracy theory, and it was they who were in charge when he was shot and thus silenced.
>
> The matter has been handled thus far with neither dignity nor conviction. Facts have been mixed with rumor and speculation. We can scarcely let the world see us totally in the image of the Dallas police when our President is murdered.
>
> The only other step would be the appointment of a Presidential Commission of unimpeachable personnel to review and examine the evidence and announce its conclusions.
>
> I think, however, that a statement that all the facts will be made public property in an orderly and responsible way should be made now. We need something to head off public speculation or Congressional hearings of the wrong sort. [23]

The same day, LBJ called Hoover to report that "apparently some lawyer in [the Justice Department, probably Katzenbach] is lobbying the [Washington] Post because that's where the suggestion came for this presidential commission, which would be very bad and put it right in the White House." LBJ reiterated he'd rather just have the FBI and Carr – whom Johnson called a "good conservative fellow" – handle the investigation.

LBJ asked Hoover to pressure the Post against the idea of a commission. But Hoover replied, "I don't have much influence with the Post because I frankly don't read it. I view it like the [communist] Daily Worker." At that, LBJ laughed wildly. However, Hoover would lobby certain members of the press. [24]

Johnson then called Washington Post columnist Joseph Alsop, who at times fed the CIA and other government agencies information, according to colleague Carl Bernstein. Alsop, who called his government work a duty while others questioned whether it compromised his supposed impartial journalistic position, advised LBJ to accept the idea of a commission partly because many on the left would not believe the FBI. The journalist maintained it would not be an investigative body, but merely a public-relations vehicle to take the evidence the FBI gathered and produce a report. When Johnson balked, calling the matter a "local killing," Alsop reminded him that "it does happen to be the killing of the president." The Post editorialized the following day for a national solution, and by November 28, LBJ publicly supported a commission. [25]

Meanwhile, most in the media fell in line. On November 25, The New York Times proclaimed that Oswald was the "president's assassin" in a banner headline. The Associated Press reported that Hoover said that "all available information indicated that Lee Harvey Oswald acted alone in the assassination of President John F. Kennedy." In its first report on the assassination, Newsweek called Oswald the "dead assassin" and "Marxist marine." Despite no one seeing Oswald pull a trigger and only circumstantial evidence linking him to the crime, most media outlets relied mostly on the official account for their reports.

Behind the scenes, some FBI officials objected to the rushed investigation. And there were some mainstream reporters who went beyond the official line. Richard Dudman of the St. Louis Post-Dispatch wrote one of the first stories in a major newspaper questioning the lone gunman theory just a week after the killing. He noted that doctors said JFK's throat wound came from the front. In addition, Dudman wrote that he saw what looked like a bullet hole in the windshield of the presidential vehicle. Dorothy Kilgallen of the New York Journal-American strongly questioned the lone-assassin theory in her columns. Golz of The Dallas Morning News was one of the few in the major media who referred to Oswald as an "accused assassin," rather than "the assassin." In subsequent years, most journalists would call Oswald "the assassin;" this author would argue forcefully to use "accused assassin" numerous times, sometimes successfully, sometimes not. [26]

LBJ consulted Hoover before naming certain members. Hoover told LBJ that Allen Dulles, the ex-CIA director fired by Kennedy who lobbied hard to be named to the commission, "would be a good man." But Hoover wasn't enthusiastic about banker and Council on Foreign Relations Chairman John McCloy or New York Sen. Jacob Javits.

Johnson strong-armed several members. To get Supreme Court Chief Justice Warren to lead the panel, LBJ told the reluctant Republican about "a little incident in Mexico City" in which Oswald might have obtained money from the Cuban Embassy and how some, such as certain Dallas police officials, blamed Castro and the Soviets. Possibly "40 million lives" were at stake to thwart a potential nuclear war, Johnson declared.

LBJ used a similar argument on Sen. Richard Russell Jr., a conservative Democrat from Georgia and strong civil rights opponent. Russell told Johnson that he was "highly honored," but he "couldn't serve on it" with Warren, who many far-right Republicans considered a traitor. "I don't like that man," Russell said. "I don't have any confidence in him at all." [27]

LBJ repeatedly called Russell "my man on that commission" and that he would do it for "the good of the country." He chose Warren because "we've got to have the highest judicial people we can have."

"Don't go giving me that kind of stuff about you can't serve with anybody," Johnson snarled. "I can't arrest you and I'm not going to put the FBI on you, but you're goddamned sure going to serve." [28]

On November 29, LBJ formed the commission through an executive order. Within a few days, the seven-member panel took shape: Warren, Russell, Dulles, McCloy, future President and Michigan Rep. Gerald Ford, Kentucky Sen. John Cooper, and Louisiana Rep. Hale Boggs Jr.

The Warren Commission would become more of a "Dulles Commission," Stone would say in a 2021 interview in Jacobin magazine. Dulles would control "a lot of the proceedings and made sure the CIA did not reveal any information. They did not even know there were Cuban assassination plots. They did not know about the history of assassinations by the CIA. They were kept in the dark," Stone said. [29]

The FBI would also keep key documents and interviews from the entity. Hoover and Katzenbach would lobby commission members to quickly support the lone-assassin theory. As early as December 9, Katzenbach urged members to announce publicly that the FBI had singled out Oswald and there was no conspiracy. Ford was among the commision members to oppose doing that so soon.

Tampered evidence, box of Oswald-Ruby papers

LBJ took other measures to control the investigation. He ordered the presidential limousine to be shipped to Detroit to have the body replaced and interior refurbished. That effectively destroyed important evidence that could have helped determine how many bullets were fired and from what direction. Connally's clothing was also taken away by Secret Service agents sent by a Johnson aide to be cleaned and effectively stripped of evidence. [30]

A week after the assassination, LBJ asked Hoover about details of the FBI's investigation. Hoover admitted the agency did not have a photo showing Oswald firing the gun, but he said they had other evidence and there was "no question" that he did the deed alone. He claimed Oswald received money from the Cuban Embassy when he was in Mexico.

Johnson asked if Oswald and Ruby knew each other, and Hoover said they were checking out reports that Oswald was seen in the Carousel Club. "So far as tying Rubenstein and Oswald, we haven't *yet* done so," Hoover stated. Apparently, the FBI was initially *trying* to link Oswald and Ruby, which would have strengthened the idea of a conspiracy, not weakened it. In its final report, the commission would claim that Oswald and Ruby never met. [31]

LBJ also asked Hoover if any shots were fired at him. Hoover said no, that three were aimed at Kennedy. Hoover claimed the bullet found on Kennedy's stretcher fell out as someone massaged JFK's heart on the way to Parkland. Hoover added that Connally was hit by the second shot and kept Kennedy from being struck by that shot, a stance the Warren Commission would not support. "Kennedy would have been hit three times," if Connally had not turned, Hoover claimed.

In addition, Hoover said Oswald went to his home and then came "back downtown" and shot Tippit, which was false. Tippit was shot in South Dallas. Hoover claimed the woman selling tickets at the Texas Theatre saw Oswald carrying a gun, another false statement. Hoover called Melvin Belli, Ruby's lawyer, "almost as much of a shyster" as Edward Bennett Williams, who had represented mobsters like Giancana and Costello.

LBJ, obviously concerned about his own safety, asked if Hoover ever used a bulletproof car. Hoover replied he did and advised Johnson to employ one, even bulletproof a vehicle on his Texas ranch "very quietly." Hoover added that the FBI had received letters and calls that there were threats against Johnson. He criticized Kennedy's family and Johnson for walking down Pennsylvania Avenue in the middle of the street during JFK's funeral. [32]

Around then, Dallas County Constable Billy Preston picked up a box full of handwritten notes and other papers that appeared to link Oswald and Ruby, Dallas reporter Golz wrote. One was a receipt for a motel in New Orleans with Ruby and Oswald's names on it, dated several weeks before the assassination. It showed that several phone calls were made to the Cuban and Russian embassies in Mexico City, Preston and Constable Ben Cash said.

Other papers detailed an air landing strip near Mexico City and handwritten notes about a plan to kill Kennedy during the "dedication of a lake or dam in Wisconsin," Preston told Golz. The registry of a restaurant in Hubertus, Wis., that appeared to have Oswald's signature a week before JFK visited some area towns was also among the items.

Preston said a Dallas woman who was "really scared that she had all that stuff" gave him the box. He and another constable transferred the box of papers to District Attorney Wade. Wade would claim more than a decade later that the papers "didn't amount to nothing." He would say his office checked out potential Oswald-Ruby links and never found anything.

Cash said the woman's roommate hid the papers for her Hispanic boyfriend. The constables kept quiet about the box. The Warren Commission would not mention ties to Cubans or Russians in its report. They would think that was done "because it might put us in World War III," Cash said. [33]

Instead of pursuing such leads, Hoover attempted to sow discord by telling Robert Kennedy that Martin Luther King Jr. allegedly said "derogatory" remarks during JFK's funeral. Many believed Hoover told RFK that hoping he would sour on the civil rights leader. [34]

Johnson soon issued another executive order to lock many FBI, CIA, and other government documents away from the public for decades. Perhaps to help divert suspicion from himself, Johnson initially told aides that Castro might have had something to do with the assassination. LBJ would later admit that the CIA could have been involved. [35]

CIA agents admit agency involvement

LBJ would not be alone in suspecting the CIA. On the day Kennedy died, many agents and other employees in the CIA's Tokyo station "rejoiced," said Jim Wilcott, a finance officer at the branch on that day. [36]

Some agents told Wilcott that Oswald couldn't have pulled off the assassination on his own, that only the "CIA could have set up such an elaborate project." Wilcott noted:

> There was nobody [else besides the CIA] with the kind of knowledge or information that could have done this....They said they were having trouble with Oswald and that there was dissatisfaction with Oswald after he came back from the Soviet Union. And they would say things like, "Well, you know this was the way to get rid of him – to get him involved in this assassination thing and put the blame on Cuba as a pretext for another invasion, or another attack against Cuba." [37]

In addition, high-level CIA officials ordered on November 23 that all of Oswald's files from the New Orleans office were to be transported to headquarters in Langley, Va. There were so many files that it took a rented trailer to carry them. Oswald also had a 201 file, which indicated that he was employed by the CIA, some researchers said. [38]

Wilcott's wife, Elsie, also worked as a secretary for the CIA from 1957 until 1966, when they both resigned. Elsie endured years of sexism; for instance, she was asked during the job interviewing process whether she ever had sex with a farm animal. Such inappropriate queries were apparently regular occurrences in government job interview processes; even a male applicant to the Secret Service reported that farm animal question in a polygraph exam. But then, there were also wildly offensive questions hurled at job applicants for private-sector jobs in the 1950s.

Gradually, the Wilcotts "became convinced that what CIA was doing couldn't be reconciled to basic principles of democracy or basic principles of humanism," Wilcott said. They would not speak out for several years afterwards because they were "scared" and thought someone else would speak out about Oswald, he said. [39]

When no one did, the Wilcotts would speak at some college campuses and with some media outlets. They would receive threatening phone calls and notes signed by "The Minutemen" on their cars' windshields, he said. Their tires would be slashed and sugar poured into the gas tank. Wilcott would be forced to resign from a job with the city of Utica, Calif., due to FBI surveillance.

But their consciences led them to speak out "for the good of the country and for the good of the people," he said. In later years, they would join protests against the CIA-sponsored contra war in Nicaragua. [40]

'Get rid of this'

A few hours after Kennedy died, Hosty said J. Gordon Shanklin, the special agent in charge of the Dallas office, called him into his office. Shanklin stated that Hoover would "lose it" if he knew about the note – which Nannie Fenner, the secretary who read it, thought was threatening that Oswald delivered to Hosty around November 12. Hoover would be concerned about the FBI's image, that people thought the FBI messed up and should have known Oswald was a threat, Shanklin said. [41]

Hosty did not think the note was a "big deal." He maintained that Oswald had not threatened JFK or the FBI. His view was they should merely explain the circumstances to Hoover and the general public. [42]

Shanklin directed Hosty to write a memo explaining what happened, which Shanklin put with Oswald's letter in a "do not file" drawer. But the situation became more crucial after Oswald's death. On that day, Hosty was again called to Shanklin's office. Shanklin handed Hosty Oswald's note and his memo. "Oswald is dead now," he said. "Get rid of this." [43]

Hosty began to tear up the documents in Shanklin's office. "No!" his supervisor shouted. "Get it out of here! I don't even want it in this office."

Hosty carried the documents out of the office. He tore them up and flushed them down an FBI toilet. [44]

When Fenner asked Hosty about the letter a few days later, he replied, "What letter?" She was told by her supervisors to forget that Oswald's hand-delivered note ever existed. Shanklin would publicly deny he knew about the note. [45]

Hosty would be placed on probation and demoted to Kansas City. He would receive letters of censure from Hoover. Meanwhile, Shanklin would get letters of commendation from Hoover. [46]

In his April 1964 testimony before the Warren Commission, Hosty, whose name and phone number were later found among those in Oswald's address book, would not mention the Oswald note. But he would admit to the House Assassinations Committee that he destroyed the letter shortly after the assassination upon his supervisor's orders.

In addition, Hosty and Agent Bookhout would admit they destroyed at least some of their notes made during the interrogation of Oswald. Hosty would apparently keep some notes that appeared in a book he wrote. Bookhout would testify to the Warren Commission that agents' notes were "normally destroyed" after they completed a report. That was not the case, judging by the thousands of FBI reports that have been released, many of them dating back decades. [47]

Marina brainwashed?

For several weeks after Ruby killed Oswald, Secret Service agents and local police guarded the Oswald family at the Inn of the Six Flags in Arlington. The motel was owned by Great Southwest Corp., a real estate investment group with investors that included Murchison.

The Oswalds were not able to have a proper funeral for Lee on November 25. Numerous ministers turned down Robert, with one telling him, "Your brother was a sinner." A minister from the Fort Worth Council of Churches who happened to drive to the cemetery that day agreed to speak. The Oswalds arrived a couple minutes late to discover that Lee's body had already been carried to the grave, so they could not hold a service in the chapel. [48]

Marguerite left the inn on November 28, well before Marina. She didn't see her much after that, except on television. In one interview, Marina stated that she thought Lee did shoot JFK. That really angered Marguerite, who accused the Secret Service of brainwashing Marina.

"What an awful thing for this 22-year-old foreign girl to think," Marguerite said. "She doesn't know... Marina Oswald was brainwashed by the Secret Service, who have kept her in seclusion for eight weeks." [49]

Robert and Marina denied any ill treatment or "brainwashing" by government agents. Marina said she was told by federal agents, including immigration officials, that she had not committed a crime and could live in the United States without fear. She didn't see that as being threatened with deportation if she did not cooperate but said, "There was a clear implication that it would be better if I were to help." [50]

Hoover told LBJ on November 29 that Marina was "very hostile" and would only cooperate if "we could give assurance she would be allowed to remain in the country." Hoover added that he "told our agents to give that assurance and sent a Russian-speaking agent to Dallas." [51]

Marina auctions off ring for $108k

Authorities took most of Marina's belongings, including passports and Oswald's wedding ring. But she would receive the ring back and auction it off for $108,000.

Marguerite wanted her "share" of the money sent from people addressed to both her and Marina. She noted that reports estimated Marina received about $35,000 by early 1964. A 1977 article would report that Marina had obtained between $200,000 and $300,000 in donations, interview fees, and item sales in the aftermath. [52]

"Lee Harvey Oswald had finally become a real money-maker after his death," de Mohrenschildt ironically noted. "Poor fellow, even his tomb was stolen and desecrated." [53]

De Mohrenschildt said that Marina never once thanked him or his wife for their aid. Marina "created an appearance of a helpless victim, of a woman searching for God, and naturally God-fearing Americans sent her substantial contributions or donations, all tax-free," he wrote. "We heard from some reporters that donations were sent frequently stuck between the pages of Bibles, and she would grab the money and [throw] the Bible furiously on the floor." [54]

Ruth Paine told the Warren Commission that she talked with Marina after the assassination, and "she expressed her gratitude.... I think she always felt terribly indebted to me in a way she couldn't resolve." Marina thanked her again in a card, even saying she was sorry that "our friendship had ended so badly." [55]

Soon after the assassination, Marina made some curious visits, including one to the office of H.L. Hunt. Marina agreed to hire Katya Ford, who knew associates of Ruby, as her business agent. Ford's first husband, Stanley Skotnicki, also knew Ruby associates, including mob-affiliated John Grizzaffi, according to Pulte. [56]

Loomis, the lawyer who some saw with Ruby and Oswald, would buy five houses on the same side of 10th Street where Tippit was shot just east of the scene within a few months of that killing. Loomis would have the homes razed and build an apartment complex. The effect was to clear out witnesses to the crime and limit future investigations, Pulte noted. [57]

Marina's lifestyle would become wilder in 1964. She would date several men and spend a lot of time at a Dallas nightclub called the Music Box. Perhaps she was trying to mask her depression over losing Lee and being burdened with the accusations, she said. [58]

"After the assassination, there were times when she was close to ending her life," wrote Mailer, who interviewed Marina. "The worst of the pain was that maybe she loved [Lee] more by the end than in their beginning.... There was some goodness in [Lee] to hold on to." [59]

'Mostly circumstantial evidence'

In February 1964, Marina, Marguerite, and Robert appeared before the Warren Commission in Washington, D.C. Marguerite provided the most headaches for commissioners, telling them numerous times that she suspected her son was a U.S. government agent. That commission, the House Assassinations Committee, and other investigative bodies would conclude that Oswald did not work for the CIA, though they would acknowledge he was in contact with intelligence agencies.

Marguerite, who died in 1981 of cancer at age 73, would believe in a conspiracy to her grave:

> Nobody saw him with a rifle shoot the president. So you have mostly circumstantial evidence....I think my son was framed because, gentlemen, would his rifle be in the sixth-floor window of the depository, unless you want to say my son was completely out of his mind? And yet there has been no statement to that effect. [District Attorney] Wade has publicly said on the television when it happened that he is sane, he is well reasoned, he knows what he did. And Lee never did break, with his black eyes. He kept saying he was innocent. [60]

Robert said based on "circumstantial evidence" it appeared his brother shot Kennedy. But he added that it was "very difficult for me to feel that Lee Harvey Oswald acted entirely on his own without any assistance whatsoever. Now, whether this assistance was from any member of any government agency or just individuals, I do not know.... I do feel that he did have assistance to the extent that perhaps some money was given to him, and that other types of assistance, such as perhaps training and orientations as to perhaps the method to be used." [61]

He also suspected that Ruby "perhaps assisted Lee in this assassination." Robert, a sales coordinator at a brick company in Denton in 1963, added that he thought Ruby knew his brother before he shot him, and he was "paid to silence" him. [62]

Marina was most adamant that Lee shot Kennedy, though she would back off that contention in ensuing years. She told commissioners about Lee returning on the evening someone took a shot at Edwin Walker and saying he had tried to kill him because he was "a very bad man...a fascist." She told them about Lee saying he wanted to hijack a plane to Cuba. She told them that her mother-in-law's contention that Lee was a government agent was "untrue, of course," a belief she would change. She told them that on November 21, Lee did not say anything to indicate he was contemplating a shot at Kennedy. [63]

Then Marina related what commissioners really wanted to hear. She said that she came to the conclusion that her husband did kill JFK "perhaps a week after it all happened, perhaps a little more. The more facts came out, the more convinced I was." [64]

In early February – almost eight months before the commission would issue its report entirely blaming Oswald – chief counsel J. Lee Rankin obviously had his mind made up. At one point, Rankin asked Marina, "Do you have any idea of the motive which induced your husband to kill the president?"

Marina replied that eventually she concluded "that he wanted in any way, whether good or bad, to do something that would make him outstanding, that he would be known in history." But she added that was her opinion and she didn't know "how true that is." [65]

Years later, Marina would tell a reporter that she was a "blind kitten" when questioned by the Warren Commission and had feared that she might be deported if she did not say what she thought officials wanted. [66]

The government & media vs. 'defenseless dead man'

Many of those who testified before the Warren Commission lent statements that helped the panel's notion that Oswald was the lone assassin. Many witnesses were nervous and, like Marina, wanted to please commissioners, especially those who weren't naturalized citizens, de Mohrenschildt said.

They spoke "very unkindly and untruthfully of Lee just because they were frightened," said de Mohrenschildt. "It was like a McCarthy hearing, the government and media against a defenseless dead man." [67]

Commissioners and their lawyers "were obsessed with the idea that Lee was the sole assassin," de Mohrenschildt wrote. "The idea of Cuban refugees with mortal grudges against Kennedy did not interest them. Any time we said anything favorable to Lee, they passed it up." Dulles, in particular, was "a distant threat," implying that his presence as a former CIA director intimidated witnesses.

Commission lawyer Albert Jenner Jr. at one point asked if Oswald was a "homosexual," to which de Mohrenschildt replied he was more "asexual." Marina countered that Lee was more sexually active than many thought. Jenner also asked if Oswald had a Christmas tree in his apartment during holidays. [68]

Judge Warren "had a weakness for Marina" and "advised her to incriminate" the de Mohrenschildts by saying they had prior knowledge of Oswald shooting at Walker "to take pressure from herself," de Mohrenschildt charged. "This would take away the sting of her guilt, because she did know that Lee tried to shoot Gen. Walker and missed." [69]

Besides Marina, the testimony of alleged CIA assets Ruth and Michael Paine helped cement the government's case more than others. Ruth stated that she did not doubt that Oswald shot at JFK, based on the police evidence. However, she "never thought of him as a violent man." [70]

Her husband agreed that Oswald likely shot at JFK. Michael called it "a very spur of the moment idea that came into his head when he realized that he would have the opportunity....to change the course of history." Oswald thought that changes of a "rather drastic nature" were needed in American society, Michael said. [71]

Even de Mohrenschildt – one of the few to defend Oswald made statements that supported the Warren Commission's case. He said Oswald had no money and was a "miserable failure in everything he did." He might have been "jealous" of JFK since he was "extraordinarily successful," the older man theorized. [72]

De Mohrenschildt would later write that calling Oswald a failure was "most unfair." Jenner, who would become counsel to the House Judiciary Committee during Nixon's Watergate hearings, "played me as if I were a baby." Oswald was not a "bloodthirsty revolutionary" and knew "it would not have made him a hero to have shot a liberal and beloved president," de Mohrenschildt said. He ultimately believed there had been a plot involving government agencies and Cuban exiles hatched after the Bay of Pigs. [73]

At one time, Oswald told de Mohrenschildt he did not resent JFK's wealth and social status. Since Oswald didn't have many possessions to load him down, he revealed, "I will die free, death will be easy for me." [74]

RFK privately suspected plot

After testifying before the Warren Commission, the de Mohrenschildts attended a Georgetown gathering. Among those present was Janet Auchincloss, the mother of Jacqueline Kennedy. They got up the nerve to ask Auchincloss why JFK's relatives, with all their resources, didn't pursue an investigation of their own.

"But the [assassin] was your friend, Lee Harvey Oswald," replied Auchincloss, who had supported Nixon in 1960 rather than her son-in-law. "Jack is dead, and nothing will bring him back." She added that Jacqueline didn't want to see de Mohrenschildt again, and that was the last time he would speak with a Kennedy family member. [75]

At the same party, Allen Dulles, who would push the lone assassin tale stronger than other Warren Commission members, asked de Mohrenschildt if

Oswald had a reason to hate JFK. His friend replied that the accused assassin admired Kennedy. "It seemed to me that I was facing a conspiracy, a conspiracy of stubbornness and silence," de Mohrenschildt wrote. [76]

Robert Kennedy privately suspected the CIA, Mafia, and anti-Castro Cubans from the moment he heard the news, although he didn't publicly pursue an investigation, according to Talbot. Kennedy asked John McCone, who directed the CIA in 1963, the day his brother was killed if the CIA did it. McCone said it did not, and Kennedy believed him. But he also knew that McCone, a businessman with no previous intelligence background, "was not in firm control of his own agency," Talbot wrote. [77]

"Bobby.... had asked the wrong man," Talbot said. Dulles, the dominant figure on the commission, and Helms, another Kennedy foe who was covert operations director in 1963, would have been better to ask. [78]

RFK would remain attorney general until September 1964, and his department would continue to pursue mafiosos and related cases. In March 1964, Hoffa would be convicted for trying to bribe a juror during a previous trial for accepting illegal payments. He would be sentenced to eight years in prison. While out on appeal, Hoffa was convicted in another trial in July for mail and pension fraud and sentenced to five years. Appeals would reach the Supreme Court but ultimately be unsuccessful. Hoffa would start serving the prison sentences in 1967 but would be released in 1971 after Nixon commuted his sentence. Nixon would soon be derailed by Watergate, and Hoffa would disappear in 1975, presumed to be murdered by Mafia members. [79]

By 1968, Marcello and Giancana would be convicted for various crimes, as well. Trafficante would steer clear of prison. Dulles would avoid legal troubles for the rest of his life, dying of pneumonia at age 75 in 1969, but Helms would plead no contest in 1977 to misleading a committee investigating the CIA and receive a suspended sentence. Hunt and Sturgis would be sentenced to prison in 1973 for Watergate crimes. Anti-Castro leader Veciana would be convicted of drug charges in 1974. So some alleged JFK plotters would be held accountable, if for other crimes.

In 2013, Robert Kennedy Jr. would tell a forum in Dallas that his father believed that civil rights for minorities was more important and it would have been "a distraction for him to make [JFK's death] a principal issue." RFK wondered if his crusade against the Mafia led to JFK's death and thought the Warren Commission was a "shoddy piece of craftsmanship," his son said. "He publicly supported the Warren Commission report, but privately he was dismissive of it," RFK Jr. said. [80]

After his brother was gunned down, RFK would read works of philosophers and religious scholars, "trying to figure out kind of the existential implications of why a just God would allow injustice to happen of the magnitude he was seeing," his son said. Like many who asked such questions, he never really found a satisfying answer.

Under pressure to change statement

While CIA officials publicly denied the agency had any contact with Oswald, de Mohrenschildt experienced some pressure that made him think otherwise.

Soon after the assassination, Dallas FBI agent W. James Wood visited de Mohrenschildt in Haiti, where the latter man had settled in April 1963 to work on a government contract to explore mineral resources there. The purpose of Wood's visit was to pressure de Mohrenschildt to change his statement about Dallas CIA head Moore telling him Oswald was a "harmless lunatic," the enigmatic figure claimed.

"Unless you change your statement, life will be tough for you in the states," Wood said, according to de Mohrenschildt. [81]

De Mohrenschildt refused to change his statement. Sure enough, life would be tougher for him from then on. Marina claimed he had prior knowledge of Oswald taking a shot at Walker. Friends shunned him. He lost work. Despite that, he refused to take money for interviews. The Warren Commission would conclude in 1964 that it found "no signs of subversive or disloyal conduct on the part of either of the de Mohrenschildts."

De Mohrenschildt, who Oswald described as his best friend in Dallas, doubted Oswald was a formal intelligence agent:

> It never occurred to me that he might be an agent of any country, including [the] United States. Although he might have been trained in Russia for some ulterior motive – Lee was too outspoken, naively so.
>
> Occasionally Lee's constant search for truth, for the answers to the mysteries of life, seemed tragic and disturbing to me. But this proves also that it seems highly improbable that any government would try to make an agent of such a man. His own element of self-inquiry, self-denial and self-doubt, mixed with instability worried Lee. But I told him not to worry, in my opinion instability, doubt, constant search were elements of youth and were indicative of exuberant life. [82]

Of course, if de Mohrenschildt was a CIA informant or asset, as CIA memos show, his denial of Oswald being one rings hollow. Since the CIA traditionally operates its projects on a "need to know" basis in which participants only know as much about their role as they need to carry it out, it's entirely likely that de Mohrenschildt did not know he was helping to put Oswald in compromising positions. It's entirely likely that de Mohrenschildt, like Oswald and others, was a mere pawn in a high-stakes chess game ultimately played by some of the country's power elite. In turn, de Mohrenschilt used the CIA and other intelligence agencies to help him obtain lucrative contracts like the oil exploration one for almost $300,000 from the Haitian government.

De Mohrenschildt would continue to maintain that he was not knowingly involved in a plot, writing that he and his wife "had nothing to do whatsoever with the JFK assassination."

The FBI harassed him because he "often expressed an opinion that Lee was a patsy," he wrote. "Often we think of shady aspects of this gruesome [Warren Commission] 'investigation,' of the harm done to this country and especially to the damage to the memory of Lee, my dead friend." [83]

Magic-bullet critics

When the Warren Report was released in late 1964, most parties, including mainstream media pundits, embraced it as the gospel. But some found holes.

One of the biggest sources of criticism was the commission's magic-bullet theory, which postulated that one shot Oswald allegedly fired struck Kennedy in the back and then caused all of the wounds to Connally. The bullet was then found virtually undamaged on a stretcher at Parkland Hospital.

Lt. Col. L. Fletcher Prouty, chief of special operations for the Joint Chiefs under Kennedy and the inspiration for the "Mr. X" character in Stone's *JFK* film, noted:

> Pictures of that undamaged bullet show it as clean as a brand-new slug. It looks as though it had hardly been fired at all, let alone having traveled through two men, broken three bones, and lodged in a fourth.
>
> I have never seen an undamaged slug, no matter what substance it had been fired into, except when fired carefully into cotton. But even then there are scars, lines, and even deformity. The "Specter Miracle Bullet" does not even show that much damage. [84]

In ballistics tests with Oswald's rifle, every bullet was "squashed completely out of shape from impact with various simulated human targets," Garrison said. [85]

Connally himself said he didn't buy the theory; he thought he had been struck by a separate shot from one that hit Kennedy. Four members of the commission – Russell, Cooper, Boggs, and McCloy – expressed skepticism of the theory. Russell disagreed with the conclusions so much that he lobbied for the final report to include a statement that the possibility that Oswald had help "cannot be rejected categorically." Rankin had the disclaimer taken out of the report, however. [86]

The Warren Report claimed, "It is not necessary to any essential findings of the commission to determine just which shot hit Governor Connally." But Wecht, former president of the American Academy of Forensic Science who would be the only member of the House Assassinations Committee's nine-member medical panel to support a second gunman, noted that without the single-bullet theory, there would have to be another gunman:

> The major disagreement is the single-bullet theory, which I deem to be the very essence of the Warren Commission report's conclusions and all the other corroborating panels and groups since that time. It is the sine qua non of the Warren Commission report's conclusions vis-a-vis a sole assassin. Without the single-bullet theory, there cannot be one assassin, whether it is Oswald or anybody else.
>
> I believe that the president was struck definitely twice, one bullet entering in the back, and one bullet entering in the back of the head. I believe that Gov. John Connally was struck by a bullet, and I believe that another bullet completely missed the car. I think that there were four shots, most probably, fired. [87]

Wecht said that the angles at which JFK and Connally were hit do not permit a straight-line trajectory, which was needed for the magic-bullet theory to have validity. "In order to accept the [magic-bullet theory], it is necessary to have the bullet move at different vertical and horizontal angles, a path of flight that has never been experienced or suggested for any bullet known to mankind," he wrote. [88]

But Oswald did have a "straight-line" shot, claimed former Sen. Specter, who was credited with advancing the magic-bullet theory with the commission. "You can really only appreciate [it] to the fullest when you're right there, look out of that window, and see it as we saw it on the reconstruction," Specter said. "[The fatal shot to Kennedy's head] ended up at about 275 feet, I think… That is reasonably close with a four-power scope, and it is not a very difficult shot for a guy with Oswald's background – so said the Marine experts who know this whole line." [89]

Fonzi said Specter was almost searching for answers as they talked, which he found peculiar. Fonzi would later write, "After those interviews with Arlen Specter, my belief in that government would never be the same." [90]

At one point, Specter said, "If you postulate a second gunman, which I think there's no evidence at all to support, you still get a guy above to the rear. You get a guy from Oswald's position [on the sixth floor of the depository building]. You know, it could have been from the fifth floor. It could have been from the seventh floor. But you get that general position." [91]

Wecht raised questions about another shot fired from the right side or lower right rear that could have struck Kennedy at the same time a shot pierced him in the back of the head:

> There is a small piece of some material that is present at the base of the external scalp, just above the hairline, which has never been commented on before except by me following the 1972 investigation of the material at the Archives, and later commented upon by this forensic pathology panel. There is a total deformation of the right side of the cranial vault with extensive fractures of the calvarium, the top portion of the skull, and extensive scalp lacerations and loss of soft tissue, so that we cannot exactly know where the exit wound was.
>
> It is, therefore, possible that that extensive deformity of the scalp, underlying galea, underlying bone calvarium, could also be the locus of the second shot of some kind of frangible ammunition which would not have penetrated deeply or at all through the calvarium. I want to emphasize that this is remote, but I have pointed this out because it is a possibility. [92]

James Sibert, a former FBI agent who took notes in the Bethesda autopsy room for the federal agency, told author William Law that he wondered if a shooter used an exploding bullet. "He thought the back wound was too low to be part of the single-bullet theory," said Law. [93]

Garrison also thought some gunman could have used frangible bullets, which explode on impact into tiny fragments. "This type of bullet was issued by the CIA for use in anti-Castro exile raids on Cuba," he said. [94]

On the other side, author Gerald Posner cited ensuing "ballistics and computer studies" that confirmed the magic bullet theory. He also wrote that two of Oswald's fingerprints were later discovered on the trigger guard of his rifle, and that rifle was "ballistically proven" to be the origin of the fatal shots. DiEugenio and others said that was false, and that no one saw Oswald on the sixth floor shooting at Kennedy. [95]

Neck wound: Entrance or exit?

Another point of debate in the Warren Report concerned whether a hole in the front of Kennedy's neck was an entrance or exit wound. The Warren Commission called it an exit wound.

"All of the surgeons in Parkland's Trauma Room No. 1 and numerous others believed President Kennedy was shot at least once from the front," wrote Charles Crenshaw, one of the physicians who tried to save Kennedy's life. "Testifying under oath, nine physicians who viewed the president's head wound at Parkland reported seeing a large defect in the back of the president's head, indicative of an exit wound caused by a shot from the front." [96]

Crenshaw said he saw four gunshot wounds in Kennedy and thought the neck wound was also caused by a shot from the front. [97]

Paul Peters, another physician who attended to JFK at Parkland, testified before the Warren Commission that the neck wound was a "wound of entry" and there was a "large defect" with brain and bone loss towards the back of his head. [98]

Secret Service agent Elmer Moore would admit he intimidated Malcolm Perry, the Parkland physician who performed the tracheostomy on JFK, into changing his testimony about the neck wound. Shortly after the surgery, Perry described the throat wound at a news conference as an "entrance wound." [99]

But before the Warren Commission, Perry testified that he "was unable to determine" whether it was an entrance or exit wound, and it "could have been either." When pressed by Specter, Perry said it was an exit wound. Moore would claim he was given "marching orders from Washington" to intimidate Perry. [100]

Former New York City chief medical examiner Michael Baden, who headed the House Assassinations Committee medical panel, said that emergency room personnel were not "trained in distinguishing some of the fine points of differences between entrance and exit gunshot wounds because this does not have much pertinence to treatment and therapy." Committee panel members unanimously agreed the neck wound was an exit perforation, Baden said. [101]

Lt. Commander William Pitzer, who headed the audio-visual department at the Bethesda Naval Medical School, took photos and a 16-millimeter film of the autopsy. He thought JFK was shot from the front based on a small hole on the right temple that looked like an entry wound and a large hole in the back of JFK's head that appeared to be an exit wound. [102]

Pitzer would be found shot to death in 1966 in his office. His death would be ruled a suicide, which family members and friends would dispute. FBI tests would conclude the gun that fired upon Pitzer was from a distance of more than three feet. Moreover, paraffin tests on Pitzer were negative. His autopsy film would vanish and never be found. [103]

Marina remarries

In June 1965, Marina married Kenneth Porter, an electrician who worked for Collins Radio Co., which did work for the CIA. They were introduced by a friend, with Porter riding a horse to meet Marina, who had reportedly received hundreds of marriage proposals through the mail. [104]

Collins Radio founder Arthur Collins was also a friend of Byrd, the oilman who owned the TSBD building. Another Collins executive knew de Mohrenschildt, while Mather, whose car was spotted near Tippit's murder site with someone who looked like Oswald in it, also worked for Collins.

The business supplied military aircraft and ships with sophisticated, top-secret electronic gear. In March 1963, the company won a contract from the CIA-affiliated U.S. Information Agency worth more than $2 million to build short-wave transmitters to be used in Southeast Asia. Assistant Secretary of the Navy Kenneth BeLieu was charged a few months later with giving false data about the Collins contract to a Congressional subcommittee. [105]

Shortly before marrying Marina, Porter had quit Collins Radio suddenly. Fellow employees said he did not have any work-related problems and did not know why he quit. Porter divorced his previous wife and left his kids, despite friends not hearing about any domestic problems. [106]

His union with Marina featured problems from the start. Just three months into the marriage, Marina sought a peace bond against her new husband for allegedly threatening her with a gun. Porter told the judge he returned home from work and found their daughters alone and Marina away at a neighbor's party. The judge declined to issue a bond but admonished them for their actions.

Marina and Porter bought a house from Skotnicki and lived across the street from Grizzaffi. The Porters had a son, Mark, in 1966. [107]

Kenneth Porter would file for divorce in 1974 and win custody of their son, the farmhouse, and land. Marina would maintain custody of her two daughters. Despite there not being records of a remarriage, the Porters would resume living together by 1977, according to neighbors. [108]

In 1974, Marina worked as a night manager of a 7-Eleven convenience store in Dallas and later was employed by a Titche's Department Store in a suburban mall. During a conversation, Pulte commented that it must have been difficult to leave the Soviet Union. "Not the way I did it," she replied. [109]

Oswald's body exhumed

Marina continued to maintain friendships with right-wing Russian emigres. Ilya Mamantov, a native of Latvia who moved to Dallas in 1952 after finding work with an oil exploration company, befriended Marina after serving as a translator for Dallas police when they questioned her in late 1963. By that time, Mamantov lectured about the "Red menace," and some said he had helped guide Marina into making statements against her husband.

Mamantov sometimes hand-carried letters from Marina to the Soviet Union, but he stopped doing that without telling her why by 1976. Mamantov would refuse to discuss Marina with Pulte. [110]

Another interesting friendship Marina had was with Michael Eddowes. The British author suspected that Oswald's body had been removed from its grave, or even that a Russian spy was buried there. Eddowes convinced Marina to go along with his exhumation plans, which Robert Oswald opposed.

She won the case, and the body at Rose Hill Cemetery in Fort Worth would be exhumed in 1981. Officials would confirm through dental records that it was Oswald. A couple years later, the alternative rock band Butthole Surfers, led by Lake Highlands High alum Gibby Haynes, would release an album that featured a song entitled, "The Shah Sleeps in Lee Harvey's Grave." The album would rise as high as 21st on one best-selling list. [111]

Marina would say in 1981 that "some people in powerful places made a mistake, and they wanted to cover it up." Then in 1988, Marina would tell Ladies' Home Journal that her late husband was a U.S. government agent "caught between two powers: the government and organized crime," and that Ruby killed him to "keep his mouth shut." Lee could have still been part of the "very complicated" and "brilliantly executed" plot, but he was "not necessarily guilty of murder," she said. She would become a U.S. citizen in 1989. [112]

By 2013, Oswald's two daughters would manage to forge their own lives. June worked in business and had two sons, while Rachel earned a medical degree and reportedly worked as a nurse. Marina would still live in the Dallas area in 2013 with Porter, according to news reports. [113]

In later years, Lee Oswald's grave would be decorated with flowers at times, rather than dug up or urinated on, by people who believed he tried to save Kennedy's life in 1963.

Paines reunite, then divorce

Soon after Kennedy's killing, Michael Paine returned to his Irving home. The Paines continued to have problems and divorced in 1970.

Ruth moved with her children to Philadelphia in 1971, becoming principal of a Quaker school. She later moved to Florida and then California, working at one point as a school psychologist. As of 2022, she had not seen Marina since 1964.

Some continued to report unusual activity by Ruth. When she volunteered with a Quaker peace group called ProNica in the early 1990s, some fellow volunteers suspected Paine was doing intelligence-gathering work. Researcher Steve Jones wrote:

> Ruth would take copious notes of everything she saw or heard; she asked people many inappropriate personal questions as if she were trying to gather information; and she took photographs of people for supposed purposes that were later proven to be false. She was confronted about this but consistently and vehemently denied that she had anything to do with the CIA or any other governmental intelligence agency. [114]

Ruth was asked to take a leave of absence from ProNica. When she was taken to a camp in nearby Costa Rica, she was asked to leave there, too, because some suspected that she was an agent. She would later settle in Santa Rosa, Calif., near her son and former husband.

Michael Paine would move to Concord, Mass., working as an aeronautical engineer and continuing to support the ACLU and environmental causes. In 2004, he would move to Sebastopol, Calif., passing away in 2018 at the age of 89. [115]

In 2009, the city of Irving would purchase the Paines' old house and recreate it as a museum, with furnishings resembling 1963. It would still be open in 2022, charging $7 admission. The rooming house where Oswald stayed in Oak Cliff would also become a recreated museum, owned by Patricia Hall, granddaughter of Oswald's former landlord, Gladys Johnson.

FBI investigation coordinator maintains stance

Robert P. Gemberling, an FBI agent and CPA who coordinated the Dallas bureau's investigation into the JFK assassination that was sent to the Warren

Commission, would remain vehement that Oswald was the lone assassin until the day he died in 2004. "I've stopped reading all the conspiracy books because there's too many to keep up with," Gemberling said in 1988. [116]

Oswald was a "confused individual who was prone to violence and had a psychological passion for notoriety," said Gemberling, who retired from the FBI in 1976. "The only reason people listen to those who make money writing about conspiracy theories is that they don't believe a man like Oswald could have pulled off such a heinous crime by himself." [117]

Ordered to the Dallas Police Department immediately after the shooting, Gemberling was there until late that evening. He then spent much of that Friday night and Saturday interviewing witnesses. After Ruby shot Oswald, he was given the responsibility of supervising the work of some two dozen agents and shoe-horning what they discovered into a report for D.C. headquarters. Hoover appreciated his work enough that he promoted him a few months later.

The KGB considered Oswald to be of "questionable character," and Gemberling discounted witnesses who claimed to see Oswald with Ruby before the killing. He noted evidence like Oswald's right palm print on the underside of the barrel of the rifle that he said Oswald brought to the building that day. Some believed that print was planted, or that it was normal for the rifle's owner to have his print on it.

To Gemberling, who was a consultant to NBC News and appeared on the *Today Show* in the late 1970s, no one had "come up with any credible, solid evidence that proves beyond a shadow of a doubt that Oswald was part of a conspiracy." As for those who respond that the FBI never proved "beyond a shadow of a doubt" that Oswald did it alone, he stated, "To expect any investigative body to prove, beyond a reasonable doubt, that there was no conspiracy is impossible. You can't prove a negative." [118]

Gemberling testified in executive session before the House Assassinations Committee in 1977, but that panel declined his requests for a copy of his testimony transcript. He was told his testimony "was to remain confidential for 50 years," he said, adding that he thought the committee did that because he did not support the "probable conspiracy" conclusion. The committee ignored experts who disagreed that four shots were fired, he charged.

Gemberling supported Dallas County's work in preserving the depository building and establishing The Sixth Floor Museum. While I didn't know in 1988 when I last interviewed him about the plots in Chicago and other cities, he believed he was doing the best job possible under the circumstances. Hoover might have given the institution a black eye with his paranoia and overzealous pursuit of alleged communists – he even thought MLK was a communist. But the large majority of FBI agents and employees tried hard to perform their duties with honor and integrity under the parameters and pressures of the job, Gemberling and other former FBI agents said.

The FBI was not given the full picture of Oswald's CIA involvement, and if it wasn't for the FBI reports still available in commission exhibits and other places, researchers would not know much of what they do, Garrison noted.

"While the CIA has behaved like a cross between the Gestapo and the [Soviet] NKVD, the FBI has worked assiduously in many different areas and gathered facts that have proved of great value to those interested in uncovering the truth about the assassination," Garrison wrote in 1967. "It isn't the FBI's fault that dozens of its reports have been classified top secret in the archives by order of certain officials in the Department of Justice." [119]

James Shay Jr., who worked for the FBI for 25 years, starting as a clerk and later becoming an agent, once told me, "The CIA is a whole different agency." Even someone as formidable as J. Edgar Hoover said, "People think I'm so powerful, but when it comes to the CIA, there's nothing I can do." [120]

That may be the only matter on which Hoover and Garrison agreed.

Fritz's notes found

For more than 30 years, Gemberling and others said there were no notes or tapes of the roughly 12 hours of interrogation of Oswald. Gemberling told me in 1988 that was merely "the way [Dallas Police Capt. Will] Fritz worked." But Marrs and others said Fritz often took notes on other cases, and others took notes during Oswald's interrogation. [121]

Fritz's rental storage unit burned after he died of cancer in 1984, according to a relative. "They have things well organized," the relative said. She said Fritz never discussed the case with family members. "He never knew when there might be a plant," she said. [122]

In 1997, an anonymous donor gave some handwritten notes that officials said were made by Fritz during that interrogation to the Assassination Records Review Board, researcher Larry Haapanen reported. The notes included a reference to Oswald admitting that he left a letter for FBI agent Hosty around November 12, which was not in police and FBI reports. [123]

Sixth-floor window controversy

Almost no moves in this case were made without controversy. That included moving the sixth-floor window of the former Texas School Book Depository building from which Oswald allegedly fired.

In January 1964, Byrd, the building's owner who was believed to have intelligence ties, had the "Oswald window" removed. He reportedly kept it as a souvenir, bizarrely hanging the framed window in his Dallas-area mansion like a trophy piece until the mid-1980s. His son, Caruth Byrd, kept it locked in a vault before loaning the piece to the Sixth Floor Museum in the mid-1990s.

But Aubrey Mayhew, a Nashville, Tenn., music producer and memorabilia collector, disputed that was the real window. In 1970, he purchased the building in an auction and said he found out that the worker who removed the window in 1964 took the wrong one. Mayhew said he had the right window removed and put it in storage. [124]

After local officials blocked Mayhew's plan to turn the TSBD into a museum, he defaulted in 1973. Mayhew claimed he was framed, a stance that fit in well with anything remotely tied to the JFK assassination.

Byrd repurchased the structure again and sold it to the county several years later. Mayhew, who died in 2009, claimed the county stole his idea that it blocked, opening the Sixth Floor Museum in 1989. The parties would continue arguing in court about whose window was the actual "sniper's perch" one. [125]

Another committee deceives public

The House Assassinations Committee concluded in 1979 that there was "probably" a conspiracy linked to organized crime. But there could have been so much more to that investigation, said staff investigator Fonzi.

The committee spent its first few months lobbying for funding, eventually spending about $6 million. Richard Sprague, its first chief counsel, was forced to resign after he insisted that agencies such as the CIA and FBI be included as targets, Fonzi said.

New counsel G. Robert Blakey's top priority was "to get a report done within what was left of the committee's limited time and budget," Fonzi wrote. "What we did was to again deceive the American people and add enriching manure to the ever blooming distrust in government planted by the Warren Commission Report." [126]

Lane, the most prominent early Warren Report critic, wrote that Blakey, who served on RFK's organized-crime task force, "had not subpoenaed even a single document from the FBI, CIA, or any other intelligence organization." Lane said the House Assassinations Committee "cleared the FBI and the CIA, while conceding that there had been a conspiracy to murder the president." [127]

The committee fingered Marcello, Trafficante, and Hoffa, who it said "had the motive, means, and opportunity" to assassinate Kennedy. But the panel, chaired by Democratic Representatives Thomas N. Downing of Virginia, Henry B. Gonzalez of Texas, and Louis Stokes of Ohio, could not obtain "direct evidence" against the crime bosses and union leader.

The committee was less sure about the involvement of Hoffa, noting that he "hated the president and his brother." But he "was not a confirmed murderer, as were various organized crime leaders whose involvement the committee considered, and he cannot be placed in that category with them," the panel concluded. [128]

Marcello, as head of the nation's oldest Mafia family, was given special privileges that included "conducting syndicate operations without having to seek the approval of the national commission," the committee noted. [129]

The committee's conspiracy conclusion was based, in part, on a recording picked up by a motorcycle policeman who had his microphone on in Dealey Plaza that fateful day. Committee scientists identified four gunshots, three from the school book depository and one from the grassy knoll.

But in 1982, a committee organized by the National Academy of Sciences did its own investigation and discounted the fourth shot. Blakey would say in 2003 that another analysis of the acoustics put the probability of random noise at less than one percent. "It's a 99 percent chance that....the sound from the grassy knoll is not random noise," he said. [130]

Blakey did note that the CIA withheld key information from the Warren Commission, such as the CIA-Mafia plots to kill Castro. "The Warren Commission's conclusion that the agencies of the government cooperated with it is, in retrospect, not the truth," he would say. [131]

The House Assassinations Committee's report might have been more truthful than the Warren Report, but the committee still falsified known facts about Oswald and Ruby that "raised the possibility that official forces" were part of JFK's assassination, Scott wrote. The House committee was under intense time pressure itself to produce a report and was unable to force the FBI and CIA to fully cooperate, he said. Even the finding of a probable conspiracy "aroused feverish and derisive dismissals" from the Washington Post, New York Times, and other "guardians of sane non-conspiratorial thinking," Scott wrote. [132]

Certain CIA figures continued to deceive in the 1970s, according to House Assassination Committee researchers, who complained of obstruction by George Joannides, the CIA's liaison to that panel. Blakey said he wrote off the complaints in the 1970s, but he later learned he was wrong.

"I no longer believe that we were able to conduct an appropriate investigation of the agency and its relationship to Oswald," he would say. [133]

Author Robert Groden, sitting at far right, holds court at the grassy knoll on a hot August day in 2016. [Shay photo]

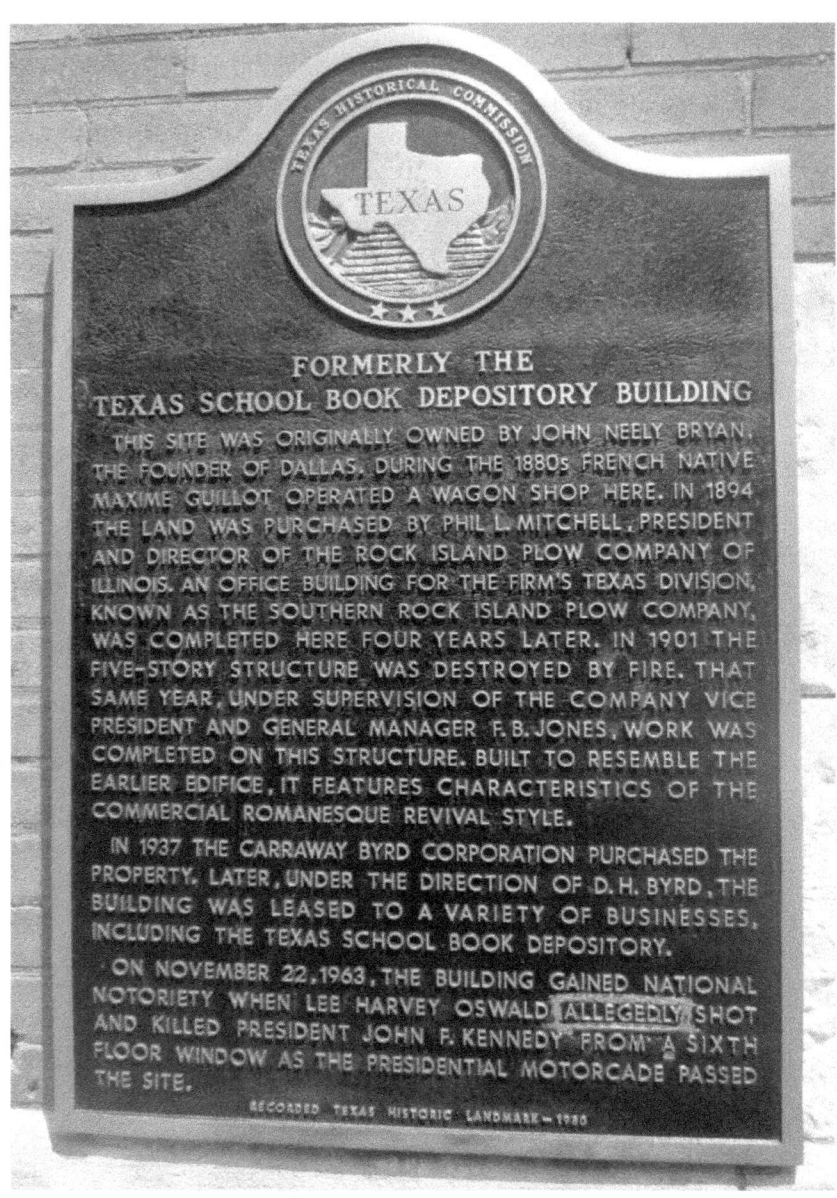

In 1980, the Texas Historical Commission dedicated the former Texas School Book Depository building as a historic landmark. In the plaque, the group noted Oswald "allegedly" shot Kennedy. Someone carved a box around the word. [Shay photo]

Chapter Ten

Ghosts of Dealey Plaza

This is what is going to happen to me, also. I keep telling you, this is a sick society.
– MARTIN LUTHER KING JR., November 22, 1963

Less than a week after JFK's assassination, the body of struggling 22-year-old actress Karyn Kupcinet was found in her Los Angeles apartment. The daughter of longtime Chicago Sun-Times columnist Irv Kupcinet, Karyn had been trying to place a call shortly before Kennedy's death. A telephone operator said that, in an apparent moment of telepathic prognostication or insider's knowledge, she stated that the president was going to be killed. [1]

Kupcinet's apartment "was all torn up," said a detective. "There must've been a tremendous struggle." Some wondered if she was killed to send a message to her journalist father, who knew Ruby from his younger days. [2]

Thus began a string of deaths – some with more ties to the Kennedy assassination than others. Some called the deaths coincidental, others called them conspiratorial. Penn Jones Jr., the crusading editor and publisher of the Midlothian Mirror, put the strange death total at more than 100 in 1983. "I am certain I know of only a fraction," Jones wrote. [3]

Somehow, Jones escaped death himself in the assassination aftermath despite his persistent reporting that cracked holes in the government's lone-assassin theory. A few people tried to kill or severely injure him. His office was firebombed, among other attempts on his life. That could have been mostly due to his risky stances against the KKK and John Birch Society. But he believed some powerful people wanted the Kennedy assassination swept under the rug.

"They tried to scare me with phone threats, tried to run me off the road," said Jones, a World War II veteran who won the Elijah Parish Lovejoy Award for courageous journalism in 1963. He would live until 1998, passing away of natural causes at age 83. "But I had to do what I had to do." [4]

What's My Line? star, men at Ruby apartment meeting die by 1965

A few hours after Ruby shot Oswald, five people met in the club owner's apartment. No one said what Ruby lawyer Tom Howard, roommate George Senator, and associate Jim Martin discussed with journalists Jim Koethe and William Hunter. Or what they found in Ruby's apartment. But most assumed they didn't meet there to play poker.

Hunter, a Texas native and award-winning crime reporter for the Long Beach Press-Telegram, was shot by a Long Beach police officer in April 1964 in the police station media room. An off-duty officer claimed to be playing a game of "quick draw" with Hunter when his pistol discharged. [5]

Five months later, Koethe, a reporter for the Dallas Times Herald, was killed by a karate chop to the throat executed by an assailant, apparently as he climbed out of a shower in his apartment. Among items taken from his residence were notes that Koethe might have been using to write a book. A week later, ex-con Larry Reno was arrested as he tried to sell some of Koethe's possessions, but a grand jury refused to indict Reno. [6]

Six months later, Howard died of a heart attack not long after cutting ties with Ruby. He was 48 and had no prior history of heart problems.

Then, *What's My Line?* star Kilgallen, who interviewed Ruby after he killed Oswald and stated that she was "going to break this case wide open," perished at age 52 in November 1965 in her New York townhouse. The cause was officially listed as a drug overdose and heart attack. Her hairdresser found her sitting up in a bed she hadn't slept in for several years with a book, as if she had been reading. But she had already read that book, he said. Her reading glasses weren't in the room. Shortly after she died, witnesses observed men taking files from her home before police arrived. All of her files on the JFK assassination would disappear.

Attorney and author Mark Shaw, who wrote a book examining whether Kilgallen was murdered over what she knew about the Kennedy case, said that she was poisoned by a man who was likely spying on her for the Mafia or FBI. Shaw called Kilgallen "the first true female media icon, a woman who stood tall while competing in a man's world." [7]

Though some called Kilgallen a "gossip columnist," she had a nose for serious news. She was the first journalist to report that the CIA and Mafia were working together to kill Castro in 1959, which caused the FBI and CIA to monitor her. In a February 1964 column, Kilgallen detailed a private interview with Ruby, in which he talked about wanting to do some good by bringing "people to God." In other columns, she wrote about how Police Chief Curry had originally thought shots were fired from behind the triple underpass, how witnesses had been intimidated, how the Tippit shooting was questionable, how a strip-joint owner like Ruby could stroll into Dallas police headquarters "as if it was at a health club," and whether Oswald and Ruby previously met. Kilgallen had also questioned aspects of Marilyn Monroe's 1962 death, such as why her bedroom door was locked when she didn't usually lock it and why the light was on when she was trying to sleep.

Shaw wrote that her enemies included Sinatra, government officials, and "those in the underworld." He concluded that she believed Kennedy was killed as part of a "mob operation based on revenge," and that Joseph Kennedy shouldered much responsibility for "ordering" JFK to name his brother attorney general "when he had to know RFK would target the underworld figures." [8]

In 1977, Lou Staples, a radio broadcaster who had done shows regularly on the Kennedy assassination for several years and also told friends he would break open the case, was shot in an Oklahoma wheat field. His death was ruled a suicide, but the bullet entered behind his right temple and Staples was left-handed. Staples' increasing interest in Kilgallen's case might have gotten him in trouble, some said. [9]

Mob-related deaths

Numerous strange deaths were tied to the mob. The bullet-riddled body of Mafia-connected motel owner Jack Zangretti was found floating in Lake Lugert near Altus, Okla., two weeks after JFK's assassination. He had told some friends on November 23 that "three other men – not Oswald – killed the president." He also had said, "Ruby will kill Oswald tomorrow, and in a few days, a member of the Frank Sinatra family will be kidnapped just to take some of the attention away from the assassination." [10]

Sure enough, Ruby did shoot Oswald the following day. And Frank Sinatra Jr. was kidnapped on December 8 and released two days after the singer paid a ransom. Three men were convicted but served only short sentences.

Several employees of Ruby's Carousel Club met untimely demises. Rose Cherami, who told authorities that two men she rode with from Florida to Dallas were going there to kill Kennedy after she was thrown from the car, died herself in 1965 when a car ran over her. The driver claimed she was lying in a West Texas road and he could not avoid crushing her skull.

Marilyn "Delilah" Walle, a regular exotic dancer at the Carousel Club, was shot to death in 1966 by her husband, Leonard Walle, after just one month of marriage. She said she saw Oswald speaking with Ruby in the club in 1963 and reportedly planned to write a book. Also in 1966, former Carousel dancer Karen Carlin was shot to death.

Other Carousel employees skipped town. Kathy Kay, who reportedly told co-workers that she even danced with Oswald or someone who resembled him a few days prior to JFK's death, left the day Ruby shot Oswald. She was not heard from again for about a decade. [11]

Hank Killam, a painter, knew Ruby since his wife, Wanda, was a dancer in the Carousel Club. He also worked with John Carter, who lived in the same rooming house as Oswald in November 1963. After the assassination, he said he was "hounded" by federal agents and moved to Tampa, Fla, and then Pensacola, Fla., to try to get away. But in March 1964, he was found dead near a broken department store window, his jugular vein cut.

Police ruled Killam's death a suicide, but the county coroner said he had never heard of a person committing suicide by jumping through a department store window. Family members and his minister said he had special knowledge of the assassination, possibly how Oswald and Ruby knew each other, and had feared for his life. [12]

'They told him not to talk'

Earlene Roberts, the housekeeper of the rooming house where Oswald lived, complained about police harassment after her Warren Commission testimony that she saw Oswald in the house about the same time the panel claimed he shot Officer Tippit. Roberts died in 1966, officially due to a heart attack.

William Whaley, the cab driver who picked up Oswald at a bus station and drove him to his Oak Cliff room on November 22, was killed in a head-on collision in 1965. When Jones went to interview the manager of the cab company about Whaley's death, the man pushed him. "If you're smart, you won't be coming around here asking questions," the manager told Jones. [13]

Edward Benavides, a brother of Tippit murder witness Domingo Benavides, was shot in the back of the head in a club in 1965. Domingo was convinced his brother was mistaken for him. Benavides told authorities the Tippit shooter looked like Oswald but his hairline was different from photos. Police told him not to talk.

Lee Bowers Jr., the railroad supervisor who saw cars cruising through the lot near the grassy knoll shortly before the assassination, died in 1966 when his new company car veered from the road and crashed into a bridge abutment. His wife told Jones, "They told him not to talk." [14]

CIA agent talks, dies

CIA contract agent Gary Underhill died in May 1964, soon after he told some friends that Kennedy was killed by a small group within the CIA. His death was ruled a suicide. The right-handed Underhill was shot behind the left ear.

The Pentagon considered Underhill "one of the country's top authorities on limited warfare," Garrison said. "He was not the type of man to make wild or unsubstantiated charges. He was on good personal terms with the top brass in the Defense Department and the ranking officials in the CIA." [15]

Five months later, Mary Pinchot Meyer, the former wife of CIA agent Cord Meyer, was shot to death while walking in the D.C. wealthy enclave of Georgetown. She reportedly had an affair with JFK a few years after her 1958 divorce, which allegedly involved experimenting with drugs that included marijuana. Her killer was never caught, and CIA official Angleton, a family friend, reportedly retrieved her diary and burned it. [16]

Casualties surrounding Garrison investigation

As Garrison started his inquiry into the New Orleans side of the alleged assassination plots in late 1966, some potential witnesses and targets turned up dead or were intimidated into not talking.

A key target, Ferrie, had dropped out of anti-Castro exile activities shortly after the Kennedy assassination, left the pay of the CIA, and took more tranquilizers and barbiturates. "In his last months, he was a tortured man," Garrison said. [17]

After the New Orleans States-Item broke the Garrison investigation story in February 1967 and named Ferrie as a target, the pilot became hounded by reporters who staked out his apartment. Perhaps others were watching him, as well. He told Louis Ivon, an investigator for the DA's office, "I'm a dead man, now." The DA paid for a hotel room for him, but it wasn't long before Ivon received a call from someone saying Ferrie had died.

His death was ruled due to an aneurysm and "natural" causes, but Garrison suspected something more sinister. At Ferrie's apartment, Garrison and his team found two typed suicide notes and several medicine bottles on a table near the sofa where his body was found. One empty bottle was for Proloid, which was often prescribed for low metabolism. But Garrison noted that Ferrie had hypertension, not low metabolism.

An LSU pathologist told Garrison that someone suffering from hypertension could die due to an aneurysm if he or she took a lot of Proloid. The coroner had not checked for drugs in Ferrie's bloodstream and did not take any blood samples. Garrison faced more questions. [18]

Another Ferrie associate, Eladio del Valle, an ex-Batista official who identified men in photos for Garrison, died on the same day as Ferrie in Miami. His skull was split open by an axe, and he was shot through the heart. The anti-Castro Del Valle reportedly paid Ferrie as much as $1,500 for each airborne mission against Castro's military installations. [19]

Then there were those who died well before Garrison's investigation, but they knew Ferrie, Shaw, or Oswald. Banister and partner Hugh Ward died in 1964 before the Warren Commission could question them. Banister's death was ruled a heart attack, but some witnesses said he had a bullet hole in his back. Ward was killed in a plane crash in Mexico. Cancer researcher Sherman, who had worked with Ferrie, died in another weird incident in July 1964. [20]

Dallas Deputy Sheriff Craig was shot in 1975, with his death ruled a suicide. In 1967, Craig was dismissed from the sheriff's department, despite having a good record that included being named "Officer of the Year" in 1960. Decker suspected he was feeding Garrison information, which Craig said he wasn't doing at the time. However, Craig later testified in the Garrison case. He said he had several attempts on his life, including his car being firebombed in 1970. [21]

Campaign against Garrison continues

While Garrison himself didn't become a casualty in the only trial that charged someone with JFK's murder, there were reported plots against him. Ferrie and Shaw tried to hire criminal Edward Whalen in early 1967 to kill Garrison, according to Whalen. When Whalen learned that a district attorney was the target, he said he backed out. [22]

Garrison's enemies found other ways to retaliate. Less than two months after reports exposed Garrison's investigation in early 1967, CIA Director

Helms formed a program to discredit Warren Commission critics. Counterintelligence chief Angleton developed a group that surveyed Garrison for some two years and likely engaged in dirty tricks and leaks to journalists. Garrison "actually underestimated the extent of the [CIA's] interest in accused assassin Lee Harvey Oswald," Morley wrote. Angleton's staff had monitored Oswald since his 1959 defection to the Soviet Union, and an Angleton aide said some CIA officials had "keen interest" in Oswald in late 1963, Morley reported. [23]

Garrison believed that at least one CIA asset infiltrated his team in 1967 and stole files. William Wood claimed to be a former CIA case officer who worked as a journalist in Austin. Garrison also accused Wood of trying to set him up in a sex-crime sting at a Los Angeles airport. When attorney and Warren Report critic Vincent Salandria voiced suspicions about Wood, the latter man returned to Texas before Garrison could confront him. Wood claimed he quit because Garrison was "addicted to drugs." [24]

In addition, Garrison was visited by oilman John J. King, who offered to help get Garrison a federal judge position if he dropped his case, according to the DA. Garrison sent him packing. King had tried to buy Oswald's rifle and pistol from Marina and could have been a friend of Ruby's. [25]

The media attacks on Garrison included those authored by journalists with government ties. Aynesworth not only wrote unflattering articles about Garrison's efforts for Newsweek, but he became an informant for the CIA, FBI, and Shaw's defense team, according to government documents and media reports. Shaw attorney Irvin Dymond told Texas Monthly that Aynesworth's help was "crucial." [26]

In April 1967, Aynesworth visited the Houston FBI office and told an agent about his interview with Garrison, according to an FBI memo. Aynesworth stated his "personal opinion that Garrison's investigation and sensational charges alleging a conspiracy in connection with the assassination of President Kennedy are a complete farce." He added that Garrison's case was "disintegrating" and Garrison was "losing his sanity." Aynesworth also said some witnesses who turned against Garrison were in "danger of being harmed and possibly killed" if authorities did not intervene. [27]

About eight months later, Aynesworth informed George Brown of construction company Brown & Root, which had CIA ties, that Garrison might try to implicate Brown in his investigation, according to a CIA memo. Aynesworth reportedly offered to get Brown documents from a former assistant district attorney who worked for Garrison. [28]

Aynesworth, who was a finalist for the Pulitzer Prize several times and did some excellent work on other topics such as Henry Lee Lucas, admitted to

Texas Monthly in 1976 that he "took [the Garrison investigation] all way too personally. I'm still not sure if I went too far on the Shaw thing. But if I hadn't come along and helped him, they would have had nobody. I wasn't being a newsman, I guess." [29]

At least Aynesworth expressed some regret about the lines he crossed, though he was wrong about Shaw having no one else on his side. NBC special correspondent Walter Sheridan, who worked for Naval intelligence in World War II and led RFK's team that prosecuted Hoffa, didn't regret his aid to Shaw's side under the guise of journalism.

Sheridan claimed to be in New Orleans to investigate the Kennedy case but in reality was spying on Garrison for RFK, who feared Garrison might implicate the Kennedys for the CIA-Mafia plots against Castro, according to several authors. Key Garrison witness Perry Russo claimed Sheridan offered to bribe him if he recanted his grand jury testimony about the 1963 meeting in which Ferrie, Shaw, and Oswald allegedly discussed killing JFK. [30]

Sheridan's June 1967 segment included the claim of convict Miguel Torres that Garrison's office offered Torres drugs and a Florida vacation if he would say he knew Shaw used the fake Bertrand name. Others accused Garrison of offering bribes, while another tried to discredit a witness who claimed he observed Shaw give Oswald money a few months before the JFK assassination. But when a grand jury asked Torres and others to repeat their charges, they invoked the Fifth Amendment. [31]

In 1968, before Garrison appeared on Johnny Carson's show, Sheridan flew to the talk show host's studios in New York and briefed him. Carson had typed questions to fire at Garrison, mostly provided by Sheridan. Many of them accused Garrison of not supporting his contention that elements of the CIA were behind the JFK killing with "facts." Garrison held his own and even got Carson to show a photo of some detained men being led away by uniformed officers. [32]

Life magazine ran some more hit pieces against Garrison in September 1967 by Hoover ally Sandy Smith, who author Joan Mellen claimed worked for the FBI. The stories alleged that Garrison was "friendly with some Marcello henchmen" and took trips to Las Vegas on the mob's dime. [33]

Justice Warren piled on suring a 1967 speech in Japan, where he claimed that Garrison had not presented "one fact" to refute the Warren Commission's conclusions. Officials in Ohio and Nebraska blocked Garrison's attempts to extradite witnesses. The U.S. Attorney's office in D.C. refused to serve Allen Dulles with a subpoena that Garrison sent. Ronald Reagan refused Garrison's extradition requests for corporate records of Ochsner's Information Council of the Americas in California. [34]

Ochsner himself tried to undermine Garrison by sending a newspaper publisher friend World War II military records that included Garrison being temporarily grounded for battle fatigue and seeing a counselor. Using his anti-communist friends in Congress, Ochsner also attacked Mark Lane, who helped Garrison's case. [35]

Garrison blamed losing the case mostly on a witness being shown to be overly paranoid to the point of fingerprinting his daughter and the judge not allowing key evidence like Shaw telling the officer who booked him that he used the "Bertrand" alias. Lone-assassin theorists and most major media outlets trumpeted the 1969 verdict as a confirmation of the Warren Report's conclusions. But Garrison noted that most jurors questioned afterwards said they believed there was a conspiracy to kill JFK; they just didn't think Garrison had made Shaw's motivation clear and proved conclusively that Shaw participated in a plot.

"The New Orleans jury had heard evidence concerning only one small corner of what necessarily was a large enterprise," Garrison wrote. [36]

Two years after a jury cleared Shaw, a federal prosecutor indicted Garrison for supposedly taking bribes to protect illegal pinball machine operations. A jury found him not guilty in 1973, with evidence showing that the government had doctored tapes. Garrison lost re-election to the district attorney position that year, but he won election as an appeals judge in 1978. After portraying Earl Warren in Stone's *JFK*, Garrison died of cancer in 1992 at the age of 70. [37]

More journalists help CIA

More journalists than just Aynesworth, Sheridan, and Smith were accused of working for the government. Just about every major media outlet, including The New York Times, The Washington Post, CBS, ABC, Reuters, Hearst Newspapers, Scripps-Howard, Newsweek, Miami Herald, and The Saturday Evening Post, had reporters or executives who fed the CIA information, according to Carl Bernstein, the journalist most famous for his Watergate stories.

"Many CIA officials regarded these helpful journalists as operatives," Bernstein wrote. "The journalists tended to see themselves as trusted friends of the agency who performed occasional favors – usually without pay – in the national interest." [38]

The Times even provided about ten CIA employees newspaper credentials in the 1950s and 1960s, he wrote. The CIA operated a formal training program for its agents in the 1950s, providing tips like how to "make noises like reporters," Bernstein said. [39]

In such an environment, most journalists parroted the party line advanced by the CIA and FBI. The Washington Post's Bradlee admitted to Talbot that he didn't pursue an extensive investigation of JFK's death because he was concerned about his career, "that I would be discredited for taking the efforts [of the Post newsroom] down that path." Don Hewitt, the creator of *60 Minutes*, said he didn't believe the lone-gunman theory and his show "tried and tried and tried" to break a major story on the assassination. Some journalists continued to break important stories. [40]

Mark Lane did more than investigate as a lawyer, writing a long piece for the National Guardian in December 1963 that detailed questions about how many shots were fired and Oswald's background. Lane said he tried to sell the story to more mainstream publications such as Life and was rebuked. One editor friend told him, "We have decided not to touch that subject." [41]

Cubans attempt to kill LBJ

While assassination attempts against Castro continued after Kennedy's death, LBJ also faced such threats shortly after his predecessor's murder. The thought of being killed became so real to Johnson that he told Agent Clint Hill that he had been having premonitions that he would be assassinated, too. [42]

The danger was real. Between 1964 and 1966, threats made against the president about doubled from the period between 1962 and 1964. While the Secret Service boosted its ranks, Johnson sometimes ignored their commands not to wade into crowds.

Just two weeks after Kennedy's assassination, Cuban immigrant Omar Padilla was arrested in New York for threatening to kill LBJ when he visited the city for the funeral of former Senator Herbert Lehman, who died December 5. Padilla had reportedly told coworkers at a manufacturing plant that JFK had been "asking for it" and he was "going to shoot LBJ." Authorities found a .22-caliber rifle in 19-year-old Padilla's apartment and a makeshift target range at his work. [43]

That same month, unemployed kitchen worker James Francis Burns told a Veterans administration employee that if he didn't get a dishonorable discharge changed, he would "pull an Oswald" and kill the president. He was soon arrested.

In October 1964, a man claiming to be with a right-wing Minuteman group was arrested in Buffalo, N.Y. A rifle was discovered on the edge of his window on the route of the presidential motorcade.

In 1965 and 1966, about twelve people were found intruding on the White House grounds. Some had weapons. In March 1966, Air Force veteran Oswald Pick, 27, called the FBI and said he planned to kill LBJ. Two Cubans put him up to it, said Pick, who ironically not only shared Oswald's last name but had the surname of Oswald's half-brother, who spelled it "Pic." Pick was tracked down and arrested as he was about to board a Washington, D.C.-bound train. [44]

Johnson was fortunate to survive such attempts, especially considering how he treated many Secret Service agents. He ordered numerous agents to do menial jobs like clean his pool and walk his dog. He sometimes physically pushed them and even knocked an agent off a motorcycle. One agent reportedly slugged LBJ in the eye after LBJ hit him several times with a newspaper. [45]

Secret Service agent framed

Then, there was the unjust treatment of Secret Service agent Bolden under the Johnson administration. Bolden had raised the possibility of a connection between the November 2 Chicago plot and the Dallas assassination to some fellow agents. Most agreed there could be something to that, but Maurice Martineau, the agent in charge of the Chicago office, ordered them to forget about what occurred on November 2. [46]

In January 1964, the Secret Service ordered all agents to turn in their passport-sized identification booklets so they could be replaced. Bolden suspected that was because Secret Service credentials had been used by some possible conspirators in Dallas on November 22. [47]

That May, Bolden was in D.C. for training when he tried to contact a Warren Commission lawyer to tell him what he knew. His call was overheard by a fellow agent apparently assigned to monitor Bolden. The next day, Bolden was ordered back to Chicago on pretenses of participating in an investigation of a counterfeiting ring, but he was arrested by agents when he arrived and accused of trying to sell Secret Service files. [48]

The first trial resulted in a hung jury, despite the presiding judge, Alabama-born Joseph Sam Perry, recommending that the jury issue a conviction. The second resulted in a conviction. Among those to testify against Bolden was a counterfeiter who later admitted to perjury and also said prosecutors instructed him to lie. Mobster Roselli reportedly was involved in framing Bolden. [49]

Perry later presided over the wrongful-death lawsuit filed by relatives of Black Panther Party leaders Fred Hampton and Mark Clark and survivors of the 1969 raid. Hampton and Clark were killed and others wounded, after authorities fired more than 80 shots at them, while Clark got off one shot as he fell, according to reports. Hampton's autopsy showed he had been shot twice in the head at point-blank range while unconscious. Perry "frequently slept" through the trial testimony, according to a Chicago Tribune article. He dismissed the lawsuit against law enforcement officials after the jury could not reach a verdict. But the case was overturned by a federal appeals court, and the families eventually won almost $2 million from the city in a settlement. [50]

After losing appeals, Bolden was sent to federal prison in 1966. He said he was committed to a psychiatric ward in a prison medical center in Missouri and subjected to mind-altering drugs, which he learned to fake swallowing. As he was imprisoned, his family endured more threats, including an attempted house bombing and a shot fired through a window. His wife, Barbara, Mark Lane, and an assistant to Garrison lobbied to stop Bolden's unjust imprisonment. After more than three years in prison, Bolden was finally released and continued to speak out. [51]

Bolden wrote that he was framed for disclosing the Chicago plot, Secret Service security lapses, and racism among agents that included a supervisor saying the "n-word" to his face. The House Assassinations Committee report in 1979 confirmed his charges about security lapses, concluding that the Secret Service was "deficient" in performing its duties and failed to use information that could have better protected Kennedy.

"I have sacrificed too many years of my life to this quest for justice," Bolden wrote in 2008. "Still, I could not have done anything differently. I never could have rolled over and accepted my fate. I could not have accepted punishment gracefully, knowing that my only crime had been to hold my fellow agents to the same standards I set for myself, and which our government and our president expected of us." [52]

Ruby injected with cancer?

Jack Ruby was among those who died quickly of cancer. Under the state's "sudden passion" murder defense in 1964, Ruby could have received as little as five years, Waldron said. But attorney Melvin Belli went with the harder-to-prove insanity defense. A jury sentenced Ruby to death in 1964, but that was overturned on appeal in 1966. [53]

In the county jail, Decker ordered deputies to only give Ruby small blankets so his feet would not be covered and he might catch pneumonia and die, Richard Aubrey charged. [54]

Some believe right-wing leader Edwin Walker had something to do with Ruby's death. When Ruby was transferred to Parkland Hospital for treatment of pneumonia in December 1966, Walker wrote to an associate that he feared Ruby might talk more and vowed to "not allow Ruby to leave the hospital alive," according to Caufield. [55]

In 1964, Ruby had enraged Walker by inferring to the Warren Commission that he might have had something to do with killing JFK. "There is a John Birch Society right now in activity, and Edwin Walker is one of the top men of this organization," Ruby told the Warren Commission. "Take it for what it is worth, Chief Justice Warren. Unfortunately for me....because of the act I committed, [that] has put a lot of people in jeopardy with their lives." [56]

Ruby also told Kilgallen in 1964 that he didn't "want to go back to what I was. I want to be something better." Kilgallen wrote that as she left, she didn't know "what I really believed about the man."

Ruby was diagnosed with lung cancer soon after leaving Parkland. He died in early January 1967. Ruby claimed he was injected with cancer cells, similar to the way Ferrie and others injected mice. He told former Carousel dancer Shari Angel that medical officials were giving him "shots of something to kill me."

"I do find it interesting that Jack Ruby died of cancer a few weeks after his conviction for murder had been overruled in appeals court and he was ordered to stand trial outside of Dallas – thus allowing him to speak freely if he so desired," Garrison said. [57]

Strange deaths in midst of committee investigations

A few months after the Church Committee began hearings in 1975, Chicago boss Giancana was murdered in his home. Giancana, who had served a year in prison shortly following JFK's death after refusing to speak to a grand jury, had been scheduled to testify before the committee. He was shot in the back of the head as he was cooking in a basement kitchen. The gunman turned his body over and shot him several more times around the mouth, which some believed was a message not to talk.

Trafficante was suspected of ordering the hit of Giancana and another of Roselli. The latter man was found stuffed and cut up inside a 55-gallon drum floating off the coast of Miami in July 1976 soon after he testified about the

CIA-Mafia plots before the Church Committee. He was slated to appear before that panel again when he disappeared.

Trafficante appeared before the House Select Committee on Assassinations, which started hearings into Kennedy's and King's deaths in 1976, but refused to answer questions. He died of natural causes in 1987, having never spent a day in prison.

In 1977, Oswald's alleged CIA handler George de Mohrenschildt reportedly committed suicide by gunshot at a Florida residence shortly after being contacted by a House Assassinations Committee investigator. He had written a letter to former President George H.W. Bush, then CIA director, in 1976 claiming he and his ex-wife, Jeanne, were being followed and his phone bugged. He asked Bush to "remove the net around us." [58]

Bush responded that while he could appreciate his "state of mind," the CIA did not have "any interest in your activities." He speculated that the media may be following him as the House Assassinations Committee investigated JFK's killing.

Six top FBI officials died after being scheduled to speak before the House Assassinations Committee. Those deaths included William Sullivan, Hoover's number three man. He was shot with a high-powered rifle in 1977 near his home by a young hunter, the son of a state policeman, who claimed to have mistaken him for a deer. Sullivan had become an outspoken critic of Hoover.

Also in 1977, mob hitman Charles Nicoletti was shot to death in his car outside a restaurant. Some suspected him of involvement in JFK's assassination.

Another odd death occurred in 1972, well before those committees formed. Warren Commission member Boggs died in a mysterious plane crash in Alaska, which also claimed the life of Alaska Rep. Nick Begich. Boggs had been the most outspoken member against the commission's conclusions, expressing strong doubts about the magic-bullet theory. Though he said publicly he thought Oswald killed JFK, he had also believed Hoover lied to commissioners and Dulles was working for the interests of the CIA. [59]

The bodies of Boggs, Begich, an aide, and the Cessna pilot were never found.

Confession by Marcello?

New Orleans boss Marcello was imprisoned several times throughout his life, including for armed robbery, selling drugs, bribing a judge, and racketeering. In 1983, he returned to prison for conspiring to bribe a federal judge and violating racketeering laws.

Fellow inmate and FBI informant Jack Van Laningham said that the mob boss admitted during a 1985 chat on the patio of the Texarkana prison that he "had that son of a bitch [JFK] killed," according to an FBI memo. "I'm glad I did," Marcello, who was released in 1989 and died of natural causes in 1993, supposedly said. "I'm sorry I couldn't have done it myself." [60]

Van Laningham, a former air traffic controller and car salesman, had been imprisoned for robbing a bank with a TV remote control and bag of laundry in Tampa, after he had fallen on hard times. He got away with the robbery but felt guilty to the point he turned in himself.

As the inmate closest in age to Marcello in that prison, they became friends. The FBI targeted Van Laningham to be a paid informant in an investigation into whether Marcello continued to run his criminal operation from prison. Besides the taped confession, Marcello told Van Laningham he had brought two hit men from Europe to shoot at JFK. Some suspected one of those was Lucien Sarti, a Corsica-born convicted drug trafficker, though others claimed he was imprisoned at the time. Sarti died in 1972 during a drug raid in Mexico. [61]

Van Laningham's courage was rewarded with an early release in 1989, but by that time, Marcello had found out he was an FBI informant. Two goons jumped him on a street, but they were forced to flee before they could shoot Van Laningham since a motorist stopped. Van Laningham passed polygraph tests about the attack and Marcello confession, and he kept a low profile until doing some interviews in 2009. [62]

Men who know too much die

The double agent Nagell, who likely foiled a September 1963 attempt on JFK, reportedly survived three attempts on his life after being released from prison in the late 1960s. He met with Garrison, but the DA thought his story was too risky for his case. Afterwards, Nagell said he made a deal to remain quiet in return for government benefits. [63]

In 1994, Nagell called Russell, who asked him what he thought of the 1992 book he had written on him. Nagell said he never received a book or many of the letters Russell sent him, and none of his friends read the book. Nagell said his mail and other materials often went missing. The following year, Nagell was found dead in his Los Angeles home of an apparent heart attack. That came right after the Assassinations Records Review Board contacted him to request to do a deposition. Friends and family members said his health had been fine up to that point. Some suspected the heart attack was chemically induced. [64]

Even after his death, someone was interested in Nagell. He told family members about a purple trunk that contained key evidence such as the August 1963 tape. His son, Robert, found in Nagell's home a key and address of a storage unit in Arizona. As Robert drove there, his own home was broken into and ransacked. He found only personal items, not the trunk, in the unit. [65]

In 1971, LBJ protégé Mac Wallace was killed when he appeared to fall asleep in his car. The vehicle crashed, hitting a bridge abutment. Some claimed the exhaust pipe of Wallace's car was blocked, causing carbon monoxide to flow into the vehicle.

Texas Ranger Clint Peoples, who investigated killings that some believed were committed by Wallace, died in another traffic accident in Texas himself in 1992. A few days before, he had supposedly told a friend that he had evidence that Wallace fired at least one shot at Kennedy in Dealey Plaza. But many researchers doubted that someone that close to LBJ would be involved in the actual shooting.

Did Wallace and Peoples also know too much? One thing was certain: A lot of people connected to the JFK case died in auto accidents, suicides, and heart attacks – all of which could be manipulated to cover up murders.

Some escape with their lives

Some were threatened without being killed. Rev. William A. Holmes, then at Northaven United Methodist Church in North Dallas, and other preachers were instructed not to say anything detrimental about Dallas in their sermons two days after JFK died. Holmes ignored the threats.

Holmes criticized officials who refused to take any responsibility for the death of JFK. That inaction was highlighted by the words of former Mayor R.L. Thornton Sr., who said shortly after the assassination, "Dallas hasn't done anything. We have nothing to be ashamed of. Forget it and go about your business." [66]

"There is no city in the United States which in recent months and years has been more acquiescent toward its extremists than Dallas, Texas," Holmes charged in his sermon. His account of elementary school children in a North Dallas school clapping and cheering when told that Kennedy died enraged people – not so much against the parents of the kids as against Holmes for daring to expose the hate. [67]

Parts of Holmes' sermon made national news broadcasts. Holmes' home and the local CBS affiliate were inundated with threats. Police advised Holmes and his family to leave town, and they did for a week, traveling by police car. "I've never been in such trauma in my life," Holmes said. He later said Dallas was "more a city of silence than we were of hate." [68]

Oil executive John Shea wrote an article for Look magazine in March 1964, saying, "Dallas feels shame, not guilt....When the hate throwers came along, [Dallas leaders] simply stood back and let the stones fly." Within a month he resigned from his job, believing that some Dallas leaders were pressuring his company to fire him. [69]

Used-car lot manager Warren Reynolds heard shots near where Tippit was killed and saw a man running away as he tucked a gun in his belt. He told FBI agents that he was hesitant to identify the man as Oswald. Two days later, Reynolds was shot in the head but recovered. He changed his story to say the man he saw running away was definitely Oswald. [70]

Beverly Massegee was threatened by former husband George McGann, who allegedly had mob ties. Their 1966 wedding guests included Civello. After telling McGann and others at Campisi's that she observed Ruby and Oswald together and thought the fatal shot came from the grassy knoll, she said McGann told her he would kill her if she talked about the assassination again.

Massegee said she was poisoned soon afterwards and witnessed her husband shoot someone and throw the murder weapon into White Rock Lake in northeast Dallas. McGann, who was murdered himself in 1970, told her there were many such weapons on the bottom of that lake and that he also dumped at least one body in Lake Texoma. She later married southern Baptist evangelist Charles Massegee, moved to a small West Texas town, and traveled with her husband doing revivals. [71]

Witness Jean Hill said a man who claimed to be with the Secret Service visited her home shortly after the assassination and warned her to stop talking. She mentioned the threat to the Warren Commission, but it was left out.

The deaf-mute Hoffman kept trying to tell authorities about the grassy knoll gunman he had seen. He claimed an FBI agent told him to keep quiet or "you might get killed." [72]

Numerous assassination researchers reported repercussions, even decades after the fact. Bill Pulte said in the 1990s he was warned by someone tied to Dallas oilmen to "watch" himself. Pulte said his wife, Kathleen, then had her supervisor at a Dallas middle school tell her to resign despite receiving great performance evaluations. Her supervisor alluded to her "unusual philosophy" outside school, and Bill said the only "unusual" activity Kathleen, who died in 2015, had was to help him research the Kennedy assassination.

The supervisor once lived across the street from Roscoe White, a former Dallas officer who some believed had a tie to the assassination, Bill said. As a marine, White was stationed at the same Japan base as Oswald. Pulte said he saw a man in a beige Oldsmobile following them near his home. He traced the license plate to a man whose wife was an accountant for Murchison and also worked for one of Byrd's companies. In addition, there was a suspicious break-in at his home. [74]

MLK family wins conspiracy case

Less than five years after JFK's killing, Martin Luther King Jr. and then Robert Kennedy were gunned down. Many suspected they were assassinated by some of the same people involved in JFK's death. Threats on King's life had been made as early as the 1950s when he led bus boycotts and other actions. The threats against RFK had long occurred, as well.

Hoover was obsessed with King and the Kennedys. He believed that MLK was "an instrument of the Communist Party," and he wanted agents to spy on him constantly to find dirt he could use, such as whether King was embezzling money, former FBI official Sullivan wrote. At one point, Hoover called King "the most notorious liar in America." FBI wiretaps did not find evidence of ties to communists, but Hoover tried to blackmail King after discovering he had extramarital affairs. [75]

On April 3, King spoke at the Mason Temple in Memphis, where he was also supporting a sanitation workers' strike for better pay and conditions. His plane from Atlanta had been delayed for about an hour by a bomb threat.

"Like anybody, I would like to live a long life," King preached. "But I'm not concerned about that now. I just want to do God's will. And He's allowed me to go up to the mountain. And I've looked over. And I've seen the promised land. I may not get there with you. But I want you to know tonight, that we, as a people, will get to the promised land."

The next evening, he stood on the second-story walkway outside his room at the Lorraine Motel. He spoke to musician Ben Branch, asking him to play, "Take My Hand, Precious Lord," at that evening's meeting.

Then at least one shot rang out at 6:01 p.m. King fell, as a bullet entered his right cheek, running along his spinal cord to his shoulder. King died in a local hospital at 7:05 p.m.

Two months later, 40-year-old James Earl Ray, a George Wallace supporter who escaped from prison in 1967 after being sentenced to 20 years for armed robbery and other crimes, was captured at a London airport. He eventually pleaded guilty to shooting MLK.

King family members believed in a wider plot to the extent that they filed a civil lawsuit. A jury agreed in 1999 that retired Memphis cafe owner Loyd Jowers was involved, along with federal, state, and local government agencies that included the FBI and Memphis police. In a unanimous decision that only took an hour, the jury awarded the King family damages of $100, a low amount they sought to show they pursued the case for justice and truth, not money. [76]

Jowers said in a 1993 TV interview that he was paid by Mafia-connected grocer Frank Liberto to hire a Memphis police officer to kill King from bushes behind Jowers' restaurant, Jim's Grill. The bushes provided cover for a closer shot at King than the second-story rooming house bathroom window from where federal authorities alleged Ray shot King. The Lorraine Motel was across Mulberry Street from those bushes. [77]

Jowers' lawyer, Lewis Garrison, agreed his client participated in a conspiracy but did not know it was a plot to kill King. The U.S. Justice Department, however, accused Jowers of fabricating his allegations and denied that former FBI agent Donald G. Wilson took papers from the car of accused assassin Ray. The documents reportedly included a page torn from a 1963 Dallas phone book that listed numbers for H.L. Hunt's family and a handwritten phone number for Ruby's nightclub. [78]

Ray recanted his confession that he killed King. He was reportedly offered money by police and publishers to admit he did it. He refused and died in prison in 1998.

"There is abundant evidence of a major high-level conspiracy in the assassination of my husband," Coretta Scott King, who passed away in 2006, said in a 1999 statement. "The jury was clearly convinced by the extensive evidence that was presented during the trial that, in addition to Mr. Jowers....the Mafia, local, state, and federal government agencies were deeply involved in the assassination of my husband. The jury also affirmed overwhelming evidence that identified someone else, not James Earl Ray, as the shooter, and that Mr. Ray was set up to take the blame." [79]

The King family had no interest in retribution, she said. "Our sole concern has been that the full truth of the assassination has been revealed and adjudicated in a court of law," she stated.

Author James Douglass covered the trial, saying he was disappointed in its relatively scant media coverage.

"What I experienced in that courtroom ranged from inspiration at the courage of the Kings, their lawyer-investigator William F. Pepper, and the witnesses, to amazement at the government's carefully interwoven plot to kill Dr. King," he wrote. "The seriousness with which U.S. intelligence agencies planned the murder of Martin Luther King Jr. speaks eloquently of the threat Kingian nonviolence represented to the powers that be in the spring of 1968." [80]

Jowers said in a tape recording that he thought Memphis Police Lt. Earl Clark fired the fatal shot at King from the bushes behind his restaurant, which fronted South Main Street. But Jowers was not the King family's primary concern, Douglass said.

"The real defendants were the anonymous co-conspirators who stood in the shadows behind Jowers," Douglass said. "The Kings and Pepper were, in effect, charging U.S. intelligence agencies – particularly the FBI and Army intelligence – with organizing, subcontracting, and covering up the assassination." [81]

The Justice Department released a report denying that the FBI or any government agency played a role in King's murder. Officials said they did not vigorously defend the government's case at the trial since Jowers was the only named defendant.

"Our investigation of these most recent allegations, as well as several exhaustive previous official investigations, found no reliable evidence that Dr. King was killed by conspirators who framed James Earl Ray," the department concluded. [82]

That statement contradicted the House Assassinations Committee's conclusion that there was "a likelihood" of a conspiracy involving some associates of Ray's. [83]

FBI and Miami police informant Somersett told Miami police Lt. Charles Sapp of the existence of a plot against King the day before he died, according to Miami Magazine. Sapp said he didn't recall relaying the information to the FBI before King died since it was "so vague." But he did afterwards, and Somersett might have told the FBI directly himself before King died.

Somersett continued to risk his life to help authorities stop other plots of attempted racially-based killings and bombings in the South before he died in 1970. While some questioned Somersett's reliability, the FBI reported that he was "one of the few Klan informants that possesses the ability, incentive, and appropriate cover to go anywhere in the southeast section of the United States concerning [FBI] matters."

Caufield called him "an unsung hero" in the efforts against the racist violence of the 1950s and 1960s. "His work likely prevented untold numbers of bombings, burnings, and murders," Caufield said. [84]

Hoover aide calls for RFK's death

By June 1968, Kennedy was on the verge of winning the Democratic Party presidential nomination. A few weeks before he was assassinated, FBI associate director Clyde Tolson, Hoover's alleged lover, shocked a group of high-level FBI officials by blurting out, "I hope that someone shoots and kills the son of a bitch [Kennedy]." [85]

On June 4, RFK won Democratic Party primaries in California and South Dakota. He addressed supporters late that night in a ballroom of The Ambassador Hotel in Los Angeles. As he shook hands with a busboy in the hotel kitchen, 24-year-old Palestinian Sirhan Sirhan fired numerous shots with a .22 revolver. Three reportedly hit Kennedy, and five others were wounded. Following extensive surgery, RFK died at 1:44 a.m. on June 6.

Coroner Thomas Noguchi told a Los Angeles grand jury that "powder burns indicated the murder gun was fired not more than two to three inches from Kennedy's right ear," Penn Jones wrote. "Witnesses testified that Sirhan was never closer than four or five feet to the senator." Cyril Wecht said that RFK's autopsy showed that the fatal shot was fired one inch to an inch-and-a-half behind Kennedy's right ear. There were as many as 13 shots fired, while Sirhan's gun only held eight bullets, Wecht said. [86]

The CIA and other government agencies began experimenting with mind-control techniques a few years after it formed in 1947 under the code names Project Artichoke and MKUltra. Sirhan attorney Lawrence Teeter believed the alleged assassin was hypnotized, saying that Sirhan had no recollection of shooting Kennedy. Some witnesses remarked that Sirhan seemed to be under a hypnotic spell as he was firing the gun. [87]

Hoover's enmity towards RFK was so intense that he purposely waited a full day before releasing news that MLK supposed assassin James Earl Ray had been caught so "he could interrupt TV coverage of Bobby's burial," FBI official Sullivan wrote. Hoover also kept graphic autopsy photos of RFK's remains locked away in his infamous confidential files, reportedly the only such gruesome photos he preserved. The photos also found their way into the safe of the CIA's Angleton.

Not everyone at the FBI shared Hoover's and Tolson's hatred of the Kennedys. Sullivan wrote a critical book, while younger FBI agents in New Orleans pursued Marcello more aggressively in later years. One even provoked the mobster to hit him so he could file charges. [88]

The Kennedy curse seemed more in play than ever after RFK's death. In 1969, Ted Kennedy drove his car off a bridge on Chappaquiddick Island, fatally trapping a young campaign worker, Mary Jo Kopechne. Kennedy escaped and claimed he tried to free Kopechne, but he did not immediately report the accident to authorities. Kopechne died of drowning or suffocation.

Then, David Kennedy, the fourth of RFK's eleven children, died in 1984 of a drug overdose. Jackie passed away in 1994 of cancer at age 64. Michael Kennedy, another RFK son, died in 1997 in a skiing accident. John Jr perished in 1999 at age 38 in an aviation accident. The small plane he was piloting crashed near Martha's Vineyard, also killing his wife, Carolyn Bessette-Kennedy, and her sister, Lauren. In 2020, RFK granddaughter Maeve Kennedy McKean and her young son, Gideon, drowned while canoeing in a Maryland bay.

Assassination plots against U.S. presidents continued. John Hinckley Jr., who shot Reagan and others in 1981, had family ties to the Bush family and CIA. Some said he could have been hypnotized to fire at Reagan. [89]

Barack Obama was targeted at least 16 times with assassination threats while president, according to *Wikipedia*. That was more than Clinton [4], George W. Bush [3], Trump [2], and George H.W. Bush [1]. [90]

Another alleged CIA asset dies weird death

In 1981, I received a stranger-than-normal call in the office of the North Texas Daily. The caller, who declined to give his name or number, said he was with a government watchdog group and had information that University of North Texas political science professor Stephen Michael Gorman was a CIA informant or asset. Gorman infiltrated groups opposed to regimes in El Salvador and other countries, and even passed on information from students' research papers to the agency, the caller said.

Something made me look into this, sensing a link to Latin American politics, if not the Kennedy assassination. I found that Gorman had lived in Peru, Ecuador, and British Honduras and wrote extensively on politics for publications such as the Journal of Latin American Studies. He was particularly interested in the explosive conflicts in El Salvador and Nicaragua. In an article Gorman wrote for the Spring 1981 issue of the North Texan, he sought a middle ground in the U.S. position on the El Salvadoran civil war. That conflict would last until 1992 with the United Nations reporting that more than 75,000 people were killed.

So I tracked him down in his university office late one afternoon in 1981. I told Gorman about the call and asked him point blank if he did work for the CIA.

He denied any involvement, saying his students' papers didn't have information worth passing on to anyone. Dealing with graduation and a job search, I dropped the matter.

Two years later, I read a short story under the headline, "NTSU prof struck by train, killed in Denton County." Gorman was only 32 and had traveled through dangerous territory in Central and South America. At one point, he had been held at gunpoint for 45 minutes by an army patrol in El Salvador and had narrowly escaped being blown up. Yet, he met his demise by being hit by a train early one Saturday morning in a rural part of North Texas.

His death was ruled an accident, according to an Associated Press story. Gorman was hit by the train "while walking on a railroad track adjacent to a state highway," the story read. The story did not say how many other adults in that area went for leisurely walks on the railroad track at 3 in the morning. [91]

In a tribute, C. Neal Tate, who chaired the university's political science department in the early 1980s, wrote that Gorman was a "skilled and popular teacher." He was completing final revisions for a new anthology on "Leftist Opposition in Democracies" at the time of his death. [92]

Descending to ridicule and name calling

In later years, lone-assassin advocates descended to name calling and ridicule to try to discredit Warren Commission critics. In his book, prosecutor Vincent Bugliosi Jr. called conspiracy theorists "as kooky as a $3 bill," though he thought most were patriotic and sincere while being misguided. [93]

In a New York Times review of that book, Bryan Burrough went even farther than Bugliosi, calling for anyone who didn't buy the government line to be "shunned." The truth seekers should be isolated in "the way we've marginalized smokers; next time one of your co-workers starts in about Oswald and the CIA, make him stand in the rain with the other outcasts," he wrote. That's despite polls that showed most Americans believed Oswald was not alone; Burrough wanted the majority to be "outcasts." [94]

Former Yale history professor Beverly Gage called lone-assassin critics "nutjobs and wackos" in a 2013 article in The Nation. Jim Marrs was a "conspiracy and UFO guru" to her, even though Marrs earned a journalism degree and wrote for newspapers like the Fort Worth Star-Telegram before working on books. Meanwhile, Gage called Warren Report-defending author Gerald Posner an "investigative journalist," even though Posner earned a law degree, not a journalism one, and resigned as a reporter for the Daily Beast in 2010 after allegations of plagiarism. Author and former BBC journalist Anthony Summers, who did some of the earliest work on CIA and Mafia involvement, received better treatment from Gage than some conspiracy-supporting authors as an "investigative journalist." [95]

Some name-calling, lone-assassin advocates had interesting ties to the government. Bugliosi and Phillips, the CIA chief who some said helped to frame Oswald, were letter-writing friends. In a 1986 letter, Phillips basically asked Bugliosi to pick up the torch against any evidence that disputes the Warren Report. [96]

Former Marquette political science professor John McAdams was probably the most active anti-conspiracy crusader before he passed away at age 75 in 2021. He was once Marquette's official representative of the Inter-university Consortium for Political and Social Research. That group, which maintains a detailed data archive, was part of the Institute for Social Research at the University of Michigan, which received funding from the CIA. [97]

McAdams didn't exactly dispel the rumors over his possible CIA ties when he attended a 1995 conference organized by the Coalition on Political Assassinations using an alias, "Paul Nolan." He also fabricated his background, saying he was a "jet-propulsion expert" and computer store owner from Sherwood, Wis. McAdams took the disguise so far that he duped journalist Matt Labash and the alternative weekly Washington City Paper, which published his false background and name, complete with quotes on his lone-assassin theory. "Oswald shot him. I'm in a small minority here. Don't ever tell anyone I said that," Labash quoted "Nolan" as saying. [98]

McAdams claimed the debunking was a "hobby" for him that should be "fun." He once responded to charges that he was paid by the CIA with, "Those people think the CIA cares a lot about them. It does not!" [99]

That led to another question: If McAdams was not associated with the CIA in some way, how did he know for sure that the CIA did not care about Warren Report critics?

Real spooks?

This section isn't really related to a conspiracy. But there have been enough reported sightings of the ghosts of Kennedy and others related to the assassination that they deserve mention. Perhaps some alleged conspirators who passed away relatively young   officially of natural causes – like Banister and Ferrie were haunted in their dreams by nightmarish visions.

In the early 1990s, Nibor Noals was working in a retail store in Bowling Green, Ky. The sales manager started walking towards the back of the store when "it seemed like time had stood still," he wrote.

Suddenly, Noals and a fellow sales manager near him both observed an elderly man walk towards them. They recognized him as JFK but at an older age in his 70s. He had a massive scar on the side of his head. "He looked right at me and continued walking until he got out of sight," Noals wrote.

The pair stared at each other. "Did you just see what I saw?" Noals asked his coworker.

"Yes, but I'm sure not going to tell anybody about it," he replied.

Noals wrote that he kept quiet for years but then decided to write about it. He described himself as a "Christian" who placed importance on honor and dignity. [100]

Author R.D. Whitaker detailed numerous sightings at Dealey Plaza in an ebook. For instance, Bill Hinton and Jewel Marshall both reported seeing a woman whom they later identified as Kupcinet at the grassy knoll of Dealey Plaza in 1969. They reported seeing her ghostly image at separate times while taking breaks during a work training meeting before it vanished. [101]

Some reported being haunted in dreams. Officer Hargis, one of the motorcycle cops next to JFK's limousine, talked about a recurring dream in which he chased a killer he believed was Oswald up and down the stairs of the TSBD, almost catching him.

"It starts out a normal dream and ends up a nightmare," Hargis said before passing away in 2014. "Every single time." [102]

The Texas Theatre, where Oswald was caught by police in 1963, continued to host movies and concerts in 2022. Some say another man who resembled Oswald was detained and then let go there. [Shay photo]

Conclusion

There are thousands who would have been glad to pull the trigger. There are millions who secretly rejoice that Kennedy is gone.
— **DEAN GORDON HANCOCK**, 1963

In the years since JFK was assassinated, more than 2,000 books have covered some aspect of that monumental event. Two of the best books – Jim Garrison's *On the Trail of the Assassins* and Jim Marrs' *Crossfire* – hit the shelves way back in the late 1980s before many government documents were released that helped clear up a few issues while raising more questions. Numerous conclusions by Garrison and Marrs back then ring true today.

Garrison wrote in 1988: "What happened at Dealey Plaza in Dallas on November 22, 1963, was a coup d'etat. I believe that it was instigated and planned long in advance by fanatical anticommunists in the United States intelligence community; that it was carried out, most likely without official approval, by individuals in the CIA's covert operations apparatus and other extra-governmental collaborators, and covered up by like-minded individuals in the FBI, the Secret Service, the Dallas police department, and the military; and that its purpose was to stop Kennedy from seeking détente with the Soviet Union and Cuba and ending the Cold War." [1]

While many agreed on the involvement of intelligence operatives, some researchers widened the net to the Mafia, Cubans, and others. Some pointed to purposes beyond the Cold War, such as revenge for not providing air support during the Bay of Pigs, JFK's advancement of civil rights, crackdown on oil profits, political slights, and threats to dismantle the CIA. In short, there were a helluva lot of people angered enough at Kennedy for many reasons to support and execute his assassination. That's why some believe there were multiple plots occurring at the same time, some known to each other, some not.

Planning for the CIA-dominated plot might have started as early as 1960 after Kennedy won election and the CIA prepared an analysis on him to use to manipulate foreign policy, wrote Garrison. "When Kennedy had veered toward détente and conventional means of controlling policy had failed, that assassination became an option in the minds of some of the CIA's Cold War establishment," he said. The planning for that apparently intensified after Kennedy forced the dismissals of Dulles and others.

After the coup d'etat worked, "major changes in American foreign policy would be arriving not in months or weeks but in the next several days" following JFK's death, Garrison wrote. LBJ immediately reversed Kennedy's course in Vietnam and escalated that conflict. His foreign policy blunders led to more deaths in Indonesia and other nations. [2]

In later years, we have learned more about schemes that occurred in the months before Kennedy's assassination, including in Chicago, Tampa, and Miami. As Bleau wrote, links between those attempts are not difficult to unearth. That alone proves that Oswald was not the only one trying to kill the president. In the Chicago and Tampa cases, two potential patsies emerged with similar profiles to Oswald.

"There was a tall building in both cases, which the motorcade was supposed to go by," Oliver Stone said to Jacobin. "They were look-alike assassination sites, exactly the same, with the same kind of profile. And also, both of these other men had also joined the Fair Play for Cuba Committee and were involved in pro-Castro activities. So, whoever was going to take the fall for the assassination had to have Castro links. Which indicates that they were trying to blame Cuba and the USSR for the assassination." [3]

The latest documents released by the National Archives through 2021 provided more clues on the enormous number of threats against Kennedy. One detailed how a CIA employee was told that a CIA contractor knew before November 22 that not only JFK would be killed, but his presumed assassin would. Others provided more information about Vallee, including how he had lived in Tennessee at the same time a man approached Kennedy with a gun in Nashville before he moved to Chicago to apparently join a plot there. The polite response that Vallee received from FBI Director Hoover shortly before the killings of King and RFK was mind-blowing. The details about Lopez and his incredible trip from Texas through Mexico to Cuba right after JFK was executed are also provocative.

Stone pointed out in 2021 how the declassified documents also showed "clear evidence" that Kennedy was about to withdraw from Vietnam, that JFK's autopsy discovered a huge hole in the back of his skull indicating an exit wound, that the final report in the Warren Commission ignored other key evidence. "All of the original evidence from day one was corrupted," Stone said.

Jefferson Morley noted that some of the latest documents helped identify more CIA officials who read Oswald's agency file and monitored him before Kennedy's killing. Others lent more details about CIA plots to assassinate Castro and the FBI paying informants in the early 1960s to report on meetings of anti- and pro-Castro groups. More documents were planned to be unveiled by late 2022 after an "intensive one-year review," Biden said, citing national security concerns. Morley and others called that the typical excuses. [4]

Likely villains

Garrison wasn't clear who exactly in the CIA or U.S. higher military establishment the ultimate mastermind was. Perhaps there was a loosely-defined group of masterminds so each one could deflect blame and deny involvement.

Based on the latest evidence from government documents, a scenario has emerged: After the failed Bay of Pigs invasion in 1961, many hard-liners in the CIA, military, and anti-Castro Cuban community blamed JFK for not providing direct support, as Eisenhower had done with a similar operation against Guatemala in 1954. They were infuriated when Kennedy made Dulles, Cabell, and others resign, believing they were scapegoats. Some of those involved in the CIA-Mafia plots against Castro, including Sturgis, Hunt, and Bill Harvey, continued that campaign before directing it against their own president.

Mafia leaders such as Giancana had helped JFK win the White House in 1960. But when Attorney General RFK kept going after them, they felt more than betrayed. RFK deported Marcello in 1961. The Kennedy Justice Department was trying to get Hoffa and Trafficante, as well. While anti-Castro Cubans targeted Kennedy, Castro could have sent his own agents to infiltrate and join the plots to avenge the schemes against him that started under Eisenhower. Kennedy's domestic policies cut into the profits of wealthy oil families like the Hunts and Murchisons, who had broad connections to the CIA. His stance on civil rights enraged racists. Some of these parties joined forces, while others targeted JFK on their own.

After threats or plots in Nashville, Los Angeles, Washington, D.C., Chicago, Tampa, and Miami were foiled, all paths led to Dallas. The North Texas metropolis was not only one of the most conservative large cities in the country in 1963, but it was a center for oil, bigoted conservative movements, mobsters, Cubans, and government intelligence activities.

Garrison saw no real evidence that LBJ, Hoover, Warren, and Allen Dulles were involved in a plot, calling them "accessories after the fact." Shortly after he took over the presidency, LBJ feared a Cuban and even Soviet plot, as he sought to pin blame on a lone scapegoat supposedly to avoid a catastrophic war. While some blamed LBJ as the main mastermind and wondered whether he was involved in other killings, there is little hard evidence linking him to planning JFK's assassination. Perhaps the most damning new incident – unearthed by fellow researcher Bill Pulte, which I haven't seen reported anywhere else is a statement in which LBJ reportedly said in 1948 that he would "kill any SOB" who got in his way of the presidency. But even such a provocative statement as that is only circumstantial evidence and doesn't prove he actually had anyone murdered. It does, however, show a part of his mindset.

There was little question that Johnson could be petty, even in the aftermath of tragedy. Shortly after Kennedy was assassinated, LBJ questioned why he and RFK were so popular. JFK "was pathetic as a congressman and as a senator," LBJ said on tapes that were later released. "He didn't know how to address the [Senate] chair." Johnson apparently thought how you addressed leaders was among the most important duties of a senator. LBJ expressed jealousy that JFK got mostly positive press, when his was mostly negative. [5]

LBJ was similarly jealous of RFK's better relations with the media. "I never did understand how the press built him into the great figure that he was," Johnson said of Robert Kennedy. He blamed him for tapping MLK's phone when that was mostly the doings of Hoover, an ally of Johnson. LBJ supported civil rights mostly for public relations purposes. He regularly was known to call African Americans the "n-word." He also praised Nixon, who was known to use derogatory language towards almost every minority and became associated with one of the biggest political scandals in U.S. history.

LBJ and Hoover both faced being fired by the Kennedys, and word of plots against JFK "must have reached the ears" of Hoover, who likely kept LBJ informed, Marrs wrote. Alleged LBJ mistress Madeleine Brown claimed that Johnson met with several high-profile men on the night before Kennedy died and told her that the Kennedys would "never embarrass me again." The account has been discredited by some researchers. If LBJ knew that at least one gunman would be firing upon the presidential motorcade that day in Dallas, he would have made some excuse to wait inside a safer building, or at least not been in the third car. However, LBJ seemed like he had been preparing for a transition mentally when he was one of the few officials at the scene right after Kennedy was shot who overcame his shock quickly and took forceful action. [6]

Whatever occurred beforehand, Johnson, Hoover, Warren, and military officials definitely worked to cover up the crime. Phone records show that LBJ and Hoover discussed on November 29 how to control the investigation's outcome and who to pick for the Warren Commission. At the same time, LBJ asked if Ruby and Oswald knew each other, and Hoover responded that they hadn't found a link *yet,* while mentioning that Oswald might have been paid by someone in the Cuban Embassy.

Talbot and Stone pointed out that Dulles was likely more involved in a plot than the others, but finding a smoking gun to directly link him would probably not occur. Talbot called Dulles "one of the wiliest masters of secret power ever produced by America." Under the cloud of secrecy, Dulles led the violent overthrow of governments, such as in Iran in 1953 and Guatemala in 1954, and the assassination attempts of foreign leaders like Castro and Lumumba. But Dulles directed his "most ambitious clandestine efforts" against Kennedy and his own government, Talbot charged.

Kennedy was the only president to actually do something to block Dulles' power. The spymaster could have sought revenge through a secret plot hatched out of his Georgetown home, Talbot said. CIA spy Hunt said under oath that he was cooking a meal with his family the day JFK died. But his eldest son said he wasn't home that day, and others testified under oath that Hunt was in Dallas. Other CIA figures, including Harvey, Morales, and Cabell, raised suspicions. [7]

Guy Banister is another who emerges as a potential prominent conspirator. No other single figure in this narrative has as many ties to the groups that were likely involved, from the CIA and anti-Castro operatives to military intelligence and the FBI. Banister, unlike Dulles, was seen with Oswald, and he had a violent reaction right after JFK's death when an associate mentioned the people who had met in his office that previous summer. Banister died a few short months after Kennedy, officially of a heart attack. However, some witnesses claimed he had been shot in the back.

Marrs ultimately blamed "powerful men in the leadership of U.S. military, banking, government, intelligence, and organized-crime circles." The operation was conducted on a "strict need-to-know" basis, Marrs noted. "Many people on the lower end of the conspiracy truthfully could say they didn't know exactly what happened," he wrote. [8]

Former SMU professor Pulte did some excellent work – some of which is included in this book   showing more examples of the links between Oswald, Ruby, right-wing businessmen, Cubans, intelligence figures, and organized crime in Dallas. They met and operated out of "safe" houses and apartments in Dallas, he noted.

Pulte also found more people who saw Ruby and Oswald together shortly before the assassination. It wasn't just people who worked in or visited Ruby's night club, whom lone-assassin theorists attempt to discredit by claiming they were drinking or hallucinating. He found people like classical piano instructor Myrtle McKay, who saw them on her Oak Cliff street in broad daylight. Of course, it was possible that the person who looked like Oswald was someone who resembled him, to implicate him in the crime of the 20th century.

Mafia bosses Marcello and Trafficante, as well as Hoffa, were identified by the House Assassination Committee as possible conspirators. All three were prosecuted by the Kennedy administration and had reason to retaliate. All three made suspicious statements, such as Hoffa's "I'll never forget what Carlos and Santo did for me." Associates have said Marcello admitted his involvement.

Besides Banister, New Orleans right-wingers Ferrie and Shaw likely played some role, numerous researchers said. Shaw and Ferrie were also observed with Oswald and Banister. They made some suspicious moves after the assassination; Shaw reportedly tried to find a lawyer for Oswald, while Ferrie drove to Texas and waited by a phone.

Oilmen Hunt and Murchison were shadowy figures, perhaps financiers, some researchers said. Their hatred of the Kennedys was legendary, as seen in Murchison's poor-taste, champagne-flowing parties that reportedly lasted a full week right after Kennedy died. Why would Marina Oswald visit Hunt's office shortly after the assassination? The hate-filled ad that ran in The Dallas Morning News the day Kennedy died was partly financed by a Hunt son and another crony.

Castro is another matter. Garrison made sense when he argued that Castro would not have wanted to see the more open-minded JFK, who was moving towards a fairer relationship with Cuba, be replaced by the conservative, Cold War hardliner LBJ. Castro had to like Kennedy not providing air support to the Bay of Pigs, refusing to invade Cuba during the missile crisis, and assuring the Soviets that the U.S. would not make further attempts to invade Cuba.

As Garrison said, Cubans could not have penetrated the Dallas police or acquired the cooperation of the FBI and CIA. But Castro still could have sought revenge for the plots on his life, since they continued so long. He could have made some anti-Castro operatives who he caught face a choice: either return and join a plot against Kennedy and tell no one of that arrangement, or die in a Cuban prison.

Castro also could have sent a few operatives who were more loyal to him to pose as anti-Castro advocates and infiltrate the plot to give it more depth. That would have been risky, but Castro was used to taking risks. He even advocated that the Soviets fire off nuclear weapons and sacrifice Cuba, if necessary, during the 1962 missile crisis, according to a PBS special report. And he might have thought that he had to do more to counter the plots against him, or the CIA and Mafia would continue them indefinitely until one succeeded in killing him. [9]

When you study the Bay of Pigs invasion and the Kennedy assassination, similarities like the diversionary tactics arise. There are more similarities between the plots against Castro and what happened to JFK. The Bay of Pigs and Castro plots were proven CIA operations. When some of the same tactics emerge in the Kennedy assassination, can they be ignored as mere coincidence?

Oswald's role

The role of Oswald is one of the most hotly-debated aspects of this mystery. Was he a mere patsy? Was he deeply involved to the point of firing his rifle? Was he a government informant trying to infiltrate and stop the plot?

Most agree that Oswald at least had contact with intelligence agencies and the FBI. Marrs and Garrison wrote that his contacts were to the extent that he was either working on behalf of the U.S. or believed he was. Posner, whose work seemed more objective than many other lone-assassin theorists, did not believe Oswald was a government agent, but left open whether he informed agencies at times. [10]

While the FBI's Gemberling argued that the evidence against Oswald would have resulted in a murder conviction, even Posner said in 2010 that a good attorney like Mark Lane "would have won an acquittal." Witness Howard Brennan saw a man who he later identified in a police lineup as Oswald shooting at the motorcade from the sixth floor of the TSBD. But he also said he could not make a positive identification, and he might have been influenced by seeing Oswald's picture on television right before the lineup. No one else came close to saying they saw Oswald actually shoot a rifle at Kennedy. [11]

Oswald's background lends further clues about his intelligence ties. He came from a military family and joined the Civilian Air Patrol, which groomed teens for military service. He was so gung-ho about following his older brothers into the Marines that he forced his mom to lie about his age. His favorite TV program as a youth was an FBI propaganda show about spying on communists.

While stationed in Japan, Oswald frequented a club reserved for elite officers and pilots, despite being a lowly private. A Marine officer was told by his superiors not to worry about Oswald reading communist literature and repeating Marxists slogans. A CIA officer testified under oath that Oswald was paid by the agency while stationed in Japan. Oswald also had a 201 CIA personnel file.

Oswald had little trouble obtaining passports and returning to the U.S. after he had defected and supposedly renounced his citizenship. He even had offered to give secrets to the Soviets, but U.S. officials didn't seem concerned. He gave FBI agent John Quigley extensive reports on Russian life and the Fair Play for Cuba Committee.

Oswald had no communist friends. His closest associate in Dallas was a Russian exile with primarily anti-communist views twice his age who worked for the CIA at times and knew Hunt and other oilmen. He associated with CIA-connected, anti-Castro advocates in New Orleans while acting like he supported Marxism. His knowledge on communism was superficial.

In short, Oswald was no communist loner. Even opponents said he was intelligent, so it is perplexing to understand how he could let himself fall into the trap of being a patsy. He had to have seen some clues. Marrs said he likely convinced himself he would stop the plot or figured it wasn't really going to go through with assassinating Kennedy.

"Oswald was a perfect fall guy," Marrs wrote. "His capture or death…implicated Russia, Cuba, and leftists – drawing attention away from the true right-wing perpetrators." [12]

Garrison added that Oswald's superiors might not have explained to him that his role was "to establish his left-wing bona fides so unshakably" that police would focus on him and the real shooters could escape. He might have thought even when he was captured that fellow conspirators were working to get him off. Indeed, that's what he told Marina after being arrested. [13]

Oswald's role as an FBI informant "may have given him a reason to believe he was actually penetrating the plot to assassinate the president," Garrison said. The FBI and Secret Service likely did not actively participate in plotting but might have looked the other way "when activity was called for," he said. [14]

Mailer portrayed Oswald as an intelligent, ambitious young man who tried to act on his beliefs but was tragically misguided and "had the character to kill Kennedy." He could "become hysterical on one occasion and, on another, be the coolest man in the room," Mailer wrote. [15]

A note on conspiracies

Conspiracies have been around since the dawn of man they're in the Bible, Shakespeare's works, and even on caveman drawings. The assassination of Julius Caesar was judged by mainstream historians to be the result of a conspiracy executed by some Roman senators.

The 1865 assassination of Abraham Lincoln in Washington, D.C., was a less risky crime than Kennedy's 1963 killing. The only "security" Lincoln had that evening was an unreliable D.C. officer named John Frederick Parker. Instead of remaining outside Lincoln's Ford's Theatre box during the play, Parker left his post to watch the play and then reportedly went to a local bar. There were far fewer journalists to deal with, and the federal government was in disarray with the Civil War still occurring. [16]

And in that "easier" crime, John Wilkes Booth had at least eight co-conspirators.

While I believe there was more than one physical conspirator in the killings of JFK, MLK, and RFK, there were even more mental conspirators. I call this the cycle of hate factor.

As Dean Gordon Hancock wrote shortly after the JFK killing, there were many who would have gladly pulled the trigger. There were many more who contributed to the mental hatred of the Kennedys. While not as bad as physical violence, of course, this intense psychic hatred spoke volumes of what the Kennedys were up against.

The hatred was seen in the distasteful celebratory parties at the homes of the Murchisons, Cabells, and others. It was seen in the voice of Hoover, who broke the news to Robert Kennedy that his brother had been shot via a phone call. RFK said Hoover sounded gleeful.

It was seen in the response of average people interviewed by FBI agents shortly after the killing. For example, James Robert Reed, a 40-year-old World War II Army paratrooper, told at least one patron of a café in the West Texas town of Colorado City, "I respect the man who killed Kennedy more than I do Kennedy." When an agent spoke with Reed the day after Kennedy died, he confirmed saying that statement and added that he would "repeat the remark in good faith." [17]

It was seen in the treatment of pastors such as Rev. Holmes, then at Northaven United Methodist Church in Dallas. He received death threats and had to leave town for a week after preaching about how Dallas officials refused to accept any blame. Federal Judge Sarah T. Hughes said there was "a climate of hate in Dallas that was not evident in any other place" at that time. Despite LBJ's Texas roots, Dallas supported Nixon in the 1960 election by a larger margin than any other major U.S. city. [18]

The hatred displayed in Dallas "comes off the pages [of 1960s newspapers] with an acrid smell, like a whiff of old sulphur," journalist Molly Ivins wrote. "Dallas was full of people who hated Jack Kennedy with livid passion because he was liberal." [19]

Some say there are still plenty of folks who hate liberals in Dallas to this day. That may be true in a lot of areas. At the same time, Obama faced more reported assassination attempts than other modern-day presidents, according to *Wikipedia*. Most did not get past the threat stage. One that involved an attempt occurred in 2011, when Oscar Ramiro Ortega-Hernandez fired seven rounds with a semi-automatic rifle at the second floor of the White House. Ortega-Hernandez claimed Obama was the anti-Christ. No one was injured, but almost $100,000 in damage was done. [20]

Dallas turned around from its informal title as the "U.S. Capital of Hate" in 1963 to vote for Biden, who was perceived by most as the more progressive presidential candidate in 2020, by 32 percentage points. Many other Southern cities moved away from their racist past by 2020. Even former anti-integration bastions like Birmingham, Ala., Little Rock, Ark., and Charleston, S.C., supported Biden. Richmond, Va., the former capital of the confederacy that voted for Nixon by 21 percentage points in 1960, went for Biden by a whopping 68 points. Oklahoma City, Colorado Springs, and Knoxville, Tenn., were among cities that supported Trump.

That such cities can change lends some evidence that perhaps we, as a nation, are not destined to forever be stuck in a cycle of hatred. Personally, I don't like to stereotype, even a country in which bigotry seems to be supported, or at least tolerated, by many. We are a nation of many aspects, a complex society that often has divergent interests competing mightily to emerge with the upper hand.

There are times I get down on the country, and there are times it uplifts me. The same United States that made Allen Dulles and J. Edgar Hoover raised Abraham Bolden, Dorothy Kilgallen, Penn Jones, and Jim Garrison. My message is one of, if you don't like the villains, be more like Bolden, Kilgallen, Jones, and Garrison. Expose the hate, the lies, the dastardly deeds. Stand up to the bullies. Let justice be done though the heavens fall.

As far as hatred of Kennedy in Dallas, I was told by numerous people decades after the fact that they were glad Kennedy didn't finish his term in office. For example, a conservative, 50-something corporate pilot for wealthy Dallas businessmen told me in 1988 that he didn't "support assassination," but it would have been "disastrous" for the country had Kennedy continued as president. He didn't seem sorry he had died. Some would make a bad joke of it, such as, "In Dallas, if we don't like the president, we kill him." They would laugh, but I wouldn't. They might have been in the minority. Or they might have, like Trump, been saying what many people really thought.

Some justice has been done

The Kennedys and King paid the ultimate price for their crusades and beliefs. Many say that their murders have not been vindicated since the higher-up plotters have not been convicted for their killings.

Yet, consider what happened to some of the prime suspects. Jimmy Hoffa was sentenced to 13 years in prison, then was murdered by alleged Mafia members. Sam Giancana was murdered, supposedly by other gangsters. Carlos

Marcello served several prison sentences. Some CIA agents suspected of involvement, including Frank Sturgis and E. Howard Hunt, went to prison. Anti-Castro leader Antonio Veciana did as well. They didn't get held accountable for the ultimate crime, but like with gangster Al Capone convicted of tax evasion after being connected to numerous murders, some justice was served.

Other suspects, such as Guy Banister and Clay Shaw, saw their lives shortened through the stress of being investigated. Others had their careers and reputations ruined. Some have made serious campaigns to rename Dulles Airport in the D.C. area after someone other than the former Secretary of State John Foster Dulles. While he was not as cruel as his CIA brother, John Dulles still aided violent regime changes. Despite knowing decent agents like my father and Robert Gemberling, I can't help but think of Hoover's petty campaigns against RFK and MLK when I think of the FBI.

Why continue this quest?

So some 59 years after Kennedy's assassination, how close are we really to a resolution? It seems like there will be questions a century from now.

So why continue this quest? Even when a case is taken to court, as Garrison did in 1969 and the King family did in 1999, many don't believe the conclusions of those trials.

One reason is that there is no statute of limitations on murder. Oswald was never tried in court. If there were other physical conspirators who remain alive, they should be pursued.

Another reason is to set our history books and websites straight. And to further expose the trends and forces that shape our government and institutions in ways both negative and positive, from the CIA assassination plots to the campaigns for truth and "liberty and justice for all." We should highlight the stories of heroes along the way, including Garrison and Bolden. Even if we don't get closer to finding out who really killed JFK, RFK, MLK, and others, the quest can unearth some important, inspiring stories, making the process worthwhile.

As someone who has researched this tragedy for many hours of my adult life, I'm not resigned to the theory, like many, that it will always remain a mystery. Like Talbot says in *Brothers,* such a theory is "a self-fulfilling prophecy that relieves [the media] of any responsibility to search for the truth."

I believe some people really know what happened on November 22, 1963, as well as on April 4, 1968, and June 6, 1968. Government records that can be accessed on websites such as MaryFerrell.org and jfk.hood.edu, books by authors like Marrs, Garrison, Talbot, Douglass, Lane, and Waldron, and the 1999 King family civil trial contain many good clues. You can even find some useful information in books by lone-assassin theorists, such as Mailer and Posner. You should consider a wide variety of sources before coming to a conclusion.

My position on the conspiracy vs. lone assassin controversy is I lean 90 percent to the conspiracy side, but almost 100 percent that Oswald was involved in some way. I give a bone to lone-assassin supporters with a 10 percent chance they are right.

Some of the more hard-to-refute pieces of this puzzle that lean me in the conspiracy direction include:

* The powerful story of Secret Service agent Abraham Bolden and the Chicago plot just three weeks before Kennedy died.

* The taped conversation between Klansman extremist Joseph Milteer and associate Willie Somersett two weeks before JFK died. Milteer admitted there was a plot to kill Kennedy and even named Klan leader Jack Brown as someone who could carry out the killing. Brown had also stalked King, Milteer said.

* The plots in Tampa, Miami, and Los Angeles, and attempts on Kennedy's life during his final year in Nashville, Miami, and other cities.

* The similar profiles of Thomas Vallee, Gilberto Lopez, and others to Oswald, making it seem like numerous people were being manipulated into becoming a patsy.

* The newly released government documents that give more details, including a CIA employee being told of another employee saying that Kennedy and his presumed assassin would die shortly before that occurred.

* The ludicrous magic-bullet theory.

* The admissions that autopsy doctors destroyed evidence under military officials' orders.

* Kennedy's head wounds and the blood-splatter evidence in the limousine that indicate a shot from the front. Medical students and others also saw an entry bullet hole in the windshield.

* The admission by Hoover that a photo that CIA officials said was Oswald in Mexico City appeared to be someone else, perhaps someone posing as Oswald.

* The more than a dozen people who saw Ruby and Oswald together in the months before Kennedy's death. The likelihood that all of these people are lying or mistaken is small. And if they saw someone who looked like Oswald, they

were not alone. That adds to suspicions that there was a double, a standard part of CIA diversion operations.

* The testimony of Gordon Arnold. The uniformed soldier had just returned from basic training and set up a movie camera on the grassy knoll. He felt a bullet pass mere inches over his left shoulder as he stood about three feet from the grassy knoll fence. He hit the ground and felt a second shot pass over. Then someone kicked him and took his film. As a soldier, he knew more than most when a bullet passed over him or not.

* The testimony of Deputy Sheriff Roger Craig. He saw a man who looked like Oswald run from the TSBD right after the shooting and get in a Rambler station wagon driven by a dark-skinned man. He later identified the man running as Oswald.

* The ease with which Oswald returned from the Soviet Union to the U.S. as the Cold War raged. Oswald had offered to give the Soviets secrets about a U-2 spy plane base where he worked when he defected but had little problems returning to the U.S.

* The fact that documents continued to be locked up away from public scrutiny some six decades later. The deadline for releasing them all keeps getting moved back, and was at late 2022.

* LBJ and others believing there was at least a Cuban connection that might have led to calls for a wider war on Cuba and eventually the Soviet Union, if it had been proven in 1964. If that was really the case, then at least they had a good reason for advancing the lone-assassin theory.

Most lone-assassin supporters – particularly the ones who refrain from insulting conspiracy theorists by calling them kooks and worse – bring up some good points. Those include:

* Oswald did have a rifle at the Paines' home in Irving, and he took something to work on November 22, 1963, in a long brown bag.

* Several other witnesses, including trained newsmen, saw a rifle pointed at the motorcade from an upper floor window of the TSBD.

* Oswald left the TSBD, rather than stay as other employees did. If he really had nothing to do with the assassination, he would have remained pat.

* Oswald likely did take a potshot at Gen. Walker.

* Oswald's suspicious behavior in the Texas Theatre.

A good approach to this case is from a spiritual perspective, which Christian theologian James Douglass takes in *JFK and the Unspeakable*. Though no one really knows for sure what happens in the afterlife, perhaps the threat of eternal damnation will cause more guilty consciences to crack and tell what they know before they pass away.

That is probably the only trump card those seeking the truth in this case can own against the CIA. Garrison couldn't beat the CIA in the late 1960s. Besides many employees, contractors, secret budgets, and secret bases, the CIA has many "assets" throughout the mainstream media, government, corporate, academic, religious, and other societal institutions.

On a spiritual level, some believe JFK's near obsession with death which seemed to grow in the months before his assassination played a role in his risky decisions at that time. When he turned against the powerful warmongering forces of his time, as seen in speeches like one at American University in June 1963 in which Kennedy called for an end to the Cold War, he was almost signing his own death warrant. Perhaps Kennedy sensed that his demise was inevitable, that he had no choice but to be a public sacrifice so that mankind could once again see the horror of its hatred in one awful act and perhaps work harder to avoid destruction.

Obviously, Kennedy was no superman. He had faults like anyone, sometimes glaring ones like the lengths he would take to cheat on his wife. He danced with the Mafia and other devils and got burned.

Robert Kennedy tried hard to contain sordid details of the Castro plots and other maneuvers. That was seen in moves like immediately calling McGeorge Bundy when he heard his brother was dead to get the national security adviser to change the combinations to JFK's locked files so LBJ's people could not raid them, according to Hersh. RFK was often a "personal watchdog for an older brother who reveled in personal excess and recklessness," Hersh noted. [21]

But like Marrs said, "History will eventually record that Kennedy truly believed he had the best interests of his nation at heart." [22]

Some of the same players seen in the Kennedy assassination crop up in Watergate and other scandals. Kennedy's killing "may come to be seen as a mere bump in the road of a series of national scandals and conspiracies which have plagued the United States right up to today," Marrs said. [23]

More than four decades after I began looking into the crime of the 20th century, my conclusion written in a column of a college newspaper in 1979 hasn't really changed. So I'll leave with that:

> Maybe there is not much we can do for the Kennedy family, and all this research will not bring back JFK.
>
> But it may set history straight and allow the American people to see more clearly who calls the shots in the government.[24]

The filming of Oliver Stone's *JFK* movie in Dealey Plaza, above, in 1991 attracted a crowd. Below, people flock to Dealey Plaza on a hot August day in 2016 to stand at the site where JFK was shot. [Shay photos]

Appendix

Acknowledgments

Bill Newman got me into this mess. A first-hand witness to the crime of the 20th century, he has to be at the top of this section. Without him waltzing into my college newspaper office one afternoon in 1978 and introducing me to a host of sources that ran contrary to the established government account, I doubt I would have found this maze on my own. At least not as quickly.

While I can blame someone for getting me into this, it's my fault I have yet to let go. Many have inspired me to keep searching through their own quests. In 1988, I met Jim Marrs at a meeting of the Dealey Plaza Irregulars that he led. He wrote a book that provided some research for Oliver Stone's *JFK* movie and continued to be a leader in this field until his death in 2017.

Mary Ferrell, who amassed tens of thousands of pages of government documents, provided more inspiration when I interviewed her. The organization that bears her name has been a beacon for researchers for decades. Early researchers such as Penn Jones Jr., Harold Weisberg, and Mark Lane sparked my studies and led the way for the later work of thought-provoking researchers, a class that includes David Talbot, James Douglass, James DiEugenio, Joan Mellen, and Jefferson Morley. There are many other researchers and authors who should be acknowledged, such as Robert Groden, Dick Russell, J.G. Lowrey, Sylvia Meagher, Anthony Summers, Bernard Festerwald, and Gaeton Fonzi. Judyth Vary Baker and Edward Haslam provided interesting accounts of the New Orleans connections. Director Oliver Stone was another inspiration in shining more light on this dark subject, including with an excellent documentary released in 2021. His *JFK* drama led to the JFK Records Act.

Gary Shaw and Larry Howard kept the JFK Assassination Information Center in downtown Dallas going for years as a counter to The Sixth Floor Museum. It was a great place to spend an afternoon. The tough reporting of Earl Golz, who was a force on The Dallas Morning News and other papers, proved that not all in the mainstream media stuck to the official story. Much thanks goes to the staffers and webmasters of various research libraries and sites that I visited, from the National Archives in College Park, Md., near Washington, D.C., to the LBJ Library in Austin, Tx. Most of those are listed in the resources section.

I spent many hours comparing notes with former SMU linguistic anthropology professor Bill Pulte, Dallas journalist Jim Erwin, and Dallas civil rights advocate Roy Williams, developing numerous interesting leads. In particular, Bill was an inspired investigative force, pursuing numerous back alleys that often led to closed doors. Some of his research, which opens up fresh avenues of discovery, is contained for the first time in this book. Bill, who won the Higher Education Honoree award from the Texas Association for Bilingual Education, has also written books on Cherokee language and culture with Cherokee Nation linguist Durbin Feeling.

Journalism professors, including Delores Griffin at Richland College in Dallas and Richard Wells at the University of North Texas in Denton, broadened my horizons, helping me to develop the critical thinking skills needed to take on such a topic. I'm grateful for the support of editors and publishers who allowed me to pursue stories on the subject in mostly mainstream newspapers and magazines. Those include Bronson Havard, Ben Miller, Russ Rian, Roger Cramer, Douglas Tallman, Bob Rand, Steve Monroe, Frank Kelly, Gene Lantz, Susan Herrbold, Judy Howard, Gary Jacobson, and the late great Lawrence Young. Thanks to cousins Mike Shay, Barbara Pignotti, and Tim Shay for their help and enthusiasm, as well as those who provided reviews and editorial support, including Stephen Berberich, Frank Cassano, and Joanne Mollica.

I'm also grateful for the support displayed by my parents, Dorothy Shay and James Shay, and siblings, Kathy Roffee, Patrick Shay, and Sharon Shay. I thank my kids, Preston and McKenna, for putting up with me as I toiled on this project many a day and night. This book is dedicated not just to them, but to their generation. May they not lose hope and carry the torch high. I really believe their generation will lead us to a better day.

Finally, I have to acknowledge people who risked their lives to try to stop the plots against Kennedy. Richard Nagell, a decorated military officer who lived until 1995 and was not a known racist, probably deserves more kudos than Willie Somersett, who died in 1970 and was a Klansman. But still, you have to acknowledge that what Somersett did   inform on fellow Klan members   was gutsy, even if he did get paid for doing so. Nagell paid for his whistle blowing with a prison sentence after he reportedly decided he didn't want to kill Oswald and there wasn't any other way out but to get himself arrested.

Abraham Bolden, the whistle-blowing Secret Service agent, spent several years in prison after trying to expose what he knew about the Chicago plot to the Warren Commission. His account, detailed in his first-person book, remains among the toughest pieces of evidence that lone-assassin theorists have to refute. He maintains he was framed for speaking out. After looking over his case, in which the main witness against him was a counterfeiter who later admitted to perjury and accused prosecutors of instructing him to lie, I have to agree. The man who Kennedy called the Jackie Robinson of the Secret Service deserves to be exonerated. He was honored with a special award at a Dallas conference in 2016. Most lone assassinologists ignore his story or take the government's position that his conviction was somehow justified.

Witnesses who told what they knew in the midst of intense pressure and mysterious deaths should be honored, as well. Those include Lee Bowers Jr., Roger Craig, Beverly Massegee, and Jean Hill.

There should be a special place in Heaven for Jim Garrison, who went through Hell attempting to prosecute the only criminal case brought against an alleged member of a plot. Garrison's investigation wasn't perfect and he took some excesses, but it was amazing what he was able to uncover about a plot in the late 1960s with the bulk of the government and media against him. If he had just a smidgen of help from those in powerful places, he and his staff might have broken the case wide open.

What is the truth, and where did it go?
Ask Oswald and Ruby, they oughta know
They mutilated his body and they took out his brain
What more could they do? They piled on the pain
But his soul's not there where it was supposed to be at
For the last fifty years they've been searchin' for that
Was a hard act to follow, second to none
They killed him on the altar of the rising sun
                     − **BOB DYLAN**, "Murder Most Foul," 2020

Notes

We're old-school when it comes to sourcing work. We always want to know where a writer gets a fact or quote, so we provide full disclosure for this work. Too many books these days have gotten away from that.

Throughout this book, we did not use periods for acronyms where they have traditionally not been used. For example, "FBI" is better than "F.B.I." Some use the latter, believing it is more consistent, but then they don't use periods for acronyms such as "NASA." We don't use periods for "USSR" but do for "U.S." The issue gets confusing, but we try to go with what has generally looked right in the past.

We also didn't capitalize "communism" since we don't generally capitalize "capitalism." But if it is a proper name of a political group like "Communist Party," we capitalized that.

When it comes to italicizing media company and even journal names, we follow the major newspapers in not using italics for The New York Times, CNN, Newsweek, and others. But if it is a specific title of a program or book, such as *60 Minutes*, we use italics.

Introduction

[1] Molly Ivins, "Liberals can testify to hatred in Dallas at time of JFK killing," Dallas Times Herald, November 22, 1988.

[2] Michael Granberry, "Those who rode by Kennedy remember," The Dallas Morning News, November 22, 2003.

[3] Sheila Taylor, "Age of innocence, optimism came to an end," The Dallas Morning News/ The Anniston Star, November 20, 1983.

[4] "Public Trust in Government: 1958-2021," Pew Research Center, May 17, 2021.

[5] Oliver Stone, *The Joe Rogan Experience*. Spotify podcast, no. 1759, January 5, 2022.

[6] JamesDiEugenio, "James Kirchick and his JFK Assassination Gurus." Kennedy and Kings, February 19, 2022.

[7] Kevin Shay, "Bill Newman: Assassination eyewitness," Richland Mandala, May 1, 1978.

[8] Shay, "A remembrance of JFK: Awakening the future," Park Cities News, November 25, 1983.

[9] David Talbot, *Brothers: The Hidden History of the Kennedy Years*. Free Press, 2007, p. 245.

[10] Shay, "It's been 25 years since Kennedy's death and the mystery continues," SR Dallas, November 1988.

[11] Shay, "The Sixth Floor exhibit explores November 22, 1963," The Addison-North Dallas Register, February 23, 1989.

¹² Shay, "A powerful experience," The Addison-North Dallas Register, December 26, 1991.

¹³ "The top news stories of the 20th century," Newseum, October 20, 1999.

¹⁴ Art Swift, "Majority in U.S. still believe JFK killed in a conspiracy," Gallup, November 15, 2013; Harry Enten, "Most people believe in JFK conspiracy theories," FiveThirtyEight, October 23, 2017.

¹⁵ DiEugenio, op. cit.; Gerald Posner, *Case Closed: Lee Harvey Oswald and the Assassination of JFK*. Random House, 1993.

¹⁶ Norman Mailer, *Oswald's Tale: An American Mystery*. Random House, 1995, pp. 775-80.

¹⁷ Robert Basham and Robert Anderson, FBI Report DL 89-43, November 27, 1963.

Chapter One: Winning at All Costs

¹ John F. Kennedy, "The Election of John F. Kennedy, President of the United States, 1960," U.S. Information Service video, Hearst Metrotone News Inc. John F. Kennedy Presidential Library and Museum, November 9, 1960.

² Jack Doyle, "JFK's 1960 Campaign," The Pop History Dig, 2016.

³ David Greenberg, "Was Nixon Robbed? The legend of the stolen 1960 presidential election," Slate, October 16, 2000.

⁴ Anthony Summers, *The Arrogance of Power: The Secret World of Richard Nixon*. Penguin Books, 2001, p. 212.

⁵ Jim Marrs, *Crossfire: The Plot that Killed Kennedy*. Carroll & Graf Pub., 1989, p. 294; Nigel Turner, "The Men Who Killed Kennedy: The Guilty Men, Episode 9." Nigel Turner Productions, The History Channel, 2003.

⁶ Peter Carlson, "Another Race to the Finish," The Washington Post, November 17, 2000.

⁷ Judy Keen, "Rumors of fraud in Chicago cast shadow on 1960 win." USA Today, September 27, 2010.

⁸ William E. Leuchtenburg, *In the Shadow of FDR: From Harry Truman to Barack Obama*. Cornell University Press, 2009, p. 80; Robert Shogan, "Mafia Helped JFK to Win, Book Claims," Los Angeles Times, November 9, 1997.

⁹ Carlson, op. cit.

¹⁰ Talbot, op. cit., pp. 136-37.

¹¹ Carlson, op. cit.

¹² Carlson, op. cit.; Greenberg, op. cit.

¹³ Herman Finer, Jerome Kerwin, and C. Herman Pritchett. "An Analysis of the Press Coverage of the 1960 Election in Chicago." John F. Kennedy Presidential Library and Museum, 1961, pp. 3, 6, 32.

¹⁴ David Stebenne, "Who Really Won the 1960 Election?" History News Network, November 14, 2010.

¹⁵ Ibid.

[16] Robin Erb, "Kennedy presidency almost ended before he was inaugurated," The Blade, Toledo, Ohio, November 23, 2003.

[17] Ibid.

[18] Mel Ayton, *Hunting the President: Threats, Plots and Assassination Attempts – From FDR to Obama*. Regnery History, 2014, pp. 60-63.

[19] Erb, op. cit.

[20] Ayton, op. cit., p. 57.

[21] Dawn Turner Trice, "Secret Service agent Abraham Bolden of Chicago served President John Kennedy as the first African-American on the White House security detail," Chicago Tribune, January 18, 2010.

Chapter Two: Fearing the Beard

[1] Noam Chomsky, Peter Mitchell, and John Schoeffel, *Understanding Power: The Indispensable Chomsky*. The New Press, 2002, p. 148.

[2] Aaron Maté, "Chomsky on Cuba: After Decades of U.S. Meddling & 'Terrorism,' Restoring Ties is Least We Could Do," Democracy Now! March 3, 2015; Natasha Geiling, "Before the Revolution: Socialites and celebrities flocked to Cuba in the 1950s," Smithsonian, July 31, 2007.

[3] John F. Kennedy, "Speech by Senator John F. Kennedy," Democratic rally, George Washington High School Stadium, Alexandria, Va.," August 24, 1960, Gerhard Peters and John T. Woolley, The American Presidency Project.

[4] John F. Kennedy, "Speech of Senator John F. Kennedy," Democratic dinner, Cincinnati, Ohio, October 6, 1960.

[5] Ibid.

[6] Geiling, op. cit.

[7] Peter G. Bourne, Fidel: A Biography of Fidel Castro. Dodd, Mead & Co., 1986, pp. 275-76.

[8] John F. Kennedy, "Speech of Senator John F. Kennedy," Democratic dinner, op. cit.; Anonymous CIA operative, "Working the Cuban beat," CIA report, 1991. Released September 3, 2014, case number C01149365.

[9] John Foster Dulles, "Memorandum from the Secretary of State to the President," U.S. Department of State, Office of the Historian, January 7, 1959.

[10] Noam Chomsky, *Hegemony or Survival: America's Quest for Global Dominance*. Henry Holt & Co. 2003, p. 80.

[11] Chomsky, Mitchell, and Schoeffel, op. cit., pp. 148-151.

[12] Fred Kaplan, "When Castro Met Nixon," Slate, March 21, 2016; "Castro visits the United States," History.com, A&E Television Networks.

[13] Richard Nixon, "Rough Draft of Summary of Conversation Between the Vice President and Fidel Castro," April 25, 1959; Bay of Pigs, Chronology of Events, National Security Archive.

[14] Kaplan, op. cit.; "Castro visits the United States," op. cit.

[15] Tim Weiner, "Word for Word/The Bay of Pigs; Blast From the Past: Recipe for a Never-Ending Fiasco," The New York Times, March 25, 2001.

[16] J.C. King, "Cuban Problems," December 11, 1959.

[17] President Dwight D. Eisenhower, "Memorandum of Conference with the President," March 18, 1960.

[18] Centro de Estudios Sobre America, "Crisis de Octubre: Cronologia," Informe Especial, 1960.

[19] "Timeline: Post-Revolution Cuba," Fidel Castro, American Experience. PBS, December 21, 2004; Don Bohning, *The Castro Obsession: U.S. Covert Operations Against Cuba, 1959–1965*. Potomac Books, 2005, p. 303; Bay of Pigs, Chronology, op. cit.

[20] Daniel P. Sheehan, "Affidavit of Daniel P. Sheehan." Christic Institute, December 12, 1986; Ibid.

[21] Sheehan, op. cit.; Chomsky, Mitchell, and Schoeffel, op. cit.; Peter Wyden, *Bay of Pigs: The Untold Story*. Simon and Schuster, 1979, p. 30.

[22] R. Hart Phillips, "75 die in Havana as munitions ship explodes at dock," The New York Times, March 5, 1960.

[23] David Atlee Phillips, *The Night Watch*. Ballantine, 1977, pp.112-14.

[24] "Cuba: That Martial Fever." Time magazine, May 23, 1960.

[25] Chomsky, *Hegemony or Survival*, op. cit., p. 81; Bay of Pigs, Chronology, op. cit.

[26] David Belin, "Summary of Facts: Investigation of CIA Involvement in Plans to Assassinate Foreign Leaders." Rockefeller Commission, May 30, 1975, released September 11, 2017; J.S. Earman, "Report on Plots to Assassinate Fidel Castro," CIA reports, May 23, 1967.

[27] Ibid.

[28] Ibid.

[29] Ibid.

[30] Ibid.

[31] Kennedy, "Speech by Senator John F. Kennedy," Democratic rally, op. cit.

[32] Wyden, op. cit., pp. 67-68.

[33] Glenn Garvin, "The Miami Herald, the CIA, and the Bay of Pigs scoop that didn't run," Miami Herald, April 17, 2015.

[34] Ibid.

[35] Ibid.

[36] Centro de Estudios Sobre America, "Crisis de Octubre: Cronologia," Informe Especial, 1960.

[37] Bay of Pigs, Chronology, op. cit.

[38] Amy Goodman, "A CIA tie to JFK assassination? Book on ex-director Allen Dulles questions agency's role," Democracy Now! October 19, 2015; Oliver Stone, *Joe Rogan Experience*, op. cit.

[39] "Memorandum of Meeting with the President," November 29, 1960; Bay of Pigs, Chronology op. cit.

[40] Whiting Willauer, "Memorandum to Under Secretary Merchant, The Suggested Program for Cuba," January 18, 1961.

[41] Ibid.

[42] "Memorandum of Meeting with the President," January 3, 1961, January 9, 1961; Bay of Pigs, Chronology, op. cit.

[43] "Meeting in the Cabinet Room, The White House." January 19, 1961.

[44] Gen. Andrew Goodpaster, "Memorandum of Conference with President Kennedy," January 23, 1961.

[45] McGeorge Bundy, "Memorandum of Discussion on Cuba," January 28, 1961.

[46] Myra MacPherson, "The Last Casualty of the Bay of Pigs," The Washington Post, October 17, 1989.

[47] Ibid.

[48] Lyman Lemnitzer, "Memorandum for the Secretary of Defense, Military Evaluation of the CIA Paramilitary Plan, Cuba," February 3, 1961.

[49] Sherman Kent, "Is Time on Our Side in Cuba?" Memorandum to Allen Dulles.

[50] Bundy, "Memorandum from the President's Special Assistant for National Security Affairs to President Kennedy," February 8, 1961.

[51] Bundy, "Memorandum of Meeting with President Kennedy," February 8, 1961.

[52] Arthur Schlesinger Jr., "Memorandum from the President's Special Assistant to President Kennedy," February 11, 1961.

[53] Sen. J. William Fulbright, "Memorandum, Cuba Policy," Senate Foreign Relations Committee, March 29, 1961.

[54] Abbot Smith, "CIA Memorandum for the Director," Board of National Estimates, February 11, 1961.

[55] Bay of Pigs, Chronology, op. cit.

[56] "Diminishing Popular Support of the Castro Government," CIA information report, March 16, 1961.

[57] Wyden, op. cit., p. 116.

[58] Arthur Schlesinger Jr., *A Thousand Days: John F. Kennedy in the White House*. Houghton Mifflin, 1965, pp. 233-34.

[59] Ibid., p. 240.

[60] Wyden, op. cit., pp.153-54.

[61] Vernon Loeb, "Soviets Knew Date of Cuba Attack," The Washington Post, April 29, 2000.

[62] "Signs of Discontent Among the Cuban Populace," CIA memo, April 6, 1961; Scott Monje, *The Central Intelligence Agency: A Documentary History*. Greenwood, 2008, pp. 33-35.

[63] Monje, op. cit., p. 35.

[64] Wyden, op. cit. p. 160.

[65] Haynes Johnson, *The Bay of Pigs: The Leaders' Story of Brigade 2506*. W. W. Norton and Co., 1964, p.86.

[66] CIA Memorandum for General Maxwell D. Taylor, April 26, 1961.

[67] Richard Bissell Jr., *Reflections of a Cold Warrior*. Yale University Press, 1996, p. 183.

[68] Philip Agee, "Terrorism and Civil Society as Instruments of U.S. Policy in Cuba." CounterPunch, August 8, 2003.

[69] Johnson, op. cit., pp. 90-91.

[70] Quintin Pino Machado, "La Batalla de Girón – Razones de una Victoria," Editorial de Ciencias Sociales, La Habana, 1983.

[71] Johnson, op. cit., p. 100.

[72] Haynes Johnson, "American Jets That Never Came." Chicago Tribune, May 17, 1964.

[73] Wyden, op. cit., p. 208.

[74] R. Ediciones, "Playa Girón Derrota del imperialismo," first of four volumes, La Habana, 1961, pp. 91-111.

[75] Wyden, op. cit., p. 230.

[76] Quintin Pino Machado, op. cit., p. 94.

[77] Wyden, op. cit., p. 208.

[78] Haynes Johnson, "A Day for Heroes." Chicago Tribune, May 18, 1964.

[79] Wyden, op. cit., pp. 264-65.

[80] Jack Pfeiffer, "The Taylor Committee Investigation of the Bay of Pigs," Zapata report, Appendix F, November 9, 1984.

[81] John F. Kennedy, "Message to Chairman Khrushchev Concerning the Meaning of Events in Cuba," April 18, 1961. Gerhard Peters and John T. Woolley, The American Presidency Project; Johnson, op. cit., pp.151-52.

[82] Michael O'Brien, *John F. Kennedy: A Biography*. Thomas Dunne Books, 2005, p. 530; Howard Zinn, *A People's History of the United States, 1492-Present*. HarperCollins Publishers, 1995, p. 432.

[83] Wyden, op. cit., pp.235-36.

[84] Howard Jones, *The Bay of Pigs*. Oxford University Press, 2008, p. 114.

[85] O'Brien, op. cit., p. 531.

[86] Ibid.; Bill Surface, "Four U.S. pilots – they died while 'serving their country'," Life, March 15, 1963.

[87] Johnson, "A Day for Heroes," op. cit.

[88] Johnson, "American Jets That Never Came," op. cit.

[89] Liz Balmaseda, "Her long vigil ends in a common grave," Miami Herald, May 15, 1982; Albert C. Persons, *Bay of Pigs: A Firsthand Account of the Mission by a U.S. Pilot in Support of the Cuban Invasion Force in 1961*. McFarland & Co., 1990, pp. 1-4.

[90] Mark Fineman and Dolly Mascarenas, "Bay of Pigs: The Secret Death of Pete Ray," Los Angeles Times, March 15, 1998.

[91] Ibid.; Balmaseda, op. cit.

[92] Balmaseda, op. cit.; Surface, op. cit.

[93] Surface, op. cit.

94 Earl Golz, "1963 tape reveals threat to JFK," The Dallas Morning News, August 14, 1978.

95 Johnson, "A Day for Heroes," op. cit.

96 Ibid.

97 Wyden, op. cit., p. 294.

98 Garvin, op. cit.

99 Tom Wicker, John W. Finney, Max Frankel, and E. W. Kenworthy, "CIA.: Maker of Policy, or Tool? Survey Finds Widely Feared Agency is Tightly Controlled." The New York Times, April 25, 1966; Oliver Stone, *Joe Rogan Experience*, op. cit.

Chapter Three: From 'Get Castro' to 'Get JFK'

1 "Record of Action." 483rd Meeting of the National Security Council, May 5, 1961; Robert McNamara, "Cuban Contingency Plan," May 1, 1961; Wyden, op. cit., p. 305.

2 "Chronology of Cuban events, 1963," U.S. Information Agency memo, October 23, 1964; "The Bay of Pigs Invasion and its Aftermath, April 1961 – October 1962," U.S. Dept. of State, Office of the Historian, October 31, 2013.

3 Bay of Pigs, Chronology, op. cit.

4 Ibid.

5 Talbot, op. cit. pp. 5-7.

6 James DiEugenio, *Destiny Betrayed: JFK, Cuba, and the Garrison Case*. Sheridan Square Press, 1992, p. 238; Jim Garrison, *On the Trail of the Assassins: My Investigation and Prosecution of the Murder of President Kennedy*. Sheridan Square Press, 1988, p. 104.

7 Richard Bissell, *Reflections of a Cold Warrior: From Yalta to the Bay of Pigs*. Yale University Press, 1996.

8 Earman, op. cit.

9 Robert Scheer, "On Cuba, JFK Was Married to the Mob." Los Angeles Times, November 11, 1997.

10 Tim Weiner, "Stupid Dirty Tricks; The Trouble with Assassinations." The New York Times, November 23, 1997.

11 "Alleged Assassination Plots Involving Foreign Leaders," Church Committee, November 20, 1975, p. 140; Sheehan, op. cit.; Stone, op. cit.

12 Earman, op. cit.; Bohning, op. cit., p. 4.

13 Ibid.

14 Ibid.

15 Belin, op. cit.; National Security Action Memorandum 181, "Actions and Studies in Response to New Soviet Bloc Activity in Cuba," August 23, 1962.

16 Ibid.

17 "Alleged Assassination Plots Involving Foreign Leaders," op. cit., p. 147.

[18] Ibid., pp. 147-48; "Chronology of John McCone's Suspicions on the Military Build-up in Cuba Prior to Kennedy's October 22 Speech," November 30, 1962.

[19] John F. Kennedy, "Cuban Missile Crisis Address to the Nation," October 22, 1962.

[20] "Castro and the Cold War," "Letter from Fidel Castro to Nikita Khrushchev October 26, 1962." PBS, December 21, 2004.

[21] David Talbot, *The Devil's Chessboard: Allen Dulles, the CIA, and the Rise of America's Secret Government*. HarperCollins Publishers, 2015, p. 453.

[22] Bohning, op. cit., p. 1.

[23] Aaron Maté, "Chomsky on Cuba: After Decades of U.S. Meddling & 'Terrorism,' Restoring Ties is Least We Could Do," Democracy Now! March 3, 2015.

[24] "Testimony of Richard Helms," House Select Committee on Assassinations, September 1978.

[25] "Timeline: Post-Revolution Cuba," op. cit.

[26] "Kennedy Sought Dialogue with Cuba," National Security Archive, Gelman Library, George Washington University, November 24, 2003.

[27] "Adlai Stevenson and Lisa Howard," White House memorandum, Top Secret, July 7, 1964.

[28] Stacy Conradt, "10 Ways the CIA Tried to Kill Castro." Mental Floss, February 16, 2012; Anthony Boadle, "Closest CIA bid to kill Castro was poisoned drink." Reuters, July 5, 2007.

[29] Todd Benson, "Bush wishes Cuba's Castro would disappear." Reuters, June 28, 2007.

[30] Anonymous CIA operative, "Working the Cuban beat," op. cit.

[31] MacPherson, op. cit.

[32] Ibid.

[33] Ibid.

[34] Ibid.

[35] Ibid.

[36] John Simkin, "John Roselli." Spartacus Educational, August 2014.

[37] Jack Anderson, "Roselli version says JFK killed in retaliation." United Feature Syndicate, October 23, 1978.

[38] Kevin James Shay, interview with Andres Manso Rojas, Miami, Fla., July 26, 2016.

Chapter Four: Enemies Unite?

[1] Amy Goodman, "The Rise of America's Secret Government: The Deadly Legacy of Ex-CIA Director Allen Dulles, Part 2." Democracy Now!, October 14, 2015.

[2] Madeleine G. Kalb, "The CIA and Lumumba." The New York Times, August 2, 1981.

[3] Stephen Kinzer, "When a CIA Director Had Scores of Affairs." The New York Times, November 10, 2012.

[4] James K. Galbraith, "A Crime So Immense." Texas Democracy Foundation, 2000.

[5] Glenn C. Altschuler, *"The Devil's Chessboard,* by David Talbot." San Francisco Gate, October 16, 2015; Talbot, *The Devil's Chessboard,* op. cit.; Stone, op. cit.

[6] Greg Poulgrain, *JFK vs. Allen Dulles: Battleground Indonesia.* Skyhorse Publishing, 2020, p. 201.

[7] James A. Warren, "Did CIA Director Allen Dulles order the hit on JFK?" The Daily Beast, October 13, 2015.

[8] Evan Thomas, *Robert Kennedy: His Life.* Simon & Schuster, 2002, pp. 156, 162; Robert F. Kennedy, Letter to June Holloway, General Services Administration, Office of the U.S. Attorney General, November 16, 1961.

[9] Thomas, op. cit., p. 173.

[10] Ronald Goldfarb, "JFK, RFK, the Mob and Dallas," Cosmos Journal, 1996.

[11] Thomas, op. cit., p. 163.

[12] Stone, "Did JFK Steal The 1960 Election?" op. cit.

[13] Marrs, op. cit., p. 164.

[14] Simkin, "Jimmy Hoffa." Spartacus Educational, November 2014.

[15] Bill Rockwood, "Interview: G. Robert Blakey. Who Was Lee Harvey Oswald?" Frontline, PBS, November 19, 2013; Lamar Waldron, *The Hidden History of the JFK Assassination.* Counterpoint, 2013, pp. 157-58.

[16] "Testimony of Jose Aleman," U.S. House Select Committee on Assassinations, 1978; "Santo Trafficante – It Should Have Been Bobby," Mary Ferrell Foundation.

[17] "Findings of the Select Committee on Assassinations in the Assassination of President John F. Kennedy," House Select Committee on Assassinations, 1979.

[18] Ibid.; Talbot, Brothers, op. cit., pp. 120-22; Rockwood, "Interview: G. Robert Blakey," op. cit.

[19] "Interview: G. Robert Blakey," op. cit.

[20] Sandy Grady, "Mafia talked of bomb in Bobby Kennedy's golf bag." Philadelphia Bulletin, October 1, 1978.

[21] Ibid.

[22] Marrs, op. cit., p. 277.

[23] Ibid., pp. 277-78.

[24] Scott K. Parks, "Extremists in Dallas created volatile atmosphere before JFK's 1963 visit," The Dallas Morning News, October 12, 2013.

[25] Dick Russell, *The Man Who Knew Too Much.* Carroll & Graf, 1992, p. 377.

[26] Bill Pulte, "Richard Aubrey" memo, April 3, 1990.

[27] Marrs, op. cit. p. 295.

[28] Robert Dallek, *An Unfinished Life: John F. Kennedy, 1917–1963* (Little, Brown & Co., 2003), pp. 500-01.

[29] Thomas, op. cit., pp. 262, 268.

[30] Joan Mellen, *Faustian Bargains: Lyndon Johnson and Mac Wallace in the Robber Baron Culture of Texas.* Bloomsbury, 2016.

[31] Phillip F. Nelson, *LBJ: The Mastermind of the JFK Assassination.* Skyhorse Publishing, 2013, p. 209-13.

[32] Ibid., pp. 215-17.

[33] Simkin, "Malcolm (Mac) Wallace." Spartacus Educational, August 2014.

[34] Garth Jones, "Federal official's death certificate ordered changed." Associated Press, August 14, 1985.

[35] Ibid.

[36] Mellen, op. cit.

Chapter Five: Mystery Wrapped in an Enigma

[1] Diane Holloway, *Autobiography of Lee Harvey Oswald: My Life in My Words.* iUniverse, 2008, pp. 2-6.

[2] Frederick Ziv, *I Led Three Lives*, Season One, "Army Infiltration." Ziv Television Programs, 1953.

[3] Rockwood, "Interview: Robert Oswald." Frontline, PBS, November 19, 2013.

[4] "Testimony of Mrs. Marguerite Oswald." Warren Commission, Washington, D.C., February 10, 1964.

[5] "Biography of Lee Harvey Oswald," Report of the President's Commission on the Assassination of President John F. Kennedy, U.S. Government Printing Office, Washington, D.C., 1964, Appendix XIII, p. 670.

[6] "Testimony of Robert Edward Lee Oswald," Warren Commission, Washington, D.C., February 22, 1964.

[7] "Testimony of Mrs. Marguerite Oswald," op. cit.

[8] "Findings of the Select Committee on Assassinations in the Assassination of President John F. Kennedy," House Select Committee on Assassinations, 1979.

[9] Ibid.; Rockwood, "Interview: G. Robert Blakey," op. cit.; Don Fulsom, "Richard Nixon's Greatest Cover-Up: His Ties to the Assassination of President Kennedy." Crime Magazine, October 2, 2009.

[10] "Testimony of Mrs. Marguerite Oswald," op. cit.

[11] "Biography of Lee Harvey Oswald," op. cit., pp. 672-73.

[12] Ibid., pp. 674-76.

[13] Ibid., pp. 676-78.

[14] "Testimony of Edward Voebel," Warren Commission, New Orleans, April 7, 1964, Vol. VIII, p. 7, 10-12.

[15] "Testimony of Mrs. Marguerite Oswald," op. cit.

[16] "Testimony of Edward Voebel," op. cit., p. 5.

[17] Ibid., p. 14.

[18] Steve N. Bochan, "The Bolton Ford Dealership Story." The Assassination Chronicles, Vol. 1, Issue 4, December 1995, JFK Lancer Productions & Publications.

[19] George de Mohrenschildt, *I am a Patsy! I am a Patsy!* Staff Report of the Select Committee on Assassinations, U.S. House of Representatives, March 1979, p. 81.

[20] Russell, op. cit., p. 82.

[21] Ibid., pp. 76-77.

[22] Ibid., pp. 71-76.

[23] Edward Jay Epstein, *Legend: The Secret World of Lee Harvey Oswald.* McGraw-Hill, 1978, pp. 357, 359.

[24] Ibid., p. 366; Rockwood, "Interview: Robert Oswald," op. cit.

[25] "Biography of Lee Harvey Oswald," op. cit., Appendix XIII, pp. 686-87.

[26] Russell, op. cit., p. 98.

[27] Anthony Summers and Robbyn Swan, "Lee Harvey Oswald: A Simple Defector?" WordPress blog, November 19, 2013.

[28] Rockwood, "Interview: G. Robert Blakey," op. cit.

[29] Summers and Swan, Robbyn, op. cit.

[30] Ibid.

[31] Russell, pp. 98-99.

[32] "Testimony of James B. Wilcott, a Former Employee of the Central Intelligence Agency," U.S. House Select Committee on Assassinations, Washington, D.C., March 22, 1978, pp. 8, 24.

[33] James W. Douglass, *JFK and the Unspeakable: Why He Died and Why It Matters.* Orbis Books, 2008, pp. 146-47.

[34] "Testimony of James B. Wilcott," op. cit., p. 47.

[35] Rockwood, "Interview: Robert Oswald," op. cit.

[36] Ibid.

[37] "Biography of Lee Harvey Oswald," op. cit., Appendix XIII, p. 691.

[38] Mailer, op. cit., p. 321.

[39] "Report of the President's Commission on the Assassination of President Kennedy," op. cit., Chapter 7, Lee Harvey Oswald: Background and Possible Motives, pp. 392-93.

[40] Ibid.

[41] Richard Snyder, "The Soviet Sojourn of Citizen Oswald," Washington Post Magazine, January 31, 2012 (first published April 1, 1979).

[42] Ibid.

[43] Simkin, "Priscilla Johnson McMillan," Spartacus Educational, August 2014.

[44] Donald Jameson, Chief SR/CA, CIA memo, No. 17456, December 11, 1962.

[45] "Biography of Lee Harvey Oswald," Appendix XIII, p. 696.

[46] Warren Commission exhibit, Vol. XVI, pp. 287-336.

[47] "Biography of Lee Harvey Oswald," op. cit., Appendix XIII, p. 698.

[48] Warren Commission exhibit, Vol. XVI, pp. 287-336.

[49] Summers and Swan, op. cit.

[50] Francis Gary Powers, "Was I betrayed by Lee Harvey Oswald?" Excerpt from *Operation Overflight: The U-2 Spy Pilot Tells His Story for The First Time*. Holt, Rinehart and Winston, 1970.

[51] Ibid.

[52] Ibid.

[53] Mailer, op. cit., p. 327.

[54] John Newman, *Oswald and the CIA: The Documented Truth About the Unknown Relationship Between the U.S. Government and the Alleged Killer of JFK*. Skyhorse Publishing, 2008, pp. 635-36; Carl Gibson, "16 Mind-Blowing Facts About Who Really Killed JFK," Nation of Change, November 22, 2013.

[55] "Biography of Lee Harvey Oswald," op. cit., Appendix XIII, pp. 699-701.

[56] Ibid.

[57] Warren Commission exhibit, Vol. XVI, pp. 287-336.

[58] Ibid.

[59] Ibid.

[60] Warren Commission exhibit 932, Vol.XVIII, p. 133.

[61] Mailer, op. cit., p. 173.

[62] "Biography of Lee Harvey Oswald," op. cit., Appendix XIII, pp. 701, 704.

[63] KGB transcripts, OLH-2658, August 11, 1961, Mailer, op. cit., pp. 230-32.

[64] Ibid., pp. 193, 207-08, 244, 251.

[65] Memo from American Embassy to State Department, July 11, 1961, Warren Commission exhibit 977, Vol. XVIII, pp. 378-80.

[66] Warren Commission exhibit 1122, Vol. XXII, p. 87.

[67] KGB transcripts, July 26, 1961, Mailer, op. cit., pp. 216-20.

[68] Ibid., pp. 273-74, 292.

[69] Warren Commission, James exhibit No. 2, Vol. XX, pp. 236-37.

[70] Snyder, op. cit.

[71] Lisa Rose, "Retired scholar looks back on his meeting with Lee Harvey Oswald," Star-Ledger, New Jersey Online, November 17, 2013.

[72] "Biography of Lee Harvey Oswald," op. cit., Appendix XIII, pp. 712-13.

[73] Warren Commission exhibit 100, Vol. XVI, pp. 436-39.

[74] Rose, op. cit.

[75] Ibid.

[76] Ibid.

[77] Ibid.

[78] Bill Kelly, "Journalists & JFK – The Real Dizinformation Agents at Dealey Plaza," Citizens for Truth about the Kennedy Assassination, July 2011.

[79] Summers and Swan, op. cit.

[80] Paul Comstock, "Who Killed JFK? – An Interview with Lamar Waldron," California Literary Review, April 3, 2007.

[81] "Testimony of Mrs. Marguerite Oswald," op. cit.

[82] Ibid.

[83] John W. Fain, FBI report, July 6, 1962, Warren Commission exhibit 823, Vol. XVII, pp. 728-29.

[84] Rockwood, "Interview: Robert Oswald," op. cit.

[85] Ibid.

[86] "Testimony of Mrs. Marguerite Oswald," op. cit.

[87] Mailer, op. cit., p. 458.

[88] "George de Mohrenschildt." Staff Report of the Select Committee on Assassinations, U.S. House of Representatives. March 1979; Edward Jay Epstein, *The Assassination Chronicles*. Carroll & Graf Pub., 1992, pp. 558-59.

[89] Staff and wire reports, "Oswald friend labeled CIA informant in memo," Dallas Times Herald, July 27, 1978.

[90] Epstein, op. cit., pp. 558-59.

[91] Ibid.; De Mohrenschildt, *I am a Patsy! I am a Patsy!* p. 209; HSCA Appendix to Hearings, Volume XII, House Select Committee on Assassinations, AARC, 1979.

[92] De Mohrenschildt, op. cit., pp. 76, 81, 95; Anthony Summer, *Not in Your Lifetime*. Marlowe & Company, 1998, p. 154.

[93] De Mohrenschildt, op. cit., pp. 86, 91, 104, 106; "Testimony of Mrs. Lee Harvey Oswald," Warren Commission, February 3, 1964.

[94] Garrison, op. cit., p. 56.

[95] Gibson, op. cit.

[96] Comstock, op. cit.

[97] Garrison, op. cit., pp. 52-53.

[98] "Testimony of Mrs. Marguerite Oswald," op. cit.

[99] "Testimony of George S. de Mohrenschildt," Warren Commission, Washington, D.C., April 23, 1964.

[100] Epstein, op. cit., p. 647.

[101] De Mohrenschildt, *I am a Patsy! I am a Patsy!* op. cit.

[102] "Testimony of Mrs. Lee Harvey Oswald," op. cit.

[103] Ibid.

[104] Ibid.

[105] "Testimony of Mrs. Lee Harvey Oswald," op. cit.

[106] "Testimony of George S. de Mohrenschildt," op. cit.

[107] Priscilla Johnson McMillan, *Marina and Lee*. Harpercollins, 1977, p. 349; "Testimony of Mrs. Lee Harvey Oswald," op. cit.

[108] "Testimony of Mrs. Lee Harvey Oswald," op. cit.

[109] Alan J. Weberman and Michael Canfield, Coup D'Etat in America: The CIA and the Assassination of John F. Kennedy. Third Press Review of Books, 1975, p. 14; Marrs, op. cit., pp. 262-63; Simkin, "Edwin Walker." Spartacus Educational, August 2014.

[110] Eric Norden, "Jim Garrison: A Candid Conversation with the Embattled District Attorney of New Orleans," Playboy, October 1967, p. 160.

[111] Rockwood, "Interview: G. Robert Blakey," op. cit.

[112] Bruce L. Solie, "Paine, Ruth," CIA memorandum, December 5, 1963; Douglass, op. cit., pp. 170-71; Steve Jones, "Regarding Ruth and Michael Paine," Kennedy Assassination Chronicles, Vol. 4, Issue 4, Winter 1998, pp. 18, 20.

[113] "Testimony of Ruth Hyde Paine," Warren Commission, Washington, D.C., March 21, 1964.

[114] Ibid.

[115] "Testimony of Michael R. Paine," Warren Commission, Washington, D.C., March 17, 1964.

[116] Nany Wertz, "Michael Paine – A Life of Unanswered Paradoxes," Kennedy Assassination Chronicles, Vol.4, Issue 4, Winter 1998, pp. 19-23.

[117] "Testimony of Michael R. Paine," op. cit.

Chapter Six: New Orleans Connections

[1] William Davy, *Let Justice Be Done: New Light on the Jim Garrison Investigation*. Jordan Publishing, 1999, p. 36.

[2] Garrison, op. cit., pp. 57-58.

[3] Ibid., pp. 70-78.

[4] Ibid., p. 73-75.

[5] Ibid., pp. 25, 37-8.

[6] "Testimony of Mrs. Lee Harvey Oswald," op. cit.

[7] Warren Commission exhibit No. 2, Vol. XX, pp. 514-16.

[8] Warren Commission exhibit 986, Vol. XVIII, pp. 521-22.

[9] James DiEugenio, *Destiny Betrayed*. Skyhorse Publishing, 2012, pp. 115-116.

[10] Norden, op. cit., pp. 160-61.

[11] Garrison, op. cit., p. 25.

[12] Norden, op. cit., pp. 160-61.

[13] Jefferson Morley, "Celebrated authors demand that the CIA come clean on JFK assassination," Salon, December 17, 2003.

[14] "Findings of the Select Committee on Assassinations in the Assassination of President John F. Kennedy;" Lamar Waldron, *The Hidden History of the JFK Assassination*. Counterpoint, 2013, pp. 180-83; Garrison, op. cit., p. 25.

[15] Warren Commission testimony, Vol. XI, pp. 171-75.

[16] James Fetzer, "14 Reasons to Believe in Judyth Baker," Blogspot, March 1, 2010.

[17] Judyth Vary Baker, *Me & Lee: How I Came to Know, Love and Lose Lee Harvey Oswald*. Trine Day, 2010; Edward T. Haslam, *Dr. Mary's Monkey*. Trine Day, 2007, pp. 56-58.

[18] Haslam, op. cit., pp. 175-76, 181-85.

[19] Haslam, op. cit., pp. 46-47; "Biography of Judyth Vary Baker," Amazon Books.

[20] Baker, op. cit.

[21] Haslam, op. cit., pp. XVIII-XIX.

[22] Baker, op. cit.

[23] Fetzer, op. cit; Garrison, op. cit., pp. 115-16.

[24] Adriane Quinlan and Naomi Martin, "In the death of Doctor Mary Sherman, strange myths pale next to stranger facts." New Orleans Times-Picayune, July 19, 2014.

[25] Aaron Kohn, "Letter to Maj. Lawrence J. Casanova, New Orleans Police Department," Metropolitan Crime Commission of New Orleans, July 27, 1964; Quinlan, op. cit.; Haslam, op. cit.

[26] Davy, op. cit. p. 90; Garrison, op. cit., pp. 156-58.

[27] Haslam, op. cit., pp. 56-58.

[28] Ibid. pp. 56-58.

[29] Spoonmore, John M., "Polygraph Examination Report for Sergio Arcacha Smith." Scientific Security Service, March 8, 1967. Accessed from University of North Texas Libraries, The Portal to Texas History.

[30] Garrison, Jim. "Opening statement." *State of Louisiana vs. Clay L. Shaw*, Criminal District Court, New Orleans, February 6, 1969.

[31] J. Kenneth McDonald, "Survey of CIA's Records from House Select Committee on Assassinations Investigation," Covert History, February 10, 1992; Russell, op. cit., p. 90; Garrison, *On the Trail of the Assassins*, p. 251.

[32] Garrison, op. cit., p. 146.

[33] Joan Mellen, "Clay Shaw Unmasked: The Garrison Case Corroborated," Address at Passing the Torch: An International Symposium on the 50th Anniversary of the Assassination of President John F. Kennedy, Cyril H. Wecht Institute of Forensic Science and Law, October 18, 2013.

[34] Marrs, op. cit., p. 413.

[35] Waldron, op. cit., pp. 190-192.

[36] "Organized Crime Expert Sees Mob Connections," ABC News, November 20, 2003.

[37] Kevin J. Shay and Roy H. Williams, *And Justice for All: The Untold History of Dallas*. CGS Communications, 1999, pp. 99-100; David E. Scheim, *Contract on America: The Mafia Murder of President John F. Kennedy*. Shapolsky Pub., 1988, pp. 83, 94-95, 98-99; "Testimony of Mr. Jack Ruby," Warren Commission, Dallas County Jail, June 7, 1964.

[38] Earl Golz, "Testimony shows gambling not new on Ross." The Dallas Morning News, April 26, 1972; Shay and Williams, op. cit., p. 100; Waldron, op. cit., p. 187.

[39] Golz, "Jack Ruby's gunrunning to Castro claimed." The Dallas Morning News, August 18, 1978; "Findings of the Select Committee on Assassinations in the Assassination of President John F. Kennedy," op. cit.; Waldron, op. cit., p. 186.

[40] Mario Machi, "Dallas, Texas," American Mafia, 1999; Dallas Det. G.D. Gandy, "Egyptian Lounge, 5410 E. Mockingbird." Memo to Dallas Police Lt. J.M. Souter, April

26, 1957; "Sworn testimony of Joseph Campisi," U.S. House Select Committee on Assassinations, May 22, 1978.

[41] Marrs, op. cit., p. 391.

[42] Kevin J. Shay, "My life with the mob: 'Babushka Lady' writes of JFK's assassination, marriage with alleged mafioso," Arlington News, November 24, 1994.

[43] Jefferson Morley, "Ex-flame says Jack Ruby 'had no choice' but to kill Oswald," JFK Facts, March 21, 2013.

[44] Shay, "My life with the mob," op. cit.; Shay personal notes of interview with Becky Oliver Massegee, 1994.

[45] Ibid.

[46] Russell, "Oswald and the CIA." Probe Magazine, November-December 1995; Douglass, op. cit., pp. 154-56.

[47] Russell, "Oswald and the CIA," op. cit.; House Assassinations Committee report, 1979, p. 136; Gaeton Fonzi, *The Last Investigation*. Thunder's Mouth Press, 1993, pp. 141-42.

[48] Russell, "Oswald and the CIA," op. cit.; Douglass, op. cit., pp. 154-56.

[49] Ibid.

[50] Russell, *The Man Who Knew Too Much*, op. cit., pp. 437, 673.

[51] Douglass, op. cit., pp. 154-56.

[52] Russell, op. cit., p. 45.

[53] Douglass, op. cit., p. 155.

[54] Ibid., p. 158.

[55] Warren Commission exhibit 410, Vol. XVII, pp. 102-04.

[56] "Testimony of Ruth Hyde Paine," op. cit.

[57] Thomas Estep, "Lee Harvey Oswald," FBI report CI 105-2505, December 5, 1963.

[58] Ibid.

[59] Oleg Nechiporenko, *Passport to Assassination*. Birch Lane Press, 1993, pp. 70-71.

[60] Ibid., pp. 76-78.

[61] Ibid., pp. 76-78.

[62] Ibid., pp. 80-81.

[63] Norden, op. cit., pp. 160-61; Canfield, op. cit., p. 47.

[64] Talbot, *Brothers*, op. cit., p. 285; Douglass, op. cit., p. 80; Simkin, "David Atlee Phillips," Spartacus Educational, August 2014.

[65] Simkin, "David Atlee Phillips," op. cit.

[66] Garrison, op. cit., pp. 64-65.

[67] "Telephone Conversation between the President and J. Edgar Hoover," Mary Ferrell Foundation, November 29, 1963.

[68] "Testimony of Ruth Hyde Paine," op. cit.; "Testimony of Mrs. Lee Harvey Oswald," op. cit.

[69] "Testimony of Mrs. Lee Harvey Oswald," op. cit.; Gibson, op. cit.; Douglass, op. cit., pp. 169-73.

70 "Testimony of Linnie Mae Randle," Warren Commission, Washington, D.C., March 11, 1964.
71 Martin Hay, "Who are the Paines?" The Mysteries of Dealey Plaza, August 9, 2010.
72 Richard Bartholomew, "Byrds, Planes, and an Automobile." Fair Play Magazine, April 20, 1997.
73 James P. Hosty Jr., with Thomas Hosty, *Assignment: Oswald*. Arcade, 1995, pp. 20-21.
74 Nannie Lee Fenner, sworn statement, FBI, Dallas, Tx., July 15, 1975.
75 Ibid.; James P. Hosty Jr. affidavit, FBI, April 24, 1964, Warren Commission exhibit No. 831.
76 Hosty, op. cit., pp. 20-21.
77 Hugh Aynesworth, "FBI knew Oswald capable of act, reports indicate." The Dallas Morning News, April 24, 1964.
78 "Testimony of James Patrick Hosty Jr.," Warren Commission, Vol. IV, April 8, 1964. pp. 457, 473.
79 Aynesworth, op. cit.

Chapter Seven: Multiple Threats

1 Russell, op. cit., p. 165; Debra Conway, "Castro Assassination Plots." JFK Lancer Productions & Publications, November 2007.
2 Abraham Bolden, *The Echo from Dealey Plaza: The True Story of the First African American on the White House Secret Service Detail and His Quest for Justice after the Assassination of JFK*. Harmony Books, 2008, pp. 48-49.
3 Jeffrey H. Caufield, *General Walker and the Murder of President Kennedy: The Extensive New Evidence of a Radical-Right Conspiracy*. Moreland Press, 2015, pp. 174, 197-98.
4 Ibid., p. 141.
5 Ibid., p. 94.
6 Dan Christensen, "JFK, King: The Dade County links." Miami Magazine, September 1976.
7 Ayton, op. cit., p. 64; Nashville Banner, January 25, 1992; Wayne Wood, "When Nashville was Camelot." Nashville Scene, May 29, 2003.
8 Agent Francis Uteg, "Thomas Vallee, Description and Identification." U.S. Secret Service report #00-2-33,991, June 28, 1966.
9 Ayton, op. cit., p. 64.
10 Russell, op. cit., pp. 210-219.
11 Simkin, "Vaughn Marlowe," Spartacus Educational. August 2014.
12 "Baltimore Hearing Set in JFK Threat Case." Associated Press, July 30, 1963.
13 Andrew J. Sciambra, "Trip to Mobile, Ala., on May 5, 1967 thru May 7, 1967." New Orleans District Attorney's office memo, May 8, 1967.

[14] Golz, "Papers link Ruby, Oswald." The Dallas Morning News, March 28, 1976; Douglass, op. cit., pp. 154-56.

[15] Jesus, op. cit.

[16] Earl Golz, "1963 tape reveals threat to JFK." The Dallas Morning News, August 14, 1978.

[17] Russell, op. cit., pp. 349-52.

[18] Ibid., pp. 156-58, 197-98.

[19] John R. Pherson, "Mrs. Ruth Taden," CIA memo marked "secret." May 18, 1964, released October 26, 2021.

[20] Robert Basham and Robert Anderson, FBI Report DL 89-43, November 27, 1963.

[21] Ibid.

[22] Emory E. Horton, FBI Report DL 89-43, November 24, 1963.

[23] Gil Jesus, "Threats against JFK – 1963," October 26, 2002.

[24] Ayton, op. cit., pp. 66-67; Kyle Clark, FBI Report DL 89-43, December 3, 1963.

[25] Edwin Black, "The Plot to Kill JFK in Chicago." The Chicago Defender, November 1975; FBI Rushing Jr. report, Warren Commission Document #117, December, 5, 1963.

[26] "Findings of the Select Committee on Assassinations in the Assassination of President John F. Kennedy," op. cit.

[27] Ibid.

[28] Black, op. cit.

[29] Ibid.

[30] "Vallee, Thomas Arthur, 1933-1988, Personal Authority Record." National Archives, no. #10600562; Bolden, op. cit., pp. 49, 55-56.

[31] John Edgar Hoover, letter to Thomas A. Vallee, February 15, 1968, Thomas A. Vallee, letter to J. Edgar Hoover, February 11, 1968, National Archives Record No. 124-10335-10278, unclassified by FBI in 1998; FBI Shanahan report, Warren Commission Document #460, February 5, 1964; Document #462, February 12, 1964.

[32] FBI report, "Comparison of photos with Thomas Arthur Vallee." Mary Ferrell Foundation, National Archives, October 1, 1974.

[33] Chuck Goudie, "JFK murder plots planned in Chicago before Dallas assassination." ABC-7 News, November 5, 2013; Bolden, op. cit., pp. 47-50; Douglass, op. cit., pp. 213-17.

[34] "Threats on Kennedy Made Here." Tampa Tribune, November 23, 1963.

[35] Dan Christensen, "A Miami police informant, a prophetic racist and fresh questions about JFK's death." Miami Herald, November 15, 2013; Donald E. Wilkes Jr., "The Georgian who knew a sniper would kill JFK." Flagpole, October 23, 2013.

[36] "Transcript of Milteer-Somersett Tape," Mary Ferrell Foundation website; Harold Weisberg, "The Milteer Documents," *The Assassinations: Dallas and Beyond.* Random House, 1976.

[37] Wilkes, op. cit.

[38] FBI Gemberling Report, Warren Commission Document #1107, May 15, 1964; Ayton, op. cit., p. 66; Fred Ligarde and Howard K. Rutherford, FBI report TP 62-455.

[39] Frank DeBenedictis, "Four Days Before Dallas: JFK in Tampa." Tampa Bay History, Fall/Winter 1994, Vol. 16; "Findings of the Select Committee on Assassinations in the Assassination of President John F. Kennedy," op. cit..

[40] Vince Michael Palamara, Survivor's Guilt: The Secret Service and the Failure to Protect the President. Trine Day, 2013; William Kelly, "The Tampa Plot in Retrospect." JFK CounterCoup, July 7, 2012.

[41] Lamar Waldron and Thom Hartman, *Ultimate Sacrifice: John and Robert Kennedy, the Plan for a Coup in Cuba, and the Murder of JFK*. Counterpoint, 2008; Jennifer Liberto, "New book tells of JFK plot in Tampa," Tampa Bay Times, November 23, 2005.

[42] "Book V - The Investigation of the Assassination of President John F. Kennedy: Performance of the Intelligence Agencies." Church Committee report, 1976, pp. 61-63.

[43] "Cuban-American." CIA files, House Assassinations Committee, unclassified November 4, 2021; Liberto, op. cit.

[44] Church Committee report, p. 60-62; "Cuban-American," op. cit.

[45] S. D. Breckinridge, "Final review of House Select Committee on Assassinations draft reports," marked "secret." National Archives record #104-10146-10093, released December 15, 2021.

[46] Evan S. Benn, "JFK toured Florida only days before he was assassinated in Dallas." Miami Herald, November 16, 2013.

[47] Paul Bleau, "The Three Failed Plots to Kill JFK: The Historians' Guide on how to Research his Assassination." Kennedys and King, November 18, 2016; U.S. Senate Subcommittee Hearings on Castro, Fair Play for Cuba Committee, February 8, 1963, p. 51.

[48] Jeff Rense, "Jim Marrs – Lee Harvey Oswald – American Hero." Jeff Rense Program, 2013; Ligarde and Rutherford, op. cit.

[49] Secret Service Agent Joseph E. Noonan, "Lee Harvey Oswald, Assassination of President Kennedy." U.S. Secret Service declassified memorandum report, #CO-2-34,030, December 3, 1963; Bolden, op. cit., pp. 56-58.

[50] Willie A. Somersett, "I Charge Robert F. Kennedy with Murder." National Federation of Labor News, March 26, 1967.

[51] Melissa Ross, "*The Devil's Chessboard* draws CIA connection to JFK assassination." Florida Politics, October 14, 2015; Poulgrain, op. cit., p. 53.

[52] Joseph Cosco, "Hunt Loses Libel Case." Sun-Sentinel, February 7, 1985; Mark Lane, *Plausible Denial*. Thunder's Mouth Press, 1991, pp. 129-132, 296-305; "Allegations by Cuban diplomat." CIA Secret memo, #110665, October 17, 1977; "Ilona Marita Lorenz," CIA confidential memo, March 2, 1982; Erik Hedegaard, "The Last Confessions of E. Howard Hunt." Rolling Stone, April 5, 2007.

[53] Marrs, op. cit., pp. 401-02.

[54] "Bottom Line: How Crazy Is It?" Newsweek, December 22, 1991.

[55] Robert Groden and Marshal Evans, *JFK: The Case for Conspiracy*. New Frontier Publications, 2015, p. 34.

[56] John Craig, Phillip Rogers, and Gary Shaw, "Chauncey Holt interview." Newsweek, October 19, 1991.

[57] Nelle M. Doyle, Letter to Pierre Salinger, Press Secretary, The White House, October 28, 1963; Rebecca Onion, "In a Prophetic Letter, a Dallas Citizen Begged JFK Not to Visit." Slate, November 15, 2013.

[58] Talbot, *Brothers*, op. cit., pp. 324-25; Comstock, op. cit.; Marrs, op. cit., p. 401.

[59] Shay, SR Dallas, op. cit., personal notes of Jarnagin interview, 1988.

[60] Shay, "My life with the mob," op. cit.; Shay personal notes of interview with Becky Oliver Massegee, 1994.

[61] Ibid.; Don Fulsom, "Did Jack Ruby Know Lee Harvey Oswald?" Crime Magazine, March 27, 2009.

[62] Shay, op. cit.

[63] Harrison E. Livingstone, *The Radical Right and the Murder of John F. Kennedy*. Trafford Publishing, 2006, p. 342.

[64] Bill Pulte, "Dick Loomis," personal memo, January 1, 1990.

[65] Pulte, "Interviews with Mack Pate," memo, January 1, 1990.

[66] James DiEugenio and Lisa Pease, *The Assassinations: Probe Magazine on JFK, MLK, RFK and Malcolm X*. Feral House, 2003, p. 122.

[67] Marrs, op. cit., pp. 408-09; Williams, and Shay, op. cit., pp. 125-26; personal notes of Esther Mash interview, 1988.

[68] Shay, SR Dallas, op. cit.; personal notes.

[69] DiEugenio, op. cit., p. 121.

[70] Douglass, op. cit., pp. 225-26, 335.

[71] "Oswald didn't act alone, widow says." Associated Press, September 28, 1988.

[72] DiEugenio, op. cit., p. 123.

[73] Ibid., p. 124; Douglass, op. cit., pp. 351-56.

[74] Ibid.

[75] Douglass, op. cit., pp. 160-62.

[76] Ibid.

[77] U.S. House Select Committee on Assassinations hearings, Vol. X, pp. 18-35; Sylvia Meagher, *Accessories After the Fact* (Skyhorse Publishing, 1967).

[78] Earl Golz, "Kennedy witness 'owed' FBI." The Dallas Morning News, September 17, 1978.

[79] U.S. House Select Committee on Assassinations hearings. Vol. X, pp. 18-35.

[80] Pulte, "Research on Kennedy assassination," July 26, 1992; Pulte, "Memo on harassment," August 4, 1993.

[81] Pulte, "Research on Kennedy assassination," op. cit.

[82] Ibid.; Golz, "1963 tape reveals threat to JFK," op. cit.

[83] Norden, op. cit., p. 162.

[84] Golz, op. cit.

[85] Rense, op. cit.

[86] Ray and Mary LaFontaine, *Oswald Talked: The New Evidence in the JFK Assassination*. Pelican Publishing, January 31, 1996, pp. 300-01.

[87] Ibid.

[88] Rense, op. cit.

[89] Baker, Amazon biography, op.cit.; Hedegaard, op. cit.; Baker, op. cit.

[90] Rense, op. cit.

[91] John Guare, "21 November 1963." The Huffington Post, November 18, 2013.

[92] A. Rosen, "Assassination of President Kennedy." FBI Memorandum #62-109060-5020, April 4, 1967.

[93] Timothy Noah, "The day before JFK was assassinated." MSNBC, November 21, 2013; Kitty Kelley, *The Family: The Real Story of the Bush Dynasty*. Doubleday, 2004, pp. 212-213.

[94] Oliver, *Nightmare in Dallas*, op. cit., pp. 110-12; Shay personal notes of interview with Oliver, 1994; Martha A. Moyer and R.F. Gallagher, "Where was Jack Ruby on November 21 and November 22?" The Fourth Decade, January 1997.

[95] McMillan, op. cit., pp. 515-16.

[96] Mae Brussell, "The Last Words of Lee Harvey Oswald," *The People's Almanac #2*. Bantam Books, 1978, pp. 47-52.

[97] "Testimony of Mrs. Lee Harvey Oswald," op. cit., Vol. I, pp. 65-66.

[98] Ibid.; Mailer, op. cit., p. 786.

[99] Ibid.

[100] McMillan, op. cit., p. 524; Mailer, op. cit., pp. 787-88.

Chapter Eight: The Sun Goes Out in Dallas

[1] William Manchester, *The Death of a President: 25 Years* (Harper & Row, 1988), pp. 106-07, 114.

[2] Ibid., p. 112.

[3] Ira David Wood III, *JFK Assassination Chronology*. Smashwords, 2013.

[4] Scott K. Parks, "Co-worker who drove Oswald to school book depository recounts Dallas' darkest day." The Dallas Morning News, April 1, 2013.

[5] Ibid.

[6] Simkin, "Bernard Weissman." Spartacus Educational, August 2014; Parks, "Extremists in Dallas created volatile atmosphere before JFK's 1963 visit." The Dallas Morning News, October 12, 2013.

[7] "Testimony of Bernard William Weissman," Warren Commission, Washington, D.C., June 23, 1964.

[8] Ibid.

[9] W. Harlan Brown and Edwin D. Kuykendall, FBI Report #DL 100-10461, Dallas, Tx., May 15, 1964.

[10] Ibid.

[11] Manchester, op. cit., pp. 110, 113.

[12] Ibid., p. 121.

[13] Marrs, op. cit., p. 7.

[14] James H. Fetzer, *Assassination Science: Experts Speak Out on the Death of JFK*. Open Court, 1998, p. 371; personal interview with Mike Niebuhr, 1989.

[15] Talbot, op. cit., p. 245.

[16] Earl Golz, "SS 'imposters' spotted by JFK witnesses." The Dallas Morning News, August 27, 1978.

[17] Marrs, op. cit., pp. 18-19.

[18] Marrs, op. cit., pp. 17-18.

[19] Marrs, op. cit., pp. 75-77.

[20] Bill Pulte, "McFadin/Wallace involvement," September 26, 1990.

[21] Golz, "SS," op. cit.

[22] Sherry P. Fiester, *Enemy of the Truth: Myths, Forensics, and the Kennedy Assassination*. JFK Lancer Productions, 2012.

[23] "Testimony of Arnold Louis Rowland," Warren Commission, Washington, D.C., March 10, 1964.

[24] Marrs, op. cit., pp. 20-26; Wood, op. cit.

[25] "Testimony of Howard Leslie Brennan," Warren Commission. Washington, D.C., March 24, 1964.

[26] Jesse Curry, *JFK Assassination File*. American Poster and Printing Co., 1969, p. 21.

[27] Marrs, op. cit., p. 11.

[28] Manchester, op. cit., p. 156.

[29] Granberry, "Those who rode by Kennedy remember," op. cit.; Marrs, op. cit., pp. 30-31.

[30] Cyril Wecht and Dawna Kaufmann, *The JFK Assassination Dissected: An Analysis by Forensic Pathologist Cyril Wecht*. Exposit Books, 2021; "Windshield Removed from the Presidential Limousine that Carried President John F. Kennedy During the Assassination." U.S. National Archives, Record Group 272, ID #305143.

[31] "Testimony of Howard Leslie Brennan," op. cit.

[32] Ibid.

[33] "Testimony of Mrs. Earle Cabell," Warren Commission, Dallas, Tx., July 13, 1964.

[34] "Testimony of Tom C. Dillard," Warren Commission, Dallas, Tx., April 1, 1964.

[35] "Testimony of Robert Hill Jackson," Warren Commission, Washington, D.C., March 10, 1964.

[36] "Testimony of Malcolm Couch," "Testimony of Tom C. Dillard," April 1, 1964.

[37] "Testimony of Robert Hill Jackson," op. cit.

[38] Golz, "SS," op. cit.

[39] Ibid.

40 Oliver, *Nightmare in Dallas*, op. cit., pp. 116-23.
41 Ibid., pp. 132-34.
42 Marrs, op. cit., pp. 37-38, 79, 324.
43 Groden and Evans, op. cit.
44 Marrs, op. cit., pp. 64-67.
45 Ibid., p. 38.
46 Golz, op. cit.
47 Marrs, op. cit., pp. 325-27.
48 Ibid.
49 Ibid., pp. 56-58.
50 Ibid., pp. 70-71.
51 Bill Pulte, Memo on "Eddie Younger," November 9, 1989.
52 Kathryn Jones, "The Skeptic's lot." Dallas Life Magazine, November 22, 1992.
53 Marrs, op. cit., pp. 81-85.
54 Ibid.
55 Shay, interview with Michael Brownlow, Dallas, August 2016.
56 Roger Craig, "When They Kill a President." Ratical, 1971.
57 "Testimony of Roger D. Craig," Warren Commission, Dallas, Tx., April 1, 1964.
58 Ibid.
59 Douglass, op. cit., pp. 276-77.
60 Brussell, op. cit., pp. 47-52; Craig, op cit.
61 Bartholomew, "Possible Discovery of an Automobile Used in the JFK Conspiracy." Fair Play Magazine, 1993.
62 Groden and Evans, op. cit.
63 Ibid., pp. 2, 30-31.
64 Ibid. pp. 30-31.
65 Ibid., p. 43.
66 Marrs, op. cit., pp. 47-48.
67 Ibid., p. 48.
68 Ibid., pp. 49-50.
69 "Testimony of Marrion L. Baker," Warren Commission, Washington, D.C., March 25, 1964.
70 Ibid.
71 Marrs, op. cit., p. 53.
72 Shay, "My life with the mob," op. cit.
73 Ibid.
74 Bill Pulte, "Interviews with Mack Pate," January 1, 1990.
75 Staffan H. Westerberg and Pete Engwall, "Looking at the Tippit Case from a Different Angle: A Theory." Assassination of JFK.net, June 6, 2014.

[76] J.G. Lowrey, "Mystery lingers 25 years after killings." The Oak Cliff Tribune, June 30, 1988.
[77] Garrison, op. cit., p. 194.
[78] Marrs, op. cit., pp 350-51; Brussell, op. cit., pp. 47-52.
[79] Brussell, op. cit., pp. 47-52.
[80] Marrs, op. cit., p. 352.
[81] Ibid., p. 353.
[82] Lowrey, op. cit.
[83] Douglass, op. cit., pp. 292-98.
[84] Brussell, op. cit., pp. 47-52.
[85] Scott P. Johnson, *The Faces of Lee Harvey Oswald: The Evolution of an Alleged Assassin*. Lexington Books, 2013, p. 43.
[86] Rense, op. cit.
[87] Marrs, op. cit., pp. 355-56.
[88] "Cabell Says Dallas Shocked by Slaying." The Dallas Morning News, November 23, 1963.
[89] Rense, op. cit.
[90] Simkin, "Hal Hendrix." Spartacus Educational, March 2015; Bernstein, Carl. "The CIA and the Media: How Americas Most Powerful News Media Worked Hand in Glove with the Central Intelligence Agency and Why the Church Committee Covered It Up." Rolling Stone, October 20, 1977.
[91] Marrs, op. cit., p. 356.
[92] Brussell, op. cit.
[93] Hosty, op. cit., pp. 20-21.
[94] "Testimony of James W. Bookhout," Warren Commission, Dallas, Tx., April 8, 1964, p. 312; "Testimony of James Patrick Hosty Jr.," Warren Commission, Vol. IV, April 8, 1964, p. 468.
[95] Brussell, op. cit.
[96] Ibid.
[97] Brussell, op. cit.
[98] Norden, op. cit., p. 165.
[99] Craig, op. cit; Mark Lane, "Oswald innocent? A lawyer's brief." National Guardian, December 19, 1963.
[100] Craig, op cit.
[101] Lane, op cit.
[102] Brussell, Mae, op. cit.
[103] Shay, "Kennedy: Will 2039 provide answers?" Richland Mandala, May 1, 1978.
[104] W.E. Chambers, Dallas Police Department arrest reports, November 22, 1963.
[105] Ibid.

[106] John Craig, Phillip Rogers, and Gary Shaw, "Chauncey Holt interview." Newsweek, October 19, 1991; Holt, Self-Portrait of a Scoundrel, TrineDay, 2013.

[107] John Hanchette, "Sleuths plan JFK assassination conspiracy convention." Gannett News Service, September 29, 1994.

[108] Bill Pulte, "Links between groups and individuals," November 22, 1990; "Belmont update," September 27, 1990.

[109] Ibid.

[110] Pulte, "Research on Kennedy assassination," July 26, 1992.

[111] Russell, op. cit., pp. 576, 788.

[112] James P. Johnston and Jon Roe, *Flight from Dallas: New Evidence of CIA Involvement in the Murder of President John F. Kennedy.* Trafford Publishing, 2005; Douglass, op. cit., pp. 298-304.

[113] Ibid.

[114] Garrison, "Opening statement," op. cit.

[115] House Assassinations Committee, Appendix, Vol. X, p. 113.

[116] Garrison, On the Trail of the Assassins, op. cit., pp. 6-7.

[117] Judyth Baker, *David Ferrie.* Trine Day, 2014; Ibid., pp. 7-8, 11.

[118] "Testimony of Mrs. Lee Harvey Oswald," op. cit.; "Testimony of Ruth Hyde Paine," op. cit.

[119] Robert C. Lish, FBI report, JFK Document No. 105-82555-1437, November 26, 1963; Martin Hay, "Who are the Paines?" The Mysteries of Dealey Plaza, August 9, 2010.

[120] "Testimony of Michael R. Paine," op. cit.

[121] Hay, op. cit.

[122] Talbot, *Brothers*, op. cit., pp. 2, 24; Waldron, op. cit., pp. 383, 386-87.

[123] Summers and Swan, "The Claims that Mafia Bosses Trafficante and Marcello Admitted Involvement in Assassinating President Kennedy." WordPress, November 23, 2013.

[124] Grady, op. cit.

[125] Ibid.

[126] Turner, op. cit.

[127] Livingstone, op. cit., p. 82.

[128] Wilkes, op. cit.

[129] Caufield, op. cit., pp. 112-14.

[130] Ibid., pp. 115-16.

[131] Ivins, op. cit.

[132] "1963: 'Stunned into silence' by JFK's death." BBC, 2005; Jarvis DeBerry, "Hatred of Catholics led some to cheer JFK's assassination." The Times-Picayune, November 21, 2013; Manchester, op. cit.

[133] "1963: 'Stunned into silence' by JFK's death," op. cit.

[134] John Guare, "21 November 1963." The Huffington Post, November 18, 2013.

[135] Philip F. Nelson, *LBJ: From Mastermind to "The Colossus."* Skyhorse Publishing, 2014.

[136] Goodman, "A CIA tie to JFK assassination?" op. cit.

[137] Marrs, op. cit., pp. 296-97.

[138] David Lawler, "How Richard Nixon learned of John F. Kennedy's death." The [London] Telegraph, November 22, 2013.

[139] Garrison, Assassins, op. cit., pp. 29-32.

[140] Garrison, "Opening statement."

[141] Joseph Hanley and William Johnson, FBI report DL 89-43, December 5, 1963.

[142] Ibid.; Pulte, "Individuals at Level One & Level Two," November 3, 1990.

[143] "Testimony of Mrs. Lee Harvey Oswald," op. cit.

[144] Ibid.

[145] Robert L. Oswald, *Lee: A Portrait of Lee Harvey Oswald by His Brother.* Coward McCann, 1967, p. 144.

[146] Brussell, op. cit.

[147] Jay Lipp, "Did Oswald Attempt to Call a Military Counterintelligence Agent from the Dallas Jail?" The JFK Assassination from Both Sides.

[148] Bolden, op. cit., pp. 53-54.

[149] "Testimony of Dean Adams Andrews Jr," Warren Commission, New Orleans, La., July 21, 1964.

[150] "Testimony of Ruth Hyde Paine," op. cit.

[151] Brussell, op. cit.

[152] Ibid.

[153] "Testimony of Ruth Hyde Paine," op. cit.

[154] "Testimony of Mrs. Marguerite Oswald," op. cit.; "Testimony of Robert Edward Lee Oswald," op. cit.

[155] "Testimony of Harry N. Olsen," Warren Commission, Los Angeles, Calif., August 6, 1964.

[156] Posner, op. cit., pp. 375-76.

[157] Bill Pulte, "November 22: New story on what Jack Ruby was up to." The Addison-North Dallas Register, November 21, 1991.

[158] Ibid.

[159] Marrs, op. cit., pp. 415-16.

[160] Newseum with Dan Rather, Cathy Trost, Susan Bennett. *President Kennedy Has Been Shot.* Sourcebooks, 2003, p. 109.

[161] Marrs, op. cit., pp. 416-17.

[162] Russell, op. cit., pp. 376-77.

[163] Ibid.

[164] "Testimony of Mr. Jack Ruby," op. cit.

[165] "Bottom Line: How Crazy Is It?" op. cit.

[166] "Findings of the Select Committee on Assassinations in the Assassination of President John F. Kennedy," op. cit.

[167] Brussell, op. cit.

[168] "Testimony of Mr. Jack Ruby," op. cit.

[169] Pulte, "Finley interview," March 1, 1989.

[170] Marrs, op. cit., pp. 419-20.

[171] "Testimony of Mr. Jack Ruby," op. cit.

[172] Ibid.

[173] J. Edgar Hoover, "Memorandum for Messrs. Tolson, Belmont, Mohr, Conrad, DeLoach, Evans, Rosen, Sullivan," FBI, November 29, 1963; Niebuhr interview, op. cit.

[174] Posner, op. cit., pp. 396-97.

[175] "Testimony of Mr. Jack Ruby," op. cit.; Marrs, op. cit., pp. 430-31.

[176] Morley, "Ex-flame," op. cit.; "Sworn testimony of Joseph Campisi," op. cit.

[177] Shay, SR Dallas, op. cit.

[178] "Testimony of Mrs. Marguerite Oswald," op. cit.

[179] Ibid.

[180] "Testimony of Mrs. Lee Harvey Oswald," op. cit.

[181] "Testimony of Mrs. Marguerite Oswald," op. cit.

Chapter Nine: The Fix Is In

[1] "Interview of Drs. James J. Humes and J. Thornton Boswell by the Forensic Pathology Panel," National Archives, House Select Committee on Assassinations, September 16, 1977.

[2] "The Deposition of Dr. James Joseph Humes," Assassination Records Review Board, College Park, Md., February 13, 1996.

[3] Jan K. Herman and Andre B. Sobocinski, "Navy Medicine and President Kennedy's Autopsy: Recollections from a former White House Physician," U.S. Navy Bureau of Medicine and Surgery, transcript of James Young's 2001 interview, published November 19, 2013.

[4] Ibid.

[5] Jeremy Bojczuk, "Richard Sprague: Memo re Dr George Burkley," *22 November 1963: A Brief Guide to the JFK Assassination*. Boxgrove Publishing, 2014; Talbot, *Brothers*, op. cit., pp. 16-17.

[6] "The Deposition of Dr. J. Thornton Boswell," Assassination Records Review Board, College Park, Md., February 26, 1996.

[7] "The Deposition of Dr. James Joseph Humes," op. cit.

[8] Shay, "Kennedy's autopsy in Bethesda continues to raise questions 50 years later." The Gazette of Politics and Business, November 20, 2013.

[9] Ibid.

[10] Gary L. Aguilar and Kathy Cunningham, "How five investigations into JFK's medical/autopsy evidence got it wrong." History Matters, May 2003.

[11] John R. Tunheim and Laura A. Denk, "Chapter 6, Part II: Clarifying the Federal Record on the Zapruder Film and the Medical and Ballistics Evidence," Final Report of the Assassination Records Review Board, September 1998.

[12] "Overwhelming Evidence Oswald was the Assassin: A 1966 U.S. News & World Report interview with Arlen Specter, assistant counsel for the Warren Commission." U.S. News & World Report, November 14, 2013.

[13] Douglas P. Horne, "The James Curtis Jenkins Revelations at JFK Lancer Confirm a Massive Medical Cover-up in 1963." Inside the ARRB, November 26, 2013.

[14] Ibid.

[15] "Interview of Drs. James J. Humes and J. Thornton Boswell by the Forensic Pathology Panel," op. cit.

[16] Ibid.

[17] "The Deposition of Dr. James Joseph Humes," op. cit.

[18] "Findings of the Select Committee on Assassinations in the Assassination of President John F. Kennedy," op. cit.

[19] Cyril Wecht and Dawna Kaufmann, *The JFK Assassination Dissected: An Analysis by Forensic Pathologist Cyril Wecht*. Exposit Books, 2021; Shay, "Kennedy's autopsy," op. cit.

[20] Herman, op. cit.

[21] Dennis L. Breo, "JFK: The Autopsy. Doctors Say The Examination Was Not Impeded." Journal of the American Medical Association, Chicago Tribune, May 24, 1992.

[22] Peter Dale Scott, *Deep Politics and the Death of JFK*. University of California Press, 1996, pp. 44-46; "Testimony of Nicholas Katzenbach," Select Committee on Assassinations, U.S. House of Representatives, September 21, 1978; "CIA files related to Ruby's Cuban activities," #180-10143-10176. Select Committee, 1978.

[23] Nicholas Katzenbach, "Memorandum for Mr. Moyers," U.S. Justice Department, November 25, 1963.

[24] "Phone call between President Johnson and FBI Director Hoover," 10:30 a.m., November 25, 1963, Walkthrough: Formation of the Warren Commission, Mary Ferrell Foundation.

[25] "Telephone Conversation between the President and Mr. Joe Alsop," 10:40 a.m., November 25, 1963, LBJ Library, Mary Ferrell Foundation; Bernstein, op. cit.

[26] Scott, op. cit., pp. XVIII, 38; "The Marxist marine." Newsweek, December 2, 1963; Richard Dudman, "Uncertainties Remain Despite Police View of Kennedy Death." St. Louis Post-Dispatch, December 1, 1963.

[27] "Telephone Conversation between the President and Senator Russell," 8:55 p.m., November 29, 1963, LBJ Library, Mary Ferrell Foundation.

[28] Ibid.

29 Ed Rampell, "Oliver Stone talks to Jacobin about JFK's killing." Jacobin, November 23, 2021; Talbot, *The Devil's Chessboard*, op. cit., p. 8.

30 Marrs, op. cit., p. 297.

31 "Telephone conversation between the President and J. Edgar Hoover," transcript, Mary Ferrell Foundation, November 29, 1963.

32 Ibid.

33 Golz, "Papers link Ruby, Oswald." The Dallas Morning News, March 28, 1976.

34 Rick Klein, "Jacqueline Kennedy on Rev. Martin Luther King Jr." ABC News, September 8, 2011.

35 Marrs, op. cit., pp. 297-98.

36 Warren Hinckle, "Couple talks about bad days in CIA." San Francisco Examiner, September 12, 1978.

37 "Testimony of James B. Wilcott," op. cit., p. 44.

38 Waldron, op. cit., p. 414; Johnson, op. cit., p. 43.

39 "Testimony of James B. Wilcott," op. cit., p. 48.

40 Ibid.

41 Hosty, op. cit., pp. 29-31.

42 Ibid.

43 Ibid.

44 McMillan, op. cit., p. 625.

45 Nannie Lee Fenner, sworn statement, FBI, Dallas, Tx., July 15, 1975.

46 McMillan, op. cit., p. 626.

47 "Testimony of James W. Bookhout," p. 313.

48 Oswald, Robert, op. cit., pp. 158-59, 162.

49 "Testimony of Mrs. Marguerite Oswald," op. cit.

50 "Testimony of Mrs. Lee Harvey Oswald," op. cit.

51 Hoover, op. cit.

52 Lynn Callison, "Hiding is over for Marina." New York Post, July 14, 1977.

53 De Mohrenschildt, I am a Patsy! I am a Patsy! op. cit., p. 249.

54 Ibid., pp. 259-260.

55 "Testimony of Ruth Hyde Paine," op. cit.

56 Bartholomew, "Byrds, Planes, and an Automobile," op. cit.; Russell, op. cit., pp. 376-77.

57 Pulte, "Dick Loomis," January 1, 1990.

58 McMillan, op. cit., p. 563.

59 Mailer, op. cit., p. 787.

60 "Testimony of Mrs. Marguerite Oswald," op. cit.

61 "Testimony of Robert Edward Lee Oswald," op. cit.

62 Ibid.

63 "Testimony of Mrs. Lee Harvey Oswald," op. cit.

[64] Ibid.
[65] Ibid.
[66] "Oswald didn't act alone, widow says," Associated Press, September 28, 1988.
[67] De Mohrenschildt, *I am a Patsy! I am a Patsy!* op. cit., p. 220.
[68] Earl Golz and Don Fisher. "Campisi subpoenaed in JFK probe." The Dallas Morning News, March 9, 1978; Ibid.
[69] De Mohrenschildt, op. cit.
[70] "Testimony of Ruth Hyde Paine," op. cit.
[71] "Testimony of Michael R. Paine," op. cit.
[72] "Testimony of George S. de Mohrenschildt," op. cit.
[73] De Mohrenschildt, I am a Patsy! I am a Patsy! op. cit., pp. 240-41.
[74] Ibid., p. 93.
[75] De Mohrenschildt, I am a Patsy! I am a Patsy! op. cit.
[76] Ibid.
[77] Talbot, Brothers, op. cit., pp. 6-7.
[78] Goodman, "A CIA tie to JFK assassination?" op. cit.
[79] "Hoffa is guilty of trying to fix a federal jury." The New York Times, March 5, 1964.
[80] James Stengle, "RFK children speak about assassination in Dallas." Associated Press, January 12, 2013; David Flick, "Kennedys make rare visit to Dallas, say RFK questioned 'lone gunman' theory in JFK assassination." The Dallas Morning News, January 12, 2013.
[81] De Mohrenschildt, *I am a Patsy! I am a Patsy!* op. cit., pp. 209-11; FBI report, June 9, 1964, Warren Commission Exhibit 2823.
[82] De Mohrenschildt, op. cit., pp. 111-12.
[83] Ibid.
[84] Lt. Col. L. Fletcher. Prouty, "The Guns of Dallas." Ratical, 1975.
[85] Norden, op. cit., p. 165.
[86] Talbot, *Brothers*, op. cit., pp. 281-82; Wanda Carruthers, "Cokie Roberts: Warren Commission Dad Doubted Single Bullet Theory." Newsmax, November 22, 2013.
[87] "Testimony of Dr. Cyril H. Wecht," House Select Committee on Assassinations, September 7, 1978.
[88] Cyril H. Wecht, "Dissenting View Part VI: Addendum to the Forensic Pathology Panel Report," House Select Committee on Assassinations, Volume VII, 1979.
[89] Gaeton Fonzi, "Transcript of Fonzi-Specter Interview," Mary Ferrell Foundation, June 28, 1966.
[90] "Fonzi-Specter interviews," Mary Ferrell Foundation, 2012.
[91] Fonzi, "Transcript of Fonzi-Specter Interview," op. cit.
[92] "Testimony of Dr. Cyril H. Wecht," op. cit.
[93] Shay, "Kennedy's autopsy in Bethesda continues to raise questions 50 years later," op. cit.

[94] Norden, op. cit., pp. 167-68.

[95] Posner, op. cit., pp. XV-XVI.

[96] Charles Crenshaw, "Official version of JFK death is questionable." The Dallas Morning News, March 20, 1995.

[97] Myrna Oliver, "Charles Crenshaw, 68; Disputed JFK Findings." Los Angeles Times, November 21, 2001.

[98] "Testimony of Dr. Paul Conrad Peters," Warren Commission, March 24, 1964, Dallas, Tx., Vol. VI, p. 71.

[99] Crenshaw, op. cit.

[100] Douglass, op. cit., pp. 309-10.

[101] "Testimony of Dr. Michael Baden," House Select Committee on Assassinations, September 7, 1978.

[102] Douglass, op. cit., pp. 315-18.

[103] Ibid.

[104] Callison, "The Elusive Marina Oswald – Back in the Limelight." New York Post, July 14, 1977.

[105] Bartholomew, "Byrds, Planes, and an Automobile," op. cit.

[106] Ibid.

[107] Pulte, "Links between groups and individuals," November 22, 1990; "Belmont update," September 27, 1990.

[108] Callison, "The Elusive Marina Oswald," op. cit.

[109] Pulte, Memo on "Ilya Mamantov," August 5, 1989.

[110] Ibid.

[111] Dan Carmichael, "Oswald's widow files suit to open grave," UPI, August 19, 1981.

[112] "Oswald didn't act alone, widow says." Associated Press. September 28, 1988; Jennifer Bolch, "Marina: 18-year nightmare contains one less mystery." Dallas Times Herald, October 5, 1981.

[113] Daniel Crowley, "Lee Harvey Oswald's widow Marina convinced he did not kill JFK – and thinks her phone is still bugged." Daily Mirror, November 2, 2013; Granberry, "As paparazzi stalk her, Kennedy assassin's widow lives quiet Dallas-area life." The Dallas Morning News, November 9, 2013.

[114] Steve Jones, "Regarding Ruth and Michael Paine." Kennedy Assassination Chronicles, Vol. 4, Issue 4, Winter 1998, pp. 18, 20.

[115] Chris Smith, "Michael Paine, debated politics with JFK assassin Lee Harvey Oswald, dies at 89." Santa Rosa Press-Democrat, March 15, 2018.

[116] Shay, notes from interview with Robert P. Gemberling, Dallas, October 1988.

[117] Ibid.

[118] Ibid.

[119] Norden, op. cit., pp. 170-71.

[120] Lisa Pease, "Sirhan and the RFK Assassination Part II: Rubik's Cube." Probe Magazine, May-June 1998, Vol. 5, No. 4.

[121] Shay, notes from interview with Robert P. Gemberling, op. cit.
[122] Pulte, "Will Fritz," March 3, 1990.
[123] Larry Haapanen, "Lost and Found Oswald Interrogation Notes." Kennedy Assassination Chronicles, Vol. 7, Issue 3, 2001.
[124] Ann Zimmerman, "Stained glass." Dallas Observer, November 27, 1997.
[125] WFAA staff. "Was this window used by JFK's assassin?" WFAA-TV, October 30, 2013.
[126] Gaeton Fonzi, "In Government We Don't Trust." Open Secrets, Coalition on Political Assassinations, January 1995, p. 2.
[127] Lane, *Plausible Denial*, op. cit., pp. 34-35.
[128] "Findings of the Select Committee on Assassinations in the Assassination of President John F. Kennedy," op. cit.
[129] Ibid.
[130] "Organized Crime Expert Sees Mob Connections." ABC News, November 20, 2003.
[131] Rockwood, "Interview: G. Robert Blakey," op. cit.
[132] Scott, op. cit., pp. 68-69.
[133] Rockwood, op. cit.

Chapter Ten: Ghosts of Dealey Plaza

[1] Penn Jones Jr., *Forgive My Grief II*. The Midlothian Mirror, 1967, pp. 20-21.
[2] Benzkofer, Stephan. "Karyn Kupcinet 1963 death still unsolved." Chicago Tribune, November 24, 2013.
[3] Jones, "Disappearing Witnesses." The Rebel, November 22, 1983.
[4] Kathryn Jones, "The Skeptic's lot," op. cit., pp. 10-11.
[5] Tim Grobaty, "Long Beach reporter Bill Hunter was in the midst of the JFK conspiracy." Long Beach Press-Telegram, November 16, 2013.
[6] David Martindale, "The bizarre deaths following JFK's murder." Argosy, March 1977; Jones, "Disappearing Witnesses," op. cit.
[7] Sara Jordan, "Who Killed Dorothy Kilgallen?" Midwest Today, Summer 2003; Mark Shaw, *The Reporter Who Knew Too Much: The Mysterious Death of What's My Line TV Star and Media Icon Dorothy Kilgallen*. Post Hill Press, 2016, pp. 294-95.
[8] Dave Price, "Local author says columnist cracked the JFK case in 1965, just before she was murdered." Palo Alto Daily Post, December 3, 2018; Shaw, op. cit., pp. 294-95.
[9] Liz Burleson, "Panel discusses lingering questions and eerie Oklahoma connection with the JFK assassination." Red Dirt Report, November 4, 2013.
[10] Jones, "Disappearing Witnesses," op. cit.

[11] Bill Sloan, "FBI eyes on Ruby strippers in JFK case." *Dallas Times Herald*, May 22, 1975; Douglass, op. cit., pp. 244-46.

[12] Richard Belzer and David Wayne, *Hit List: An In-Depth Investigation into the Mysterious Deaths of Witnesses to the JFK Assassination*. Skyhorse Publishing, 2013.

[13] Jones, "Disappearing Witnesses," op. cit.

[14] Ibid.

[15] Norden, op. cit., p. 70.

[16] Talbot, Brothers, op. cit., pp. 199-202.

[17] Norden, op. cit., p. 176.

[18] Garrison, op. cit., pp. 140-43.

[19] Norden, op. cit., p. 176.

[20] Jones, "Disappearing Witnesses," op. cit.

[21] Craig, op. cit.

[22] Garrison, op. cit., pp. 122-24.

[23] Morley, "The CIA's secret files on Jim Garrison, the prosecutor celebrated in 'JFK'," JFK Facts, August 19, 2016.

[24] Garrison, op. cit., pp. 122-24,187-92.

[25] Oliver Stone and Zachary Sklar, *JFK: The Documented Screenplay*. Applause Theatre & Cinema Books, 2000; Garrison, op. cit., pp. 132-36.

[26] William Broyles, "The Man Who Saw Too Much." *Texas Monthly*, March 1976.

[27] FBI memo, "Assassination of President John Fitzgerald Kennedy, November 22, 1963, Dallas, Tx.," May 3, 1967.

[28] Ernest A. Richel, "James Garrison/George Brown possible attempt to embarrass agency," CIA memo, December 27, 1967.

[29] Broyles, op. cit.

[30] Garrison, op. cit., pp. 165-71.

[31] Ibid.

[32] Joan Mellen, *A Farewell to Justice: Jim Garrison, JFK's Assassination, and the Case That Should Have Changed History*. Potomac Books, 2005.

[33] Mellen, op. cit., pp. 255-57.

[34] Garrison, op. cit., pp. 181-82.

[35] Norden, op. cit., pp. 188-89.

[36] Garrison, op. cit., pp. 250-51.

[37] "Jim Garrison," Spartacus, October 2021.

[38] Bernstein, op. cit.

[39] Ibid.

[40] Talbot, *Brothers,* op. cit., pp. 393-94.

[41] Lane, Plausible Denial, op. cit., p. 19; "Oswald innocent?" op. cit.

[42] Ayton, op. cit., p. 73.

[43] Ibid., pp. 79-81.

[44] Ibid., pp. 82-83.
[45] Ibid., pp. 74-75.
[46] Douglass, op. cit., pp. 214-15.
[47] Bolden, op. cit., pp. 54-55, 61-85.
[48] Ibid.
[49] Liz Smith, "JFK assassination gets another look." Toledo Blade, March 15, 2006.
[50] Maurice Possley and Matt O'Connor, "U.S. Judges in for Life – Even When Not Fit for It." Chicago Tribune, October 15, 1996; Jeffrey Haas, "What the FBI's Murder of a Black Panther Can Teach Us 40 Years Later." The Nation, December 2, 2009.
[51] Bolden, op. cit., pp. 265-77; Douglass, op. cit., pp. 215-17.
[52] Bolden, op. cit., p. 285.
[53] Waldron, op. cit., pp. 450-51.
[54] Pulte, "Richard Aubrey" memo, April 3, 1990.
[55] Caufield, op. cit., pp. XVI-XVII.
[56] "Testimony of Mr. Jack Ruby," op. cit.
[57] Dorothy Kilgallen, "Nervous Ruby feels 'breaking point' near." New York Journal-American, February 23, 1964.
Sloan, op. cit.; Norden, op. cit., pp. 175-76.
[58] Russ Baker, Family of Secrets. Bloomsbury Press, 2009, p. 268.
[59] Marrs, op. cit., pp. 465-66.
[60] Summers and Swan, op. cit.; Raymond A. Hult and Thomas K. Kimmel Jr., FBI memo DL 183A-1035, March 7, 1986.
[61] Waldron, op. cit., pp. 61-75, 182.
[62] Ibid., pp. 486-87.
[63] Douglass, op. cit., p. 156.
[64] Ibid., pp. 156-57.
[65] Ibid., p. 157.
[66] Craig Flournoy, "All Eyes Turn to Dallas." The Dallas Morning News, November 20, 1983.
[67] Ibid.
[68] Ibid.
[69] Ibid.
[70] Simkin, "Warren Reynolds." Spartacus Educational, August 2014.
[71] Oliver, *Nightmare in Dallas*, op. cit., pp. 151-54, 157-58.
[72] Marrs, op. cit., p. 84.
[74] Pulte, memos and interview.
[75] William C. Sullivan, "Hoover: Life with a Tyrant." The Washington Post, September 23, 1979.

[76] Emily Yellin, "Memphis Jury Sees Conspiracy in Martin Luther King's Killing." The New York Times, December 9, 1999; "Assassination Conspiracy Trial," The Martin Luther King, Jr. Center for Nonviolent Social Change, 1999.

[77] Yellin, op. cit.

[78] Yellin, op. cit.; Mike Dorning, "U.S. Report Debunks King Conspiracies." Chicago Tribune, June 10, 2000.

[79] News release, "Assassination Conspiracy Trial," The Martin Luther King, Jr. Center for Nonviolent Social Change, 1999.

[80] Douglass, "The Martin Luther King Conspiracy Exposed in Memphis." Probe Magazine, Spring 2000.

[81] Ibid.

[82] Vanita Gupta, "King v. Jowers conspiracy allegations." U.S. Department of Justice, Civil Rights Division. August 6, 2015.

[83] "Findings on Martin Luther King, Jr. Assassination." Report of the Select Committee on Assassinations of the U.S. House of Representatives, Washington, D.C. United States Government Printing Office, 1979.

[84] Dan Christensen, "King Assassination: FBI ignored its Miami informer." Miami Magazine, October 1976. Caufield, op. cit., p. 94; Ligarde and Rutherford, op. cit.

[85] Thurston Clarke, "The Last Good Campaign." Vanity Fair, May 1, 2008.

[86] Jones, "Disappearing Witnesses," op. cit.

[87] Lawrence Teeter, "Sirhan Sirhan: A True 'Manchurian Candidate'." Ebony Showcase Theatre website, 2004.

[88] Susan Donaldson James, "J. Edgar Hoover: Gay or Just a Man Who Has Sex With Men?" ABC News, November 16, 2011; Waldron, op. cit., p. 457.

[89] Russ Baker, "Bush angle to Reagan shooting still unresolved as Hinckley walks." Who What Why, August 16, 2016.

[90] "List of United States presidential assassination attempts and plots," Wikipedia, 2022.

[91] "NTSU prof struck by train, killed in Denton County." The Dallas Morning News, July 3, 1983; "Texas road accidents kill at least 18." Associated Press, July 3, 1983.

[92] C. Neal Tate, "Stephen M. Gorman." Political Science and Politics, The American Political Science Association, Vol. 16, Issue 4, Fall 1983, p. 767.

[93] Vincent Bugliosi Jr., *Reclaiming History: The Assassination of President John F. Kennedy*. W.W. Norton & Co., 2007, p. XV.

[94] Bryan Burrough, "Or No Conspiracy?" The New York Times, May 20, 2007.

[95] Beverly Gage, "Who Didn't Kill JFK?" The Nation, December 18, 2013; "Gerald Posner," Wikipedia, 2016.

[96] "JFK Cover-Up Artist: Vincent Bugliosi." JFK Players and Witnesses, January 15, 2013.

[97] Ami Chen Mills, *CIA Off Campus: Building the Movement Against Agency Recruitment and Research*. South End Press, 1999, p. 35; Bill MacDowall and Jim Hargrove, "The Official McAdams FAQ," The Col. L Fletcher Prouty Reference Site.

[98] Matt Labash, "Oswald's Ghosts: Searching for Signs of Intelligent Life at the National Conference on Political Assassinations." Washington City Paper, October 27, 1995.

[99] "JFK Cover-Up Artist: Vincent Bugliosi," op. cit.; Jack Dickey, "The Debunker Among the Buffs." Time, November 5, 2013.

[100] Nibor Noals, "We saw John F. Kennedy in early 1990s." About.com, April 11, 2016.

[101] R.D. Whitaker, Ghosts of Dealey Plaza, Amazon, 2015.

[102] Granberry, "Those who rode by Kennedy remember," op. cit.

Conclusion

[1] Garrison, op. cit., p. 277.

[2] Ibid., pp. 277, 281-82.

[3] Rampell, op. cit.; Bleau, op. cit.

[4] Amy B. Wang, "Biden administration released previously classified JFK assassination files." The Washington Post, December 15, 2021; Morley, "Oswald was known to a dozen senior CIA officials." The Deep State, May 18, 2018.

[5] Michael Beschloss, "Lyndon Johnson on the record." Texas Monthly, December 2001.

[6] Marrs, op. cit., p. 582; Simkin, "Madeleine Brown." Spartacus Educational, August 2014.

[7] Talbot, *The Devil's Chessboard*, op. cit., p. 3; Goodman, "The Rise of America's Secret Government," op. cit.

[8] Marrs, op. cit., pp. 583, 588.

[9] "Letter from Fidel Castro to Nikita Khrushchev, October 26, 1962." PBS, December 21, 2004.

[10] Posner, op. cit., p. XVI.

[11] Page Six staff, "Posner has new ally in plagiarism battle." New York Post, May 13, 2010.

[12] Marrs, op. cit., p. 584.

[13] Norden, op. cit., pp. 162-63.

[14] Garrison, op. cit., pp. 278-79.

[15] Mailer, op. cit., pp. 777-78.

[16] Paul Martin, "Lincoln's Missing Bodyguard." Smithsonian, April 7, 2010.

[17] Coleman Mabray and Ronald E. Brinkley, FBI report #DL 89-43, November 25, 1963.

[18] Flournoy, op. cit.

[19] Ivins, op. cit.

[20] "Assassination threats against Barack Obama." Wikipedia, November 11, 2016.

[21] Seymour M. Hersh, *The Dark Side of Camelot*. Little, Brown & Co., 1997, p. 2.

[22] Marrs, op. cit., p. 589.

[23] Haslam, op. cit., foreword.

[24] Shay, "JFK theories: Can the truth be found?" Richland Chronicle, January 26, 1979.

A historical landmark signs marks the Oak Cliff site where Dallas Police Officer J.D. Tippit was killed soon after Kennedy. Below, the ramp where Ruby entered the police building to shoot Oswald has a "do not enter" sign. [Shay photos]

Resources

Here are a few resources where you can research the JFK assassination and other matters. There are many more good sites out there.

U.S. National Archives and Records Administration
College Park, Md.
archives.gov/research/jfk
Government agency containing records of investigations into JFK killing.

Assassination Archives and Research Center
Washington, D.C.
aarclibrary.org
Founded in 1984 by Bernard Fensterwald Jr. and Jim Lesar to preserve records and educate the public on the JFK assassination and other political killings. Center is part of a coalition working on the release of the rest of the JFK assassination documents.

Mary Ferrell Foundation
maryferrell.org
Nonprofit organization that stores some 1.3 million pages of documents, government reports, books, and more related to the political assassinations of the 1960s. Most items were collected by the tireless Dallas researcher Mary Ferrell.

Kennedys and King [former CTKA]
kennedysandking.com
Group led by James DiEugenio dedicated to the political vision and legacies of the Kennedys, King, and Malcolm X, and to hte investigation of their murders. Began in 1993 as Citizens for Truth about the Kennedy Assassination. Works for full disclosure of all records relating to the assassinations.

Harold Weisberg Archive
jfk.hood.edu
Another large collection of documents related to the JFK killing, maintained by Hood College in Frederick, Maryland.

John F. Kennedy Presidential Library and Museum
Boston, Mass.
jfklibrary.org
JFK's official library with many online resources and more on site.

Martin Luther King Jr. Center for Nonviolent Social Change
Atlanta, Ga.
thekingcenter.org
Resource center and community institution dedicated to King and his teachings. Formed in 1968 by his widow, Coretta Scott King.

National Civil Rights Museum at the Lorraine Motel
www.civilrightsmuseum.org
Memphis, Tn.
Museum dedicated to the life of King and others who worked for civil rights. Converted from the former Lorraine Motel where King was assassinated in 1968.

LBJ Presidential Library
Austin, Tx.
lbjlibrary.org
LBJ's official library that also contains online resources.

Spartacus Educational
spartacus-educational.com
Great Britain-based website founded by John Simkin that provides educational information about historical events, including the JFK assassination.

JFK Facts
jfkfacts.org
Fact-based investigation and forum overseen by Jefferson Morley, former Washington Post reporter and author of *Our Man in Mexico*.

JFK CounterCoup2
jfkcountercoup2.blogspot.com
Blog by Bill Kelly, research coordinator for Citizens Against Political Assassinations.

History Matters
Ipswich, Mass.
history-matters.com
Contains many documents on the JFK assassination and Cold War history.

JFK Lancer Productions & Publications
jfklancer.com
Provides resources, books, magazines, films, and more. Has hosted an annual conference in Dallas since 1996.

JFK Assassination Conference

jfkdallasconference.com

Annual conference in Dallas organized by Judyth Baker and others.

The National Security Archive

Washington, D.C.

nsarchive.gwu.edu

Research institute and library at The George Washington University formed in 1985 by journalists and scholars to check rising government secrecy. Collects and publishes declassified government documents related to the Kennedy assassination and other historical events.

John F. Kennedy Assassination Information Center

jfkassassination.net/home.htm

Detailed transcripts of mostly government investigations into JFK assassination, including Warren Commission hearing testimony.

A Brief Guide to the JFK Assassination

22november1963.org.uk

British author Jeremy Bojczuk explores many of the key issues about the assassination.

Kevin James Shay Books and Blog

www.amazon.com/Kevin-J.-Shay/e/B004BCQRTG

kevinjshay44.medium.com

Books on Amazon and articles on Medium by writer and researcher Kevin James Shay.

The Memphis motel, above, where Martin Luther King Jr. was assassinated was turned into the National Civil Rights Museum at the Lorraine Motel. The wreath on the second story balcony, far right, marks the spot where King was killed.

Rays of sunshine, below, reach the tomb of Martin Luther King Jr. and Coretta Scott King, which rests on a stone platform surrounded by a reflecting pool at the Martin Luther King Jr. Center in Atlanta. [Shay photos]

Index

Alpha 66 organization, 53, 111-12, 121, 124-25, 144

Arlington National Cemetery, 9-11, 176

Arnold, Gordon, 153-54, 158, 257

Aynesworth, Hugh, 15, 118, 225-26

Baker, Judyth, 104-5, 107, 145, 173, 260, 302

Banister, William Guy, 99-103, 106-7, 112, 119-20, 172, 177, 192, 224, 242, 249

Bay of Pigs, 26, 34-52, 57-59, 62, 96, 99-101, 121, 125, 138, 143-44, 203, 245, 247, 250

Bissell, Richard, 30-31, 34, 37-38, 40-41, 45, 50-51, 53, 62

Bolden, Abraham, 26, 122, 129-30, 132, 179, 229-30, 254-56, 261

Bowers, Jr., Lee, 153, 223, 262

Brennan, Howard, 154, 156-57, 163, 251

Brigade 2506, 26, 36, 40-48, 59

Brownlow, Michael, 161, 171, 185

Byrd, D. Harold, 70, 117, 174, 210, 215, 236

Cabell, Charles, 30-32, 42, 50-51, 62, 68, 106, 176, 249, 253

Cabell, Earle, 50, 68, 152, 157, 168, 183

Campisi, Joseph, 109-10, 147, 183, 235

Carousel Club, 12, 108-10, 139, 141, 165, 183, 195, 221-22

Castro, Fidel,
  anti-Castro movement, 16, 31, 49, 75, 99-103, 104-05, 119-21, 137, 143-44
  attempt to blame JFK assassination on, 11-12, 164, 171, 194-96

Castro
  Bay of Pigs conflict, 36-50, 57-58, 250
  CIA-Mafia plots against, 31-33, 51-56, 226
  death, 56-57
  guerrilla war campaign, 27-30
  possible role in JFK assassination, 58-59, 247, 250

Church Committee, 56, 135, 231

Civello, Joseph, 108-09, 171, 235

Connally Jr., John, 13, 139-40, 152, 155-56, 159, 195, 206-07

Craig, Deputy Roger, 155, 161-62, 164, 167, 170, 224, 257, 262

Crenshaw, Dr. Charles, 209

Cuban Missile Crisis, 54-55, 91-92, 112-13, 121

De Mohrenschildt, George
  CIA ties, 90, 200
  harassed by FBI, 192-93
  Jackie Kennedy ties, 90, 203
  link to Oswald, 90-93, 192, 204
  suicide, 232
  Warren Commission, 200-03

DiEugenio, James, 10, 14-15, 142, 208, 260, 300

Douglass, James, 16, 112, 237-38, 256-57, 260

Dulles, Allen
  activities after CIA, 61-63, 137, 176, 226
  as CIA director, 29-34, 39, 44, 48
  family background, 60-61
  resignation, 50-51, 247-49
  Warren Commission, 194, 202, 204

Eisenhower, Dwight D., 25, 28-30, 33-35, 39, 55-56, 61, 81, 247
Fair Play for Cuba Committee, 101-03, 120, 124, 135-36, 181-82, 246, 251
Ferrell, Mary, 12-13, 255, 260, 300
Ferrie, David, 75, 100-02, 104-07, 117, 119, 140, 144, 172-73, 177, 192, 223-24, 226, 250
Fritz, Capt. Will, 138, 168, 181, 214

Garrison, Jim
  beliefs on case, 51, 91-92, 95, 99-103, 106-07, 115, 144, 165-66, 169, 172-73, 207-08, 214, 223, 245
    harassment, 16-17, 223-27
    investigation and trial of Clay Shaw, 107-08, 223-27
Gemberling, Robert, 212-14, 251, 255
Giancana, Sam, 23, 32, 51-52, 63-65, 195, 204, 231, 247, 254
Golz, Earl, 14, 143, 153-54, 193, 196
Groden, Robert, 138, 159, 162-63, 217

Hargis, Bobby, 9, 156, 243
Harvey, William, 51-56, 62, 137, 247
Hill, Jean, 159, 235, 262
Hoffa, Jimmy, 11, 23, 25, 66-67, 139, 174, 204, 216, 226, 247, 249-50, 254
Holt, Chauncey, 138, 170-71, 182
Hosty Jr., James, 117-18, 168-69, 198, 214
Hoover, J. Edgar
  animosity towards Kennedys, King, 196, 236, 238-39, 248, 253
  closeness to LBJ, 69, 191-92
  letter to JFK killing suspect, 121, 130-31
  organized crime, 64, 68, 140
  rush to blame Oswald, 116, 167-68, 177, 191-96
  secret files, 69, 213, 236-39, 248

Hunt, E. Howard, 30-31, 42, 62, 130, 137-38, 145, 170, 204, 247, 249, 255
Hunt, H.L., 12, 60, 68, 150-52, 174, 180-81, 200, 237, 250

JFK Records Act, 14, 260
John Birch Society, 47, 68, 94, 97, 100, 125, 129, 150, 152, 219, 231
Johnson, Lyndon Baines
  1948 threat to kill, 68-69
  belief in conspiracy, 196, 228-29, 247
  cover-up after JFK assassination, 191-93, 195
  Cuba concerns, 56. 196, 228-29
  questionable elections, 20-21
  reverses JFK policies, 10, 49, 246
  suspicious deaths, 69-71, 234
  Warren Commission, 191, 194
Jones Jr., Penn, 14, 160, 219, 239, 254

Kennedy, Jacqueline
  actions after husband shot, 156
  others' anger towards, 174-75
  Dallas reaction, 149-52
  Ruby concerned about, 181-82
Kennedy, John F.
  1960 presidential campaign, 19-24
  1960 stalker, 24-25
  actions day of assassination, 149-56
  autopsy of, 187-91, 208-10
  Bay of Pigs criticism, 48
  Castro plots involvement, 52, 226
  Chicago plot, 128-32
  CIA dealings, 48-52
  civil rights, 26, 121, 123, 125
  Cuban Missile Crisis, 54-55
  détente/peace issues, 10, 54-56, 81
  extramarital affairs alleged, 223
  funeral, 9, 176, 196
  ghost sighting, 242-43

Houston, San Antonio threats, 146-47
Kennedy, John F.
  KKK threats, 122-23, 132-33
  Los Angeles threat, 124-25
  Mafia threats, 65-67
  Nashville threat, 123-24
  oilmen's anger, 68, 250
  Oswald praise of, 97, 145, 203
  others gleeful about death, 174-77
  Tampa plot, 132-36
  Vietnam policy, 10, 121, 129-30, 246
Kennedy Sr., Joseph, 23-24, 221
Kennedy, Robert
  assassination, 238-39
  belief in conspiracy, 203-04
  campaigns against Mafia, Hoffa, 53, 63-67, 174
  Castro dealings, 39-40, 53, 57
  cover-up moves, 69, 187-88, 236, 250
  LBJ rift, 176, 248
  Nixon charges, 20
Kennedy, Ted, 239
Khrushchev, Nikita, 44, 54-55, 81
Kilgallen, Dorothy, 51, 193, 220-21, 231, 254
King Jr., Martin Luther
  assassination, 236-37, 301
  civil trial and verdict, 237-38
  Hoover campaign against, 196, 236
  House Assassinations Committee investigation of, 238
  plots against, 123, 133, 175, 219
Ku Klux Klan, 122-23, 132-33, 219

Lane, Mark, 202, 213-14, 216, 236, 245
Lincoln, Abraham, 12, 252-53
Lopez, Gilberto, 134-36, 256

Maheu, Robert, 31-32, 51

Mailer, Norman, 15-16, 84, 90, 95, 101, 200, 252
Marcello, Carlos, 65-67, 73, 108-11, 139, 172, 174, 204, 216, 232-33, 249
Marrs, Jim, 12, 137, 145, 167-68, 214, 241, 245, 248-52, 258, 260
Masferrer, Rolando, 16, 144, 171
Mash, Esther, 12, 141, 184
Massegee, Beverly Oliver, 110-11, 140, 147, 158-59, 164, 235
McMillan, Priscilla, 79-80, 86-87, 95
Milteer, Joseph, 122-23, 132-33, 137, 174-75, 256
Monroe, Marilyn, 221
Morales, David, 62, 115, 249
Morley, Jefferson, 14, 225, 246-47, 260, 301
Murret, Charles, 73-74
Murchison Sr., Clint, 14, 225, 246-47, 260, 301

Nagell, Richard Case, 76, 111-12, 124-25, 233-34, 261
Newman, William, 11, 160, 190, 260
Nixon, Richard, 19-24, 29-30, 33, 56, 66, 68, 96, 177, 203-04, 248, 253-54

Ochsner, Alton, 104-05, 226-27
Oswald, Lee Harvey
  actions on day JFK died, 149, 163-70
  bioweapon project, 104-05
  burial and exhumation, 199, 211
  childhood, 72-75
  CIA ties, 76-80, 90-91, 99-101, 104-07, 172-73. 179-80
  Cuban ties, 102-04, 111-12, 144
  De Mohrenschildt friendship, 90-93, 192, 204
  defects to Soviet Union, 78-81
  double sightings, 140-44, 161-62, 165-67, 172-73, 256

FBI ties, 88-89, 117-18
interrogation, 168-71
Oswald, Lee Harvey
   Japan ties, 76-77, 92-93
   married life, 83-85, 91-92, 115-17
   Mexico City visit, 114-16
   Paines defense, 178-79
   Ruby possible meetings, 139-41
   Ruby stalking and shooting, 180-84
   Walker shooting suspicions, 93-95
Oswald, Marguerite
   belief that son was government agent, 87-88, 201
   commission testimony, 201
   raising Lee, 72-75
   relationship with Marina, 91-92, 199
   suspicions of Paines, 180
Oswald, Marina
   changed view of husband's guilt, 202
   commission testimony, 201-02
   double sighting, 142
   life in Soviet Union, 83-85
   making money after husband's death, 199-200
   marital problems, 92-93, 114
   moving in with Paines, 95-97
   second marriage, 210
Oswald, Robert
   commission testimony, 201
   growing up with brother, 72-75
   speaking with brother in jail, 178-79
   military career, 75
   suspicions of brother's guilt, Paines, 180, 201

Paine, Michael
   CIA family background, 96-97
   return to Irving home, divorce, move to Mass., Calif., 212
   surprised Oswald's rifle stored in garage, 173

Paine, Michael
   tells commission Oswald is guilty, 203
   views toward Oswald, 97, 203
Paine, Ruth
   calls Communist Party lawyer for Oswald, 179
   CIA family background, 95-97
   drives to New Orleans to convince Marina to return to Dallas, 113-14
   file cabinets of Cuban contacts in garage, 173
   helps Oswald get TSBD job, 116-17
   moves to Philadelphia, Florida, California, 212
   suspicious activity in Central America, 212
   tells commission Oswald is guilty, 203
   vehicle allegedly seen at assassination scene, 162
Phillips, David Atlee, 30-31, 42, 111, 115-16, 144, 242
Pic, John Edward, 72-75, 229
Posner, Gerald, 15, 208, 241, 251
Powers, Francis Gary, 50, 81, 167
Pulte, William, 14, 16, 140, 144, 160, 171, 180-81, 200, 210-11, 235-36, 248-49, 261

Ray, James Earl, 236-38
Rockefeller Commission, 31, 53, 56
Roselli, Johnny, 31-33, 51-54, 58, 63, 65, 100, 139, 229, 231-32
Ruby, Jack
   Chicago days, 108-09
   Mafia ties, 108-09, 139-40

meeting in apartment after shooting Oswald, 220-21
seen at assassination site, 159-60, 166
seen with Oswald, 139-41
Ruby, Jack
stalks, shoots Oswald, 180-84
trial and death, 230-31
views toward Kennedy, 110-11

San Roman, Jose "Pepe," 36, 42, 45-47, 57-58
Shaw, Clay, 15, 106-08, 177, 179, 224-27
Sherman, Mary Stults, 104-05, 224
Sirhan, Sirhan, 239
Sixth Floor Museum, 13, 213, 215, 260
Smith, Sergio Arcacha, 101, 106, 111, 138
Somersett, William, 122-23, 132-33, 136-37, 174-75, 238, 256, 261
Stone, Oliver, 10, 13-14, 48, 52, 55, 63, 137, 194, 206, 227, 246, 248, 259-60
Sturgis, Frank, 30, 130, 137, 145, 170, 204, 247

Talbot, David, 14, 16, 34, 50, 55, 61-62, 137, 149, 176, 204, 228, 248-49, 255-56, 260
Texas School Book Depository building, 13, 70, 117, 142, 146, 152-59, 162-63, 178, 188, 210, 215, 218, 243, 251, 257
Texas Theatre, 164-67, 172, 178, 195, 244
Tippit, Officer J.D.
death, 165-66, 299
diversion incident, 171
Oswald charged, 169
seen with Ruby and Oswald, 139, 141-42
suspicious car, 167, 210

witnesses threatened, 222, 235

Trafficante Jr., Santo, 32, 52, 58, 63, 65, 67-68, 109, 134, 174, 204, 216, 231-32, 247, 249

U.S. House Select Committee on Assassinations, 11, 55, 67, 129, 143-44, 162-64, 182, 190-92, 198, 201, 207, 209, 215-17, 232
U.S. National Archives and Records Administration, 14, 191, 246, 260, 300

Vallee, Thomas Arthur, 121, 124, 128-32, 134, 170, 192, 246, 256
Varona, Antonio, 16, 32-33, 52, 54, 144
Veciana, Antonio, 111, 144, 204, 255

Walker, Edwin, 58, 68, 93-95, 122, 149-50, 152, 201-03, 205, 231
Wallace, Malcolm, 69-71, 234
Warren Commission, 13-16, 94, 100, 105, 117-18, 142-43, 153-54, 161-66, 189-91, 194-96, 200-07, 215-16, 224-26, 231-32
Warren, Earl, 181, 194, 226-27, 231
Weisberg, Harold, 260, 280, 300
Wilcott, Jim, 78, 196-97

Yarborough, Ralph, 12, 139, 146, 152

Zapruder, Abraham, 158-59

www.ingramcontent.com/pod-product-compliance
Lightning Source LLC
LaVergne TN
LVHW011415080426
835512LV00005B/65